PZ 2417
.H3
1981

The Chinese
Vernacular Story

Harvard East Asian Series
94

The Council on East Asian Studies
at Harvard University,
through the Fairbank Center for East Asian Research,
administers research projects designed
to further scholarly understanding of
China, Japan, Korea, Vietnam,
Inner Asia, and adjacent areas.

The Chinese Vernacular Story

PATRICK HANAN

Harvard University Press

Cambridge, Massachusetts
and London, England

1981

Library of Congress Cataloging in Publication Data

Hanan, Patrick.

The Chinese vernacular story.
(Harvard East Asian series ; 94)
Bibliography: p.
Includes index.
1. Short stories, Chinese—History and criticism. 2. Chinese fiction—
History and criticism. 3. Folk literature, Chinese—History and criticism.
1. Title. II. Series.
PL2417.H3   895.1'30109   80-17840
ISBN 0-674-12565-7

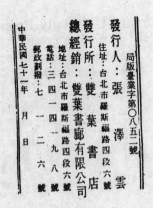

局版臺業字第○八五二號

發行人：張　澤　雲

發行所：雙　葉　書　店
住址：台北市羅斯福路四段六號

總經銷：雙葉書廊有限公司
地址：台北市羅斯福路四段六號
電話：三四一四一九八號
郵政劃撥：七一一二六號

中華民國七十一年　月　日

To the memory

of

Frederick Arthur Hanan

Ida Helen Dewes Hanan

Preface

This critical history of the vernacular short story is related to an earlier, technical work of mine, *The Chinese Short Story: Studies in Dating, Authorship, and Composition* (Cambridge, Mass.: Harvard University Press, 1973). The dating and attributions in Chapters 2-3, 5, and 6 broadly reflect the earlier book's conclusions. The *huaben* genre, referred to before as the "short story," is here renamed the "vernacular story."

Part of Chapter 7 appeared, in an earlier version, as "The Nature of Ling Meng-ch'u's Fiction" in Andrew H. Plaks, ed., *Chinese Narrative: Critical and Theoretical Essays* (Princeton: Princeton University Press, 1977).

The Pinyin system of transliteration is used, except in a few place names. All translations, unless otherwise noted, are my own.

The tale of my indebtedness is long. Cyril Birch, James R. Hightower, and Victor Mair all read a draft of the manuscript and gave valuable advice. Y. W. Ma shared with me his exceptional knowledge of modern scholarly writing on Chinese fiction. Numerous others helped by elucidating problems or procuring copies of rare materials, among them Jerome T. Cavanaugh, Chan Shing-cheong, Stephen H. L. Cheng, Ronald C. Egan, Achilles Fang, Joseph F. Fletcher, Jr., Howard Hibbett, S. F. Lai, Sally Wo-kwun Loh, Loh Wai-fong, Rulan Pian, Benjamin I. Schwartz, Tseng Yong-yih, Wang Ch'iu-kuei, Ellen Widmer, Susan Wilf, Yang Lien-sheng, and Yü Ying-shih. I owe a long-standing debt of gratitude to Wu Xiaoling in Peking and to Enoki Kazuo and Ono Shinobu in Tokyo.

A fellowship from the American Council of Learned Societies enabled me to write much of the book, and a grant from Harvard's Seminar on High and Popular Cultures in East Asia, funded by the Mellon Foundation, helped me to complete it. Something of what I owe to libraries in East Asia, Europe, and the United States is indicated in the Bibliography. I am particularly grateful to Eugene Wu and the staff of the Harvard-Yenching Library for their unfailing assistance, and to the Peking, Peking University, and Shanghai Libraries for making rare books available at short notice during a recent visit.

Finally, and most deeply, I am indebted to Anneliese Hanan for her help at every stage of the book's writing.

Contents

The Chinese
Vernacular Story

DYNASTIES

Shang 1751–1112 B.C.
Zhou (Chou) 1111–249 B.C.
Qin (Ch'in) 221–206 B.C.
Han 206 B.C.–A.D. 220
Three Kingdoms 220–280
Eastern and Western Jin 265–420
Southern and Northern Dynasties 420–589
Sui 581–618
Tang (T'ang) 618–907
Five Dynasties 907–960
Northern Song (Sung) 960–1126
Jin (Chin, Jurchen) 1115–1234
Southern Song (Sung) 1127–1279
Yuan (Mongol) 1271–1368
Ming 1368–1644
Qing (Ch'ing, Manchu) 1644–1912

1
Language
and
Narrative
Model

The functions and relationships of China's languages can be more easily illustrated than explained. Take the case of Feng Menglong (1574-1646), a great figure in the vernacular fiction. As a member of a highly educated Soochow family, Feng undoubtedly spoke an upper-class variant of the Soochow dialect, which belongs to the Wu dialect group current in much of Jiangsu Province and most of Zhejiang. He knew a more popular variant of it as well, for he collected Soochow songs and composed his own in imitation. He must also have known an upper-class variant of one of the great Northern group of dialects, of which the most prominent was the dialect of the capital, Peking. A language based on the educated speech of the capital served as a lingua franca for officials, merchants, and other travelers, but it amounted to something far less than a standard spoken language, and its norms must have been capacious indeed. It was called *guanhua* ("officials' language"), for which the usual English equivalent is "Mandarin," although both "guanhua" and "Mandarin" have also come to describe the Northern dialects as a group. Feng's main contacts with the Northern dialects must have been with their southeastern variety, spoken along the lower Yangzi, in Anhui, and in those parts of Jiangsu where the Wu dialects did not hold sway.[1] As a neighbor of the Wu dialects, it exerted some influence upon them and received some in return, especially in its lexicon.

As to written languages, Feng's education was, inevitably, in the

1

reading and writing of *wenyan,* the "literary language," for which I shall
use the term "Classical Chinese," preferring to retain "literary language"
for a different purpose. Classical Chinese had long ceased to be a normal
medium of speech. It was a written language that, according to modern
belief, had been developed two thousand years before as a stylistically
refined version of a common spoken language of that time; the classical
literature of the Zhou (Chou) dynasty provided its principal models.
Most of Feng's writings were in Classical Chinese. In this respect, he
resembles the great majority of his peers, in whose voluminous works we
find nothing but Classical Chinese, except perhaps for a rare vernacular
word used in a poem to capture some earthy or familiar effect or an even
rarer conversational sentence reported verbatim. What sets Feng apart
from the great majority is that he wrote also in genres that required the
vernacular: novels, stories, plays, and songs. I pass over for the moment
the fact that none of these works, except for some of the songs, is exclusively in the vernacular.

The spoken language of which Feng's written vernacular is a stylistically refined development was not his native Soochow dialect but a semistandardized version of Northern. The vernacular literature associated
with the other great dialect groups, the Wu, the Min (Fujian), and the
Yue (for example, Cantonese), is meager by comparison with the literature in Northern. The Northern group included in its territory by far the
greatest number of speakers as well as the capitals (and hence, usually,
the cultural centers) of almost all the major dynasties. Some version of
Northern had been used, at least since the Tang dynasty, as the norm for
vernacular writing even by writers who, like Feng, lived outside the area.
Feng's vernacular writings show some features of the southeastern variety current along the lower Yangzi; but since the phonemic distinctions,
the dialects' main criteria, are masked by the Chinese character script,
the actual differences on the page amount to mere shadings, not the clear
profile. We know, moreover, that vernacular authors took some pains to
avoid words and idioms with too narrow a currency and tended to choose
a vocabulary intelligible within the whole Northern area.

Thus, Feng commanded at least two spoken languages: his own (regional and class) dialect and an upper-class version of one of the Northern dialects. He also commanded two or three written languages:
Classical Chinese; a semistandardized vernacular developed from Northern, which in his hands shows some features of the southeastern variety;
and his own Soochow dialect, in which he wrote a few songs of a locally
popular type. But even in his collection of Soochow songs, the notes and
commentaries are all either in Classical or in the Northern vernacular; he
can hardly be said to have practiced the Soochow dialect. Of the two
written languages he did practice, only one, the Northern vernacular,
was associated with a language he spoke in daily life.

The primary forces that shaped Classical Chinese were the functions it was called upon to perform in society. As first established as *the* written language in the Zhou dynasty, then further standardized and consolidated in the Qin (Ch'in) and the Han, and used in written form during the long centuries after the spoken language had parted company with it, Classical fits admirably the modern linguist's concept of a literary language.[2] (The word "literary" refers here to written communication in general.) That is to say, it served as the written medium in government and law and as the vehicle of learning, history, and tradition for the class by whom and for whom it was primarily written, the class it helped both to create and define. The language had its accepted models of style — a prerequisite for literary and standard languages — certain classical (that is, canonical and archetypal) texts that embodied the values of the high culture. China's centralized mode of government, with its reliance on a powerful bureaucracy, brought with it both the need and the opportunity to standardize the literary language. The recruitment of the higher bureaucracy in later dynasties by means of civil service examinations exerted a further stabilizing effect on the development of the language. Finally, the literary language had its own cultivated public. It was a public that, despite invasions and other upheavals, prevailed for over two thousand years, right up to the first decades of this century. During that period, the language met with hardly any significant disruption of its essential role. The most serious was probably the interlude during the Yuan (Mongol) dynasty in which the civil service examinations were suspended, the literary language suffered a temporary erosion, and some government statutes were written in a hybrid language that included the vernacular.

The general characteristics of literary languages have been summarized as selectivity, homogeneity, and conservatism.[3] Selectivity and homogeneity are the qualities of any language that, though it cannot be said to have been planned, has at least been molded by social institutions and is unduly subject to notions of decorum. Classical Chinese was selective in that it chose what to reject and what to assimilate, largely according to notions of decorum; it was homogeneous by virtue of its creation of norms — no regional or class peculiarities survive in it — and by its standardization of syntax, lexicon, and notation. Conservatism, which some linguists prefer to call stability, it had in full measure.[4] In addition to these qualities, it possessed the intellectualization that has been discerned in the making of all standard languages.[5]

It is unfortunate, in some respects, that the analogy that springs to mind in considering the function of Classical Chinese is that of medieval Latin before it was supplanted by the Romance vernaculars. Latin was the obvious analogy for the reformers in their efforts to replace Classical Chinese as literary language with the Northern vernacular. (In fact, in

the so-called Literary Revolution that began in 1917, it was not merely
the classical language that was to be replaced but also its public and their
culture.) But the analogy's disadvantage is that it makes the dominance
of Classical Chinese for thousands of years seem like some monstrous
aberration condemning Chinese literature to sterility. In the case of
Latin, the old cultivated public had ceased to exist several centuries
before. At the time of the development of the Romance vernaculars as
written media, Latin was in the service of a new ideology, Christianity,
for which the classical models of Roman culture were little more than the
relics of a pagan. past.[6] In contrast, the decline of Classical Chinese,
together with its public and their culture, was swift and painful, brought
about in a generation or two by the sons and grandsons of men who had
sustained it. There were attempts in the 1890s to adapt the language, in-
fusing it with new terminology for new, imported concepts and thus to
allow it to continue to perform its proper role as a literary language.
Such gradualism suited the first stage of reform, but it soon gave way to
wholesale change, leading to the replacement of Classical as the standard
written language by the Northern vernacular (which had to be intellect-
ualized rapidly to fit it for its new role) and also to a broad attack on the
old culture.

In the long period of its dominance, there were virtually no serious
proposals to replace Classical with the vernacular. The critics who
praised vernacular works praised them, generally, in elegant Classical
Chinese; their concern was with literary merit, not with the literary
medium, or if with the literary medium, then only as used in that genre.
The theory of historical change in literature, especially with regard to the
succession of prevalent genres, helped drama and even popular song and
vernacular fiction to gain a critical hearing in certain circles. In the latter
part of the Ming, this theory was combined, by a few critics, with the
conviction of the superior authenticity of an oral and vernacular
literature free from the artifice of the literary language. But there are few
statements to match that of Li Yu (1611-1679/80), like Feng Menglong a
great figure in the vernacular fiction and drama, that the Yuan (Mongol)
dynasty was remembered solely by virtue of its drama.[7] Li Yu writes this.
at the opening of his treatise on drama, and it appears that he is urging
the importance of the (vernacular) drama upon the monarch of yet
another alien dynasty, the Manchu. In any case, he does not go on to
draw the obvious conclusions from his argument. The numerous literary
critics who recommended simple or common diction in literary prose
were not speaking of vernacular diction; at most the features they
stressed dimly paralleled the changes in the spoken language.[8] As no major figure after the time of Wang Chong (A.D. 27-circa 100) endeavored
to write his principal works in a language consonant with the spoken lan-

guage[9] (in his time it was still possible to do so in Classical Chinese), the retention of the literary language can hardly be called an aberration.

In fact, the retention of a classical literary language no longer spoken in ordinary contexts is by no means an unusual phenomenon. The contemporary cases of Arabic and Modern Greek and the historical cases of Sanskrit and Old Church Slavonic offer parallels of a kind.[10] This situation is most likely to occur when a society feels a direct continuity with a revered past culture, a culture that possesses its own classical models.

Since the position of standard written medium was already occupied, a distinct vernacular literature could grow up only to fill some new, additional function that Classical could not perform. As a rule, it is exclusively in relation to oral literature that a written literature in the vernacular first develops. Oral literature provides the model—the sermon, the saga, the song—that the vernacular requires, as well as its sanction. The vernacular is first used in place of the literary language when it is important to record the actual words spoken or when rendering oral literature in written form or when composing a piece to be performed orally. Thus, it does not encroach directly upon the territory of the literary language but adds a new dimension to it, or restores a lost dimension.

With regard to its form, in any close relationship with oral literature, the written vernacular may be either a notation of an oral performance or a composition for an oral performance. In a more distant relationship, the written vernacular may follow the model of an oral work or a category of oral works. Typically, a folk song in written form is notational, while the text of a play is compositional, though neither has to be so. Modern research on oral literature has been carried out most frequently on literature that the researcher is the first to record; his recording, if written out, is an example of the notational use of the vernacular. In China, and in other countries in which there was a considerable literate class, the compositional form is also important.[11]

The purposes of writing in the vernacular may be set out schematically as follows: for performance only; for performance mainly but also for reading; for reading mainly but also for performance; for reading only. Actual use often varies from intended use—for instance, in the extreme case of a performance work that no one remembers how to perform—but it is the purpose of writing, regardless of the ultimate use to which the writing is put, that determines a work's literary form and style. Typically, a play is composed mainly for performance, though also for reading. (There may even be different texts, one for each purpose.) The sermons and dialogues or divines and moralists (*yulu* is the Chinese term for the genre) are often in the vernacular, purporting to represent the master's actual speech as recorded by his disciples; the aim is to preserve

it for reading. The use of the vernacular in fiction is more complex. It
may serve any of the four purposes mentioned. However, a work that is
written for reading only has severed contact with oral literature. In
China, no doubt because of the position of the vernacular in relation to
Classical Chinese, the novel and the story tended to retain a distant connection with oral literature; that is, they retained the oral literature as a
model, to some degree.

At what point did these developments occur in China? In particular,
when can a reading public be said to have existed for vernacular fiction?

A substantial literature in the vernacular survives from the Tang
dynasty. Before then, elements of a distinctive vernacular had been used
in folk song, in the Chinese translation of Buddhist texts, and in the
dialogue of the fifth-century *New Account of Tales of the World* (*Shi
shuo xin yu*). However, the corpus of Tang material discovered at
Dunhuang reveals a far more extensive use. The so-called *bianwen* narratives, including *chantefables* and other pieces solely in verse or prose,
as well as the popular songs, use a free vernacular occasionally mixed
with Classical Chinese. Most of the texts were copied in the tenth century, but some at least may have been composed as early as the eighth.
Their themes are secular as well as Buddhist. Besides the Dunhuang
texts, there exist a number of Buddhist yulu of Chan (Zen) masters of the
ninth century and after.[12] Generally, the introductory and linking prose
is in Classical, while the dialogues are in the vernacular. An extended use
of the vernacular, even for narrative, is also found in some similar texts,
for example the early-Song Buddhist work *Zutang ji*.[13]

The strong association of the vernacular literature with Buddhism in
the Tang may be understood in general terms. Buddhism was an imported ideology which owed little fealty to the dominant Chinese culture
and its canonical models, even though it was influenced by them. Its
clergy and devotees may be seen, at the height of the Buddhist monas-
teries' power, as constituting a new public. The proselytizing activities of
the Buddhist movement, sometimes encouraged by the Emperor, and
their link with popular entertainment — in the Tang, Buddhist temples
were major entertainment centers — must have helped in the growth of
the vernacular literature and stimulated the development of any existing
secular oral literature. We hear much from contemporaries of the *sujiang*
(popular exposition) of Buddhist priests, some of whom could attract
large audiences. A humbler class of performer, whose material was not
always Buddhist, may have been responsible for telling the bianwen
tales.[14]

Some of the Dunhuang texts are apparently compositional (the songs,
of course, are more likely to be notational) and were intended for performance in conjunction with pictures shown to the audience. But others,
judging from the remarks with which they close, were intended for

reading.[15] It seems clear that by the Tang, a vernacular literature had begun to take shape. Of course, this does not mean that its authors intended it exclusively for reading. There is only a small difference between composition for performance and composition for reading, and there may indeed be no difference at all; a work may be intended for both purposes from the beginning. Later chantefable genres, such as the *baojuan* and the *tanci*, were frequently written for reading. It seems certain that manuscripts circulated among readers in the Tang, how widely we do not know. The relative lack of standardization in the writing system may indicate that the vernacular fiction had not yet found its recognized models.[16]

New kinds of vernacular literature survive from the Song (Sung) dynasty, particularly the period of national division between the Jin (Jurchen) in the North and the Southern Song. The medley (*zhugongdiao*), a long and elaborate chantefable, flourished in the North under the Jin.[17] Texts survive, one of them in an early edition; it was presumably composed for performance then published for reading. In the Southern Song, Zhu Xi's (1130-1200) disciples compiled the monumental *Yu lei*, recording their master's sayings. In this case, the neo-Confucians were apparently imitating the Chan Buddhists. Buddhist vernacular yulu are also found in the Song and later dynasties. Patches of vernacular, mainly confined to dialogue, occur in the *Sanchao beimeng huibian* (Documents on the Treaties with the North during Three Reigns) of 1194, a patchwork chronicle history of the years 1117-1161.[18] But by far the most important extant work for our purposes is the *Record of How the Priest Tripitaka of the Great Tang Fetched the Sutras (Da Tang San-zang Fashi qu jing ji)*,[19] the earliest known written version of the story complex whose most famous treatment is the novel *Journey to the West (Xiyou ji)*. Two slightly different editions survive, both probably of the Southern Song. It may be described as the first mainly prose narrative that we known of in the vernacular (a severely limited vernacular) after the bianwen texts of the Tang dynasty. In the Song dynasty, the main centers of public entertainment were the *wazi*, the pleasure quarters of the cities, in which various types of oral literature were performed. The performers were professionals, specializing in a particular genre and a particular body of material. Presumably, the *Record* was related at some remove to an oral story complex on the subject, and perhaps to the drama as well.

The slight shift in the relationship of Classical to vernacular during the Yuan dynasty is apparent in a number of ways, not merely in the hybrid language of some government ordinances. The Yuan was the heyday of the Northern (*zaju*) drama, of which thirty plays survive in Yuan editions and numerous others in Ming. The *Zhongyuan yinyun* (Sounds and Rhymes of the Central Plain) attempts to set out the phonological system

of the Peking dialect for use in Northern plays and songs.[20] It is a prescriptive attempt not merely to establish a standard in phonology but
also to establish the Peking dialect, hitherto of restricted currency, as a
standard for the vernacular. The playwright is enjoined to choose
"universally intelligible words" and to avoid jargon, dialect, and
scholars' tags, both common prescriptions for standard languages. A
Peking standard became established for zaju plays in the Yuan and early
Ming; even when the plays were written in Hangchow by Southerners,
the same prescriptions were observed, such was the genre's normative
power.

From the Yuan and the early Ming, there survive eight examples of
vernacular narrative that belong together in terms of genre and
language.[21] The titles of some of them are formed from the titles of
dynastic histories with the addition of the word *pinghua*, "popular tale";
they claim to be popularized history. In fact, they develop connected
stories from the compartmentalized materials of the dynastic histories by
adding legend and folklore. Notable among them is the *Sanguo zhi
pinghua* (Popularization of the *Annals of the Three Kingdoms*), a fictional treatment of the familiar Three Kingdoms material, which is based
to some degree, no doubt, on an oral complex.[22] It is one of the sources
of the great *Sanguo zhi tongsu yanyi* (Popular Exposition of the *Annals
of the Three Kingdoms*), which was apparently written during the late
Yuan. Another is the *Xuanhe yishi*, an account in chronicle form of the
decline of the Northern Song, concentrating on the events of its last reign
period, Xuanhe. It is noteworthy for a vernacular section that gives a
brief but complete account of the Shuihu narrative.[23]

The pinghua are an odd mixture of languages, at one point more
Classical, at another more vernacular, the mixture representing their
dual origins. They are an uneasy combination—one can scarcely say a
synthesis—of two different methods of composition, those of written
history and oral narrative, with the proportions of each varying from
work to work. Just as some of the Classical sections have been copied or
thinly adapted from official or unofficial history, so the vernacular sections may, in some cases, have been copied from other works. This is
especially likely in the case of the *Xuanhe yishi*, which, in several more or
less self-contained sections, employs a narrative model that is characteristic of oral and vernacular literature. In the *Sanguo zhi tongsu yanyi*, the
dual narrative methods are brilliantly synthesized; as a result, the work
itself became the model for the long Chinese tradition of fictionalized
history.

Some of the pinghua date from the 1321-1323 reign period in Jian'an,
a publishing center in Fujian. Five of them carry captioned illustrations
in the top third of each page; they are among the earliest illustrated
books. Their language, of course, represents not a Min (Fujian) dialect

but some as yet unidentified variety of Northern. This kind of work must have been quite common in the Yuan. Two editions survive of one of the texts, and no fewer than twenty-six of them were apparently copied into the now lost sections of the *Yongle Encyclopedia*, which was compiled in 1403-1407.[24]

Besides the drama (and song) and the pinghua of the Yuan, there was a third category of vernacular literature of which we know far less: the stories (*huaben*)[25] and novels. No editions survive from this period, except for an excerpt from a work entitled *Xiyou ji* (Journey to the West), which was also copied into the *Encyclopedia*.[26] But a number of other works may be placed tentatively in the Yuan, even if their earliest extant editions are mid-Ming or later. Many of them are on subjects popular in oral narration in the Yuan (itself no criterion of date), and they exhibit linguistic and narrative features that appear to be early. They are true vernacular fiction, as distinct from the tradition of fictionalized history, which generally uses a more Classical language, and they provide the immediate models for the Chinese novel and story. A dozen or so stories may date from the Yuan, as may the conjectural earliest versions of the *Shuihu zhuan*. All of these works present the familiar problem of how to relate written fiction to oral literature. Their narrative method is apparently based, to some degree, on that of oral narrative. Their themes existed in oral literature. But what is the process, and what is the purpose, of their composition? It is likely that, in a period in which there evidently existed a reading public for vernacular fiction, they were composed for reading from material current in oral literature, but we cannot rule out other possibilities in some cases.

The often fluent vernacular of these works differs in dialectal type from that of both the plays and the pinghua. Though based on a Northern dialect, it must reflect, in a shadowy way, some southern or southeastern variety. It has been suggested that the language it distantly reflects is that of Kaifeng, the Northern Song capital, as transposed along with the court to Hangchow, the capital of the Southern Song.[27] Hangchow is in the heart of Wu dialect country, but the effects of a long period (1128-1276) as capital made a deep impression on its spoken language, an impression that survives to the present day. But even if, as appears likely from its topical references, much of this fiction originated in Hangchow, one should be wary of a simple equation with the local dialect; I have already noted the normative power of the genre concept.

From this point on, the vernacular tradition was no longer periodically buried or lost, as it had been in the past. The bianwen of the Tang, popular as they must have been in their heyday, were forgotten in the Song and—such is the fate of a subliterature—remained so until the Dunhuang caves were opened in the early years of this century. The pinghua were known in the Ming, and at least two were incorporated in

Ming works. The *Sanguo zhi tongsu yanyi* and the *Shuihu zhuan,* the two great models of the later novel, were rediscovered in the middle of the Ming and kept in print thereafter. By 1550, there were at least two editions of the *Ping yao zhuan* (Suppressing the Demons' Revolt), an early-Ming novel. And at midcentury too, many of the surviving early stories were collected and published, along with Ming fiction, in a series entitled *Sixty Stories* (*Liushijia xiaoshuo*). By that stage, a broad public was assured for vernacular fiction, and the fiction itself became an institution. The Northern vernacular can be thought of as a second literary medium, provided one remembers that it was restricted to certain genres which, with the exception of drama and the art song, enjoyed little prestige.

This restriction, which is even more severely applied in the sparse literature of the other major dialect groups, implies a close connection between genre and language. If the vernacular is restricted to a small number of functions that seem to call for its use, it is also true that those functions are confined to the vernacular. For example, the novel is, with the exception of a few virtuoso experiments, always mainly in the vernacular, or at least in some intermediate language between Classical and vernacular. On the other hand, the author's or editor's preface, if there is one, is always in Classical, even though it is addressed to the same reader. This can be justified in a number of ways, but the immediate reason is simply genre convention. A preface belongs to a different genre, one conventionally written in Classical.

Thus the vernacular is confined to the novel and story as a matter of convention (although there are good historical reasons for the choice) and to the drama, chantefable, and song partly as a matter of necessity. Outside of these forms, it is used for notational purposes, for example in the yulu or in oral depositions. And consistently, beginning with the Buddhist works, it is also used for the purposes of education and propaganda, in didactic texts and in moral and religious tracts, in order to reach a wider, less lettered readership.

That use of the vernacular did give access to a wider readership can scarcely be doubted, despite the fact that education was in Classical Chinese. It is easier to learn to read a language one already knows than a language that has to be studied. In the first case, to put it oversimply, one is learning a notation merely; in the latter, language and notation must be learned together. Li Yu, in his urbane instructions on how to educate a concubine (one does not educate one's wife, he tells us, for wives are for serious duties, not for pleasure) advises the reader to start her on vernacular fiction for this very reason.[28] If the concubine can recognize a few characters in a sentence, he says, she will be able to guess the rest, because she knows the language and knows what to expect. In Classical Chinese, of course, she would not, unless she had studied enough for it to become second nature.

It is not quite true to say that education was exclusively in Classical Chinese. The first stage of the traditional education, lasting about a year, consisted of a concentrated course in learning characters, most of which would be needed anyway in reading the vernacular.[29] But there were also other kinds of text that served as the medium of instruction in families outside the highly educated class. These texts listed common words, not just characters, of the vernacular language along with pronunciations and occasionally explanations as well. Even the second and third stages of the regular education indirectly helped students master the written vernacular. Generally, in the second stage, they would study rhymed maxims of rather limited syntax which served mainly to teach characters. At least two widely used texts were in the vernacular. Thus, in the area of the Northern dialects, and to some extent also in the Wu dialect area, the traditional education helped the student to read vernacular as well as Classical Chinese.

Readership depends on many things, of course, in addition to relative literacy — price and accessibility of reading matter as well as social values, constraints, and even leisure time — about most of which our knowledge is sketchy. But it is noticeable that works designed for a wide readership are either in simple Classical (characterized by a restricted choice of vocabulary and syntax combined with an expansive, even redundant use) or in the vernacular or, most often, in some mixture of the two. In all three cases, and particularly in the last two, potential readership must have exceeded that for the ordinary Classical literature by the addition of some boys and women and also of the less lettered classes — merchants, shopkeepers, shop assistants, lower functionaries, and the like. Writers often take cognizance of this broader public, not merely in the pious educational intent so often expressed in their prefaces but also in the actual level of explanation of the texts themselves. Feng Menglong is an excellent example; his stories regularly explain facts that the Classical tale which served as his source took for granted. Like some of his peers, he is writing down to his audience.

Circulation figures do not exist for the scholar of this literature, as they do for his counterpart in English or European literature. He is dependent on prefaces to fictional works, which are often self-serving, and on moral tracts, which tend to exaggerate the menace of fiction, or on clumsy criteria such as the number of known editions. Probably the most objective assessments, simplistic though they are, are those given by the late-Qing reformers who were intent on enlisting the power of fiction in their campaign to remake Chinese culture. Xu Nianci, in "My View of Fiction," written in 1907, remarks of the youthful shop assistants, presumably of Shanghai, that "they always have a volume in their hands whenever they have no customers to see to" and that the volumes are those of familiar historical and heroic fiction (*Sanguo, Shuihu*) or of "filthy and decadent" literature.[30] Women, he tells us, were great devourers of the prudish, idealistic romances of the *caizi jiaren* (brilliant youth and beautiful girl) type. These two kinds of reader were clearly, in his view, at the bottom of the reading public in terms of literacy.

In generalizing about the social position of the authors of the vernacular literature, one must draw a sharp distinction between drama and fiction. Leading dramatists were in some cases successful men in public life who received acclaim for their plays as well as their other writings. By contrast, no novelist or story writer ever received this kind of acclaim during his lifetime in respect of his fiction. Many a leading dramatist left a body of collected work in Classical Chinese; not so the writer of fiction. Li Yu is the only prominent fiction writer whose collected works have survived, and he was, of course, a well-known dramatist. The writer of fiction was often a frustrated man, disappointed in his ambitions to serve in public office, or else a professional writer of humbler status, perhaps an editor or clerk employed by a publishing house. The clearest distinction to be drawn among writers of fiction is between the gifted amateurs and these obscure and often anonymous professionals of the popular literature.

Patronage and literary commissions, those staples of the Classical author, were out of the question for the fiction writer. Li Yu tried to support his expensive tastes by writing and publishing for profit and also by seeking patronage, although not for his fiction. The professional writer of fiction, even if he was not working for a publishing house, was likely to have been engaged in a host of publishing enterprises, such as compiling textbooks and letter-writing handbooks. At the same time, there was also a very different kind of novelist who was responsible for the greatest novels and who did not, so far as we know, envisage publication for profit as a primary motive. *The Story of the Stone* (*Honglou meng*), *The Scholars* (*Rulin waishi*), and probably *The Golden Lotus* (*Jin Ping Mei*) were not even published during their authors' lifetimes.

No simple statement will suffice to describe the position of the vernacular fiction in Chinese society. It is going too far to assert that it was always held in low esteem. At certain times, in certain avant-garde circles, vernacular fiction — usually the same handful of novels — was appreciated and even exalted. But there is no denying that, in general, although it was avidly read, fiction was largely disregarded by society, and that the twentieth-century estimation of it represents one of the most drastic reappraisals in literary history. Even Classical fiction had never claimed a high place in literature, and the vernacular fiction suffered the extra cultural handicap of its language. If drama, that socially and linguistically ambivalent form, was considered a minor art, what could vernacular fiction claim to be?

The Classical, vernacular, and oral languages are media and cannot be directly equated with class-differentiated cultures in society. One can conceive of a "high" oral literature performed at court which could not be associated with a "low," or popular, culture. But in general, the Classical and oral literatures do reflect somewhat different emphases within Chinese culture. If the potential publics for the three literatures are thought of as concentric circles, the circle of the Classical literature will be surrounded by the somewhat larger circle of the vernacular, while both will be engulfed by the vastly larger circle of the oral, the only true mass literature of premodern times. (This division is, of course, too simple; the drama confuses it, and the distinction between Classical and vernacular is blurred by the existence of a simple Classical and the various mixed languages. Moreover, the oral, and to some extent the vernacular publics were divided by dialect.) The differences lie not in distinct systems of philosophical and religious belief but in different emphases among attitudes and values. The themes stressed in one may be relatively ignored in the other. The group of attitudes about physical heroism—the romance of war, military glory, machismo—that is so prominent in the oral literature is seldom stressed in the Classical, which tends to dwell instead on war's pity and terror. (The romantic figure of the knight errant is found in both literatures but in rather different guises.) Similar broad differences can be discerned with regard to love and sex, religion, and morality. The fact that fiction bulks much larger in the oral literature confuses this comparison but does not confound it.

The vernacular has a complex relationship with the other literatures. At one extreme, the vernacular author may develop and transform material that had existed in oral literature. (The same material may pass through numerous vernacular versions.) Most early works are at least partly of this kind. However, even in the process of compilation, changes are made and different values asserted, particularly by authors with some standing as literati. At the other extreme, an author may compose his own fiction with reference to the philosophical and aesthetic values of the Classical literature and with only a minimal concern for the form of the vernacular novel. But even in the latter case, the vernacular fiction, because of its ambiguous position in Chinese culture, frequently served as a vehicle for criticizing the culture's dominant values. This is true of the great novels of the Qing dynasty, *The Scholars, The Story of the Stone,* and *Flowers in the Mirror* (*Jing hua yuan*), as well as some of the later story collections, particularly Aina's *Idle Talk under the Bean Arbor* (*Doupeng xianhua*).

Language and Style

The differences between Classical and vernacular lie in lexicon rather than grammar. At not too high a level of abstraction, it can be main-

tained that there is a universal Chinese grammar, which holds good for
the vernaculars of the various dialects as well as for Classical, of which
the prime constituent—since Chinese is an extreme example of an
isolating language—is word order.[31] This universality of grammar is the
main reason why the Classical and spoken languages were not recognized
until modern times as different languages (in the sense of distinct
linguistic systems). The significant development from Classical to vernacular was in lexicon, particularly in the lengthening of words from
(mainly) one syllable in Classical to (mainly) two or more syllables in the
modern vernacular. The change was accompanied by a drastic reduction
in the phonemic stock. (Dialects such as Cantonese that have a relatively
large phonemic stock also have relatively few polysyllabic words.)
Classical Chinese remained intelligible on the page solely because it was
written in Chinese characters, which identify morphemes rather than
phonemes, as does an ordinary script. A phonemic transcription of
Classical according to modern Peking pronunciation would be
unintelligible because of the vast number of homonyms.

Since grammar is, in essence, constant, and since there are no inflec-
tions in the proper sense, Classical and vernacular may easily be allowed
to interpenetrate on the written page. They are, to a large extent, gram-
matically compatible systems with different sets of interchangeable
parts. It is therefore possible to design a language constructed of both
Classical and vernacular elements. In fact, many modern expository and
scientific styles use Classical for the syntactical words and vernacular for
the substantive words, to borrow a traditional distinction. Some such
styles use both sets of syntactical words in a hierarchical relationship.
When Classical Chinese came under attack in the second decade of this
century, schemes of just such combination were devised, and there were
also conscious efforts to merge both languages into one intermediate
form.[32] This singular property of Chinese, resulting from the nature of
its grammar, its isolating tendencies, and its script, gives the written
language an extraordinary contractile quality, for which one may borrow
the word "elasticity" from a modern critic.[33] The Chinese writer, even in
modern times, tends toward conciseness as a cultural habit, assured that
the morphemic script will keep his work intelligible.

The vernacular writer has the ever-present opportunity and inclination
to create an intermediate language, or more commonly, to adopt one
ready made. The two languages can be alternated or they can be mixed,
but although a rigorous standard is maintained for Classical, the vernacular writer always compromises to some degree. In the vernacular,
the two languages are thus effectively reduced to styles or the ingredients
of styles. The writer, being bilingual, can if he chooses work out his own
combination of styles, both serially, alternating the two languages, and
synthetically.

Vernacular fiction is written in a series of styles differentiated partly by the mix of the language. The use of different mixes is functional, but it becomes a convention. That is to say, there is a close relationship between style and context, and the language mix, as a principal stylistic variable, depends on context. The Classical styles convey dignity and loftiness and hence are used in the descriptive set piece or tableau, which, when the loftiness is inappropriate, becomes burlesque. Couplets and verse, more or less Classical, perform the same service and also give a pithiness to the style. Intermediate languages are used particularly in the functions of summary and comment, for the sake of conciseness. The vernacular itself is used in close-up narrative (scene), especially in dialogue, to which its direct, homely, even earthy force is suited. A change in the social context may result in a change of language; for example, when the action moves to Court, the narrative styles become noticeably more Classical—that is to say, more formal. When the *Shuihu* deals with the outlaws in more elevated, less domestic contexts, its language also becomes more Classical. The mix can be used to differentiate dialogue; it has been noted that Zhang Fei, the earthiest character in the *Sanguo*, speaks in the most vernacular style.[34] Major variations of language mix between different types of novels—for example, the fictionalized history and the domestic novel—can also be explained in the same way. The same vernacular author—Feng Menglong is an excellent example—will use radically different language mixes depending on the kind of novel or story he is writing.

The classification of styles is not wholly dependent on the language mix; that would be absurdly mechanical. Nor can one say that a particular effect is impossible in a given language; Classical can even suggest styles and registers in dialogue. One must also reckon with a gradual change in the acceptance of the vernacular for virtually all functions, a process that culminates in the great novels of the eighteenth century, *The Story of the Stone* and *The Scholars*.

The tendencies and affinities of the two languages result from the uses to which they were put in society, the one the main vehicle of the cultural legacy, the other based on the spoken language and restricted to certain genres of low esteem. These are the primary associations the languages bear; they lead to a polarity of elegance and refinement (*ya*) on the one hand and vulgarity and commonness (*su*) on the other. Classical aspired to a standard of good taste not unlike the *elegantia* or *urbanitas* of Classical Latin. The contrast is actually raised in the earliest known piece of fiction criticism, a 1494 preface to the *Sanguo*,[35] and it is frequently posed in criticism of the drama. The problem for the dramatist, we are told, is to write dialogue that is neither pedantic nor vulgar. Successful dramatists are said to "transmute the vulgar into the refined." "If a song has literary embellishment," says the *Sounds and Rhymes of the Central*

Plain, quoting an old saying, "it is considered an art song; otherwise, it is a popular ditty."[36] But what the Classical gains in elegance, it loses in immediacy and down-to-earth force.[37] The language of close-up narration in the *Shuihu* is effective precisely because it is in the vernacular; it has a direct physical connotation. One has only to compare a fight in the *Shuihu* with one in the *Sanguo* to see the difference, even though the latter is not completely Classical.

The Classical resounds with the echoes of the past, recalling Edward Sapir's remark, "The ghosts of the past, preferably of the remote past, haunt the cultured man at every step."[38] A contrast is often drawn by the late-Qing reformers, the only critics ever to detail the stylistic properties of the Classical and the vernacular, between the openness and direct expressiveness of the vernacular and the suggestiveness or richness of semantic and cultural implication of the Classical.[39] The main tangible difference is that the Classical is concise and the vernacular expansive, specifying relationships that are merely understood in the Classical. So ingrained was the ideal of conciseness that late-Qing champions of the vernacular felt they had also to promote the value of expansiveness.[40]

Some of the common features of vernacular fiction can be associated with, if not attributed to, this matter of language: the relatively humble social level of the life with which it deals; its preference for detailed, particularizing narrative; and its distinct emphasis on either comedy, satire, and ribaldry or on straightforward moral didacticism.

A Scheme of Narrative Analysis

For the scholarly discussion of narrative, one needs a comprehensive analytical method, something that, despite the attention given the subject in recent decades, does not yet exist. The scheme I shall present here is of my own devising, intended to fill the need. It is consciously, even deliberately, syncretic; no scheme can afford to neglect the work of Lubbock, Ingarden, Frye, Booth, Barthes, Genette, and others.[41] It is merely outlined here for the practical purposes of this book; a full exposition will have to await another occasion.

The basic notion is of levels of analysis in literature, on the analogy of levels of analysis (phonology, syntax, and semantics) in linguistic description.[42] A level is linear, sequential, extending in space to represent the sequential nature of speech and literature. No fixed hierarchy is postulated among levels, let alone the tight, "integrative" relationship that Saussure and Jakobson found among the linguistic levels of the distinctive feature, the phoneme, and the morpheme.[43] One requirement of a level, apart from its relevance to literary analysis, is universality; it must consist of elements that are both discernible in the text and that run throughout any and all texts in the same manner as linguistic levels. Such intermittent features as character, image, and symbol therefore do not exist as levels but merely as constituents of one level or another.

The levels must also derive from a general model of communication, even if literature's use of the model is simulated. Recent attempts to derive the concepts of narrative analysis from the grammar of the sentence—as if the narrative work were the sentence writ large—are, in my opinion, misguided.[44] If we fix our attention on the text itself, examining it as listeners or readers, we can discern the levels of speaker, focus, mode of discourse, style, meaning, and sound. The speaker level refers to the implied speaker or speakers of the text and to its implied audience. The focal level—the concept is taken from Genette's *focalisation*[45]—refers to the person who sees, and reflects what he sees, at any given moment in the text. In some texts it is the speaker who reflects what he sees, but not in all; certain kinds of narrative are a conspicuous exception. "Modal level" refers to the basic mode of discourse to which the text belongs (monologue, dialogue with or without action, exposition, narrative). Style, from the listener's or reader's point of view, is seen in relation to some anticipated norm of language use.[46] "Meaning level" refers to the meaning conveyed by the text, embodying the speaker's (or implied author's) intention. It is conditioned by all of the other levels. The sound or phonic level and, in the case of written texts, the graphic level, complete the list.

The levels differ greatly from one literary kind to another. By "literary kinds," I mean the four great categories of lyric, drama, epic or narrative, and exposition or theme. (The last of the four is a recent addition to the classical trinity.) Their very universality testifies to a basis in principle, and from the time of Plato and Aristotle, there have been recurrent attempts to distinguish among them on broad theoretical grounds.[47] But none of the distinctions proposed seems quite satisfactory. Positive definitions, which attempt to enumerate the essential qualities of each kind, fail in comprehensiveness, while instrumental definitions, in terms, for example, of characteristic personal pronouns and grammatical tenses, are awkward and, in the case of some languages, defective.

I suggest that the four kinds are best distinguished in terms of two oppositions, one relating to the kind of experience we perceive in literature, the other to the kind of perception by which we realize it. Drama and narrative are distinguished from lyric and exposition by the opposition of event and state; they present experience as it extends through time, as distinct from experience occurring in a moment of time or outside of time altogether, as in philosophical discussion. In the other opposition, lyric and drama are distinguished from exposition and narrative by their closeness to or distance from the focus as subject. (The focus, as in the term "focal level," is the person whose perception is presented to the reader.) Lyric and drama tend to offer subjective rather than objective perception—the use of the first-person pronoun is an indication of this tendency—and to present the particular rather than the general, existence rather than essence. The lyric, of course, deals in general concepts, but it relates them to the subject and may even render them in sensuous terms. (Its personification of abstractions is one example.) The lyric's extreme use of imagery is related to the desire for particularity; imagery can conjure up an impression of closeness that ordinary classifying language cannot. (Metaphor, in effect, creates new classes by bringing disparate terms and predicates together.) The drama, with its visible action and direct speech, is close in a way that narrative, with its recounted action and characteristic third-person pronoun, cannot equal. Individual works should ideally be placed in relation to the two axes of opposition rather than merely assigned to one of the literary kinds.

In narrative, the speaker level should be renamed the narratorial level—that is, the level of the narrator, whether or not he appears as an identifiable figure in the text. It refers to the person represented as telling the narrative, to whom, and under what circumstances. The narratorial level occupies so inconspicuous a place in most modern novels that it is frequently neglected by critics. Not so the focal level, which, as "point of view," has come to dominate modern criticism. The focus, the person who sees and reflects what he sees at any given moment in the narrative, may be identified with the narrator, as in historiography, or with one of the characters, as in autobiography and in much modern fiction. Even when the focus is identified with a character, however, what he sees must still be mediated by the narrator.

The modal level is the product of the two oppositions that serve to distinguish the literary kinds. (The kinds have, in fact, been distinguished as modes.) Critical analysis on the modal level therefore means the classification of the work and its parts along the axes of static and dynamic, close and distant. In practice, it is still convenient to use the familiar categorical terms of "scene" and "summary," crude though they are. "Scene" stands for passages that are both dynamic and close, with directly rendered speech and thought and a specific recounting of action. "Summary" stands for a more distant and general recounting of action and speech. Since "summary" covers a long stretch of the close-distant axis, all the way from a quite detailed recounting to the merest generality, it is the less satisfactory term.

In addition to summary and scene, the mimesis of action, there are also static elements in narrative—that is, narratorial comment and description.[48] Comment lies toward the distant end of the axis, corresponding to exposition. Description lies toward the close end of the same axis. *The Golden Lotus* provides an extreme example of lyrical description by its use of songs to depict the minds of its characters. The interweaving of scene, summary, comment, and description makes up the modal level. The passages of comment and description may be either coordinate with or subordinate to the passages of scene and summary. If coordinate, they stand apart, distinct from the mimesis of action; if subordinate, they are included piecemeal within it. There is subordinate comment and description in most works, whether or not there is coordinate as well.

Like the other literary kinds, narrative has its characteristic means of transition from one section of the text to another. In addition to the visual breaks (the graphic level) indicated by paragraphing (in Western fiction) and chapter divisions, it relies heavily on the modes of summary and comment.

Style can be analyzed in units ranging in size from the single word up to the whole text. In a verse epic, a relatively uniform style is a paramount requirement. In a realistic novel, with its attempt to suggest natural dialogue, there are numerous variations, all within a general stylistic conception. For the analysis of prose fiction, it is convenient to speak of general style, the style of the whole work, as well as of local style.

Three levels of narrative meaning need to be distinguished. In an ascending order, the first is serial meaning, the string of meanings in the text, without major configuration. The second is configurative meaning, the level on which plot and character are built up and questions and hypotheses provoked in the reader's mind. (This level resembles Ingarden's "stratum of created objects.") All of Barthes's codes refer to the configurative level, except the symbolic code, which refers to the serial. The third is the level of interpretive meaning, on which the reader understands and interprets the whole in general and perhaps symbolic terms. It might be objected that the process of interpretation begins only after the text has been read. But the common experience is that a tentative, continually modified interpretation accompanies reading.

The phonic and graphic levels need no explanation.

There are thus seven principal levels of analysis—narratorial, focal, modal, stylistic, phonic, graphic, and the level of meaning. Style is divided into local and general and meaning into serial, configurative, and interpretive, making ten levels in all. These ten levels provide the basic means for analyzing the composition and structure of a narrative work.

Three other terms need to be at least roughly defined. "Plot" ideally means the configurative level in its entirety, but for the purposes of discussion, it can mean a précis of the configurative level *in the same sequence.* "Stuff-material" (George Saintsbury's word) or "material" means the identifiable subject matter of a text regardless of its order and form. A novel and a film based on it share the same stuff-material but not the same plot. "Theme" denotes an abstraction from, or a generalization about, stuff-material—for example, revenge theme, knight errant theme, and so forth.

The Model of Vernacular Fiction

All Chinese vernacular fiction appears to make some use of the narrative model of professional oral fiction. No matter how great the divergences from the model—by the eighteenth century in novels such as *The Scholars* and *The Story of the Stone* they were great indeed—they never exceeded a certain point, one that can be described negatively more easily than positively. There is no vernacular work told in the first person (that is, by one of its characters) before the very end of the Qing dynasty, although such works do exist in Classical fiction. Nor is there a work that makes exclusive use of the historian's narrative method, the method of the chronicler or biographer, although it is the norm in Classical fiction.

The oral model is most apparent on the narratorial and modal levels. The former simulates the storyteller addressing his audience,[49] a common procedure in the early stages of a vernacular literature; what is remarkable about Chinese fiction is merely the persistence of the simulation. The audience is never individualized, except in *Idle Talk under the Bean Arbor*.[50] The narrator is sometimes individualized, especially in literati works of the seventeenth century and after, in which he becomes a distinctive authorial persona. The development can be seen as a feature of the Classical literature spreading to the vernacular; it springs from the different relationship of the Classical author to his literary subject.

The effects of this narratorial context are everywhere to be seen—in explicit reference to the story being told, in simulated questions asked of the audience, in simulated dialogue with the audience, in the sharp demarcation of the various modes, and even in the relative uniformity of style from work to work. The modal level is notable for its passages of coordinate comment and description. The narrator's reflexive remarks are only a small part of what is meant by comment. Virtually all vernacular fiction has a prologue, ranging from a mere poem to a whole complex of poem, prose introduction, and prologue story, all of which serve as anticipatory comment. Comment is also found at intervals throughout the story, in the form of poetry or prose offering explanation and moral evaluation, raising questions in the reader's mind, heightening suspense. (These passages have the ancillary function of sectionalizing the narrative.) In addition, there is an epilogue, a final comment by the narrator on his story, which usually includes a poem.

Coordinate description usually appears as a piece of parallel prose, less often as a poem. It is description from a general viewpoint, a tableau presented to the reader usually at the same time the character sees it but not necessarily through his psychology. Its diction tends toward an elevated Classical, full of well-worn imagery and allusion. For this reason, and also because passages of description are often borrowed from other works as part of the common currency of the novelist's art, they are known as set pieces, at least in their parallel prose form. A suitable general term to apply to both prose and verse would be *descriptio*, as it is used in medieval European literature. Like reflexive comment, descriptio is a common feature in many kinds of oral narrative.[51]

On the configurative level, there is the loose linkage between events, particularly *entrelacement* — that is, the use of an action for linking purposes only. On the level of local style, there is the array of different styles and prosodic forms used in the same work, a common feature in the oral literature yet one rarely met with in the Classical.

The use of an oral model is clearly indicated. On the one hand, the copious short fiction in Classical, written over a far longer period than the vernacular fiction, never uses these features. The narrator never asks questions of his audience, let alone conducts a dialogue with them. The only coordinate comment is placed before or after the tale, as a separate item. The tale never has a prologue and only rarely displays anything that can be called descriptio. Its narratorial stance is that of the chronicler or biographer, not the storyteller. On the other hand, such genuine notational prose fiction as we have, all of it from the modern period, displays the features expected of an oral model. The Wu Song saga of the Yangzhou storyteller Wang Shaotang, for example, shows strong evidence of all such features in its first chapter and fairly consistently thereafter.[52] What complicates the hypothetical relationship between oral and vernacular fiction is the apparent tendency of some later authors to indulge in flourishes that merely suggest oral practice. Among late-Ming authors, there is a development of the dialogue with the audience to extraordinary proportions, for both comic and didactic purposes. There is a similar elaboration of the prologue and even of the descriptio in some writers. These are to be taken as the literary man's elaboration of features inherent in the oral model.

The original model, presumably, was the professional oral fiction of the Song and Yuan periods, particularly the fictional (*xiaoshuo*) and historical (*jiang shi*) genres. This is the general opinion, and one can only echo it. (There may well have been systematic changes made in imitating the model, such as the elimination of sung or chanted parts.) Other oral forms of which we have knowledge, such as the bianwen or the medley, differ significantly on one level or the other.[53] Luo Ye, whose *Notes of the Drunken Old Man* (*Zuiweng tanlu*) describe the storyteller as composing his stories himself from Classical tales, is the main source of information on Song and Yuan oral fiction.[54] If the earliest surviving texts were created in the way Luo Ye describes, then the model is known, for the texts must have been compositional. If one remains skeptical of that view, the model can be reconstructed only tentatively from those texts with the closest thematic ties to oral fiction.

For virtually all vernacular authors, the actual model was earlier vernacular, not oral, fiction. Many authors may have been unaware of the influence of the oral model, accepting certain of its features as a successful narrative method without realizing their provenance. At the same time, the oral model is only one of the influences on vernacular narrative. Inevitable changes were produced by the vernacular fiction's very existence as written literature; by a different range of authors and public, with their different cultural emphases; and by the ever-present example of Classical narrative and its own distinct methods.

The Vernacular Story

How does the story (huaben) differ from the novel? To the student of European literature, the distinction between the novel and the novella presents no problem. Boris Eikhenbaum expresses the general view: "The novel and the novella are not homogeneous forms; on the contrary, they are fundamentally strangers to one another."[55] For him, the novel is syncretic, the novella elemental. The former derives from history and travel records, the latter from the *conte* or anecdote. The distinction is one of principle, and different cultures and writers cultivate one form or the other, not both. But the Chinese novel and vernacular story have largely the same origins, largely the same narrative models, largely the same history. The only apparent distinction is that of length, and yet it is a distinction so marked in the early stages of vernacular fiction as to imply a general structural difference.

Feng Menglong was the first to point to it, in a notice on the title page of his earliest collection of stories: "Works such as the *Sanguo zhi* and the *Shuihu zhuan* are considered the great landmarks of fiction. But the kind that concerns itself with a single character in a single action and which serves to provide entertainment should not be neglected, any more than the *zaju* as compared with the *chuanqi*."[56] The expressions "great landmarks" and "single character in a single action" point simply but effectively to the principal difference between the novel and the story. If by "plot" is meant the sequence of main events in a work, we may say that the story has a unitary plot in that no major segment of it can be removed without changing it radically, even to the point of rendering it incoherent. The novel, by contrast, has a complex master plot which may contain within itself a number of virtual unitary plots. Feng likens the relationship of story and novel to that of the zaju, or Northern drama, in which the Yuan dramatists excelled, as compared with the chuanqi, or

Southern drama of the Ming. The former's structure is simple and compact by the standards of the chuanqi, with its subplots and interweaving dramatic lines. It is also a fraction of the chuanqi's length. Although Feng's mention of the Northern drama was designed to raise the lowly story to a higher critical status, the analogy also has some merits of its own.

Character and action stand in a different relationship to each other in the novel and the story; this fact explains their difference in plot structure. The great early novels invoked by Feng may be abstracted as systems of virtual unitary plots linked by the participation of one or more of the novel's main characters. One of the functions of each adventure (or unitary plot) is to serve in the continuous revelation of character. (This is true even if the characters are not themselves complex; think of the running character joke in *Journey to the West*.) Each novel, of course, has a superstructure—a civil war, a rebellion, a quest. By calling them linked novels, one singles out their characteristic feature—the joining, on a lower level than that of the superstructure, of the virtual unitary plots.

Feng's distinction applies well enough in a comparison with the great early novels and, if modified, will serve also for the novels of the sixteenth century. But the advent in the seventeenth century of both shorter, more compact novels, especially in the vein of erotic fiction and the romance, and longer stories divided into three, five, and even ten chapters, makes a simple structural distinction impossible. Scholars have adopted the convention of classifying medium-length works as stories if they occur in collections and as novels if they occur independently.

The story also differs generally from the novel in the degree to which it is ruled by the mode of comment. Within its smaller compass, the comment, as extensive as that of a novel, bulks larger in effect. In fact, some story writers make their comment, especially their prologue, even more elaborate than in full-length novels. The prologue often contains a separate prologue story, a rare feature in the novel. Few novelists write prologues as elaborate as those of Ling Mengchu and Li Yu; one of the exceptions is Li Yu himself, in his own novel *Carnal Prayer Mat* (*Rou putuan*). If the usual function of the prologue is to direct the reader's attention to a particular angle of interpretation, the story is far more explicitly angled than the novel.

The proper contrast to the novel, in the spirit of Eikhenbaum's distinction, is not the story but Classical fiction in general. There is practically no long Classical fiction; it ranges from the anecdote, often included in the heterogeneous class of *biji* ("jottings") to the full-fledged Classical tale (chuanqi). (*Qi* means wondrous, remarkable, exotic, signifying the principal strain in the tale's ancestry.) The latter is usually distinguished from anecdote on the rough grounds of its length and complexity.

There is an extraordinary parallelism between the tale in Classical

Chinese, developed as an art form in the eighth century and written until the nineteenth, and the story in vernacular Chinese, written from the fourteenth century to the eighteenth. If the story is generally longer, that is in part because of the difference in language (and its associated stylistic values). Although different emphases could be shown in their characteristic content, they often share the same stuff-material. When they do share material, it is always the story that, as the more popular form, is the more derivative; there is hardly a single known case of a tale based on a story. When the tale was turned into a story, it was never merely translated into the vernacular; it was always transformed into the other genre, as a compelling example of the power of pure convention.

Feng Menglong's preface to his *Stories Old and New* (*Gujin xiaoshuo*),[57] the collection from which the remark about a single character in a single action was quoted, takes pains to defend the story against the Classical tale. In the course of a summary account, Feng notes the rise of fiction by literary men (*wenren*) in the eighth century and traces the development of vernacular fiction in the Southern Song to the Emperor's passion for reading huaben, which led the palace eunuchs to reward the writing of vernacular stories. (This explanation, for which there is a little evidence in the Song,[58] occurs also in earlier Ming writers in slightly different forms.) Ming dynasty vernacular fiction—Feng evidently means the story—frequently surpassed that of the Song, "yet some people regret its lack of the charm possessed by Tang fiction—a gross error!" Logically, he asserts, if we are to apply the standards of the Tang to the Song, we should also apply the standards of the Han to the Tang, and so on, back to the invention of writing and beyond. The art of the Tang writers "enters the literary mind"—that is, it appeals to the literary sensibility—while the vernacular story of the Song "is attuned to the common ear," and the literary minds are far outnumbered by the common ears. Finally, he points out that the effect of oral fiction on its listeners is far greater than that of moral texts such as *The Classic of Filial Piety* or *The Analects*. Throughout his argument, Feng never draws a clear distinction between oral and (written) vernacular literature, claiming for the latter all the impact of the former.

Despite this ambiguity, Feng's comparison sets out, for the first and virtually the only time in premodern fiction, the terms of a fascinating topic. The story and the tale present the scholar with an opportunity that is rare in any literature. Both are short fiction in prose. Their subject matter overlaps. The tale is the most common source for the story, but its stuff-material must undergo a metamorphosis of form and language before it can be transferred. The close comparison of a brilliant tale with a brilliant story based on it can illuminate the imperatives and tendencies of their respective forms and the characteristics of the literatures they represent.[59]

The main features of the comparison, which concerns every level of analysis, have already been suggested above. A few additional features can be associated with either language or oral model or both. The authority on which the fiction is narrated differs from one form to the other; the story purports to give us the storyteller's stock-in-trade, not the personal experience of the narrator or an acquaintance. The matter of the fiction may differ; the story's plot is of public importance; that is to say, its events cause a stir in society and offer a lesson to the public. Prologues often refer to the furor, scandal, delight, or admiration that the events about to be told aroused in the community at large. The perfect example of the resolution of a socially significant conflict being the law case, it is not surprising that the vernacular story abounds in lawsuits, trials, and judgments. By contrast, the tale is capable of dealing with experiences of private importance, which make no impact on the community, and even with psychological experiences. The extent in time of the plot may differ, even when both tale and story treat the same stuff-material. The story extends its recounting backward in time to specify the background and causation, and also forward to tie up loose ends and satisfy the reader's curiosity about the action's long-term effects. The order of the plot may differ; the story tends to take events chronologically from the beginning, while the tale, with greater flexibility, may begin in medias res.

Not only does the world of the story differ (it tends to deal with the less exalted elements of society in a mundane social role); the story's vision of its world differs also, with comedy and satire playing a far greater part than in the tale. The story expressly takes a didactic, even moralizing, stance toward its readers, a stance that makes the story simpler to interpret than the tale, except when the reader has to look beyond an inadequate narrator. Given their didacticism and the nature of the medium, it is not surprising to find authors disparaging fantasy and expressing a preference for tangible reality. Finally, the nature, if not the extent, of creativity in language differs in the two genres; the story, in keeping with its model, accepts formulae and *topoi*, and its creativity has usually to be sought elsewhere than in the individual phrase or figure.

In general, the story offers a different method of rendering speech and action. Its language makes possible a greater illusion of individuality and naturalness in speech. And its characteristic density of circumstantial detail, particularly evident in some of the later authors, offers a closer, more detailed account of the fictional world, satisfying better than the tale two of the three criteria for Ian Watt's notion of "formal realism": particularity of person, time, and place, and a descriptive and denotative use of language.[60]

To what extent is the vernacular story worth studying as a genre? I mean "genre" not in the critic's sense of an inductive classification but in the author's sense of an archetype that he may accept or reject or modify, the main element in his relationship to the literary tradition. The question could be expressed as: How vital is the idea of the archetype? Did writers work consciously in the tradition of the earlier story, modifying it according to their lights and their needs, or was the story for them a mere bundle of conventions accepted without question, while their real allegiance was given to other forms—the novel, the tale, the essay, the drama?

It is clear that the story tradition was important as more than a mere outer form. Types and patterns, signs of the power of the archetype, stand out clearly among the early- and middle-period stories. Feng Menglong not only collected and republished the earlier stories; he also adapted them and wrote imitations, in addition to creating new types of his own. Ling Mengchu professedly based his work on Feng's example, and there is a clear influence, although Ling is a very different writer. Li Yu parodied some of the stories collected by Feng and was heavily influenced by Ling. Even the last significant work in the genre, Du Gang's *Stories to Delight the Eye and Awaken the Heart* (*Yumu xingxin bian*),[61] is explicitly related to two or three collections written over a hundred years earlier.

Nonetheless, change is important in the story—so important as to make a synchronic study fruitless, as a glance at its social meaning, moral world, and technique will show.

The term "social meaning" refers both to the sphere of life (social locus) treated in fiction and also to the attitude taken to it. Toward the same social type and class, attitudes may range from denigrating to admiring, from patronizing to empathetic. The early stories, for example, contain a number of types of hero who figure only rarely in later fiction —outlaws, thieves, warriors—and the attitude taken toward them is in each case approving, although it sometimes contains a dash of good-natured satire. In a familiar heroic ethic, also found in the *Shuihu zhuan*, these figures are favorably contrasted with rich merchants and moneylenders. All of the stories are on topics that existed in oral literature, like the *Shuihu* itself, and we must suppose that their allegiance is to certain values of Yuan oral literature. In the middle period, there is no longer any stress on heroic outlaws but rather on merchants and shopkeepers, whose values of prudence, thrift, and hard work are upheld.

Nor is the moral world as uniform as one might imagine. Most writers worked within the idea of a morally active universe in which justice is a function of human and suprahuman ethical law, and in which ultimate tragedy is therefore ruled out. *Bao*, requital, which is usually translated "reward" or "retribution," is the moral grammar of interaction among men or between men and gods.[62] Indeed bao may be said to determine the structure of all stories on moral themes, since one requirement is that they be morally satisfying. But there are vast differences between the advocacy of utilitarian behavior in some writers and principled behavior in others, between stress on the human and suprahuman levels, and between an active and passive morality. Differences appear even within the five key social relationships of Confucianism: late-Ming adherents of the cult of feeling were inclined to stress love (husband and wife) or friendship; patriots concerned over China's fate stressed loyalty, which in this context came to mean nationalism; and writers of a more traditional cast continued to stress filial piety. There are important writers who employed other ethical systems in addition to the Confucian: the universalistic ethic of the knight errant,[63] for example, or the transcendental doctrines of Taoism or Buddhism. And there are even writers who ignored or questioned the fundamental idea of a morally active universe. The stories of the early period are noteworthy for their lack of interest in ethical questions, and Aina, writing in the aftermath of the Manchu invasion of China, was driven to see history as the product of vast, impersonal forces.

Changes in narrative method within the general practice of the story have already been mentioned in passing. They include, on the narratorial level, the substitution of a personal voice for the voice of the old narrator and, on the modal level, the profusion of comment, the number and density of scenes, and the increasing use of inside views—thought, feeling, dream, and vision. In addition, the concept of what makes a story (and especially of what makes a story complete) underwent radical change in the seventeenth century. One can, in a broad generalization, distinguish three stages in the history of the story. In the first stage, it shared a good deal of its stuff-material (and even its story types) with previous or contemporary oral literature, and its narrator's voice often resembled that of the oral narrator. These are the stories treated in Chapters 2 and 3. In the second stage, authors such as the playwrights Feng Menglong and Ling Mengchu imitated the first-stage stories, valuing them for their appeal and accessibility and also for their comparatively realistic (that is, nonfantastic) depiction of life. But Feng and Ling also introduced their own values into the story and effected a compromise between the author's individual persona and the stock narrator. These are the stories described in Chapters 4 to 7. In the third stage, the motives of imitation and of broad didacticism lost their strength, and the story developed freely in several directions, influenced by other genres. The individual voice was elaborated to an extraordinary degree by Li Yu, while the concept of what makes a story complete was dramatically loosened by Aina and others. These are the stories treated in Chapters 8 and 9.

2
The
Early
Period

Although it is clear that they arose from a tradition of artistic narrative, the earlier texts are surrounded by an almost total documentary silence. They survive only in anthologies from a later period, notably Hong Pian's *Sixty Stories* and Feng Menglong's three collections.[1] Apart from a single, problematical mention of a "huaben" written by a Yuan playwright, they are never referred to in contemporary writings. It is a puzzle even to establish the time ranges of their composition (one can scarcely speak of dates). They bear an obvious relationship to professional oral fiction as described in Song and Yuan works, sharing much of its stuff-material and fitting its typology in many instances; but this fact cannot be used to date them unless we believe they were compositional—that is, that they were written for oral delivery.

Our sole recourse is to the evidence of the texts themselves. A rough grouping quickly becomes apparent as one compares their manner of reference to historical, geographical, and literary matters with their conventions of style. The grouping is confirmed, to some degree, by typology and by the nature and identity of their source material. However, it can be fixed only tentatively to a time scale; thus a slight misjudgment could falsify the dating sytem, though the grouping itself might still be valid. The result of this investigation is to isolate thirty-four stories as written before about 1450; these are the "early stories" of this book.[2] Fourteen of them form an earliest group, Group A, most of which may well date from the Yuan dynasty. Eight others either are similar to them or else lack criteria; these are Group B. The remaining twelve stories, Group C, are clearly later than Group A; some date from the Ming, and it is likely that all do.

One can reasonably ask three broad questions of these texts. First, from what materials is the story made? Is its stuff-material derived from oral fiction, other vernacular fiction, drama, or some Classical genre? Second, for what medium was the story intended by its author — for oral performance, for reading, or for both? The fact that a story neatly fits some oral category may mean that it records oral fiction (in some fashion) or that it is intended for oral performance or that it is an imitation intended for reading. Third, by what kind of author was it written?

Four stories draw substantially on Classical tales; one is from Group A, three from Group B.[3] Another five or six stories, some from Group A, share their material with Classical tales but do not depend on them; they may well have been derived from drama or oral fiction.[4] It is unlikely that the influence of oral fiction was restricted to these few, however. Five of the six stories of linked structure use material that appeared in Song or Yuan oral narrative, and two of them suggest a knowledge of larger story cycles. Certain of the demon stories, which display a regular pattern of plot, may also derive from oral fiction. The early stories share stock subject matter and language, including set pieces and poems, with the *Shuihu* and the *Ping yao* and also with each other. There seems to have been a storehouse of narrative convention on which the vernacular fiction drew, and a few stories appear to have been constructed largely out of stock elements.

Until recently, the usual explanation of the stories' primary purpose ran as follows: the earliest huaben texts were originally scripts for storytellers to speak from; when printed, they became popular reading matter; writers then imitated them and produced a vernacular fiction. The explanation rested, in part, on the interpretation of "huaben" as "script for narrating," an interpretation that has since been challenged.[5] But removing the etymological evidence does not, in itself, make the theory untenable. Luo Ye, in his eulogy of the storyteller, describes him as composing his stories from Classical tales and interlarding them with famous poetry. According to the *Sanchao beimeng huibian,* a court eunuch compiled a saga for recital to the Emperor Shaozong from the recollections of a participant in some real-life adventures.[6] The *Huibian* is not reliable history, but it at least shows that this kind of explanation was current as early as the twelfth century and was not the invention of Ming writers, as is commonly thought. For all this, we know that there was an established public for vernacular fiction by the Yuan dynasty, and reading must surely be included in any consideration of purpose. It seems likely that it was the dominant purpose, and that the majority of texts were intended for reading, whether or not they derived their material from oral fiction.

The one author whose name we know is the playwright Lu Xianzhi, active about 1300, who is described as writing a huaben on the same subject as that of the early story "Song Four Causes Trouble for Miser Zhang"

(GJ 36). (Whether Lu's huaben can be identified with the extant story is
uncertain.)[7] The only other external reference to authorship is Luo Ye's
account of the storyteller as author. References in the stories themselves
are uniformly vague. The word *cairen* ("man of talent"), which often
refers to playwrights, is used of the author of "Madam White" (TY 28), a
Group C story.[8] It is also employed in a chantefable published in the
1470s.[9] Elsewhere it is occasionally used of the authors of poems quoted
in fiction. The word *shuhui* ("study group"), which refers in the Yuan to
groups of writers who cooperated in writing plays, is also applied to the
authors of topical poetry quoted in fiction. However, it occurs in one
more significant meaning; the *Shuihu* narrator complains at one point of
the difficulty he is having in integrating the various narratives handed
down to him by the shuhui. Unfortunately, he does not make it clear
whether he means writers or storytellers.[10]

The picture is obscure. Some of the more popular playwrights must
surely be counted among the authors. Perhaps a few highly educated
storytellers were involved. But we miss any reference to the professionals, the publishers and editors of popular books, the journeyman
class of writer responsible for the bulk of the vernacular fiction in later
periods. Presumably such men were also engaged in writing huaben.

The stories' social meaning also bears on the level of authorship. They
deal often with the middle and lower strata of Chinese society, and from
a sympathetic point of view. There is a story about a waiter, younger
brother of a wine shop owner; another about a jade carver and his wife;
another about a shop manager. There are few stories about examination
candidates or officials, and those few belong to particular types.
Moreover, most of the stories show more concern for narrative power
than for moral interpretation. Of course, these traits might be attributable to the early stories' greater reliance on the subject matter of
folklore and professional oral fiction. But the writing itself indicates that
they have also to do with authorship. Quotation is on a lower level of ac-
curacy than in late authors, allusion is more limited and more predictable, and the quantity of narrative and linguistic convention is much
greater.

Three Sample Stories

Most of the early stories fall easily into types based on thematic and
structural criteria, but before discussing them, I shall describe three
stories as specimens of early narrative. In all three, the ghost of a dead
wife or lover reappears among the living, but they cannot be said to constitute a type in a strict sense.

In "Zhou Shengxian" (HY 14), Fan Erlang, whose elder brother owns a wine shop, and Zhou Shengxian, daughter of a seagoing merchant, fall in love. Indeed, they fall sick with love. The girl's father is away on a voyage, and her mother, worried over the girl's health, and encouraged by Mother Wang, who doubles as nurse and matchmaker, consents to an engagement. The father flies into a rage when he hears of the match and repudiates it. The girl falls down in a faint, and then dies when her father refuses to let anyone go to her aid. As his wife had taunted him with meanness over the dowry, he reacts by burying his daughter in all her finery but without religious services.

A grave robber, Zhu, stripping the girl's body bare in the tomb, is overcome with lust and violates the corpse, at which point it comes back to life. Promising to restore her to Fan, he instead installs her as his own mistress. At New Year's, Shengxian escapes when a neighbor's house catches fire and makes her way to Fan's wine shop. Taking her to be a ghost, Fan hurls a cauldron at her and kills her. He is arrested and put in jail, where her ghost visits him in his dreams. (A god has taken pity on her soul.) The grave robber is exposed, and the god appears to the magistrate's clerk in a dream to assure him of Fan's innocence. Fan marries and thenceforth sacrifices regularly to the god.

Professedly a tale of strong passions and strange happenings,[11] the story is realized in six major scene sequences. The summary narrative, like the epilogue, is very brief. In the first scene, Shengxian and Fan meet on a holiday near the Jinming Pond, a pleasure resort of the Northern Song capital of Kaifeng. A set piece, the only one in the story, describes the girl in sensuous tones. The couple cannot speak openly to each other, but Shengxian thinks to herself: "How marvelous if I could marry a young fellow like him! If I let this chance slip through my fingers, when will I ever get another?" The idea she hits on is to conduct an indirect dialogue with Fan while addressing her remarks to a vendor of soft drinks. Her calculated scolding of the vendor is full of unnecessary information about herself and also of double entendres: "I'm seventeen years of age, and no one's ever taken advantage of me!" Fan follows suit, at which the exasperated vendor blurts out: "You must be out of your mind! What's the point of telling me all this?" It is a brilliant little opening scene, unmatched by anything else in early narrative.

The second sequence is that in which Mother Wang, a stock figure, divines that what ails the sick lovers is a "disease of the heart" and persuades the amiable Mrs. Zhou to agree to an engagement. The next is Mr. Zhou's return. He is offended by the thought of Fan's social position. "The most he can ever hope to be is the owner of a wine shop!" Zhou is a domestic tyrant with a violent temper, a common type in early fiction.[12]

The fourth scene causes a break in the narrative. The grave robber, Zhu, in league with the undertakers, is shown exulting over the haul he is planning. His mother warns him of the fate that befell his father--he once robbed a grave from which the corpse sat up and grinned at him, causing the robber to die of shock—but Zhu is not to be deterred. The robber's kit is described in detail, as in other stories of theft,[13] particularly the device attached to his coat that obliterates his tracks in the snow. We are told in elaborate detail how the master grave robber works. Zhu addresses the corpse: "Now, Miss, don't be alarmed. I just want to borrow some of your wealth and use it to hold a mass for you."[14] When he violates the girl's body, she sits up and embraces him, apparently believing him to be Fan, her lover. The next sequence is of her escape and confrontation with Fan, and the last is of their dream meetings in jail.

The concentration on a few exceptional scenes is characteristic of the vernacular story, particularly the early story, which often places a strong, lively scene at the beginning, where it will command attention. The scene is given here before the backgrounds of hero and heroine have been established. Such a bold beginning is unthinkable in the later story, which begins gradually, with summarized information, more in the manner of a biography.

The prologue is extremely brief, a reference to holidays in the capital in times of peace, with people straining their eyes to catch a glimpse of the Emperor as he comes out to join the festivities. It is a stock scene. We find it at the beginning of "Encounter in Yanshan" (GJ 24), where it is used for contrast. Here it is simply a way of narrowing down to a restricted scene from a broad prospect. It is a common feature of vernacular fiction. Many novels and stories run through the list of emperors in a dynasty until they come to the one in whose reign the events of the story are to take place.

The narrator's comment continually calls attention to itself. Its main function is predictive, anticipating what will result and lending weight to the incident described. For example, the fact that Fan trailed the girl home "led directly to an insoluble murder." At various points in the narrative, a common formula is used to predict disaster and convey a sense of dread: "If he had not heard this, all would have been well, but . . ." Another common remark, preceding some coincidence, is "Dear Reader"—or Audience; the words are the same—"What do you think of this for a coincidence?" The flippant tone offsets the horror of some of the events described. In accordance with common practice, couplets and poems also convey comment. After Shengxian has collapsed and died, we have the couplet:

> Alas! Three feet of loveless earth
> Now lie above this loving maid!

But there is virtually no overt moralizing. Explanation yes, such as how

Shengxian's vital breath (*qi*) caused her to faint, and how the *yang* influence of the grave robber's semen revived her. It is true that when Fan and the girl meet, we are told "people have no control over their passions," and certainly their reactions to their love are extreme. Presumably, the grave robber's lust is an example, on a lower level, of the same power. The final poem of the story, after telling us what a tale of remarkable passion this is, then offers the thought that, after all, it might be better to be without passion altogether. Behind many of the early stories — with the notable exception of the romances, which represent the ideal of a higher social class — lies the vague notion that daring in love and sex is to be equated with danger. The story makes no attempt to make a case of moral blame, as a later writer would have done, laying the tragedy at someone's door — at the girl's, perhaps, for being flirtatious; or at Fan's for responding; or at her mother's for her weakness; or at the matchmaker's for her meddling; or at her father's for his snobbery and cruelty. Nor does the author attempt to put the story into some wider context of causation, such as karma.[15]

It is told instead for its sheer narrative value. Its ingenious chain of events is intrinsically interesting, even shocking. But the reader is still not closely involved with the characters. He contemplates their plight but is not called upon to share their feelings. What he knows of their thoughts is merely functional, consisting of their plans and reactions to events, not their emotions. For all its suspense, the suspense that arises from knowing more than the hero does about his predicament, the early story's narrative technique maintains a certain detachment.

In "The Jade Guanyin" (TY 8), a jade carver in the service of a prince runs away with a maid from the prince's household. Later, in a distant city, they are recognized by someone from his staff and brought back, and the carver is beaten and exiled. On his way into exile, the maid joins him again. In fact, unknown to him, she has been beaten to death; this is her ghost. The carver is recalled to the capital to serve the Emperor, and the same man from the prince's staff recognizes the maid and tells the prince that he has seen a ghost. When the prince disbelieves him, he stakes his life on it. The girl is brought to the prince's palace, but when her sedan chair is opened, there is nobody inside. The informer escapes with a severe beating. The ghost returns home, tells her husband that she can stay no longer, and takes him away with her into her ghostly existence.

The main story, as distinct from the prologue, begins, like "Zhou Shengxian," with a number of scenes. The first starts obliquely with the prince, who is not named but who is identifiable as the famous general Han Shizhong, returning home from outside the city and catching sight of someone in the crowd whom he asks an aide to procure for his service.

Who is it? First we are given a couplet:

When will it end—
the dust that follows the horses and the carriages?
One day it must end—
the love that clings to the human heart.

She proves to be the daugher of a craftsman who has brought her out to
see the prince's cavalcade. The aide suggests that the father consider giving his daughter into princely service, and the father, who says he is too
poor to provide the dowry for a marriage, is happy to agree, in exchange
for a reward. The girl's skill in embroidery is described in a set piece, and
it is in this capacity that she is taken into the prince's household. Her first
task is to make a replica of an embroidered battle tunic that the Emperor
has given the prince.

The second sequence deals with the prince's response to the gift and introduces the jade carver. The prince has an unusual piece of jade which
he plans to have carved and presented to the Emperor. What should it be
made into? His carvers make suggestions. The third and best suggestion
is by Cui Ning; it will be a figure of the goddess Guanyin (Kuan-yin), the
image after which the story is named. He does the job so well that he rises
in the prince's favor.

The next sequence is the elopement. Cui has been out celebrating and
is in a wine shop with his friends when a hubbub outside alerts him to a
fire nearby. A set piece describes the fire, which seems to come from near
the prince's palace. The palace has been evacuated as a precaution. In its
deserted halls, Cui encounters Xiuxiu, the embroideress, clutching a
quantity of jewels. She begs him to help her and says she is exhausted and
hungry. But once inside his house, she reminds Cui that the prince had
promised them to each other and simply threatens him with an accusation of rape if he does not agree to make love. Cui agrees on condition
that they elope. They journey on and on, fearing the long arm of the
prince's vengeance. Only in the third city they reach do they feel secure.
A note of suspense has been struck.

Alone among these early stories, this is in two parts, like a two-chapter
novel. The first part ends as a man, minutely described, recognizes Cui
Ning. He is not named; and the section ends:

What boy with his fish clapper
Startles the lovebirds apart?

Who was this fellow, anyway? Listen pray, to the next installment and you'll
have the explanation.

The second part of the story does not answer this question at once. It
begins with a ci lyric, to the same tune as the opening lyric of the prologue, written by Liu Qi, who, like the prince, had been a general in the

wars against the Jurchen but who, unlike the prince, is now living in poverty and obscurity. His poem about his plight has found its way to the capital and ignited the sympathies of the prince, who has sent gifts to Liu Qi by his trusted servant, Guo Li. It is Guo Li who has recognized Cui Ning. Despite a promise to the couple not to tell the prince, Guo does just that on his return.

The next big scene is of the prince's fury as Cui and the girl are dragged before him. The prince is a general from the border area, a man of towering rages and a quick way with those who cross him. He is dissuaded from promptly killing them both by his wife, a gentle and amiable soul, who has to remind him that he is not on the frontier.

At this point, mystery is introduced. Blaming his defection on the girl, Cui is beaten and exiled. He does not know what has happened to her, and when she catches him up on his journey into exile, he is uneasy only because she has brought him bad luck in the past. There is an incident with the girl's parents that heightens the reader's suspicions but not Cui's.

The final scene is the confrontation between the girl and Cui, who now realizes she is a ghost.

> Cui Ning arrived home in utter despair, and saw his wife sitting on their bed. "My dear, spare my life, I beg of you!"
> "It was because of you that I was beaten to death by the prince and buried in the back garden. How I loathed that blabbermouth Sergeant Guo! Today I have had my revenge, for he has received fifty lashes from the prince. But now that everyone knows I am a ghost, I can stay here no longer."
> So saying, she stood up and gripped Cui Ning with both hands. He slumped to the ground with a loud cry.
> When the neighbors came to see what was amiss, this is what they saw:
>
> His pulses had completely stopped,
> His life returned to the Yellow Earth.

> Cui Ning had been dragged away, to live a ghostly existence with Xiuxiu and her parents. A later writer has an apt comment:
>
> The prince could not control his temper,
> Nor Sergeant Guo his tongue:
> Xiuxiu could not give up her mortal spouse,
> Nor Cui escape his ghostly lover.

The prologue is noteworthy for its poem chain, a series of poems linked together and connected to the story. The linking is generally fanciful and ingenious and the connection to the story tenuous. Indeed the poem chain prologue often flaunts its tenuousness; it is ostentatiously decorative rather than functional in narrative or thematic terms. The poems, ascribed to famous poets, sometimes in simplified form, are chosen for their surface meaning; all the ingenuity lies in their choice and arrangement. In this prologue, the first poem, a ci lyric, is on the first month of spring, and the fact is pointed out in a comment. But, we are told, it is not as good as another poem on the second month of spring, which, of course, is not as good as a poem on the third month of spring. This, in its turn, is not as good as a poem by Wang Anshi about the east wind being the cause of spring's departure. Then follows a statement by Su Shi that it is not the east wind but the spring showers that cause spring to end. Another poet contradicts, and is contradicted in turn, each adducing a reason for spring's departure. At length an obscure poet, Wang Yansou, says it is merely the passing of time, that the ninety days of spring are over. At this point, the end of the prologue, a simulated question is put to the narrator: "Storyteller, why do you give us these lyrics on the departure of spring?" He replies:

> "In the Shaoxing reign, there lived in the temporary capital [Hangchow] a man from Yan'an prefecture, Yanzhou, Guanxi. He was the military governor of three regions and Prince of Xian'an. Fearing that spring would soon depart, he had taken many members of his family on a spring outing and was returning to the city at nightfall . . ."

The words "spring would soon depart" constitute the sole connection between the poem chain and the story itself.

Poem chains, with various kinds of linking, occur in five Group A stories, two other early stories, and nowhere else.[16] To a late-Ming editor such as Feng Menglong, they appeared a bizarre feature of the early story.[17] Their obliqueness of approach, at least, is shared by other prologues in the early story; whereas the later stories announce a theme, expound it in a prologue, and illustrate it in the main story, the early story prefers an associative technique, with the prologue winding its way into the story. The elegant playfulness of the poem chain, the simplified version of a literary game, contrasts sharply with the mundane material of the story itself, the lives of jade carvers, sergeants, embroideresses, and the like.

"The Jade Guanyin" has many of the general features noticed in "Zhou Shengxian." It shows no sense of moral or social problem, only the implicit assumption, which it shares with much folklore, of the dangers of sexual love.[18] Our sympathies are again with the common man, this time with the jade carver and the embroideress, rather than with the prince or his retainer. But, unlike "Zhou Shengxian," it attempts to mystify the reader, as does the next story I shall consider.

"Encounter in Yanshan" (GJ 24) is atypical in several respects. In a simple reordering of its plot, it tells how, after the fall of Kaifeng, the Northern Song capital, Han Sihou, a palace official, and his wife, Zheng Yiniang, flee south. At Xuyi in Anhui, they are captured by the Jurchen. He escapes, makes his way south, and resumes his career. She kills herself rather than submit to the advances of the Jurchen general. The general's wife is so moved by Zheng Yiniang's devotion that she has the body cremated and brought back to Yanshan, the Jin (Jurchen) capital.

A close friend and sworn brother of Han's, Yang Siwen, also a former palace official, has moved from Kaifeng to Yanshan, and is eking out a living there as a scribe. At New Year's, he goes out to see the celebrations and catches sight of Yiniang in a retinue of ladies. He manages to speak to her, and she tells him that she tried to kill herself but failed, and that the general's wife took pity on her and made her a lady-in-waiting.

Shortly thereafter, Yang discovers that Han has arrived in Yanshan as the first envoy from the Southern Song. (The story's title refers to the meeting of the two old friends in Yanshan.) Yang tells the incredulous Han that his wife is still alive, but when the two men go to see her, they find only a ruined mansion. Han tries to remove her ashes for burial in the South but cannot budge them. After he holds sacrifices, his wife's ghost appears and permits him to take the ashes, on condition that he promise never to remarry.

Han eventually falls in love with a Taoist nun, the widow of a man who died in the war. She too has vowed not to remarry. Yiniang's ghost, informed by her old servant of their marriage, takes possession of the new wife's body, clutches at Han, and cannot be prised loose. A Taoist priest exorcises her spirit, but before long it repossesses the new wife. The priest tells Han to dig up Yiniang's ashes and cast them into the river. Later, when Han and his wife are out in a boat, waves spring up, and apparitions of Zheng Yiniang and the nun's first husband arise and drag them into the depths.

This story's plot is remarkable for the point at which it opens. Unlike most vernacular fiction, it begins in medias res and with a character not strictly necessary to its action. It is easy to imagine a story beginning with an account of Han and Yiniang's life before the fall of Kaifeng and of their forced separation, and then proceeding to tell of Han's mission to Yanshan, where it is *he*, not Yang, who catches a glimpse of Yiniang. It is easy, too, to imagine a late story describing Yiniang's suicide to the reader before telling of Han's mission. But it is precisely the story's unorthodox beginning that allows it to develop its first theme, nostalgia for the old order.

The prologue, a loving description of the old capital, is integrally related to this theme. It takes the high point of the calendar, the New Year's celebrations, and describes the brilliance of the capital on a festive and ritual occasion. It closes with the Emperor's own lyric on this very scene. The contrast with the rude capital of the Jurchen is made painfully clear. Yang Siwen — it is his mind through which we see Yanshan — at first cannot bring himself to watch the New Year's festivities. But the hubbub draws him irresistibly into the street, and then farther and farther away. It is an eerie experience, in which echoes of old Kaifeng keep

occurring wherever he sets foot. In a temple, he meets an acolyte with a
Kaifeng accent who once belonged to the greatest of all Kaifeng temples.
He sees a lady dressed in Kaifeng style, then a poem on a wall written by
some forlorn woman full of nostalgia for the old capital. Next day,
returning to the temple in hopes of seeing her, he notices a woman who
looks like Zheng Yiniang. She goes into the Qinlou, a vast restaurant like
the one in Kaifeng described in "Zhou Shengxian." There he meets a
waiter who is actually from the Kaifeng restaurant. The calamity of
Kaifeng's fall, the sense of loss and decline, is emphasized through
Yang's emotions and through Yiniang's and Han's poems.

The second theme, of a lover's promise broken and avenged, is just as
carefully worked into the story. When Yiniang tells Yang that she has
failed in her attempt at suicide, she mentions that Han has not remarried,
or so she has heard. The poem Yang discovers on the wall of an inn is
Han's lament for Yiniang. The old woman who leads them into the ruined mansion says Yiniang told her "she died to preserve her chastity, for
his sake," and the point is made many times thereafter. Her ghost says,
"Husband, had I been greedy for life, I would have dishonored you."
When he declares he will never remarry, she doubts his self-discipline,
knowing him a passionate man. "If I break my promise," he vows, "let
me be killed by a highwayman, or let my boat be capsized by a giant
wave." Before parting from Han, Yang cautions him not to forget his
promise. Meeting the old servant on his way back to Nanking, Han is
reminded that Yiniang died for him. After he has remarried and begun to
neglect his wife's grave, the servant accuses him of betraying his vows,
and Han, embarrassed, orders the man beaten. In the last page or two,
there are some rare examples of moral comment: "It is inconceivable that
those who betray their vows like this should escape retribution from the
Heavenly Principle." In the last desperate scene, as they set off in the
boat, Han hears the boatman singing a song he recognizes as Yiniang's
lament and feels as though "ten thousand knives were stabbing at his
heart."

> Suddenly he saw a storm springing up on the river, with misty waves swel-
> ling, strange fishes leaping and diving, and weird creatures parting the
> waters . . . Then he saw a woman, a silk scarf wound about her throat, her
> eyes preternaturally large and piercing. The woman clutched at him and
> dragged him down into the depths of the waters, and there he drowned.[19]

The silk scarf hides the marks of Yiniang's strangulation; it has been
described in all her previous appearances.

The story is, of course, an example of bao, requital. Yiniang has killed
herself for Han's honor, and he has vowed not to remarry; hence on two
counts he deserves to be punished. The broken promise of husband or
wife is a common folklore theme in Hong Mai's vast collection of supernatural tale and anecdote, the *Yijian zhi*, as is the first theme, the fall of

the capital. There are several *Yijian zhi* tales in which the ghost of a dead woman appears to people after the city's fall. Both folklore themes are actually joined in the longish *Yijian* tale "Yiniang of Taiyuan," the source of this story.[20] There is a variant in another Song work, the *Gui Dong,* which claims to amplify the end of Hong Mai's tale, and the vernacular author has apparently taken the hint and combined the two. There are several other sources, including a historical account of the New Year's festivities, a poem by the Emperor, and a well-known Song romance of nun and young poet.

Thus, the remarkable feature of this story, namely Yang's position as focus, comes from the *Yijian zhi.* The vernacular author has made brilliant use of his opportunities, however, for the *Yijian* tale, though good, is hardly an outstanding work. The story develops the two themes implicit in the tale with haunting (in both senses) effectiveness. The description of Kaifeng, of Yang's feelings, the eerie sense of illusion as he is drawn into a barbaric city that is full of memories of the old capital—all this is new. It is more than illusion, for the city is peopled by ghosts, and as Yiniang explains, "In times of peace, ghosts and human beings remain separate, but today they are intermingled."[21] Moreover, the betrayal and response are made to seem inevitable. The emphasis on the vow prepares the reader for its breaking, for Han's descent into sin—his beating of the servant, the figure of conscience, shows his sense of his own guilt—and for the desecration of his wife's ashes. The song on the lips of the boatmen, *her* lament, brings the two themes together in the end. Compared with the tale, the story contains much of the kind of extra detail that is essential for establishing a solid sense of time, place, and person. But what distinguishes it most of all is its extraordinary evocation of atmosphere, of nostalgia and tragedy, of illusion and unease, of guilt and horror.

Several ci lyrics are included, most of them represented as written by the characters. Apparently there were once more of them in another version of the story. But the disparity noted in "The Jade Guanyin" between the poem chain and the story does not exist here; these lyrics, belonging to a different world of the ci, that of nostalgia and lamentation, are central to the story's meaning.[22]

Court Case Story

Crime and punishment are an important theme in traditional literature —Classical, vernacular, and oral alike—a more important theme, perhaps, than in any other of the world's literatures before the advent of Western detective and crime fiction. Crime was seen as an offense against the social and moral order, on both the human and suprahuman levels, and the crime and punishment theme was a clear illustration of bao.

Court case literature goes back at least as far as the Song dynasty. *Gong'an,* the modern word for the court case theme, was the name of a type of puppet drama in the Song and a type of oral narrative in the Song and Yuan. Its precise meaning in those contexts is unclear, but it presumably covered court case themes. Court case plays formed a distinctive type in the Yuan drama, although the word "gong'an" was not, to the best of our knowledge, applied to it.

Obviously it is a theme that implies a structure—the commission, solution, and judicial punishment of a crime. (In the context of Chinese society, it was natural that the agent of justice would be an official, usually a local administrator.) The work typically takes this shape, showing us the criminal committing his crime and making no mystery of his identity. The reader's interest is in the judge's solution, which may be complicated by previous miscarriages of justice, the need to obtain a confession, and the like. But there are many exceptions to this shape, including a few remarkable stories in which the reader is shown the crime occurring but does not realize its nature. The three court case stories of the early period are all of this kind; they demonstrate once more the early story's penchant for mystery.

Another feature they share is a concern with sexual crime. Two are about married women, the third about a lady from the imperial seraglio; one is innocent, one guilty, the third misled. (The villains are typical: two priests, Taoist and Buddhist, and a government clerk.) Sex is the subterranean current of interest beneath much of the early fiction.

"The Monk with the Love Letter" (Hong 2) has a story rather than a poem chain for a prologue, but on close inspection, it proves not much different from a poem chain.[23] Its connection to the main story is not of theme, even less of tone, just of an element of the plot, expressed in a similar title, the prologue story being "A Letter Wrongly Sealed" and the main story "A Letter Wrongly Sent." But the prologue story is a *jeu d'esprit,* an exchange of ingenious and comic letters between a wife and husband and the misunderstanding caused by the wife's badinage. What does this have in common with the main story, apart from the similarity of title? Letters that cause trouble between husband and wife. The prologue tells of an exchange of poems between a scholar and his highly literate wife; it is on the level of parlor literature, like the poem chain prologues. Because of the gulf between it and the main story, the author might seem to be writing a two-level story addressed to different kinds of readers; but it is not so. The prologue is a deliberate piece of virtuosity which serves to put the story at a distance and establish the narrator's persona.

The story concerns a priest who, desiring the beautiful wife of a young captain, sends her an anonymous love letter, calculating accurately that the captain will intercept it. The captain is enraged, has his wife tried for adultery, and although she refuses to confess, divorces her. The divorced wife is befriended by an old woman who introduces her to a friend and creditor — the priest — and persuades her to marry him. At New Year's, the wife and her former husband happen to meet at a temple, where the captain learns the priest's identity from another victim. The priest makes the mistake of telling his wife who he is and what he has done. As she struggles with him, the captain bursts in and hauls him before the prefect. The priest is sentenced to death and the wife restored to her first husband.

The actual ordering of the plot is quite different. It begins with the sending of the letter but keeps the reader in the dark about the ruse. We see a stranger entering a teashop opposite the captain's house and summoning a boy to take a letter to the captain's lady, with instructions not to let the captain know. The first person the boy sees is the captain, and his guilty start and evasive manner ensure that the captain will seize the letter from him. The captain then slaps his wife and insists that the police interrogate her. The two scenes, told with notable objectivity, are the heart of the story. This is how the main story begins:

> In Date Spear Lane of Kaifeng Prefecture, Bianzhou, the Eastern Capital, there lived a gentleman named Huangfu Song. He was a captain on the Palace staff, twenty-five years old. He had a wife, née Yang, of twenty-three, a twelve-year-old servant girl named Ying'er, and nobody else in his family.
>
> Captain Huangfu had been on a mission to the frontier delivering winter clothing to the troops, and it was on the second day of the New Year holiday that he returned.
>
> At the head of Date Spear Lane there was a little teashop owned by Wang Two. On this particular day, about noon, when business had slackened off, a gentleman walked into Wang's teashop. To describe him:

> Thick eyebrows,
> Large eyes,
> Snub nose,
> Big mouth.
> Wearing a tall, bucket-shaped headdress,
> With a wide-sleeved, sloping-lapeled gown
> And close-fitting clothes beneath it,
> Neat shoes and socks.

> He walked in and took a seat. The proprietor, Wang Two, brought over a cup of tea, greeted him, and offered him the tea. He took it and drank it, and then said to Wang,
> "I'd like to wait here for someone, if I may."
> "By all means."
> After some time, a boy came by carrying a tray and shouting, "Get your quail fritters here." The gentleman motioned the boy over.
> "I'll have one." The boy, Seng'er, brought in his tray and put it on the table, then skewered a fritter, added a pinch of salt, and set it before him.

"Eat up," he said.

"I shall," said the man, "but first I'd like to ask a favor of you."

"Yes?"

The man pointed to the fourth house down the lane. "Do you know the people who live over there?"

"Of course. That is Captain Huangfu's house. He has just got back from delivering winter clothing to the soldiers on the frontier."

"How many in the family?"

"Just the Captain, his wife, and their maid."

"Do you know the wife?"

"She rarely appears outside the house, but she occasionally calls me over to buy some fritters, and in that way I've come to know her. Why do you ask?"

The man took out a gold-embroidered purse, shook fifty or so cash into his hand, and put them on the boy's tray. The boy was ecstatic. He clasped his hands together and made a low bow.

"What is your command, sir?"

"I want to ask you a favor."

He took a piece of white paper from his sleeve. It contained a pair of jade rings,[24] two short gold hairpins, and a note. He handed them to the boy.

"I'll trouble you to give these to the lady I was asking about. If the Captain should be there, don't on any account give them to him. When you see her, just say that a gentleman insisted you bring these trifling gifts over and that he hopes she will deign to accept them. Now, off you go. I shall be waiting for her reply."

The boy took them, left his tray on the teashop counter, and with the three presents clutched in his hand, turned into Date Spear Lane. At the Captain's house, he parted the green bamboo door curtains and peered inside. The Captain was sitting in an armchair just inside the door when he saw the boy who sold quail fritters open the curtain, give a flustered look inside, and make off. The Captain uttered a stentorian roar, such a roar

As Zhang Fei boldly uttered on Dangyang Bridge,
Facing Lord Cao and his million men-at-arms.

"What do you want?" he roared.

The boy paid no attention to him but just took to his heels. The Captain sprang after him, caught him in a couple of strides, and dragged him back inside.

"What's going on? You took one look inside and then ran off. Why?"

"A gentleman told me to give some things to the mistress. He said I wasn't to hand them to you."

"What things?"

"Don't ask! I'm not supposed to hand them to you!"

The Captain clenched a seamless fist and pounded the boy hard on the top of his head.

"You'd better show me!"

Stunned by the blow, the boy had no choice but to produce the package from his pocket, protesting all the while: "I was told to give them to the mistress. I'm not supposed to hand them to you."

The Captain snatched the package and opened it. Inside he found a pair of jade rings, a pair of short gold hairpins, and a note.

The prologue is linked to the main story in such a way as to give a hint of the plot. The passage runs:

The story I shall tell next is called "The Letter Wrongly Sent." A gentleman was sitting at home with his wife when she received a love letter, and because of this love letter, a strange, strange story evolved. In truth

> When will it end—
> the dust that flies from the horses' hoofs?
> One day it must end—
> the trouble that clings to the human heart.

There is a different version of this couplet in "The Jade Guanyin." A lyric follows on the highborn woman's beauty and is itself followed by the opening of the main story as I have translated it above. What is the lyric's function? It gives the reader a picture of the virtuous beauty and an inkling that she cannot be guilty of adultery. Second, with its trite plum blossom imagery, it anticipates the description of her, "twenty-three years old and lovely as a flower," that occurs throughout the story like a refrain. (The villain too is known only by his appearance.) Contrasted with the fragile, flowerlike wife whom the constable cannot bear to torture are the husband with his towering rages and the loyal, cloddish maid, a comic grotesque.

The story includes remarkably little comment. There is a satirical poem at the end by a "shuhui gentleman" who saw the priest being led to execution. The story ends with a tag that presumably descends from early storytelling practice:

> The story is over
> Please disperse for now.

But not much significance should be seen in its appearance here; it is also attached to stories that are remote from oral literature.

The other court case stories are "The Ghost Appears Three Times" (TY 13), a Group B story, and "The Case of the Leather Boot" (HY 13), a Group C story. The prologue of the former is about the power of the fortuneteller; it proves to be a deceptive comment on the main story, which includes gripping early scenes in which a man's death is prophesied by a fortuneteller and then actually occurs. His ghost appears to a maid and gives her cryptic clues that he has been murdered by his wife and her lover. From this point on, the story becomes a vehicle for Judge Bao, the most famous judge-detective in Chinese fiction.

"The Case of the Leather Boot," written with more circumstantial detail, makes a sharp change on the focal level as it switches from one theme to another. In its first half, we are given a moving portrait of a neglected palace lady, yearning for love. Having fallen sick and been permitted to recuperate outside the palace, she is gradually restored to health. She then falls in love with the statue of a god in a temple, and when the "god" appears in her bedroom, she is infatuated and credulous enough to accept him. Thereafter, she remains in love with him; after a moment's doubt, when he demonstrates his power against an adversary, "her joy was redoubled." Much later, when the "god" has been exposed as a magician, despite a natural fear as to what might happen to her, she still feels she has "achieved her life's desire."[25] The story is notable for the sympathy evinced for her plight and also for the many inside views, unique in the early story, by which her feelings are made known. But Lady Han and her concerns are soon left far behind as the second half of the story takes us through the intricate steps of the finest detection plot in Ming fiction.

Demon Story

The structure of the demon story, the most clearly demarcated of the types, has been abstracted as three universal actors and four universal actions. The actors, in the order of their appearance, are a young man, unmarried; a demon, that is, an animal spirit or the ghost of a dead person, in the guise of a young girl; and an exorcist, usually a Taoist master. The four actions may be labeled Meeting, Lovemaking, Intimation of Danger, and Intercession by the Exorcist. The young man goes out on a spring day to a resort on the outskirts of the city, meets a beautiful girl, and they make love. At length he realizes she is a threat to his life and calls in the help of a Taoist master who makes the girl return to her real form as ghost or animal spirit and punishes her. In the more complex plots, actions may be repeated several times, particularly the action of Intimation. The "revelation" procedure is in regular use, in which the truth is only gradually revealed to the reader as it is to the hapless young man. The stories are intended to induce suspense.[26]

There are other common, if not universal, elements. For example, in some stories there are second and third demons, one of them posing as the girl's mother. And the day of the meeting is usually the Qingming Festival, a time of services for the souls of the dead.

The stories should be judged by the art with which they are told—that is to say, by the suspense they induce or the atmosphere they evoke; by their gradual revelation of the woman's nature, raising a suspicion in the reader well before the victim is aware of it; and by their twists and turns of plot, with the victim captured, escaping, recaptured, and so forth. They are a Chinese gothic, complete with wild scenery and eerie visions, but they are also stories of exorcism behind which we can discern the dim shape of popular belief in the vampirism of animal spirits and in the search of malignant ghosts for human substitutes. Some demons eat the hearts and livers of their victims; others merely deplete their vital yang essence so that they wither and grow pale. Since the demons are succubi tempting young men to sexual love, these stories implicitly assert the same lesson as the ghost and court case stories — adventurous love is full of danger. But even in the early period there is a development of the demon's character from succubus to impish lover, and by the middle of the Ming, the gothic type of demon story has died out, leaving only the quasi-fairy story.

The demon type, obviously a folk tale, is not found in the great compendium of pre-Song Classical fiction, the *Taiping guangji*, but appears in the *Yijian zhi* and the *Gui Dong*, collections only a century or so earlier than the first of the extant demon stories. It was never popular in the drama, and although it must have been a type in the Yuan oral fiction, Luo Ye gives no titles of known demon stories.

"The White Falcon" (TY 19) is the most exotic of the demon stories, for what sets off the action is the loss of a white falcon, tribute from Korea. The prologue, which presents facts and legends about the reign of the Emperor Xuanzong of the Tang, explains that *xuan* ("darkling") refers to the morning star, which goes dark at dawn and hence signifies the decline that occurred during Xuanzong's reign. What caused the decline? The Emperor's excesses, especially in sexual love and hunting. We are given the story of his devotion to Yang Guifei, despite her infidelity. Li Bai (Li Po) compared Guifei to a notorious femme fatale and was banished, together with Minister Cui. Cui took along the white falcon that the country of Silla in Korea had presented to the Court and that the Emperor had given to him. It is Cui's son who incurs the danger, as he goes hunting with the falcon.

Hunting and sex are a current beneath the surface meaning of the story. A poem of comment refers to the twin obsessions, and after the young hero and the demon girl have made love, there is another warning:

> Sex!
> Sex!
> Hard to dispense with,
> Easy to succumb to.
> Ensconced in boudoirs,
> Hidden along willowed paths.
> It strengthens the small man's ambition,
> But ruins the gentleman's virtue.
> It made the Last Emperor betray his talent,
> And all King Zhou's power go for nought.
> It is a sword that kills without pain,
> A robber that slays one face to face.
> At length we realize that the eyes are treacherous waves.
> How many wise men and fools they have swept to their doom![27]

The connection between prologue and main story is more than one of historical background. It is a similarity of themes: sex and hunting were the ruin of the Emperor, and sex and hunting will almost be the ruin of the young man. The falcon is a token that ties the two together. The Emperor is endangering not merely himself but also the Tang line, while young Cui is courting his family's destruction. In addition, the story suggests that the Emperor's excesses have upset the natural order and given license to demons.

One's main impression is of the story's gothic elements. On his hunting jaunt, the young man stops at a wine shop kept by an evil-looking owner and peers into a wine cask full of blood. (The evil innkeeper will reappear in due course.) At the approaches to Mount Ding, a warning is posted about spirits and ghosts, a warning the foolhardy Cui ignores. He sets out in pursuit of a red hare; but not only does he fail to catch it, he loses the precious falcon. Desperate, he finally sees the falcon in the grasp of a skeleton sitting on the top of a high cliff: "The skeleton was tinkling the bell around the falcon's neck with one finger and cooing to it." At a manor house, the door is answered by the innkeeper. A girl in red (the hare) appears and says, "We have been waiting a long time for you." She proposes marriage, but is interrupted by a visitor. Cui peeps, and sees the skeleton, now in the guise of a general, swearing that if he ever catches Cui he will eat his heart and liver. Cui flees but suddenly runs up against a band of armed men. All is lost — until he sees that they are his own companions.[28] And so forth.

The distinctive formal feature of the story is its series of expanding poems of the "pagoda" or pyramid type used mainly in literary games. They are written in couplets of gradually increasing length, in this case beginning with one character and ending with seven, making fourteen lines in all, with one rhyme from start to finish. (The poem on sex given above is an example.) Seven poems are scattered throughout the story like set pieces, fitting their context in a general, not a particular, sense.[29] The story's prose is also notable for its stock metaphors: Cui's eyes are routinely referred to as "two drops of holy water, on the left and on the right, with their five cycles and their eight brilliances." The girl is described as "opening slightly her red lips, revealing two rows of splintered jade." The falcon is "round-eyed, wide-beaked," and the hunting dogs "droopy-eared, narrow-waisted, deep-jawed." The narrator issues a formulaic warning: "If this storyteller had been born in the same hour as Cui and had grown up alongside him, I would have pleaded with him not to go. The last thing in the world he should have done was to take out this white Silla falcon."[30]

I pass over "A Den of Ghosts" (TY 14) — in which the hero, a schoolmaster, actually marries the demon woman — and turn to two other demon stories, "The Three Monsters of Luoyang" (Hong 8) and "The Three Pagodas of the West Lake" (Hong 3), which appear to be interrelated.

The former has the earlier language, as early as that of any story; the latter was probably written in the early Ming. Although both share motifs with other demon stories, they have vastly more material in common. In terms of plot, one can be regarded almost as a transformation of the other. They also share text, but curiously, it is confined to six set pieces, some of which have very restricted contexts. I speculated previously that one might have been derived from the other at the oral stage, at which time only the set pieces might have existed in writing.[31] But there is too much in common between the phrases that introduce the set pieces, and we can only conclude that the set pieces were extracted from the text of the first story by the second author.

"The Meeting at Jinming Pond" (TY 30) is an excellent example of a demon story's transformation. The source is a substantial piece in the *Yijian zhi*[32] in which a rich man's son meets a pretty waitress in a tavern by the Jinming Pond during the holiday season. Returning the next year, he is told by the girl's father that she is dead. As he and his companions ride disconsolately away, they are overtaken by the girl, who invites them to her house in town. The young man stays with her, and they become lovers; but his health and looks begin to fade, and eventually his father concludes that he has been bewitched. A Taoist expert diagnoses a demon's influence and declares that the young man must move away three hundred *li*. If, in one hundred and twenty days, the demon cannot be shaken off, the young man will die. The time elapses, but the girl remains. As a last resort, the Taoist gives the man a magic sword and tells him that when the girl knocks that evening, he should open the door and strike her down. He does so and is arrested, but her parents testify that the girl died long before. When her grave is opened, only her clothes remain inside, proving that Wu has merely killed a ghost.

With its three actors and four actions, this is an example of the demon type. However, when adapted into the vernacular genre, it was matched with a prologue drawn from a well-known Tang tale that is put straightforwardly into the vernacular. This prologue story is not a demon story but merely a romantic comedy that demonstrates true love can bring people back from the dead. Some of its incident is similar, and this fact may have caught the author's eye. But he chose it mainly as a model, to serve him as a guide in adapting the *Yijian zhi* tale. The principal change is prefigured in the linking passage:

> Why have I told you this story today? Because it is about returning from the dead, that's why. There was a romantic young maiden who had the misfortune to meet a young gallant. She was not able to marry, and threw away her life in vain, but she nevertheless helped another girl to enjoy the delights of the bridal chamber.

The change is signaled by the word *duoqing*, "romantic," which bears a different set of moral expectations; we are no longer reading of implicit warnings against sex but of love's sympathetic power.

How is the new notion of love accommodated in the demon story? Much of the source material is kept. The young man wastes away, consumed by his passion, although whether the cause is sexual excess or some sinister force we do not yet know. The Taoist master who specializes in decapitating "demons of sexual desire" finds the demonic miasma thick around him, but the magic is ineffective. The girl is able to foil it because she has divine authorization to return to earth and bring with her a knowledge of heavenly secrets. But if she is a fairy, why does she sap his strength? One is left to conclude that congress with spirits, even well-meaning ones, is harmful. The obvious change from the original is that the young man kills a pageboy who comes knocking at his door as he waits for the girl. In jail for murder, he is visited in a dream by the girl's ghost, who tells him that her one hundred and twenty days of allotted marriage were up just as he played his trick on her. Using magic, she rights the situation and enables him to marry. Reassuringly, his wife has the same given name as the ghost girl and resembles her in appearance.

The demon of "Madam White" is more benign even than the ghost in "The Meeting at Jinming Pond." She is, as she tells the exorcist, a snake who took refuge in the West Lake at Hangchow during a storm and happened to fall in love with the hero, Xu Xuan. Her love is insisted on throughout; she is never depicted as wanting to devour him, although they spend a good deal of time, intermittently, as husband and wife. The trouble she gets him into by stealing money and jewels from impregnable vaults springs only from her desire to give him presents. At the end of the story, she is still devoted to Xu; reduced to her original form, she "still raised her head and looked at him."

Xu's love for her, however, is the object of censure. Here is how the subject is broached:

> Today I am going to tell of a handsome lad who, while roaming about the West Lake, met two women, an event that led to a great scandal in a number of counties and towns and created a furor in the pleasure quarters. A man of talent [cairen] was induced to take up his brush and make the event into a romantic story [huaben]. But who was this young man? What was his name? What sort of women did he meet? And what events did their meeting lead to?

This passage suggests a *schreckmärchen,* yet the word "romantic" (*fengliu*) hints at a contrary emphasis. Xu is "a rather naïve person" who cannot help falling under her spell. After they marry, we are told, they were "infatuated and enmeshed in their delight all day long." On a later occasion, when she persuades him against his better judgment to take her back, he does so because "he was led astray by lust." Finally, at the end, after a Buddhist priest has subdued her, the priest writes a poem to warn others; it contains the line "Those given to lust are deluded by lust," and it ends:

> Had I not come to the rescue
> The white snake would have devoured him

which suggests a return to the old demon story, much as the story itself belies it. At the end, Xu, showing no remorse at the subjugation of his "wife," turns to Buddhism, giving the semblance of an ascetic moral to the story.[33]

With a benign demon like the White Snake, the comedy that lurks behind the gothic terror of the demon type is allowed to emerge and predominate. The story becomes a series of comic sequences: of the snake's routing of the Taoist magician; of the snake charmer's attempt to subdue her; of her ingenious thefts and even more ingenious explanations; and of her continual turning up, a well-meaning curse that hangs over poor Xu. The sequences are told with a degree of circumstantial detail unmatched among early stories except for "The Case of the Leather Boot." The detail allows the author to pay significant attention to motives, much as in the later story and novel.

Romance

There is another, different attitude toward sexual love—that of the romance. The romance began with the Classical tales of the Tang and flourished in the Song and afterward.[34] The most striking feature of the earlier romances is the extraordinary social and cultural restrictiveness of their subject matter. They are virtually confined to heroes and heroines of the literati class and to some highly lettered courtesans. They are concerned largely with the poet as romantic subject. In most of the stories, courtship is carried on, at least in part, through poetry, a fact that sanctions the lovers' virtuosity. "The Swallow Tower" (TY 10), for example, is about Guan Panpan, a poet and the mistress of a poet, who remains loyal to his memory; it is a romance of idealistic love transcending death.

"The Pavilion of Lingering Fragrance" (TY 29) is a classic example of the romantic comedy, the type of romance that culminates in marriage. Its hero, Zhang Hao, is a man of brilliant talent who resolves to remain unmarried rather than accept anything less than the ideal beauty as his wife. He meets Li Yingying; they exchange poems and become lovers. However, Zhang is later engaged to another girl, an arrangement made by his parents. Yingying argues the priority of their engagement in court and produces Zhang's poems as evidence, winning her case. She is more resourceful than the conventional heroine and Zhang more indecisive than the usual hero. (A guilty dream dramatizes the conflict in his mind between romantic longings and Confucian propriety.) The story, like all romances, stresses the value of *qing*, love or passion, and shows the special dispensation accorded the ideal couple. It is based closely on a Song Classical tale inspired by the familiar Western Chamber stuff-material.

Linked Story

The term "linked" denotes a different relationship of hero to action than in the unitary story. The distinction between linked and unitary certainly existed in oral fiction, as Luo Ye's topics show, and if the extant linked stories are related to oral fiction (no fewer than five of the six are on topics listed by Luo Ye), their oral counterparts must have been long, diffuse narratives, each containing a string of adventures by one or more heroes.[35]

The six stories share a number of thematic patterns. "Song Four Causes Trouble for Miser Zhang" (GJ 36) and "The Toy Pavilion" (TY 37) are stories of thieves and bandits with a social meaning found also in the *Shuihu zhuan*. The former, which describes itself as a "mirth-provoking" story, takes the side of the ingenious thieves against their enemies, especially a rich and miserly pawnbroker. "The Toy Pavilion" distinguishes among its bandits, some of whom show gallantry; they include a pilfering servant driven outside the law by a harsh and vengeful master and a filial bandit who robs only to support his mother. Both main stories begin with scenes of stinginess and harshness, a patent attempt to give them moral meaning. (In the heroic code to which both stories subscribe, miserliness is the principal vice.) "The Meeting of Dragon and Tiger" (GJ 15) and "The Magic Bow" (HY 31) relate the adventures of men of destiny, for which there was a special category (*faji biantai*) in Song oral literature.[36] They deal not with the *enfances* but with the wild and wayward youth of their heroes as beggars, swashbucklers, and convicts. Both stories are about historical figures of the Five Dynasties, that turbulent period in which itinerant soldiers could hope to become warlords and eventually the rulers of petty states. In each story, a vision of the hero's destiny is vouchsafed to someone in the netherworld. "Yang Wen" (Hong 15) is related both to the bandit stories and to the men-of-destiny stories. "The Fairy's Rescue" (GJ 33), however, is quite different; it tells the adventures of a Taoist immortal in human guise. All of the stories have a large component of comedy, and the heroic stories in particular manage to make fun of their heroes even as they sympathize with them.

"Song Four" includes a lengthy prologue story on the Chinese Croesus, Shi Chong, whose wealth serves only to bring him to ruin. This version adds a folkloric explanation of how Shi, a humble fisherman, first got his money. When he is brought low, his executioner asks, "Why didn't you distribute your wealth, since you knew it would only bring you harm?"[37] The linking passage between prologue and main story attributes Miser Zhang's disaster to "a scintilla of meanness he had failed to eradicate,"[38] a reference to his rejection of a luckless *haohan* (heroic type) who came begging at his shop. But the heart of the story is the series of brilliant tricks played on their companions as well as on others by a group of men who live by their wits. One sequence in which Song sets tests for his former pupil, Zhao, resembles the folk tale type of the Master Thief. Zhao's burglary of Zhang's vault, as heavily guarded as a missile site, is the story's high point. In the end, the miser is forced to confess to a crime he has not committed. Unable to part with his wealth, he hangs himself in his own vault. The chief of police, who has earned the thieves' enmity merely by being relentless, dies in jail. And the thieves themselves?

> The band went blatantly about their nefarious ways in the capital, drinking none but the finest wines, sleeping with none but the most famous women, and nobody could lift a finger against them. During all this time the Eastern Capital was in an uproar; no one felt secure. Not until His Honor Bao Longtu was appointed prefect did the band get alarmed and disperse, restoring peace at last to the troubled city.

The subversion of authority is treated in a comic spirit, as in the early and middle sections of the *Ping yao zhuan*. Ingenious, farcical, ribald, the story is never entirely serious except in its opening moments, when the beggar is ejected from Zhang's shop.

"The Meeting of Dragon and Tiger" is a good example of the man-of-destiny story. It deals with two well-known historical figures—Guo Wei, who founded the Zhou state of the Five Dynasties period, and Shi Hongzhao, who rose to eminence under the fabled Liu Zhiyuan. The story tells of the early adventures of these two heroes in their days of total obscurity, when they were little more than brawling ruffians. It tells also of their marriages (their wives discern the aura of future greatness about them) and their rise to power. Incongruously, it seems, the prologue consists of the most ingenious poem chain of all. It begins with a poem written to Su Shi as he went to Hangchow to take up a post. (Several of the stories that are not set in Hangchow, such as "The Toy Pavilion," have Hangchow as a center of reference.) Then there is a leap to Hong Mai of the Southern Song, compiler of the *Yijian zhi*. What is the connection? Hong is the only man in the Southern Song fit to wear the literary mantle of Su Shi. After Hong's arrival to take up a magistracy, he gives a feast at which a girl plays a dragon flute, and Hong responds with a ci lyric on the subject. The guests praise its novelty, but one astute young official claims that it is a pastiche and proceeds to prove his case line by line, poem by poem. This is a poem chain similar in its rationale to the chain at the head of "A Den of Ghosts." How is all this relevant to the main story? This is precisely the question asked of the narrator by a member of his audience. He replies:

> "Today I shall confine my story to two travelers who brought to the eastern mountain, the sacred Mount Tai, wood fit for carving into a pair of dragon flutes and who there burned the wood as an offering. This act led to a Zhengzhou (Fengning-jun) courtesan's becoming a great lady with two titles and to her marrying a haohan who became a commander of four regions and whose name was recorded in history and survives to this very day. The material forms several installments of brilliant narrative. But who was this haohan who was destined to rise in the world? What was his name, and how did he succeed?"

The first scene is on Mount Tai. Wood for dragon flutes has been sacrificed, and the God of the Mountain summons the soul of a famous carver to make it into flutes. Free to roam about in the netherworld, the carver observes the God holding court and sending a man back to earth to become a military governor. When the carver asks, as a favor, that his sister, a singing girl, be allowed to enter respectable society, the God decrees that she will marry a military governor. At this point, the carver wakes up in his own bed, his soul having rejoined his body. Not long afterward, he catches sight of the man he has observed in the netherworld and urges his reluctant sister to marry him. The fellow is Shi Hongzhao, still a penniless soldier. Soon after, Shi's friend Guo Wei arrives in Zhengzhou. The reader is evidently assumed to be familiar with episodes of the early legend of Guo Wei, since these are merely alluded to. From this point on, we are taken through a series of adventures, presumably the installments referred to by the narrator, some comical at the expense of Guo and Shi, some chivalrous, several of them with analogues in the Shuihu and other works.

In "The Fairy's Rescue," the comedy arises from a realistic setting to which we soon find that rules do not apply, since the story is about supernatural beings. The art of this story is in the careful unfolding of its plot, which hides from the reader, as from the girl and her parents, the identity of the old man who insists on marrying her. "The Three Stars" (TY 39) is similar in some respects, but what is striking about this rather naïve work is its combination of elements that have already appeared in half a dozen stories of several different types.

Two or three stories escape classification, and a few others I have left
out because they anticipate trends that did not become dominant until
the middle period, the subject of the next chapter.[39]

3
The
Middle
Period

The stories of the middle period — that is, the years between 1400 and 1575, and particularly the century from 1450 to 1550 — differ markedly from the early stories. They differ in form, in structure, and in provenance, with the drama and the chantefable appearing in a larger ostensible role as sources. They differ in the nature of their thematic concern and in the degree of explicitness with which they express it. Their social meaning seems also to have changed; the merchant and the shopkeeper play a key part in shaping their values. On the other hand, Hangchow is still the main center of action and reference.

The division into periods, rough as it is, arises from the fact that the earliest surviving editions are those of the *Sixty Stories* of about 1550. With the aid of the later limit provided by the *Sixty Stories* and the earlier limit provided by the internal evidence of the texts themselves, it is possible to select a certain number of early- and middle-Ming stories and, with that group as a guide, to designate others as middle period by arguments of stylistic and thematic analogy.[1] Thus, the choice of the 1550 date is primarily a matter of convenience, not principle. However, the very fact that Hong Pian published his collection was to affect the history of the vernacular story permanently. His book was not the only means by which the early and middle stories survived to be reprinted in the late Ming,[2] but it was an important agency, and it served Feng Menglong as a model for his first collection.

Apart from Hong's edition and the catalogue of a private library that included vernacular fiction, a documentary silence almost as complete as in the early period surrounds these stories. Questions as to their provenance, purpose, and authorship have again to be answered on the evidence of the texts themselves.

Classical literature, in the form of the tale, again supplies some sources, but there is one notable development—the use of historical works. Several stories, all of them the work of the same author, are based on historical biographies. Oral literature's relationship to the vernacular appears even closer than in the early period but no less problematical. For example, all five known topics of the *taozhen*, a form of oral narrative, were also the subject of contemporary vernacular fiction,[3] but the relationship of oral to written is impossible to determine. Three middle stories exist in a form that actually suggests a chantefable. "The Lovers' Rendezvous" (Hong 14) contains a set of songs to a single pattern, spaced throughout the text, which describe, resume, and comment. They are prefaced, on each occasion, by directions to an accompanist. At the end of the story, the audience (or reader) is invited to get the full details by listening to "The Lovers' Rendezvous" of Qiushan, presumably the name of a storyteller.[4] "Zhang Zifang's Love of the Way" (Hong 10) is essentially a series of debates between Zhang Liang and the Han Emperor Gaozu on the relative merits of official service and the Taoist search for immortality. (It is a satire, in which Zhang has the better of the argument.) The topic is a celebrated item of Taoist lore, and since the story is largely in vernacular verse and at one point even mentions a *daoqing*, a type of chantefable on Taoist themes, it may well represent some such work.[5]

The third story, "Li Cuilian the Quick Tongued" (Hong 7), is by far the best of the three, a brilliant match of form and subject. It contains thirty-one verse passages in a common chantefable meter, all from the mouth of Li Cuilian, a shrew and virago; the passages are her diatribes at parents, sister, brother-in-law, neighbors, husband, parents-in-law. These last stories retain their chantefable form to some degree, because the verse passages are an essential element of the narrative. By contrast, the kind of chantefable in which the verse merely embellishes what has just been narrated in prose tended to lose its verse, as occurred in several Judge Bao court case stories derived from the fifteenth-century chantefables. Of course, derivation from a chantefable text means at most only an indirect relationship to oral narrative. In some cases, the chantefable itself may have been written primarily for reading.

The drama appears also to have been an important source, but the point is not easy to prove. There is only one extant play that could have been the source of a story—"The Contract" (Hong 4).[6] If two criteria are set—that a play must have existed on the same subject and that the story must show signs of conventional dramatic technique—five or six middle stories may have been derived from plays. Few of them are first-rate fiction, and some, including "The Contract," may be the work of a single hack writer.[7]

Hong Pian and *Sixty Stories*

Hong Pian traced his ancestry back to Hong Mai, whose *Yijian zhi* was the primary source book of the early story. (One of the first works Pian published was an edition of the *Yijian zhi*, which had already become rare in the Yuan.) In the Ming dynasty, the famous member of the Hangchow Hong family was Pian's grandfather, Hong Zhong (1443-1523), who rose to the rank of Grand Guardian of the Crown Prince.[8] His eminence allowed his son, Hong Shou, to enter the civil service without examination, where he served in the Censorate, and his grandson, Hong Pian, to serve in the Supervisorate of Imperial Instruction, which was concerned with the Crown Prince's education.[9] Giving up his minor palace post in 1545, Pian returned to Hangchow,[10] where he published a number of works, beginning probably with the *Yijian zhi*, for which he asked Tian Rucheng (*jinshi* graduate, 1526) to write the preface. Tian was a famous writer, a chronicler of Hangchow, whose *Guide to the West Lake* (*Xihu youlan zhi*) is a fascinating mixture of geographical description, local history, lore, and legend. At about the same time, Hong Pian republished a famous collection of anecdotes about Tang poets and their poetry, the *Tang shi ji shi*, asking Kong Tianyin (jinshi 1532) to write the preface. Both men write as if Hong were a protégé, and we may assume that he was still comparatively young. According to Kong's preface, Hong found the old edition of the *Tang shi ji shi* while reorganizing the family library upon returning to Hangchow. Curiously, his edition follows hard upon another of the same work. Four more editions by Hong are known, but only one is dated (1549).[11] The works he republished run from the famous literary anthology *Wen xuan* to what is apparently a handbook on art. With the possible exception of this last work, *Sixty Stories* stands apart as ostensibly intended for a wider public.

Sixty Stories comprised six groups, each with its own mildly fanciful title such as *The Rainy Window Collection* (*Yuchuang ji*) and *Leaning on the Pillow Collection* (*Qizhen ji*). There is good reason to believe that the groups were published separately and that *Sixty Stories* was, in effect, a series title, perhaps confined to a general title page when the groups were assembled and republished together.[12] The twenty-nine surviving stories, a few of them fragmentary, have the loosest organization imaginable: the general or series title never appears in them, and the group title appears only at the beginning of each of the group's two sections. The stories are not numbered, and pagination runs only to the end of each story. In only one group are the stories paired by means of parallel titles. And the printing format, although consistent within each story, differs even among stories making up the same section.

The title, *Liushijia xiaoshuo*, has a certain significance. *Sixty Stories* follows by only a few years a *Sishijia xiaoshuo* (Forty *Xiaoshuo*), which was compiled and edited by Gu Yuanqing (1487-1565) and consists of works by Gu and other Soochow writers.[13] Like *Sixty Stories*, it is strictly a collection of individual works, with no chaptering, pagination only to the end of each work, and a general title only at the head of the collection. Its contents, however, are of a very different kind. Written in strict Classical, they are the typical products of literati: essays, discussions of poets and poetry, occasional history, works on the minor arts, biographies.[14] Hong must have borrowed the title from Gu together with the format, the loose organization, and perhaps also the mode of publication. He can hardly have intended anyone to think that *Sixty Stories* was remotely akin to the Soochow collection; indeed his stories insist on their links to oral literature even when the links are spurious.

One of the groups, the *Pillow* collection, can be seen by its nature to be the work of a single author. The fact that his stories make up a group and that they are arranged by paired titles and by themes indicates that they were written for *Sixty Stories*, presumably by Hong Pian himself or some associate.[15]

But apart from the *Pillow* collection, the extant stories are an anthology without any obvious selection or arrangement by author, theme, source, or date. At least seven early stories are scattered among a majority of middle stories. At one extreme, there are the three that suggest a chantefable form; at the other, there are a few Classical tales. Hong did not draw a distinction between tale and story, as Feng Menglong was to do. It is not known how heavily he edited. Some of the superficial uniformity must be his work—for example, the regular labeling of the prologues (as *ruhua*) and possibly a few explanations in the text as well. But if "The Blue Bridge" (Hong 6) is any indication, he did not rewrite or edit heavily; it differs only in trivial instances from the Yuan edition of the same tale.[16]

The *Pillow* Collection

The *Pillow* collection is more than just the first collection by a single writer; it displays a distinct authorial personality. Its author was evidently a member of the literati who compromised with the huaben form in language and narrative method but hardly at all in attitudes and beliefs. For this reason, his stories strike us as different from those of his predecessors and similar to later fiction. Their moral attitudes are not latent, as the attitudes of virtually all the early stories are; they dictate the topic and control the work. Beliefs other than Confucianism are scarcely referred to: Buddhism is mentioned only to condemn the chanting of sutras and Taoism only as it accords with Confucian eremitism. The subject of sexual love, which dominates directly or indirectly the mass of early and middle stories, simply does not arise here. The *Pillow* stories stress the obligations of the social role and pay no attention to personal self-fulfillment outside of that role. Only in "The Red Snake" (Hong 27) does a hero win a wife—she is the daughter of the Dragon King, given to the hero as a reward for his gallantry—and no play is made of their union.

All of the stories are about men either in public office or seeking to attain it. Their study and examination taking form a major part of the action. In "Friends in Life and Death" (Hong 22), one hero learns that a desperately ill man staying at the same inn is a scholar and feels compelled to help him, despite the fear of infection. In the companion story, one hero enters the humble cottage of another and feels an immediate affinity upon seeing the bare room piled with books. Pity is shown for the good man thwarted in his quest for office. Two stories tell of generals who, despite a record of success, are dismissed through the machinations of palace underlings. There is a tendency to disparage the rash or arrogant hero such as Xiang Yu or Jing Ke, the would-be assassin. Classical poetry is frequently quoted, and heroes express themselves in commemorative verse and prose.

The morality is characteristic of this class. Much attention is given to the moral evaluation of great historical figures, particularly in the quoted poetry. The first two stories deal with the ethic of friendship in the special form of the *zhiji*, the intimate friend who alone appreciates one's worth. Friends commit suicide (or let themselves die) in the morality of self-sacrifice, by which the moral will meets an ethical obligation in its extreme form. The moral man's belief in fate (with regard to death and even worldly success) frees him for his act of heroism, of which the one sure result is fame, all that Confucianism will yield to the desire for immortality. The symbol of enduring fame is the shrine, and how many shrines there are in these stories!

The ancient past is the subject of most of them. The stories of the early period are generally set in the Song, but in this collection, there are two set in the Zhou, one in the Han, and two others that, though set later, concern the ghosts of ancient heroes. The classical sphere of the moralist allows the virtues of the past to be contrasted easily with the vices of the present. Not all of the lessons are moral, however. There is much other information—geographical identifications, descriptions of scenery, descriptions of old temples, and a good deal of history. (Much of the in-

formation is simple, and a little of it is wrong.) The keepers of historical
shrines lecture the sightseeing scholar, and the sightseeing scholar muses
on past history, expressing himself in poetry that unites the literary
culture with Confucian moralism.

The stories are heavily dependent on history and Classical fiction. "Li
Guang" (Hong 24) is quarried from Li's biography in *The Records of the
Historian*.[17] It simplifies what it finds, elaborates the settings, works the
incidents of the biography into a repetitive pattern reflecting the story's
theme, and adds comment. Although not bound by the biography, it uses
a good deal of the text and retains the implicit theme—that of the
doughty general who is continually denied his deserts and finally takes
his own life. The companion piece, "Feng Tang" (Hong 23), is also
historical.[18] It concerns a similarly mistreated figure as well as a
righteous old man, Feng Tang, who reproves the Emperor on his behalf.
More reworking of historical fact was required to establish its repetitive
sequence. From Classical fiction,[19] the author took "The Red Snake," a
fully formed Song tale, and freely elaborated it into a story. But his
finest story, "Friends in Life and Death," proves to be very different
from the Yuan play of the same title. The play represents more closely
the locus classicus.[20] The friend who kills himself to keep a commitment
and the reciprocal suicide of the other friend—these events belong to the
story alone. They serve to bring it closer to its companion story, and
hence it is possible that the author was himself responsible for them.

The *Pillow* stories begin with a short introduction or prologue and
then announce the theme of the main story. They make sparing use of the
usual stylistic features, and their language is close to Classical. They are
so clearly chosen and ordered to produce a moral effect that there is little
need for moral comment; more often, the heroes take upon themselves
the burden of moralizing. Description is also handled modestly, stopping
short of the set piece but sometimes using vivid language. Some of the
material is undeniably slight, for, like the romances, the stories tend to
concentrate on elements such as sentiment and scenic description that do
not involve conflict. Nevertheless, their plot configuration is skillful, and
even the most rambling stories prove, on close inspection, to be carefully
arranged sets of statements on a single theme.

Folly and Consequences Story

The folly and consequences type is more than a mere crime story; its plot
forms a tight chain of causation originating in some initial act of
folly.[21] The causation is constantly pointed out by the narrator, whose
warnings and predictions are the stories' most obvious feature. Predictions occur elsewhere in fiction, notably as chapter-ending devices in the

novel, but nowhere are they as prominent as here. In their most elaborate form, they comprise a cluster of three or four elements, beginning with a cause—"Because of this act"—proceeding to a consequence—"it was to develop that . . ."—and ending in a couplet and perhaps a short poem. In "The Wrongly Identified Corpse" (Hong 18), clusters occur at least eight times. Apart from their value as a structural device, their function is to make an insignificant act seem portentous, to increase the reader's sense of dread, and to supply moral comment. The folly stories reveal all to the reader and predict the general outcome; they are far removed from the early story with its tendency to mystification.

Their social locus is that of the merchant and shopkeeper and their highest value the preservation and stability of the family, including its economic basis. In only two cases are the heroes of a slightly different group: one is a shop manager, the other a government clerk. A stable family and a prosperous business may be threatened by sexual misadventure, by the idleness of a spoiled son, or even by a misplaced sense of humor, as in "Fifteen Strings of Cash" (HY 33). Sex is the principal danger in as many as six of the eight stories. Powerful sexuality in a man is dangerous because it makes him vulnerable to women. In women it is a danger because a husband may not satisfy a demanding wife—sometimes it is simply his naïveté that disappoints her—and she will turn elsewhere, cuckolding him, bringing danger to his family, and forcing him to take revenge. Or the woman may exhaust the man, draining him of vitality and even causing his death if he is very young or past his prime. The fear of woman as harlot or as succubus underlies the stories. In their social locus and attitude to sexual love, they are at the opposite pole from the romance, with its idealized view of the love of educated young men and women.

Hangchow realism is a convenient term for some of the key qualities of these stories. They are not much concerned with the supernatural. (The only clear exception, "The Golden Eel" (TY 20), is also the earliest of them.) Their action occurs on an ordinary social level. Such literati as make an appearance do so only as judges, and then the part they play is a small, often ignominious one. The highest person socially is the traveling merchant, then the shopkeeper, the manager, workers, servants, and prostitutes. There is a preponderance of people connected with the silk trade—as buyers, weavers, merchants, shop owners. The morality is, naturally, utilitarian; it persuades not by moral imperatives but by pointing to reward and punishment. The stories are cynical about motives and show a good eye for economic realities. They offer a view of the underside of society that is reminiscent of the naturalistic novel, except that the impulse behind them is moral. They never flinch from sordid detail, whether it be a case of dysentery or murder, and they often end in tragedy. Furthermore, all eight stories are set in Hangchow, nominally during the Song, and most of them refer in great detail to the city, to its gates, quarters, woods, streets, and embankments, as well as to its outlying towns and villages. Even among the early stories, set variously in Kaifeng, Luoyang, and Hangchow, the Hangchow settings are the most detailed. These stories are even more specific; one goes so far as to say, "At that time, there were no houses below New Bridge,"[22] exercising the reader's imagination in terms of a place he is assumed to know.

In general, the middle period story is freer in its narrative order. The early story avoids changes of focus and breaks in time. In the middle period, possibly under the influence of the drama, such breaks become more frequent. The sharp distinction that the early story makes between scene and summary is not so clear in the middle stories; their narrative slips smoothly from one to the other. They contain less formal description, usually just a couple of phrases, seldom the long set pieces of the early story. Many have no prologue at all, save for a short poem, which they do not comment upon. They get down to business in a traditional order: date, place ("this Hangchow," using some Song or Yuan designation for Hangchow), person (usually described in terms of his social function, name, family details, temperament, situation—especially economic situation), and then the unique event. This is how "The Wrongly Identified Corpse" (Hong 18) begins:

> The story tells how in the first year of the Mingdao reign of His Imperial Majesty Renzong of the great Song dynasty, in this Ninghai Commandery of Zhejiang Province (that is to say, present-day Hangchow), near the Guanyin Temple on the north side of Zhong'an Bridge inside the city, there lived a merchant named Qiao Jun, styled Yanjie, whose family had been living in Qiantang for generations. Qiao Jun's parents died while he was still a boy. He grew up into a big, powerful man, greatly addicted to sexual pleasure. Both he and his wife, née Gao, were thirty-nine. They had no sons, only a daughter—now seventeen, whose childhood name was Yuxiu—making a family of three. They had only one servant, a man named Sai'er.
>
> Now it was readily apparent that Qiao Jun had a vast amount of money. He specialized in buying silk in Chang'an and Chongde, selling it in the Eastern Capital, and then buying dates, walnuts, and general provisions, which he brought back to Hangchow to sell. This business kept him away from home six months out of every year. He had Sai'er run a wine shop in the front of the house, and hired a wine maker, Hong Three, to prepare the wine on the premises. His wife saw to all the financial and other matters. And there we leave the subject.
>
> In the spring of the second year of Mingdao, having sold his silk in the Eastern Capital, Qiao Jun . . . (p. 213)

Note the economical approach, in three steps, to the events themselves. The first two steps tell us most of what we need to know; the only fact missing is that Gao, the wife, is rather foolish. But the other potential causes of disaster are all there—Qiao Jun's sexual desires, the fact that he is away half the year, the fact that he has a wine shop on the premises, requiring a live-in worker, and also the fact that his daughter is seventeen and not yet married.

The folly story begins in the early period with "The Golden Eel," the only story with obvious folk-tale causation. One other early story, "Fifteen Strings of Cash," combines a folly story with one of judicial injustice. There are six middle period folly stories, one of which, after a beginning suggestive of the type, launches into the theme of revenge for cuckoldry. Three of the six are the finest fiction of the period and may well be the work of a single author. Although Feng Menglong reprinted almost all of them, he wrote none himself, no doubt because of his radically different view of human nature. Ling Mengchu was clearly influenced in writing his satires. The signal influence, however, was on the novel *The Golden Lotus*, which begins its first chapter with a page taken largely from "The Lovers' Rendezvous."[23]

"The Golden Eel" begins by telling how Ji An catches a golden eel that pleads for its life and promises Ji a fortune. "But if you kill me, I will make your whole family die unnatural deaths."[24] Ji goes home and puts down his fishing basket but is called away before he can tell his wife about the eel. When he returns, to his horror, she has cooked it for his supper. That night, the woman conceives the daughter who will prove to be their undoing. Aside from the eel incident, the story is a series of calamities caused by the girl. After it has wound its gory way through the predictable — indeed predicted — disasters, there is an epilogue comment. Later commentators, we are told, wondered why other people should die because of Ji An's mistake. Perhaps they shared the same karmic destiny as Ji An and his wife. Even if the eel incident is not true, continues the epilogue, it should still be taken as an omen of disaster.

The prologue reflects a common motif in Chinese folklore. The eel is a god — the god of Jinming Pond — and in revenge, the god incarnates himself in the form of the licentious daughter who destroys Ji and his family. But the story is also sprinkled with four elaborate warnings and several cautionary comments that are independent of the supernatural causation. In "The Lovers' Rendezvous," there is no eel and no supernatural causation; the girl's conduct is the product of her own nature and upbringing. Take away the supernatural element from "The Golden Eel," and one has something very close to "The Lovers' Rendezvous."

"The Golden Eel" appears to have influenced a number of other folly stories, notably "Fifteen Strings of Cash" and "The Wrongly Identified Corpse." Several elements in the former — robbery and murder, the execution of an innocent person, the accusation of the murderer by his own wife — are foreshadowed in "The Golden Eel." Of course other elements — the ambush and death of the family servant, marriage to the bandit — are foreshadowed in "The Toy Pavilion." Like some other Group C stories, "Fifteen Strings of Cash" is a mélange of motifs from earlier fiction.

Its first section is the ingenious story of the unseemly jest that leads to the death of the man who uttered it and to the execution of two innocent people. The man who makes the jest is from an educated family but has fallen on hard times. He is amiable enough but ineffectual. His father-in-law, a wealthy businessman, is concerned that his daughter is not being kept in an appropriate style and offers him the capital to set up a shop. It is in the afterglow of this news that he gets drunk and teases his concubine with the story that the money has come from selling her. The jest leads, by a series of logical steps and one flagrant coincidence, to the execution of the concubine and a young silk salesman. It is the sheer unlikelihood of the coincidence that impresses the judge, who is eager to tie up the case—"I simply don't believe such a coincidence could occur!"[25]—but the narrator, in a rare piece of explicit social criticism, makes the point that thorough investigation is necessary:

> With any care, this injustice could have been detected, but the examining officer was stupid and just wanted to wind up the case. He ignored the fact that by the application of torture you always get the result you want. (p. 17)

From this point on, the story departs from the folly type and turns to the correcting of the judicial wrong.

By contrast, "The Wrongly Identified Corpse" is a perfect example of the folly type. Its opening, which I have translated above, states the essential causes of the ensuing action: it is Qiao Jun's lust and his long absences from home that will bring him and his family to ruin. The story can be summarized as follows: Qiao Jun, a wealthy traveling merchant, has a wife, Gao, and an unmarried daughter. From one of his trips, he brings home a concubine, whom Gao insists he install in a separate residence. On Qiao's next trip, he falls in love with a courtesan in the capital and dallies there two years until his money runs out. During his absence, his family is destroyed and his property confiscated. The steps by which the disaster occurs are as follows: The concubine takes on a servant and, before long, begins sleeping with him. Gao, fearing scandal, invites her to join the household, but the concubine insists that she be allowed to bring the servant with her as a worker in the family wine shop. The servant soon seduces the daughter. Discovering this, Gao forces the concubine to help her murder him and throw his body into the river. The body breaks free from the rock to which it has been tied and rises to the surface. It is at first wrongly identified (hence the name of the story). A local villain recognizes it, though, and tries to blackmail Gao. Failing in the attempt, he informs on her. All three women die in jail, and the property is confiscated. At length, Qiao returns home, finds out what has happened, and throws himself into the West Lake. This is how the story ends:

> Having learned all this, Qiao wept streams of tears and took his leave. But wherever he thought of going, north or south, it was equally hopeless.

"Enough! Enough!" he sighed. "Here am I in my forties, with no children, my property, my wife, my concubine all gone! Where can I turn?" He made his way to the second bridge by the West Lake, and gazing over the clear waters, threw himself into the lake and drowned.
How deeply to be pitied are Qiao Jun and his whole family!

Up to the present, in wind and moon, on river or lake, this age-old tale has been told by fishermen and woodcutters. His body will never be coffined and buried—such is the outcome of lust.

> Flowerlike womenfolk die in jail.
> Tigerish Qiao drowns in the lake.
> Because of the shameful things they did,
> A mighty fortune reverts to the state. (pp. 229-230)

The story is built on a series of warnings and predictions, some in the tripartite cluster, others simply in prose. Here is the comment that follows the murder of the servant by Gao and the concubine:

Although Gao was personally a very virtuous woman, she was somewhat deficient in intelligence and mishandled the matter. Once she had discovered what was going on, she should have simply sent him packing, and the whole affair would have been over and done with. Strangling him was the worst thing she could possibly have done. Later she herself would be accused and would die of beatings in jail, and her whole family would be destroyed. (p. 222)

In her jealousy, her personal virtue, and her folly, Gao prefigures Moon Lady in *The Golden Lotus*.
As in other folly stories, the narrative is extremely fine meshed, leaving little to the reader's imagination. The following example, as Qiao returns home with the concubine he has just purchased, is typical. The passage could have been summarized in a short sentence.

The next day the weather cleared, the wind dropped, the waves subsided, and all the boats, big and small, set sail. After several days' travel, Qiao Jun arrived at North Xinguan. Mooring the boat, he went ashore, ordered a sedan chair for Chunxing, and accompanied her by way of Wulin Gate to his own front door. When she had alighted from the sedan chair, he dismissed it and took her into the house, but left her behind while he went to greet Gao and tell her what he had done. He then came out again and brought Chunxing in to meet her. (pp. 214-215)

"One Songbird Causes Seven Deaths" (GJ 26) is fully the equal of "The Wrongly Identified Corpse." It has the usual features of the folly story: it is built around a set of warnings and predictions; it does not break down easily into a few main scenes; it has little, though effective, description; and it places great stress on causation. The initial folly is a minor one; if the modern reader is not careful, he will miss it altogether. It is the idleness and frivolity of the first victim, the spoiled son of a Hangchow silk weaver, who instead of working for his father devotes himself to

raising songbirds. His parents dote on him as an only son and are unable
to discipline him. His folly is pointed to by the opening poem, which
refers to the bird as the source of catastrophe and urges parents not to let
their children neglect their family duty. This phrase, "source of
catastrophe," is also used by a contemporary Hangchow writer in telling
us that the stuff-material goes back to the mid-fifteenth century.[26]
Evidently it had the same moral meaning then, in an oral version, as it
has here.

Nevertheless, idleness is a venial fault, as venial as the tasteless trick
played by the victim in "Fifteen Strings of Cash," and it is not surprising
that this story too turns to the theme of judicial injustice. This is how the
story begins, after the usual orderly steps have been taken, establishing
date, place, social status, family, and character:

> Suddenly we come to late spring and early summer, when the weather was
> neither too hot nor too cold, and the flowers and willows were a brilliant con-
> trast of reds and greens. On that day, Shen Xiu got up early, washed, ate his
> breakfast, and prepared the cage with the incomparable songbird in it.
> Perhaps there was something in Heaven to match this creature;·there was cer-
> tainly nothing on earth. Whenever Shen had taken it to compete with other
> birds, it had emerged victorious, and by now it had won him a tidy sum. It was
> as precious to him as his own life. He had had a gold lacquer cage made for it,
> fitted with a brass ring, little feeding and drinking troughs of Ge porcelain,
> and a cover of green silk gauze. Now he swaggered along, his cage in one
> hand, headed for town and Willow Wood to show his bird. Who would ever
> have suspected that on this journey Shen Xiu would die an unnatural death?
> He was like
>
> A beast that enters the slaughterhouse,
> ᾿Step by step on its way to death! (p. 1b)

The details are important, for they illustrate Shen Xiu's consuming passion and also explain why the bird changes hands so often.

Two incidents show the naturalism of the best of these stories. The
first is the murder of Shen Xiu on the morning he takes his songbird to
Willow Wood. He arrives too late; the other bird fanciers have left.
Shen, because of his exertions, his disappointment, and the season, succumbs to a congenital illness. As he lies unconscious, his face the
color of wax, a cooper comes by and sees the bird in its golden cage hanging from a branch above him. The cooper attempts to steal the bird, but
Shen comes to and tries to stop him. There is a fight. The cooper kills
Shen, cuts off his head, and throws it into a hollow tree.

The second incident concerns the missing head, without which Shen's
father cannot give his son a proper burial. A reward is offered, and it
prompts a simple-minded old man, a sedan-chair bearer, now blind, to
suggest to his sons a way out of their abject poverty: to kill him and use
his head to claim the reward. This monstrous suggestion appeals to the
sons. They get their father drunk, kill him, put his head in a pond until it

is bloated beyond recognition, and then claim to have discovered it while fishing. The crime, which is suitably punished when the case unravels, illustrates the peculiar vision and narrow-based strength of the folly story: its low view of human nature, its awareness of the economic forces that persuade weak minds to ignore morality, and its unflinching description of crime and punishment.

Two other folly stories, "Han Five Sells Love at Newbridge" (GJ 3) and "The Apotheosis of Ren the Filial Son" (GJ 38), may have been written by the author of "One Songbird."[27] "Han Five" does not have a prologue story but instead offers a series of historical anecdotes on the ruin of emperors by femmes fatales. This is a traditional misogynist theme occasionally referred to by writers of folly stories about sex, even though they deal with a lesser social sphere. The hero of the story, the only son of a silk dealer, is put in charge of a branch shop that his father is setting up. He is married, and neither the lecher of "The Wrongly Identified Corpse" nor the idler of "One Songbird." Rather, he is "clever, capable, honest, and posessing a sense of morality."[28] However, he is seduced with ease by a young woman. How is the contradiction to be explained? The question is asked of the storyteller, and his answer is that the young man had only now, as manager of the new shop, escaped from parental control. The girl's background is left a mystery at first, but mysteries do not survive for long in the middle story. She is, in fact, the same kind of promiscuous woman as the concubine of "The Wrongly Identified Corpse," except that her motive is not sex but money. As the hero succumbs to her charms, she drains him of vitality. He suffers, in any case, from an illness, and sexual excess makes him vulnerable to a malignant ghost (a priest who had broken his vow of chastity and died in that very house). Just in time, Wu's father realizes that his son is a victim of ghostly possession, and has sacrifices made.

The last of these three stories is "The Apotheosis of Ren the Filial Son." The introductory poem couples the injunction against love with one in favor of thrift, two common values. The hero, Ren Gui, is the serious, hard-working manager of an herbalist's shop owned by a very rich man and is a filial son caring for a blind father. He is also, however, "a simple-hearted, naïve soul," who in his naïveté does not inquire into the character of a young woman whom a matchmaker proposes to him. Thus he makes a "careless marriage." In fact, his wife has already been involved in an affair with a local rake and remains captivated by his sophisticated charm. With his homespun manner and long working hours, Ren Gui fails to please his wife, who quickly resumes her affair with the rake. But the presence of the old man downstairs, blind though he is, impedes the affair, and in order to force her husband to send her home, the wife invents the story that the old man has attempted to rape her. "Ren Gui was so blinded by his passion for this woman that he did not ask his father if it was true or not."[29] He sends her home, where she falls into the arms of her lover.

So much for the relatively blameless folly of Ren Gui. He goes to see his wife and is thoroughly humiliated. As he waits inside the city for the gates to open, he overhears the carters joking about the way his wife is cuckolding him. From that point on, he is slowly transformed into the heroic avenger. His father and employer both counsel him against vengeance, but while sacrificing in a local temple, he receives a sign that he will take five lives. His employer asks Ren to stay the night in the hope that his anger will cool. "But in the bedroom, Ren felt as if his heart was being cut with a knife. He threw himself down on the bed, with all his clothes on, twisting and turning, enduring the slow passage of time until the end of the fourth watch. By then his rage had flared so high it could no longer be suppressed."[30] He goes to his in-laws' house, manages to slip in when the maid, who has been sent down by the adulterous couple, comes out to buy some cakes from a street vendor, and proceeds to kill his parents-in-law in their beds. Then he kills the maid as she comes back in and gives the alarm. He runs upstairs and kills his wife, who is pretending to be asleep, but cannot find her lover. Then, remembering the sign in the temple, he looks up at the rafters and sees him crouching there, naked.

> "Come down at once, and I'll spare your life," called Ren.
> Zhou had clambered up in panic, and now, seeing Ren below him, he trembled so violently that he could not move. Enraged, Ren climbed up from the bed and thrust wildly at him with the dagger, at which poor Zhou tumbled down from the rafters. Ren leaped after him, and planting his foot on his chest, stabbed him a dozen times. He then cut off Zhou's head, loosened the hair, and tied it to the woman's. He replaced the dagger in its sheath and went downstairs carrying the two heads. At the foot of the stairs, he fetched the maid's head and went to look for his mother-in-law's and father-in-law's heads. He undid their hair, tied all five heads together, and laid them out on the floor.
> By now it was broad daylight. "After this joyous work, my mind is completely at peace," he thought. "I'll be no hero [haohan] if I try to escape and am captured. It is best to hold my head high and confess to everything I have done. Then, even if I am executed, my name will go down to posterity." (p. 16b)

Reluctantly, the authorities sentence him to death, but on the execution ground a wind springs up, followed by a dust storm, and when it clears, Ren is seen to have died in the manner of a Buddhist saint. He becomes a local tutelary god.

The two other folly stories are distinctly inferior. In "The Wrongful Examination of the Stolen Goods" (Hong 17), an innkeeper, a widower, insists on marrying a prostitute against the advice of his family. It is a feeble story that shows signs of hasty adaptation from a play.[31] "The Lovers' Rendezvous," or strictly, "The Lovers' Rendezvous at Which

Murder is Committed," commands attention for its apparent chantefable
form, but it is an unsatisfactory work. The introduction, stressing the
power and universality of sexual love, is followed by a prologue story
(adapted from a Tang Classical tale) on the theme of adultery. The linking passage then talks of "an ignorant young fellow who also committed
adultery, who was constantly avid for sexual pleasure, and who set off a
catastrophe in which corpses were strewn beneath the sword . . ."[32]
However, the main story is about the sexual career of a promiscuous
woman who brings ruin to several men and one child. She seduces the
boy next door, who dies of fright when her parents return unexpectedly.
This experience turns her mind, and her father, realizing the depth of her
sexual passions, gets her out of the house as quickly as possible. A series
of marriages and infidelities ensues. She eventually marries a traveling
merchant but, unable to endure his long absences, she takes up with a
"stylish, sophisticated" young fellow. Her husband learns of the affair
and takes vengeance in the manner of Ren Gui in "The Apotheosis." As
her death approaches, like Vase in *The Golden Lotus,* she has nightmares
in which her victims come to claim her life. There is no reason why her
sexual career should not have resulted in good fiction, and there are hints
here and there of a powerful story, but the scenes are sketchy at best.
One is tempted to infer from the story's closing remarks that it is indeed a
clumsy version of something better.

Romance

The romance carries over into the middle period, where, with its idealized vision of love and its special social meaning, it contrasts as sharply
with the folly story as the early romance contrasted with the court case
and demon stories. No doubt the reason for its continuity lies in Classical
fiction, to which it still adheres in spirit. Although romantic comedy in
the early-Ming Classical tale shows some changes from the Song—it is
generally longer, more precious, more fanciful, more sentimental—it
belongs recognizably to the same type. It is reflected in "Du Liniang," a
middle period story that makes the fewest possible concessions to the vernacular.[33] Liniang pines over the long Ming Classical romances, contrasting them with her own loneliness, until she dies of the desire for
love. But idealized love transcends death, and she returns to life to fulfill
an ideal romance herself. (This unremarkable story was Tang Xianzu's
apparent source for his play *Return of the Soul,* also known as *The
Peony Pavilion.*)

, The middle period story includes other kinds of romances (a story of
Su Shi, which is full of poems; a scurrilous story of Liu Yong), but they
are no more remarkable than the comedies.[34] By far the best vernacular

romances are the mutations of the type, for example, "The Ring" (Hong 20), which combines the romance with the folly story. It tells of a clandestine affair that culminates in a secret meeting between the lovers in a temple. At the very height of their lovemaking, the boy dies, for metaphysical as well as physical reasons, as we are later told. All this is the stuff of the folly story, and the many dread warnings and predictions prepare us for an ultimate condemnation of vulnerable males, rapacious females, and the like. But along with its warnings, it also contains a series of lyrics, full of evocative description in the manner of the romance. Moreover, the love that is described is an idealized love—the boy is at the point of death from lovesickness—rather than lust, and neither he nor the girl is seen from the cynical viewpoint of the folly story.

The aftermath of the boy's death turns the story decisively in the direction of the romance. When the girl finds she is pregnant, she resolves to go on living in order to raise his child, her resolve strengthened (and the romance motivated) by a dream in which her lover explains the karmic causes of their tragic love. Sensibly, the families agree to pretend that the lovers had been engaged before his death. The girl proves to be a model mother and a chaste widow, and when her child grows up to become a high official, he sees that her virtue is commemorated. (The narrator comments sourly that such honors come more easily to the rich.)[35]

The intermediate status of this story springs from the social disparity between the lovers. While the girl is the well-educated daughter of a high official, the boy, for all his talent, is merely the third son of a traveling merchant, the class at which the warnings of the folly stories are directed. Marriage is out of the question; hence the tragedy. A similar disparity is found in another middle story, "Pei Xiuniang's Night Outing on the West Lake,"[36] in which the daughter of a high official falls sick with love for a young man whose father is merely the owner of a Hangchow silk-weaving factory. Her parents, despairing of their daughter's life, finally realize that love is the cause of her illness and reluctantly consent to a marriage. It is a standard romance, full of poetry, but with a new social meaning.

To return to "The Ring." It is precisely the closeness of its narrative, characteristic of the folly story, that raises it above the level of the middle period romance. Here is its account of the boy's death:

> She felt Ruan, prone on top of her, stop his movements. She put her arms around his waist and tried to insert her tongue into his mouth, but found his teeth tightly clenched and felt his body growing chill. She was panic stricken, this beautiful girl, right in the act of love. From her head flew the three *hun* souls, from her feet the seven *po* souls. She turned over, pushed him toward the wall, sat up, and then scrambled into her clothes and left the room. Still trying to catch her breath, afraid her mother might call her away at any moment, she replaced her hairpins with trembling hands at the dressing table, and in dazed despair renewed her make-up before the mirror.

Her mother's knock came just as she was ready. She opened the door.
"Child, the service is over. Are you just awake?"
"No, I've been awake for ages. I was just making myself presentable before joining you for the journey home."
"The bearers have been waiting for some time," said her mother. They thanked the nun, who saw them off at the main gate. (p. 256)

Religious Story

Like the folly story, the religious type originates in the early period and is set in Hangchow. It tells of priests, their deaths, and sometimes their reincarnations.[37] (In one case it is not a priest but a girl devotee who dies.) These are not the bad priests caricatured in the vernacular literature but poet-priests, men of literary distinction. The priest's death is self-willed, and the stories invariably give his valedictory poem and describe the funeral service and cremation, complete with funeral address. The reason for the death is related in some way to sex. The priest wills his own death from shame when his sexual conduct becomes known or because he has been falsely accused. (In the girl's case, she dies because she wishes to avoid sexual contamination.) The stories are concerned above all with the priest's vow of chastity and the temptations to which he is subjected; but they also preserve, together with a dash of comedy, a certain religious meaning. And although they share the folly story's interest in sexual love, they lack its narrative features, as well as its insistent detail and its emphasis on causation. Indeed, they are often implausible by ordinary standards and are written with a simple authority in a manner reminiscent of the fairy tale.

The earliest religious story is probably "The Five Abstinences Priest Seduces Red Lotus" (Hong 13). Its nucleus is the historical friendship between Su Shi and the priest Foyin, a fellow poet, around which a whole complex of fiction grew, all of it contrasting sexual love with Buddhist abstinence. This story tells of Su Shi and Foyin in their own lives and also in a previous incarnation. In their own lives, Foyin is seen instructing Su Shi and softening his hostile attitude toward Buddhism. The previous incarnation, the heart of the story, supplies the karmic causation. When Five Abstinences, a devout priest of high reputation, seduces a young orphan girl, Red Lotus, whom he has raised in the monastery, his brother priest allusively reproves him in a poem on the subject of the lotus. Five Abstinences is so ashamed—shame rather than guilt is his motive—that he wills his death, leaving a valedictory poem, at which point his friend hastily dies too in order to pursue him and save him from the fate that is in store for him. Five Abstinences is reborn as Su Shi and his friend as Foyin, and it is through Foyin that Su comes to understand and honor Buddhism. There is a related story that tells of the accidental

way in which Foyin becomes a priest and of how Su Shi tests his virtue
with the aid of a compliant singing girl, a test from which Foyin emerges
with honor.[38]

In a middle period story that derives, in part, from both of these, we
find the test of a priest's virtue given a very different meaning. This is
"Red Lotus Seduces the Priest Yutong" (GJ 29), in which the opposition
between civil official and priest leads to the latter's death and reincarnation. The text bears a complex relationship to early and middle fiction
and drama.[39] Virtually every element in it can be paralleled in other
works, including "The Five Abstinences Priest" and a number of vernacular stories. Its stuff-material was one of the subjects of the *taozhen*
chantefables performed in Hangchow in the sixteenth century, and some
of its development may have taken place in oral narrative.

"Red Lotus" appears to be a retrospective formation from material
reflected in a Yuan play, *The Yueming Priest's Salvation of Liu Cui*
(*Yueming heshang du Liu Cui*), which tells how a famous singing girl was
converted by a priest. According to this theory, the "Red Lotus" story
was developed to supply its karmic causation. In the story, Liu, an arrogant prefect of Hangchow, resenting the fact that an aged priest, a
celebrated holy man, failed to present himself together with other priests
at a ceremony, dispatches a local singing girl to tempt the priest's virtue.
In a scene that forms the story's center, by means of a stratagem, she succeeds. When the old priest, Yutong, realizes that he has been tricked, he
wills his own death and sends a valedictory poem to Prefect Liu. Yutong
is reincarnated as a baby girl born to the prefect's wife. After Liu's death,
the family's fortunes begin to decline. The girl has one unhappy experience after another as a concubine and then drifts into prostitution,
besmirching the name of the Lius and carrying out the priest's revenge.
At this point, the story as it exists in its earliest form sums up the girl's
salvation in a few phrases, commenting: "If the reader wishes to learn the
actual details, he is urged to read "The Yueming Priest's Salvation of Liu
Cui." Feng Menglong, in his version, thought it unconscionable to leave
the matter like this, and filled out the ending.[40]

"Chen Kechang" (TY 7) is another story of official and priest,
although in this case, the accusation brought against the priest is false.
The hero is a gifted young poet who becomes an acolyte after repeatedly
failing the examinations. His poetic talent impresses the Prince, the temple's patron, and the Prince obtains a priest's license for the poet and
takes him as a protégé. The story is studded with lyrics that the young
priest composes to express his own feelings and also, on occasion, at the
Prince's behest. (The lyrics, which are all of the same pattern, help give
structure to the story.) When the Prince's concubine becomes pregnant,
she accuses the priest (falsely, as it turns out), and the Prince, one of
those imperious figures found in the early stories, believes the accusation

and forces the priest into a confession. When the Prince realizes his error, the priest, knowing he is about to be vindicated, wills his own death. He receives the usual funeral orations, and at the moment of cremation, appears and explains to all that he is really an arhat who has returned to earth to repay a karmic debt. It is a compelling work, despite the implausibility of the Prince's charge and the final supernatural causation, which, as always, diminishes the significance of human action. In this and other respects, the story lacks the middle period tendency to show causation at its source.

A more religious story is "Liannu Attains Buddhahood on the Way to Her Wedding" (Hong 16), probably an early-Ming work. It is a reincarnation story that tells of a pious old woman, fond of chanting the *Lotus Sutra*, who is reborn as the only daughter of a devout middle-aged couple who have shown her kindness. It is an excellent example of religious comedy, mundane on one level, religious on another, with the comedy arising from the interplay between the two. The little girl is a rare trial to her well-intentioned parents as she insists on challenging passing priests with cryptic Chan questions (*kōan*), and then, when they cannot answer her, hitting them in the manner of the Linji school of Buddhism. At length a neighbor's son falls in love with her and haunts the family flower shop until flowers festoon his room. (The family are makers of artificial flowers; there is an association with the *Lotus Sutra* and with the girl's name, Lotus.) The boy falls ill, and when his father finds out the reason, he proposes marriage, even though, as he is an official, his family's position is vastly superior to the girl's. The climax is the wedding day. When the sedan chair carrying the bride reaches the bridegroom's house, she is found to have willed herself to death inside it.

Court Case Story

That court case fiction also remained popular during the Ming dynasty was shown by the discovery in 1967 of some texts in a fifteenth-century grave.[41] In addition to a play, they consisted of sixteen *cihua* chantefables published in the 1470s, no fewer than eight of which were court case fiction featuring Judge Bao, the most common judge figure in the Yuan drama. The chantefables resemble the Yuan plays in showing Bao attacking malefactors in high places. In fact, they go further and show him actually challenging the Emperor's relatives in the cause of justice.

No court case huaben survive from the middle period proper, but a collection of Judge Bao stories entitled *The Hundred Cases (Baijia gong'an)* exists in a Hangchow edition of 1594.[42] It was not the first edition—indeed it does not even represent the collection's original form—and parts of it may well have been written a decade or more earlier. *The Hundred Cases* stimulated a small boom in court case fiction; numbers of collections survive from the next twenty years, each pillaging its predecessors.[43] Like *The Hundred Cases*, they belong to the world of popular publishing; their authors were mostly professional publishers and editors. The boom was soon over, and it was not until the turn of this century that it was repeated, stimulated on that occasion by the appearance of the Sherlock Holmes stories in Chinese. (The so-called court case [*gong'an*] novels of the middle and late Qing scarcely qualify; the proportion of heroic adventure far outweighs that of detection.) During the late Ming and Qing, court case fiction was kept alive by the popular secondary anthology *Longtu's Cases* (*Longtu gong'an*), half of which come from *The Hundred Cases*.

Of the Ming collections, only *The Hundred Cases* can be classified as huaben; the others use neither the narrative model nor the vernacular language. To be appreciated as huaben, however, *The Hundred Cases* should be seen in its original form. On close inspection, it proves to be the work of three separate writers, the third of whom—presumably the editor of the 1594 Hangchow edition—was guilty of breaking up the order of an earlier collection and placing his own, distinctly inferior, stories at its head. Before his edition, the work had consisted of forty stories by one author followed by thirty-one stories by a second.[44]

The first author was apparently inspired by the Judge Bao chantefables; he used one of them, an enfance,[45] as his prologue and drew heavily on others. His first twelve chapters formed a connected chronological series, beginning with Bao's first appointment as a magistrate. Several of them are devoted more to illustrating Bao's mind and character than to the solution of crime. Bao appears as a tough-minded Confucian. His sympathy for ordinary folk and his ruthless pursuit of those who abuse their authority, even the Emperor's relatives, give the stories something of the flavor of social protest. In their social meaning, they certainly stand closer to the early story than to the middle. It is noticeable that the stories that pit Bao against high authority come mostly from chantefables and that later writers confine themselves to more mundane types of crime. The best of the former kind, in Chapters 74 and 75 of the 1594 edition, is based on the chantefable "Renzong Recognizes His Mother" (*Renzong ren mu*), in which Bao convinces the Emperor that the Empress Dowager is not his mother (her baby girl was switched at birth with the baby boy of another imperial concubine) and that his real mother is a woman now living in squalor in a remote village. Bao's interview with the woman, his confrontation with the Emperor, and the stratagem by which he and the Emperor induce the guilty to confess all produce high drama, even if the author's writing is never more than workmanlike. Among his more mundane detective stories, the finest is that in Chapters 76 and 77, in which Bao deduces from a woman's brilliant solution to a murder—she suggests that the invisible cause of death might be a nail driven in inside the victim's nose—that she herself had killed her first husband in that very manner. Thus one murder case leads neatly into a second.

Both authors have a far greater range than later court case writers, and both draw on a wide variety of sources, especially plays and vernacular and Classical fiction. The first author even includes a tragic romance (Chapters 93 and 94) resembling the early story "Zhou Shengxian," and the second author dabbles freely in myth.

The latter's crime stories are the more elaborate. They treat most of the aspects of the crime, from its planning to the criminal's execution, and often throw in an unjust verdict as well for Bao to overturn. By the same token, however, they rarely set out to mystify the reader. Also the second author more often shows positive actions, such as kindness to animals or charity toward Buddhist priests, that bring a supernatural reward. (Neither author exhibits the antimonasticism of other court case fiction.) The innocent young victims of his romances are also regularly brought back to life. His most notable stories are mythical, particularly "The Goldfish Spirit" (Chapter 44) and "The Five Rat Spirits" (Chapter 58). The rats, who can take on the likeness of anyone they please, impersonate people at five levels of authority, right up to the Emperor and his mother. Chaos results, since at each level there are now two identical authorities issuing contradictory orders. Bao resolves the dilemma by fetching the Jade-Faced Cat from its Buddhist guardian and setting it free to detect the impostors. Myth and comic fantasy subsist happily in this collection alongside romance, moral fable, and the crime story.

Different as their writing is, the two authors still subordinate themselves to their work; no distinct authorial personality emerges. With the exception of the *Pillow* collection, the same subordinate relationship of author to fictional tradition holds true throughout the early and middle periods. It accounts for the ease with which the stories can be divided into types and for their widespread use of shared materials and methods at all narrative levels. One reason for the relationship, which is not to be confused with the even more subordinate relationship obtaining in oral literature, may lie in the social position of the authors, who were very likely the anonymous professionals of the world of popular publishing, unlike their successors, men such as Feng Menglong and Ling Mengchu, who were literati coming into popular publishing from outside. From the beginning of the seventeenth century, most of the compilers, and all of the best authors, were of the latter kind.

4
Feng's
Life
and
Ideas

Feng Menglong was not merely the author of a large number of vernacular stories, the first whose name we know for certain. He was also the principal creator of the late-Ming story in all its diversity. The quality of the fiction he selected, adapted, and wrote, together with the fineness of the editions in which he presented it, brought a financial success that attracted other highly lettered writers to the genre, each with his own preoccupations. Though there is no typical vernacular author, in order to understand the position of the vernacular in Chinese literature, one cannot do better than examine Feng's ideas, life, and work.

For his ideas on literature, one must turn to his prefaces and introductions. Feng makes no general statement on the nature of literature and its values; instead he is always arguing a case, usually for some underrated genre, and his claims and apologias have to be considered in that light. Nevertheless, it is possible to extract certain broad principles from his criticism, especially from his prefaces to *Stories Old and New* and to the *Shange* (Hill Songs) anthology, both of which are original attempts to relate the oral and the vernacular to the Classical literature.

Feng held a low opinion of literature as belles lettres; meaning or substance was more important to him than literary virtuosity. In taking this attitude, he joined a long line of Confucian thinkers that can be traced back to Confucius himself. Wang Yangming, as Feng notes in the biography he wrote, was contemptuous of mere literature and steadily refused to join literary societies. In Wang's opinion: "The reason the world is not in order is because superficial writing is growing and concrete practice is declining . . . People devote much of their time and energy to competing in conventional writing and flowery composition in order to achieve fame."[1] There is a correlation between lack of simplicity in literature and in life: "As customs and manners become more complicated, ornament and embellishment become more prevalent."[2] Most of Feng's other ideas can be related to his contempt for virtuosity: his stress on plain diction, his belief in the direct expression of emotion as a paramount value in the lyrical forms; his concern for sheer affective power as a paramount value in fiction and drama; and even, out of this same concern, his espousal of the vernacular.

Feng supported his views with historical arguments about the course of Chinese culture. The notion of a natural succession of dominant genres had been used as early as the Yuan dynasty to promote the cause of Northern drama, and by Feng's day it had become a critical commonplace. A few bold spirits went so far as to claim that the contemporary popular song was the highest achievement of Ming literature; they were convinced that the most direct expression of feeling was the one least impeded by the cultural tradition. Feng's arguments developed from this opinion, as well as from the historical critique that Confucian thinkers like to apply to the morals of past dynasties. If one may interpret it in terms remote from Feng's own, his idea was of a schism in Chinese literature that developed at some time between the Han and the Tang and severed the oral literature once and for all from the recognized literature, to the impoverishment of both. This is, of course, the conclusion of modern scholarship with regard to the development of oral and vernacular literature. The difference lies in the reasons adduced. We attribute the schism to both the inexorable process of linguistic change and the institutional factors that form and then freeze a literary language. Feng had no conception of linguistic change; he attributed the schism to the passion for virtuosity that led writers to despise the simple folk song, as well as to the use of literature, especially poetry, in the civil service examinations.

For Feng, in his *Shange* preface,[3] the great example of the unity of Chinese literature is also the earliest: the *Poetry Classic*, which embraces both folk songs and ceremonial court songs. After this, the schism began, blamed first on the *Songs of Chu* (*Chu ci*) poets with their virtuosity and then on the Tang practitioners of regulated verse. By that time, the folk song was excluded from the realm of literature and ignored by the gentry—to its detriment. Its range narrowed until it was virtually confined to erotic subjects. Still, although there was an abundance of false Classical literature, there were no false shange. They retained their authenticity because they were not involved in the contest for social prestige.

Feng's arguments are nowhere else put as clearly as here, but in his preface to *The Celestial Air Played Anew* (*Taixia xin zou*),[4] an anthology of dramatic and art song, he returns to his criticism of the great periods of Chinese poetry: "The Tang used poetry as a means of selecting officials, and poetry became stereotyped; the Six Dynasties [sic] used it for a display of the poet's talent, and poetry became abstruse; the Song used it for discourse, and poetry became pedantic." The notion that the use of poetry in the civil service examinations was a disastrous turning point in Chinese literature occurs several times in Feng's writing and seems to have had symbolic force for him. In his preface to another volume of art songs,[5] Feng remarks that there was originally no set line length in Chinese verse, but that the use of five-syllable or seven-syllable lines hardened into a convention in the Tang when poetry came to be used in the examinations. In the Song, when essays took the place of verse in the examinations, poetry was once more allowed to develop freely, this time into the ci lyric, with its multitude of different forms. "Writers killed off by the *shi* were now brought back to life by the *ci*." Competitiveness, resulting from the prestige conferred by society on a particular genre, has condemned contemporary poetry and prose to sterility. Art songs, "no doubt because they are considered to belong to a minor genre and hence have invited no competition," are still immune.[6] Dangers loom, however. In the last few decades, these songs have come into fashion, and there are ominous signs of stereotyping and bizarre experiment. A similar, more impassioned complaint occurs in his preface to his play *A Pair of Heroes,* in which he deplores the rage for the Southern drama as leading to its current cliché-ridden mediocrity.[7]

Although arguments of this kind are often associated with demands for an exclusive literature, nothing could be further from Feng's meaning. Prestige and breadth of popularity are by no means the same thing. What Feng deplored was the convention, artifice, virtuosity, and inauthenticity of feeling that result from a scramble for social prestige. If literature were disestablished, it might exhibit true literary value. At the same time, he felt that it ought to have a broad popular appeal.

In another kind of historical approach, exemplified by the *Stories Old and New* preface, he makes just this point. In comparing the tale and the story, Feng champions the story on the grounds that its audience is larger and its impact on the audience's feelings greater. The two approaches do not conflict. In discussing poetry and song, Feng is concerned with their expressive function, with the authenticity of the feeling they express; in discussing the novel and the drama, he is concerned more with their affective function, their persuasive effect on the audience.

A broad appeal requires relatively simple writing. The preface to Feng's fictionalized history, *A New History of the States* (*Xin Lieguo zhi*)[8], praises the work for "allowing the uneducated to share in the learning of the gentry" and for combining taste and refinement (*ya*) with the common touch (*su*). In the words of the preface to *Constant Words to Awaken the World* (*Xing shi hengyan*), Feng's third collection of stories, narrative becomes too abstruse if it stresses philosophical meaning and too ornate if it stresses diction; in neither case will it be capable of "striking the common ear or affecting the constant heart." At the same time, simple writing should not be thought of as easy. Like most other highly educated vernacular writers, Feng took pains to distinguish himself from the "village schoolmaster" (*cun xuejiu*), a term that denotes not a profession but a level of education. (In fact, it usually refers to professional hacks in the employ of publishing houses.) The work of the "village schoolmaster" was derided for its inaccuracy, its tastelessness, and its conventionality. As the title-page blurb to *New History* puts it, a mediocre talent cannot hope to succeed in vernacular fiction.

All of Feng's fiction presents itself as educational in a broad sense, instructing and affecting at the same time. The titles of his collections declare this aim: to "warn the world," to "awaken the world." Even the *New Ping yao zhuan* is described as admonitory in Feng's foreword.[9] Most of the plays he wrote or adapted are concerned with moral action; indeed, many have been adapted so as to make their moral points more clearly. Of course, it is a common gambit to claim a moral force for one's fiction, and some of what Feng says can be discounted, but there is no doubt that he viewed fiction and drama as centrally concerned with broad moral issues.

Important as moral issues were to him, however, Feng was no moral philosopher. He made no attempt to be consistent from work to work, and his thinking was always governed, to a certain degree, by the assumptions of the genre in which he happened to be writing. At least some of the time, too, he indulged in humorous exaggeration. But he did write a vernacular life of Wang Yangming that dealt with Wang's ideas as well as his military campaigns. He also constantly quoted Li Zhi, who derived many of his ideas from Wang, and he was also much influenced by Yuan Hongdao, who derived many of his ideas from Li. His thinking was deeply affected by ethical issues alive in the late Ming.

It is the notion of "innate knowledge" that Feng stresses in his life of Wang rather than the "unity of knowledge and action."[10] The incident in which Wang traces the concern he feels for his family to an inner sense of filial piety is highlighted. (It convinced Wang of the truth of the Mencian notion that the cardinal virtues are innate in every human being, thus leading him to reject Taoism and Buddhism.) From the concept of innate knowledge as Wang developed it, there flowed a number of possibilities that Chinese philosophy during the rest of the sixteenth century ardently explored and disputed. In the first instance, the concept negated the notion of external forms, social rules that the individual was supposed to internalize. The "false moralists" so inveighed against by Li Zhi and by Feng were puritans who preached the importance of just such rules of behavior. Second, the concept's stress on the internal springs of moral action depreciated the doctrinal differences among religions and philosophies and gave new impetus to a "Three Doctrines" thinking that respected Taoism and Buddhism as well as Confucianism as systems of morality. Li Zhi, Yuan Zongdao, and Feng were all adherents. Third, the belief in innateness argued for nature over nurture and depreciated the importance of the cultural processes in the making of the moral man. A measure of egalitarian thinking was one consequence, since it was culture that, more than anything else, erected the barriers in Chinese society. Another consequence was the suggestion that culture could actually be a hindrance to natural or spontaneous action. Li Zhi's "childlike heart,"[11] out of which good literature is written, is not solely the property of children, though experience makes it difficult to maintain in educated maturity. Feng found support in the notion for his ideas about the value of oral literature.

What constitutes innate knowledge was another subject of inquiry. One line of thinkers, notably Yan Jun, Luo Rufang, and Li Zhi, interpreted it to include *qing*, "feelings, emotions, sympathy, sentiment." Qing had traditionally been regarded as a negative force in moral behavior; but in fact, well before Wang Yangming, it had come to occupy an honored place in literary criticism as the faculty poetry both expresses and appeals to.[12] This is the sense of the word in Feng's *Shange* preface, which shows the patent influence of Li Zhi. And in Feng's art songs, qing—in this case idealistic, headlong, romantic passion—is the ruling value. However, the songs rarely subscribe to the metaphysic of qing, that imagined world of the romance in which love may overturn the laws of nature and triumph over death itself. Feng's *Anatomy of Love* (*Qing shi leilüe*) is a classified compendium of narrative, both fact and fiction, devoted to the subject of love and sex. The preface refers to qing as a sort of ardent, universal sympathy in much the same terms that Feng applies to Wang Yangming's innate knowledge. In the commentary, qing is described as the psychological stimulus necessary for virtuous action. This is a reasonable attempt—one of many in the late Ming—to accommodate qing to Confucian morality.[13]

However, qing does not retain the same degree of importance throughout Feng's work. As one moves away from the art songs and the *Anatomy* to the vernacular fiction and the plays, one enters the familiar world of predominantly Confucian morality. Feng has still not entirely discarded his preoccupation with qing. It clearly informs those stories of his that give a sensitive, sympathetic portrayal of women in love. In Confucian terms, it led him to stress friendship and the husband-wife relationship more than filial piety.[14] When he challenges the traditional morality, it is mainly in matters of love and sex, and his belief in the power of qing is the evident cause. But apart from these challenges, Feng is himself very much in the Confucian mainstream. He does not search for any ideal of the self as apart from, or in opposition to, society, as the great eighteenth-century novelists Cao Zhan and Wu Jingzi were to do. For Feng the fulfillment of the self meant the fulfillment of one's social role, or rather of the social role to which one aspired.[15]

This subject leads to a third area of Feng's ideas: politics. He was an ardent patriot. In the last months of his life, he was still publishing tracts and documents designed to promote the resurgence of the Ming under the leadership of this or that prince in the South, and much of his writing is concerned with political issues in the broad sense. His highest ambition was to hold office himself, an ambition he finally realized, in a very modest way, in his fifties. But Feng's ideas on government and nationalism are best discussed in an account of his life and works.

Feng came from an educated Soochow family.[16] All that is known of his father is that he was a friend of Wang Jingchen's (1513-1595), a Confucian moral philosopher of great piety and personal modesty.[17] (Wang sounds just the kind of puritan Feng Menglong scorned.) Menglong was the second of three brothers, who were, so one source tells us, known in recognition of their talent as "The Three Fengs" of the locality.[18] The elder brother, Menggui, mentioned once or twice in Menglong's works as poet and gourmand,[19] was an artist who served at one stage in the educational administration of Guangdong. The younger brother, Mengxiong, highly regarded as a poet, had little success in his career and suffered poverty.[20] Menglong himself, after decades of study and examination taking, served one term as assistant county instructor and another as county magistrate.

Feng was a Soochow writer in more than a trivial sense. He spent much of his life in the city and was interested in its history, its folkways, and its personalities. He collected its anonymous popular songs, the shange, and explained them to the reader. His fiction and other prose, while not confined to Soochow, is set there more than in any other place, and makes particular use of its recent past. The term "my" or "our Soochow" recurs constantly in his prose, and his anthology Survey of Talk (Gujin tangai) teems with anecdotes about the bohemian literati of his youth.

Feng can be described as presenting himself in two distinct personae, or rather in a range of personae between two extremes. At one extreme is Feng the wit, the ribald humorist, the bohemian, the drinker, the romantic lover. This is the Feng Menglong who had celebrated liaisons with at least two beautiful and accomplished Soochow singing girls, whose reputation he helped to make. It is the Feng who compiled two volumes of popular songs, almost all on erotic or ribald themes, who supplied the comments for a work that ranks and assesses the hundred most beautiful courtesans in Nanking, who conceived and compiled a famous joke book, and who wrote two short works on a card game used for gambling in Soochow. It is also, of course, the Feng Menglong of legend, as he appears in Qing dynasty anecdote.[21]

At the other extreme is Feng Menglong the student and examination candidate, who spent twenty years, so he tells us, on the *Spring and Autumn Annals,* the classic he had chosen as his examination specialty, compiling no fewer than three handbooks on it, and who wrote *Guide to the Four Books, Sack of Wisdom*, the life of Wang Yangming, and the patriotic tracts of the Southern Ming regimes. This is the Feng Menglong who finally, after half a lifetime's effort, obtained an appointment and served in it with vigor and imagination. It is the work of the first persona that draws our interest to Feng Menglong, but the fiction and plays reveal elements of both.

With one exception, everything significant we know about Feng's life comes from his works. The exception is his relation to the Donglin and Fu She reform movements of the 1620s and 1630s.

The calamitous event of the 1620s was the purge of the Donglin movement in 1625-26 by the powerful eunuch Wei Zhongxian. The Donglin was both a society for the study of the classics and a movement for political reform which was particularly concerned about the growth of eunuch power. Some of its members attacked Wei, and Wei retaliated with arrests and executions. One of his victims was Xiong Tingbi, a general, who was executed in 1625. (In an anecdote in a Qing source,[22] Xiong appears as a patron of Feng Menglong. The anecdote cannot be vouched for, although some of its incidental details are correct.) Others were falsely charged with taking bribes from Xiong, were arrested, and in many cases executed. In 1626, when Soochow officials tried to arrest a friend of one of the accused, riots erupted that caused Wei's agents to flee the city in panic.

Although Feng's attitude to these events is not in doubt, there is no mention of them in his works. By contrast, his friends and protégés Yuan Yuling and Li Yu (Xuanyu) both wrote plays on the subject.[23] To the best of my knowledge, Xiong is not even mentioned in Feng's accessible works. But among Xiong's close friends were Mei Zhihuan (1575-1641), General Mei Guozhen's nephew, and also Li Changgeng (jinshi 1595), both of Macheng in Hubei, where Feng spent years of study and teaching prior to 1620. Li wrote prefaces to one of Feng's handbooks on the *Spring and Autumn Annals* in 1625 and to his edition of a famous collection of tales the following year. Mei was a Donglin member whose cousin, Mei Guozhen's son Zhiyun, was a close friend of Feng's and a colleague in the same study society; his preface for Feng's *Survey of Talk* is written in intimate terms.[24] Zhang Mingbi (1584-1653), who wrote a preface for *Sack of Wisdom,* was, he tells us, the victim of an informer who revealed to Wei a disparaging remark Zhang had made in a letter.[25]

The Donglin was destroyed, but other groups survived, and new groups were founded. In 1628 they merged in the Fu She, which was particularly powerful in the 1630s, its high point being a nationwide congress held in Soochow in 1632. Although Feng's name is not listed as belonging to the Fu She, the fact may not be significant. His friend Mei Zhiyun was apparently a founding member of the Ying She,[26] which was formed in 1624 and later merged in the Fu She. The majority of Feng's known friends were members of the Fu She. Even if there is no direct testimony, we can be sure that Feng was engaged in the reformist political activity of the period.

The most obvious distinction among Feng's works is between those to which he attached his own name and those for which he used a variety of pseudonyms. The difference is not quite that between Classical and vernacular, for there are several risqué or less "serious" works in Classical, such as *Anatomy of Love*, to which he attached a pseudonym. Significantly, however, there are no works in the vernacular, no matter how serious they are, that carry Feng's own name. The use of a pseudonym may, in some cases, have been merely conventional—it was common in the vernacular literature—or it may have offered a modicum of protection for an author hoping to enter the civil service and thus highly vulnerable to charges of frivolity. What is clear is that it shows the author's explicit acknowledgment of a different role.

Signed Works

Feng's choice of *Spring and Autumn Annals* as his examination specialty affected his publications as well as his course of study. His sojourns in Hubei, in the Macheng area, which began long before 1617 and continued past 1620, were ostensibly undertaken for the purpose of studying the classic in a special study group. Macheng was a center of scholarship on the *Annals*, with 80 or 90 percent of the local candidates specializing in it.[27] Several handbooks, published and unpublished, were produced in the district, some by Feng's colleagues in the society to which he belonged. Feng's were, it seems, the first of them. His *Guide to the Annals* (*Lin jing zhi yue*)[28] appeared in 1620 and a second handbook probably in 1623.[29] Zhang Wocheng's preface to the latter makes it clear that the classic was not studied in isolation but that handbooks on it were intended to bring its moral and political lessons to bear on contemporary society.[30] In this sense, study groups, particularly on the *Annals*, tended to be more than mere study groups. Feng's third handbook, entitled *Chunqiu hengku*,[31] was by far the most successful; it became a standard work during much of the Qing. In 1630, Feng also published a *Guide to the Four Books* (*Sishu zhi yue*), assisted by his former pupils from Macheng and Soochow.[32]

Sack of Wisdom (*Zhi nang*), which Feng later said[33] he put together in two months in 1626 while staying in a friend's house in Jiaxing, is a characteristic Feng production. It is an anthology of material drawn largely from earlier sources and bearing on a single broad topic: in this case, applied intelligence. ("Wisdom," although I have left it in the translated title, is too contemplative for what Feng intended.) Yet the elaborate classification into ten main types and many subtypes, with short, witty essays on each type and comments on many of the items, makes it something more than an anthology; it approaches the status of an anatomy. Feng used the same organization in three other works: in his *Treasury of Jokes,* in his *Survey of Talk*, and in his *Anatomy of Love*.

Feng should not be given credit for any originality in the conception of this anthology. It is based squarely on the *Classification of Wisdom* (*Zhi pin*) compiled by Fan Yuchong and commented on by his brother, of which one preface is dated as late as 1614.[34] In addition to the idea of classification and a few of the categories, Feng took over a good number of entries, some of them bearing the brother's comments. Although he did nothing to hide his indebtedness, it is strange that he never mentioned the work that made his rapid compilation possible. Feng's book was highly successful, and in 1634 he reissued it in expanded form.[35] Fan's work, by contrast, was never reprinted. But lest the reader see an all too familiar irony here, I should explain that Feng's is by far the livelier and more interesting; the *Classification of Wisdom* might never have met with much success anyway.

For Feng, applied intelligence is a true faculty—that is, innate—but the faculty is latent, and it takes study to draw it forth, like water from a well.[36] A further assumption is that intelligence is the factor that determines success in public affairs. Public affairs are, overwhelmingly, the subject of the book, as they were in the *Classification of Wisdom*, and success means not a personal triumph but the triumph of the national or general interest. The book is strictly concerned with rational calculation, and other determinants, such as fate or karma or the Heavenly Principle, have no place in it; its world of belief is quite different from that of Feng's fiction and drama.

The attitude is pragmatic. Feng is against all pet formulae; there are no "set strategies," he says, in the highest form of intelligence. He despises success in the examinations as a qualification. He ridicules the "fusty and pedantic" Confucian thinkers who attempt to apply theoretical formulae to problems requiring a practical solution. He values magnanimity of mind as well as of purse in leaders and a genial tolerance of peccadilloes. (The same values, and even the same anecdotes, appear in some of his

stories.) He is against the resignation of an official to protest bad
policies, quoting Shao Yong in the time of Wang Anshi's New Laws:
"This is precisely the time when the wise and upright man should exert'
himself to the utmost. The New Laws may be terribly harsh, but the people will benefit from every amelioration, no matter how slight. What is
the sense of resigning?"[37] There is a sharp difference between the first
and the supplemented versions, with the latter stressing the stern
measures needed to preserve governmental control. The reason for the
change of emphasis is clear enough: Feng was supplementing his book in
a period that saw the start of the disastrous Ming rebellions.

The *Survey of Talk* (*Gujin tangai*),[38] which appeared before *Sack of
Wisdom,* contains thirty-six categories, each introduced by a condensed,
allusive, paradoxical essay. Its anecdotes are generally shorter than those
of *Sack* and frequently have Feng's and others' comments attached.
(Many of the anecdotes and even the comments have been taken over
from other anthologies, particularly Li Zhi's.)[39] The majority are
satirical; others are comic; still others show wit in action. Some are
devoted to the eccentricities of genius, a theme suited to the in-
dividualistic trend in late-Ming thought.[40] And there are many on
positive qualities that Feng admired, such as gallantry and magnanimity.
Even when comic, they are anecdotes rather than jokes; for example,
after telling of an incident during the Soochow drought of 1589 in which
Shi Kunyu, the prefect, prayed for rain outside the temple of the city
god, Feng remarks drily that Shi prayed so long he "almost died of
sunstroke."[41] There are numerous other anecdotes about Soochow, some
of them obviously written by Feng.[42]

Behind the satirical items a set of values not very different from those
of *Sack of Wisdom* can be discerned. Taoism and Buddhism are given little attention in either book; the satire is directed against Confucian
dogma and obscurantism. The irrational is fair game: lucky and unlucky
days, taboo words, the magical value of intoning this or that classic, the
use of the hexagrams, and so forth. We hear of a devout Confucian who
always went to sleep with his hands folded in front of him in case he met
his father in his dreams. The obsessed (such as the hedonist Yan Jun) and
the absurd are both targets. (For example, there is the priest who claims
Buddhism is superior to Confucianism because it is more arcane.)[43] As
Sack of Wisdom stresses the pragmatic, the *Survey of Talk* ridicules for-
malism and dogma.[44]

In 1626, Feng carried out a drastic revision of the *Taiping guangji,* the
famous compendium of pre-Song Classical fiction, adding notes and
comments but reducing the whole to half its former size by eliminating
the more repetitious items and sharply trimming the text of the re-
mainder.[45] His justification of the collection, written over his own name,
strikes a very different note from the prefaces to his story and song an-

thologies. Here he presents literature, the work of erudite and talented men, as a remedy for the vulgarity of mind that produces "all the squalid and evil behavior in the world."

During his three-year tenure in his one important position, as magistrate of Shouning County in northern Fujian, Feng compiled a local history.[46] There was nothing unusual about his doing so; it was not even the first history of the county. But Feng's history is exceptional. In a genre that suppresses the compiler's personality in favor of fact gathering and the expression of social pieties, his work is astonishingly personal. It is largely about his own endeavors as a magistrate, and the first-person pronoun spatters its pages.

The Shouning job was no plum. Among the hills on the Zhejiang border, the county was in Feng's time entirely rural. Its population was sparse, and it was quite devoid of the culture with which Feng had always been surrounded. He notes that, although there was a county school, there were few educated people, there were no books apart from the Confucian classics, and the traveling book merchants never even bothered to visit. Feng resorted to issuing his own *Guide to the Four Books* and lecturing on it himself. All the facilities were modest or tumbledown. The local people were noted for fierce tempers and bloody vendettas. Female infanticide was a common practice, but Feng, using a mixture of prohibitions and rewards for those who took in and raised girl babies, managed to stamp it out, or so he claims. Sick people engaged shamans rather than doctors. Feng banned this practice too and, at his own expense, issued free medicine, although he acknowledges that progress was slow. The area was vulnerable to bandits and pirate marauders. And it was also menaced by tigers, which had claimed over a hundred victims in the town. As magistrate, Feng first prayed to the city god and then, when prayer had no effect, paid from his own pocket for the manufacture of some traps. Several tigers were caught, and the menace ceased. One is tempted to wonder what the Feng of the *Survey* would have said about his praying to the city god, but he remarks in this book that the responsibility of an official is "to serve the spirits as well as to govern the people."[47]

Throughout, Feng appears as a model magistrate. At some point in many of the topics discussed, there comes the clause "As soon as I took up office," heralding his own action. He devotes so much of his own salary to repairing temples, putting up a shelter for victims of palsy, and the like, that one wonders if he could have had any money left. He tells of his frustration with higher authority, with petty regulations, with his own clerks. He is prevented from adjusting the taxes on land newly broken in, and reflects ruefully how, as a subordinate in Dantu County, he had given the contrary advice to his magistrate.[48] There is practically no history, except for the pirate incursions; the work is organized under topics that are treated synchronically. Feng is self-conscious about his performance but not diffident. "I have always sought the truth before fame," he writes, "and so give the full details here." Under the topic of good omens, he notes, a trifle portentously, that an unusual weather phenomenon occurred the day before he arrived to take up office. He includes his own poems and reflects on his current reading. Indirectly, the local history gives an engagingly personal view of Feng Menglong, both active and contemplative, totally absorbed in his job.[49]

His preface is dated the spring of 1637, just two and a half years after he took up office. The proper title of the work, as he makes clear, is *A Provisional History of Shouning* (*Shouning dai zhi*), for no history is complete or final; it merely awaits (dai) the next historian. Presumably he chose the title to signify his personal approach to the impersonal face of local history.

Toward the end of his life, in the last, desperate days of the dynasty, Feng wrote and compiled several works in which his cool pragmatism was warmed by a heroic romanticism. There are really two kinds of works, entangled with each other to some degree.[50] There is the *Veritable Records of the National Resurgence* (*Zhongxing shilu*), which must have appeared in the middle of 1644 just a couple of months after the fall of Peking and the suicide of the Emperor, as the officials in the South rallied around the Prince of Fu.[51] It includes the new Emperor's proclamations, various declarations and vows of support (including some by local groups), memorials, and plans of action. Feng's preface, addressed to the Emperor, deals with the selection of officials. He urges that selection not be restricted by formal qualifications: "The poor and lowly have no way open to them." He attacks the results of the present system: "Of the hundreds and thousands of examination graduates in the land, barely twenty gave their lives in the hour of peril." He sets out recommendations for large-scale changes, and adds, "Now an elderly retired official, I have been beating my breast over the state of our country for many a long year. I am still hopeful that, in the time that is left to me, I may see true peace."

Later in 1644, in the ninth month or shortly thereafter, Feng published a larger work, *Records of the Year Jiashen* (*Jiashen jishi*).[52] The book includes the *Veritable Records*, along with much other material, particularly on the fall of Peking and the suicide of the Emperor. Feng brings together several eyewitness narratives of the debacle. He includes accounts of three revolts in other parts of the country, two of which he compiled himself, and a chapter of poems, some of which he wrote himself, on the dead Emperor, on the famous martyrs Ni Yuanlu and Ling Yiqu, and on the obscure Soochow youth Xu Yan who starved himself to death. Feng's preface expresses a mood of urgency rather than despair. The events of 1644 "are something one cannot bring oneself to

record, and, and, equally, something one cannot bring oneself not to record."
China's situation is "like sailing a holed ship through a raging storm.
Helmsman and oarsmen are straining every nerve, united in the common
effort to avoid going down. The slightest relaxation will spell certain
disaster. What do you imagine would happen if they stuffed their hands
in their sleeves and hurled insults at each other?" His particular concern
is that the Ming soldiers are out of control—it is "worse than having no
soldiers at all"—and he defends the action of several cities along the
Yangzi that locked their gates against the Ming armies.

In the middle of the following year, 1645, after the Prince of Fu had
been captured, the Prince of Tang, in Zhejiang and Fujian, rallied many
of his supporters, including Feng Menglong. The *Veritable Records* was
reissued, with some necessary adaptations and a new preface by Feng,
now an "elderly, retired official of seventy-two *sui*."[53] It is his last known
work.

Feng also wrote a volume of poetry, *Qile zhai gao,* or *Poems from the
Studio of the Seven Delights.* It survived into the Qing but is no longer
extant. The critic Zhu Yizun gives it his usual pithy appraisal: "His
Honor excelled at humorous language which he inserted into light, satiric
meters. He cannot be regarded as a poet but rather as a jester of the
literary world."[54] Although it is more generously expressed, this is the
same kind of criticism found in official Qing assessments; both the *Sack*
and the *Survey* are described as frivolous, despite their serious basis of
implicit values.[55]

Feng's signed work assumes an odd shape. Apart from the handbooks,
it consists mainly of anthologies and a local history, all of novel
character. He was not taken seriously as a poet—perhaps he did not take
himself seriously—and his Classical prose pieces were rarely included in
late-Ming anthologies.[56] Surprisingly, with the one exception of the
Taiping guangji, he did not produce any new editions of Classical works,
unlike a number of his contemporaries. Instead, he turned his efforts
away from the standard literature toward drama, fiction, and song.

Popular Songs and Jokes

Numerous collections of popular songs were made during the Ming,
especially songs to a particular tune. Commentators on social history
sometimes mention the craze for a particular tune and tell us where it
originated and how far it spread. In the sixteenth century, a number of
distinguished writers also chose to write words to the currently popular
tunes and sometimes even published their songs under their own names.
The collections that survive are either of such imitations or else of poorly
edited popular songs by unknown authors. Feng's, however, are differ-

ent; he edited the popular songs with great care and defended them by challenging Classical poetry and Confucian morality itself.

His first collection was to the tune (or tune type) *Guazher*, which became popular in north China in the second half of the sixteenth century.[57] Only four songs are actually identified as Feng's, and all four appear in his notes as analogues or ripostes. Here is the first of them, written in response to the anonymous song "In Denunciation of Du Kang" (Du Kang was the mythical inventor of wine) and entitled "In Gratitude to Du Kang":

> Brother Du, I hail you as my benefactor!
> Many's the time I've succeeded in love through your invention.
> Three cups go down, to such marvelous effect!
> Thanks to you, spring desire rises
> And spring sorrow vanishes.
> My lover, who would have left as a stranger,
> Got drunk, thanks to you, and stayed.[58]

Feng's comments are often highly personal, as in his art songs. He refers in detail to his loss of the singing girl Hou Huiqing and to the thirty agonized poems he wrote in her memory. Most of the songs are anonymous (he relates that some were sent to him by singing girls), but he also mentions half a dozen authors by name, all of them apparently his friends. One is Dong Sizhang (1586-1628), who is revealed as the author of "The Sneeze," a well-known song that, before the discovery of the collection, was thought to be of popular, anonymous authorship. In his comment on the song, Feng praises Dong as a man whose talent is "beyond estimate" and also as a remarkable "man of feeling." Qing, as romantic feeling, is the ruling sentiment of the songs. Apparently the collection bore the general title of *Tong chi* (Child's Folly), which refers to the literary views of Li Zhi, particularly to his essay "Tong xin shuo" (On the Childlike Heart).

Feng's second collection differs from the first in one important respect. The shange was a Soochow tune, and its dialect was Soochow. Feng's comments are in Classical with some Northern vernacular, in which he sometimes explains local idiom, but the occasional imitations he includes in the commentary are always in Soochow dialect. His notes and comments reveal at least as much editorial care as he lavished on the *Guazher*. No doubt he adopted this strict editorial stance to show the value he placed on the songs. In the same spirit, one of his comments points to a punning device and compares it to a feature of Li Shangyin's poetry. His sources must have included printed texts, since his notes sometimes mention an edition. One song was given him by a singing girl. Another, which Feng describes as a "traditional children's ditty," was still current in the Soochow area in this century.[59] Some are songs Feng himself remembers. In his comment on the second song, he gives us the text of "The Sixteen Discordances," a comically erotic series of double entendres he heard as a child but could not understand at the time.[60] Virtually anyone could turn a shange if necessary; he describes how a peasant and a boatman's wife compose songs impromptu.

Feng constantly points out the local character of the songs. His comments on the first song explain the rhymes of Soochow speech — "The people of Wu sing in Wu" — and liken the dialectal usage to local games. "There is no need for the songs to circulate throughout the country like written regulations handed down by the Court."[61]

Most of the songs are comic, and many are constructed like jokes, with a punch line at the end. Almost all are concerned with erotic adventure, in which they take a simple delight. There are no songs of parting, none of frustration; the shange was obviously not the vehicle for plaintive love. In his comments, Feng endorses the approach, cheering on the bold and criticizing the puritanical and the timid. In one case, he praises the mother who tells her daughter to give herself to a lover while she is still young enough to attract one. After an atypical song, which asserts that married love is best and ends with the line "When you fall sick, you need your own dear wife," Feng comments: "So puritanical, all of a sudden! Still, there are plenty of days when you're not sick!"[62] In their lewd and lusty celebration of sex, the songs are unhampered by Confucian morality. It is understandable that Feng should seek to use them in his campaign against the strictures on love and sex of the Confucian puritans. But he also deserves credit for his courage in collecting kinds of songs that, although no doubt present in all cultures, were rarely collected in any, and even more rarely printed, before our more tolerant times.

Although few of them make specific reference to singing girl prostitutes, the songs were no doubt sung most often in the pleasure quarter. In another work, *The Hundred Beauties of Nanking* (*Jinling baimei*), which is specifically on singing girls, Feng appears as a commentator and the writer of the colophon. The work was compiled by Li Yunxiang, editor of the earliest edition of the novel *Investiture of the Gods* (*Feng shen yanyi*), and was published in Soochow in 1618.[63] *The Hundred Beauties* consists of prose and verse eulogies (including popular songs) on the one hundred most beautiful singing girls the compiler has met in Nanking. They are ranked like the top hundred candidates in the metropolitan examinations, and each is matched with a particular flower. The ranking notion is common enough, and the idea of describing the girls in various literary genres is found in a work by Deng Zhimo of a decade or two earlier,[64] although not with this degree of elaboration. Li's preface explains that while staying in Nanking, he was encouraged to write this book by a friend from Soochow. There is little doubt that the friend was Feng, who appears as one of the commentators under his pseudonym Long Ziyou. Feng may have been in Nanking in 1618 for the triennial provincial examinations; he was there again in 1624 and 1627.

It is not difficult to see where the friend from Soochow got his idea. In the summer of 1617, there had appeared *The Hundred Most Beautiful Courtesans of Soochow* (*Wuji baimei*),[65] organized on precisely the same lines, even to the inclusion of popular songs. Feng (again under his pseudonym of Long Ziyou) appears as the lover of one Liu Hanxiang, the ninth in the ranking.[66] After Feng went to Chu—presumably Macheng in Hubei—the girl's love for Feng cooled. "Her door was as busy as a marketplace," and she became a famous courtesan. The editor gives Feng, whom he describes as a friend, the credit for discovering her. The book includes a picture of Liu Hanxiang in the company of a mustachioed and bearded man in scholar's robes.

Feng's *Treasury of Jokes* (*Xiao fu*)[67] was probably the most famous of Chinese joke books; it formed the basis of the still popular *Forest of Jokes* (*Xiaolin guangji*), and in Japan it became a minor classic. If a broad distinction is drawn between the comic anecdote, told of famous figures, and the joke, which is about social types, the anecdote can be seen to predominate in virtually all joke books up until the last part of the Ming. Feng actually made the distinction in his own practice; the *Survey* consists of anecdotes, mostly comic, while the *Treasury* is entirely jokes. The anecdote, which often depends on a participant's wit, will undoubtedly strike us as more original in terms of Arthur Koestler's "bisociative context."[68] Jokes depend on the staple paradoxes of Chinese society: lethal doctors, illiterate teachers, intimidating wives, sexually sophisticated brides, lecherous priests, and so on. (The joke's humor is in proportion to the subtlety and indirection with which the paradox is revealed.) Feng's choice of jokes, some of which are taken from other collections, is distinguished by irreverence, bawdiness, and simplicity of language; most are actually in the vernacular. His book is noteworthy too for the personal and local reference of its commentary, much of which has been stripped away in later versions of the *Treasury*.

Drama and Art Song

As a dramatist, Feng wrote plays and art or "free" songs (*sanqu*, songs of the same type as those of the drama), adapted the plays and songs of others, and compiled a manual of dramatic prosody. Although he never finished the manual, he took a strong professional pride in his ability: "I may lack talent," he says modestly, in venturing to amend drastically the prosody of the most famous play of his time, *The Peony Pavilion*, "but this is an art of which I do know the rudiments."[69] Through his first play, *A Pair of Heroes (Shuangxiong ji)*, written possibly as early as 1602, he gained an introduction to Shen Jing (1553-1610), one of the great dramatists of the age, and studied with him.[70] Shen was noted for his scrupulous attention to prosodic detail and also for his advocacy of plain diction, and in both respects Feng followed him. This was a time in which the Southern drama burgeoned in popularity, and many writers were aghast at the low technical quality of the new plays.[71] Several attempts had been made to provide a definitive manual of tunes, including one by Shen Jing himself. Feng's attempt, *Ink-Crazy Studio's New Manual (Mohan zhai xin pu)*,[72] was developed as a critique of Shen's, and it corrects him unmercifully, although Feng is still firmly of the school of Shen Jing, together with Shen's nephews and several other dramatists. His anthology of art song, *The Celestial Air*, in which his sharpest criticism is offered, is heavily dominated by members of the Shen family.[73]

The main purpose of his obsession with technicalities was to make the songs singable. Notes to the anthology frequently run: "This was revised by Ink-Crazy Studio and naturally it is singable."[74] In his revision of *The Peony Pavilion*, he complains: "The connoisseur looks on it as reading matter, not as a text to be performed. There is no way to make it ready for the stage without some measure of adaptation."[75] In his revision of *A Pair of Heroes*, he denounces as a fallacy the belief that the Southern drama is easy to write. He finds musical, phonetic, and prosodic distinctions neglected altogether and tunes ignored in favor of libretti, and he concludes by announcing a program of publication: "I have been deeply concerned about this art for a long time and have tried to think how I might correct the mistakes of the current trend. And so I have sought out plays of noteworthy content that do not infringe the rules too greatly and made slight emendations to them. In recent years I have gathered together several dozen and plan to issue them one by one, to instruct the specialist."[76]

If Feng were solely concerned with such matters, his work would indeed interest only a few specialists. But despite what he says, his concerns range widely over the drama, from its moral values to character, theme, structure, and the like. They are expressed in his notes and "general critiques" and are revealed in his choice of plays and his manner of adaptation. He often discusses the acting of a particular passage or scene, explaining that, because of its structural importance, actors should not be allowed to omit it and suggesting the impression they should strive to give. In several cases, Feng is revising an earlier edition and reacting to the way he has seen the play performed. Piecemeal though his criticism is, it is still, in my opinion, the most interesting practical dramatic criticism of the Ming period. His concern with structure, performance, and prose dialogue anticipates Li Yu.

There are at least sixteen surviving plays that Feng wrote, adapted, or

merely edited.[77] *A Pair of Heroes* was his first play and probably the
only one that was entirely his own work. *Happiness Complete* (*Wanshi
zu*) and *Flag of Perfect Loyalty* (*Jingzhong qi*) are major reconstructions
of old plays that he held in low esteem. *Servant in a Wine Shop* (*Jiujia
yong*) and *The Heroine* (*Nü zhangfu*) he composed by combining existing
plays on the same subject. In the case of *Servant in a Wine Shop*, Feng
helpfully apportions the credit: 40 percent comes from one play, 30 percent from another, with the remaining 30 percent his own contribution.
The other eleven plays are all adaptations. In some, the adaptation is
quite severe: in *The New Gardener* (*Xin Guan yuan*), a reworking of a
play by Zhang Fengyi, or in *Romantic Dream* (*Fengliu meng*), his adaptation of *The Peony Pavilion*, whole scenes are added, omitted, and rear-
ranged.

A *Pair of Heroes* was apparently based on the love affair of one of
Feng's friends with the singing girl Bai Xiaofan. Feng wrote a set of art
songs for his friend. They are preserved in his anthology and followed by
the comment: "Ziyou also wrote *A Pair of Heroes* representing
Bai Xiaofan as Huang Suniang and Liu as Liu Shuang. It eventually so
moved Liu that he bought Bai out [from her status as singing girl]. Who
says that a writer's brush cannot work miracles?"[78] It is a straightforward, lively play with many of the common structural elements of the
Southern drama. It has some themes characteristic of Feng; the heroes
are ambitious to serve the state in civil as well as military matters; they
are sworn brothers, and one sacrifices himself for the other; the singing
girl Suniang is a "noble and romantic" spirit;[79] and both heroes fight gallantly against the pirate invaders. There is also some satire of government relief operations and of army recruitment. It appears that as soon
as Feng turned to the drama, he became concerned with the values of
public morality. He inclined toward a drama of straightforward moral
content, written in a plain style, without undue reliance on the exotic or
the supernatural. It was, in fact, the lack of moral content, together with
the taste for fantasy and ornate language, that he criticized in the contemporary New Drama.

*Flag of Perfect Loyalty, Servant in a Wine Shop, The Heroine, The
New Gardener, Measuring the River* (*Liang jiang ji*), and *Dream of
Rocks* (*Meng lei ji*) are all historical plays to which Feng made a large
contribution. They display his attitudes toward public events as seen in
Sack of Wisdom, Records of the Year Jiashen, and in his vernacular fiction. *Flag of Perfect Loyalty* is about loyalty and treason in the fall of
the Northern Song. Its hero is Yue Fei, its villain Qin Gui. It takes us
from the fall of the capital and the capture of the Emperor through Yue
Fei's victories to his imprisonment and execution, and finally to the
vengeance of his ghost on Qin and the meting out of justice in the netherworld. It was based on an old play that Feng found "vulgar and lacking

in truth."[80] Feng tells us that he went back to the historical sources and wrote a new play that, apart from some touching up, is faithful to the facts. He wrote one story on this subject in *Stories Old and New* and several more on similar themes. Yue Fei combines the qualities of the civil and military official in a way Feng admired. He is ready to execute his son (scene 7) for an infraction of the rules. He refuses a concubine given to him. He is able to inspire the local leaders to revolt against the Jurchen (scene 15). His daughter wants to fight like a man (scene 8), and after his death, she and her mother both kill themselves (scene 28). Scenes with Qin Gui and his wife, a veritable Lady Macbeth, are alternated with these for effective satirical counterpoint.

Servant in a Wine Shop is the most interesting of the plays heavily altered by Feng. It is about a tyrant and his victims (there are stories on similar themes among those Feng wrote). Some aspects of the play, concerning political tyrants and the problems of succession, may be seen as having contemporary relevance. The two plays Feng combines here are vastly different from each other. Although both deal with the same set of historical incidents, they choose different characters as hero. Feng argues against both choices and opts for a third, Li Bian, the youngest son of the martyred minister, Li Gu. Feng also objects to one play's use of the stock separations and reunions of romantic comedy. The play shows us a galaxy of heroes resisting tyranny — Li Gu himself; his daughter, Wenji; Wang Cheng, his faithful follower; as well as the wine shop owner and Li Bian himself. On the other hand, the famous Confucian scholar Ma Rong, who is persuaded by the tyrant Liang Ji to draw up a charge of sedition against Li Gu, is an example of the intellectual who lacks integrity. In his preface, Feng stresses Ma's eternal infamy and claims that drama can serve a didactic purpose just as well as the *Spring and Autumn Annals*. In scene 7, when Ma is challenged as a Confucian, he replies: "I am the most learned Confucian of our day. I have taught thousands of disciples. How can you call me a hypocritical moralist?" In scene 27, when the young Li Bian at first resists studying the classics — "The Five Classics are the dregs of what the ancients thought!" — it is Ma Rong's hypocrisy that has caused his revulsion.

The play contains many practical comments on acting. Feng explains that he excluded scene 14, "Sun Shou's Four Styles of Make-up," from his first edition as superfluous but has included it in this edition because it is a favorite piece with performers. We are constantly told what impression an actor should seek to give. Feng complains that, in scene 17, "vulgar actors" play the hypocrite Ma Rong like a low villain, with none of the dignified presence of a high official. In scene 16, "Li Gu at his death should be played with more anger than suffering," and in scene 24, in which the daughter argues her case in court, Feng says of her speech, which is in prose: "This defense speech must be enunciated with fieriness and clarity if it is to move the audience. It must not be cut out by some vulgar actor."

The New Gardener is a reworking of Zhang Fengyi's *The Gardener,* literally *Watering the Garden (Guan yuan ji),* about an incident of the Warring States period. Feng's main objection to Zhang's treatment is a moral one: his play shows the Crown Prince, in disguise as a gardner, putting romance with his employer's daughter ahead of vengeance for his father's death.[81] (Curiously, in chapter 95 of his *New History of the States,* Feng is not so scrupulous.) Another fault is that the turncoat general who kills the king is never punished; this means that the working of bao is not watertight, as it should be in a play. There is thus a clear moral point about Feng's play that is not so clear in the original.

I shall pass over *The Heroine,* on the subject of a famous Tang tale about the founding of the dynasty, in which Feng is much concerned about the proper heroic behavior of the hero Curlybeard, and also *Measuring the River,* in which he shows no sympathy whatever for the famous poet Li Yu, ruler of the Southern Tang. (A note reads: "He is a callow ruler, and Gong and Huangfu are idlers. The frenzied hedonism of ruler and ministers must be portrayed in full."[82]) *Dream of Rocks* is a romantic comedy, but as one might expect, Feng's version is concerned with its historical background and its lesson in political morality. Feng adapted two of Tang Xianzu's plays, *Romantic Dream (Fengliu meng)* from *The Peony Pavilion* and *Handan Dream (Handan meng)* from *Handan ji.* Tang's writing is marked by its imaginativeness, its rich and sensuous language, its elaboration of detail, and its lack of concern for the technicalities of singing and performance. The contrast with Shen Jing's ideals of technical perfection and stylistic plainness, together with the moral content that is usually associated with them, was already apparent to their contemporaries. As a result, playwrights were classified as belonging to one school or the other, sometimes with justice, as in Feng's case, but often without.

The most significant change Feng makes in his adaptation is to cut down the profusion of rich and cloying language, particularly in *Romantic Dream.* He is obeying his writer's instinct for plain diction, but not without qualms: "I hope that people will not ridicule me as one who transmuted gold into base metal." But he does not shrink from major structural change either. In *The Peony Pavilion,* he thinks it illogical that, although the hero and heroine dream of each other, his dream should have taken place before he appears in the play while hers takes place a few scenes into it, and so he alters the play drastically to make them share the same dream.[83]

There is a vast difference between the public themes of Feng's plays and the private themes of his songs. The latter are not only private but particular; most of the song sets need elaborate introductions. Their subject is love—the amours of Feng and his friends with singing girls—and their primary value is also love—that is, they exhibit an extreme idealism in love and an extreme heartbreak in rejection.

The only surviving work containing Feng's songs is the anthology *Celestial Air*, which was published in 1627 with a preface by Feng. It was preceded by a lost work, some of whose songs it reprints, together with their notes. *Celestial Air* contains sixteen sets by Feng, all but one or two of which have a clear personal reference: as many as six relate to his loss of Hou Huiqing. Dong Sizhang comments on one set's "authentic feeling" and calls Feng, by virtue of his simplicity and directness, "a master of the plain drawing style." Another, anonymous comment on a different set runs: "All of his songs are quite without embellishment. However, there is one aspect in which he surpasses others—authenticity." It is Dong who tells us of the poems of lament Feng wrote after his loss of Hou. Friends contributed matching poems, and the collection was published under the title of *Anguish* (*Yutao ji*). "Feng's were just like this song, nothing but high emotion forced out without a single lovelorn cliché in them. Even now they can make you weep." Feng's other sets are on the amours of his friends, one featuring Dong Sizhang, another the Liu I have mentioned, and a third Yuan Shudu, a publisher. The set that gives the best account of qing describes a séance attended by Feng and his friends. The spirit of a boy appears and reveals that he and his lover are as much lovers in death as in life. Feng reflects:

> "People aren't spiritual," as the saying runs, "only ghosts." I say that ghosts aren't spiritual, only love [qing]. In ancient times there were the Three Eternal Things, but in the light of this experience, love should be added to them. Better to be a ghost with love than a mortal without. The only thing to fear is unconsciousness after you die. If you are conscious and the love that cannot be fulfilled in life is fulfilled as a ghost, I maintain that a ghost with love is superior to a mortal without. Moreover, to remain alive while love is dead is to cease to be human. To be dead while love remains alive is to be no ghost . . .[84]

The Anatomy of Love

The Anatomy of Love, literally *A Classified Outline of the History of Qing,* draws the great majority of its items from other works, notably the collections of female biographies, both fact and fiction, that flourished in the latter part of the Ming. A lost work, also entitled *Qing shi,* appears to have preceded it.[85] Feng's own part is unclear. In his preface, he disclaims all credit, asserting that he intended to collect items on the subject but had not the time, since he was down on his luck and had to rush about just to make a living. (This seems to put the compilation before his instructorship, which probably began in 1631.) In the meantime, he says, he was forestalled by Zhanzhan Waishi (Hairsplitting Historian), whose classification he praises and whose selection he both praises and apologizes for. In fact, of course, Feng had a great deal to do with the *Anatomy,* even if someone else collaborated. Several of his own compositions are included, accounts of amours and tragedies of which he had personal knowledge. One of them appeared among his comments in the *Guazher* songbook, and the rest may also have been reprinted from other texts.[86] The most notable of them, "The Life of Ai-sheng," is a moving account of the precocious intelligence, frustrated idealism, melancholia, and death of a young singing girl in Soochow.

There is a close, if indirect, connection with Feng's story collections; the stories use some of the same sources as the *Anatomy*, and the *Anatomy* appears to refer to the vernacular works on several occasions.[87] It has a more general connection with other works of Feng's, especially the *Shange* and the *Survey*; all contain anecdotes about the same flamboyant Soochow personalities. Perhaps an old collection of Feng's was the basis of the *Anatomy*. At the same time, Feng is credited with the commentary on some dozen items. The comments *might* have been lifted bodily, along with the item, from some earlier work of Feng's, perhaps the old collection I have postulated. But it is more likely, from the form in which some of them appear, that Feng added them in the course of the *Anatomy's* compilation.[88] Two pseudonyms are used by the writers who sum up at the end of each juan, the Master of Qing and the Historian of Qing. They alternate up to juan 8, after which the latter does most of the work. Both tend to pontificate in a manner that suggests not the witty, ironic Feng of *Sack, Survey,* or *Treasury of Jokes* but the Hairsplitting Historian of his preface. However, there is some evidence that the Master might have been Feng.

Feng interprets "qing" in his preface as an ardent, selfless sympathy for others, and he apologizes for the fact that the compiler has limited its meaning to sexual love. He says: "As a young man, I was considered a fanatic about qing. I would always open my heart to my friends and colleagues and share their joys and sorrows. If I heard of someone in dire poverty or suffering a particular injustice, even if I did not know the person, I would do my utmost to help. If I lacked the means, I would sigh over the case for days on end and toss and turn without sleep. If I met a man of qing, I would feel like bowing down before him." He had once cherished the "intention of selecting the finest examples of qing through the ages and writing a short account of each so that people might know that qing can last forever." He concludes with a long poem, a Buddhist *gāthā* in which he proclaims qing as the only material reality and announces his intention of establishing a Doctrine of Qing, a sort of universal religion, in direct contrast to Buddhist belief.

> I shall establish a Doctrine of Qing
> to instruct all living things.
> Sons shall have feeling for fathers,
> subjects shall have feeling for rulers.

The myriad things of the world are "so many scattered coins" and qing, feeling, is "the string that threads them up." Qing is here treated as a cult, with comic hyperbole, but in Feng's comments, it is rationalized in psychological terms. An anonymous commentator in juan 5 says: "All actions of loyalty, piety, chastity, and honor receive their stimulus from qing; hence Ziyou wrote his 'Discourse on Courage in Feeling.'"[89] Immediately afterward comes the Master's summary, which is on this general subject.

Feng's comments in the book show him focusing on the point at which the heroic and romantic meet. He approves of the suicide of the maiden who kills herself after sheltering the fugitive Wu Zixu. He approves also of the knight errant who kills in the cause of justice, but he has contempt for two famous objects of the romantic imagination, Yang Guifei and Li Wa.[90] He might have been expected to despise Yang, but his criticism of Li Wa, the courtesan who reforms her lover, comes as a surprise. What Feng deplores is her lack of ardor, her shallowness of commitment. If her lover had died, she would not have shed a tear. She was simply not enough of a romantic.

5

Feng's Vernacular Fiction

About 1615, according to Shen Defu, his friend Feng Menglong urged a publisher to offer a high price for Shen's manuscript of *The Golden Lotus*.[1] Shen self-righteously declined the offer, but he tells us that the novel was published soon afterward anyway. Several years earlier, Feng had assisted in the preparation of an expanded version of the *Shuihu*. The editors' claim that the version was the one Li Zhi had commented on is certainly false, and the Li Zhi commentary it includes is probably spurious. The report of Feng's involvement comes from the playwright Xu Zichang: "A follower of Li Zhi's had brought the manuscript to Soochow, where the Soochow writers Yuan Wuya, Feng Youlong, and others, who were ardent admirers of Li's theories and worshiped the man, greatly esteemed it and together checked it several times and removed its mistakes."[2] This seems reliable; Feng's songs show how close he was to the publisher Yuan Shudu (Wuya). However, Feng did not take the major part in the editing; his style differs from that of the man who rewrote the added portions.

His first novel, a reworking of the *Ping yao zhuan*, makes a similar spurious claim. Zhang Yu claimed in his 1620 preface that Feng's expanded novel was the original. But the pretense was soon dropped and Feng acknowledged as having supplemented the old novel. Feng adapted one other work, a fictionalized history, and also wrote a biography of Wang Yangming in the form of a novel.

His three forty-piece collections of old and new vernacular stories were published at intervals during the 1620s. (During that decade, Feng published so much that he must surely have been making his living by writing.) The collections were reprinted and, presumably when the blocks had worn, were brought out in new editions. He may well have been partly responsible for the famous secondary anthology *Remarkable Stories New and Old* (*Jingu qiguan*), which was selected from his three collections and Ling Mengchu's two.[3] However, he was clearly not involved in numerous other works to which his name or pseudonym is attached[4]; enterprising publishers made as free with his name in the 1630s as they had done before with Li Zhi's and Yuan Hongdao's. All of the editions Feng prepared were handsomely produced with fine illustrations, copious notes, and elaborate punctuation. Feng was spreading the vernacular literature to a wide readership but not to a poor one.

Novels

The *Ping yao zhuan* was an old work, dating back to the early part of the Ming dynasty.[5] It is about a short-lived eleventh-century rebellion, which by the Yuan dynasty at the latest had become a storyteller's topic. There were religious and magical overtones to it, as in most Chinese rebellions, and by the time the novel appeared, the magical elements far outweighed the military. Almost two-thirds of its twenty chapters are concerned with the prankish mischief of the various witches and wizards before the rebellion even begins. It is a largely comic work whose comedy consorts oddly with its serious dénouement.

What struck Feng about it was its incompleteness. It begins abruptly, "like gunfire heard in the dark." The reader does not know who Aunt Divinity (Sheng Gugu) is or where she comes from or what happens to her. There is no disposition of half the wizards and witches. These criticisms from Zhang's preface are true. It is not that the novel is formally incomplete — just that it contains mysteries and leaves loose ends in a way that vernacular fiction abhors. To improve it, Feng placed fifteen new chapters before the old text and also rewrote and stretched the text itself, inserting extra action and background detail and elaborating the ending. He made extravagant use of the mode of comment, especially in the form of the narrator's dialogue with his audience. Occasionally he even seems to mock the technique of the old novel. He flouts convention by beginning a chapter with an entirely new topic, and is fond of internal reference, as if it were a game.

But although his adaptation enjoyed a popular success, it is by no means a masterpiece. Feng failed to make the rebellion interesting, and his fifteen new chapters do not compare to the original. Only in rare instances does he attempt its comedy of mischief, and when he does (as in Chapter 15, when the girl magician is given in marriage to a eunuch), he lacks the nerve to carry it through. His most successful comedy is satirical and depends heavily on stylistic means. Someone makes the Emperor dream of a "Heavenly Text," and when the Emperor announces the dream, this same person is ready to supply the text, which proves to be a garbled version of the *Lao Zi*.[6] There are also numerous witty disquisitions by the narrator and many comic touches to the language.

Feng also provides a vernacular introduction with the trite moral that all is foreordained and we should not strive against our fate. His illustration is a pointed one:

> Take two students. One has high talent and exceptional scholarship yet leads a life of failure, never finding anyone who appreciates him and ending his days in obscurity. The other, at a tender age, when he can barely mumble a few lines, let alone write decent prose, passes all the examinations at his first attempt and is applauded and lionized. The man who fails says the examiners are blind and the heavens deaf; little does he realize that the youth may have studied and done good deeds in some previous existence, thus accumulating the early success and distinction he enjoys in this life.

Surely this is ironic! However, Feng goes on to talk of the ease with which the man destined to be Emperor attains the throne. He derides people like the Tang rebel Huang Chao, who could not pass the examinations but dreamed of being Emperor, and whose dreams led only to his own death and an evil reputation for all eternity. Huang Chao gained his temporary success only because the national fortunes were destined to decline. But there is also the kind of rebel the novel is about: "One who is ignorant of the situation in which he finds himself, and who plays out his little farce just when the dynasty is at the height of its power. Not only does he never succeed in declaring himself Emperor; he ends up with head and body in different places, an example for all posterity to observe."

The *New History of the States,* Feng's venture in fictionalized history, was to have been the first of a series. According to the publisher's notice on the title page, Feng had also begun an account of the Han, and the preface implies that he might go on to treat the rest of Chinese history (except the Three Kingdoms period, for which a masterpiece existed). He never did so, and in fact his Han history never appeared, perhaps because official duties intervened. The preface is contemptuous of existing works in the genre, the fabrications of "village schoolmasters" with no respect for history. A long catalogue follows of the mistakes and absurdities that characterize the work Feng is adapting. Feng's own statement gives further detail of the old history's weakness. Even its poetry is inadequate: "Although one doesn't expect great skill from the poetry in fiction, still, it ought not to be too vulgar."

It was natural that Feng should find a gulf between his taste and the taste of most of his predecessors in the genre. The sixteenth-century fictionalized histories are irremediably dull if read as literature; what value they have is as popularized history. And they contain ludicrous mistakes. For example, Feng's predecessor quotes poems by the famous early Ming poet Gao Qi and labels him a Tang poet![7] But the contemptuous term "village schoolmaster" has a wider significance. It indicates the cultural gap between two kinds of writers in the vernacular literature — between the Feng Menglongs on the one hand and popular publishing's regular authors on the other.

Feng's principal source was a fictionalized history by Yu Shaoyu, a member of the Fujian family of popular publishers.[8] If, to state the obvious, narrative history must be structured upon events or people or the clock (as in a chronicle) in some order of priority, Yu Shaoyu's book emphasizes the first; it is a series of more or less self-contained events. Feng recasts it into chapters none of which is self-contained. He also pays attention to the clock, constantly referring to the Zhou kings. He plants information well ahead to prepare us for some major event which is then spread over several chapters, interwoven with other events. He is continually updating.

Feng's main concern was to put fictional flesh on the bones of the source. Where the two works treat the same event, Feng's version increases the number and size of scenes, in particular the amount of dialogue, and grounds the original in specific reality. He pays minute attention to motivation and, more broadly, to causation. His plotting is intensified, his descriptive language fresher. These changes are apparent throughout, but perhaps the best example is in the story of Wenjiang of Qi and her half brother.

Feng introduces the pair in Chapter 9. They have grown up in an atmosphere in which nothing is denied them. They played together as children and did everything short of making love. The marriage her father, the Duke, proposes for Wenjiang does not take place, and she falls into a melancholia in which her dependence on her brother becomes even stronger. Finally, she is married to the elderly Duke of Lu, although by that time she and her brother are wildly in love. The climax of their story occurs when she insists the Duke take her back on a state visit to Qi, of which her brother is now the ruler. The two are reunited and make love. When the Duke of Lu becomes suspicious, the brother takes him out hunting and has him killed. The assassin's life is then offered to the state of Lu in propitiation. The problem is what to do with Wenjiang. Her son, the new Duke of Lu, is torn between his duty to her and his duty to his father, whom she has, in effect, murdered, while she and her half brother are torn by their own conflicting claims of love and propriety. She takes up residence on the border between the two states.

This conflict of passion and propriety is done in excellent detail by Feng but in feeble fashion by Yu,[9] who does not even introduce Wenjiang

until the occasion of her state visit to Qi. Although her brother is inflamed with desire on seeing her, nothing is said of any previous fixation.
Nothing at all is said of her feelings. It is true that he puts some effort into
the hunting scene, with its contrast between the sunny picture of the hunt
and the dark design in the brother's heart, but Yu's story is all too perfunctory as compared with Feng's account.

In fact, so novelistic is Feng's writing at times that certain vignettes
stand out like open-ended short stories. It is this impression—of brilliant
short sequences excellently realized—that is likely to remain in the
reader's mind. This is, of course, Feng's intention. He is professedly concerned with human action, not heavenly destiny, over five centuries, and
the narrative is bound to break down into short sequences. But one may
also speculate that his forte lay in writing stories and that he set about
composing the long work in the manner of a story-writer.

The figures that emerge from his narration are of two kinds. There are
the spectacularly wicked women, of whom Wenjiang is one example.
Feng does nothing to alter the historical stereotype of the femme fatale;
what he does is develop it in realistic terms and with detailed motivation.
The other, more important, kind are the statemen and planners. Feng
pays little attention to the warriors and ignores the life of contemplation.
Confucius exists as a man of action rather than as a moral philosopher.[10]
Respect is paid to the hegemons, whose personal faults pale beside their
gift for magnanimous leadership. But the real heroes are the advisers—
Guan Zhong, Sun Shu'ao, Yan Ying, Sun Bin, Zhang Yi, Su Qin, and so
forth.[11] These men are the key to a state's power, and it is on their
character and intellect that Feng concentrates. In this too he is not changing the interpretation of his source but simply bringing it into sharper
focus.[12]

Feng's life of Wang Yangming (*Huang Ming da ru Wang Yangming
Xiansheng chu shen jing luan lu*) is an anecdotal biography focusing on
Wang's early career, particularly the military career in which he suppressed various brigands and rebels, including Prince Ning of the Ming
royal house. Feng's Wang Yangming is a brilliant man of action, ingenious, flexible, resolute, and daring, but also wise and enlightened. He
is able to understand and even admire the bonds a bandit leader can
forge with his men, but he also governs the natives of Guizhou with a
sage's wisdom. Feng's life of Wang makes some concession to the form
of the vernacular novel, notably in its language and mode of comment,
but in other respects it resembles historical narrative: it is not organized
into chapters, it frequently mentions its sources, and it refuses to let fictional needs shape the narrative to any great degree.

Feng's preface to his *Chance Selection on the Three Doctrines*,[13] in
which Wang's life represents Confucianism, takes pains to defend
Taoism and Buddhism against familiar Confucian charges. The sage-

kings had characteristics that can as easily be called Buddhist or Taoist as Confucian. China's fortunes were no higher in the Song, when Confucian philosophy held sway, than in other periods: "The three doctrines deride each other, but they cannot do away with each other." Feng goes on to describe his own attitude and the origins of his book:

> I do not have a general grasp of the Three Doctrines, and would never be so presumptuous as to reject one in favor of another. From Buddhism, I take its compassion, from Taoism, its serenity, and from Confucianism, its sense of ordinary reality. This is what I mean by saying that when their meaning is grasped, one will be able to cope with the world. I chanced to read the chronology of [Wang Yangming's] life and sighed to myself that he was the finest type of Confucian, one who combined civil with military ability. On my free days, I worked it up into a short biography to teach all those who study Confucianism that their learning must be like Wang's if it is to be of any use. Then I recalled that novels existed about Ji Dian and Jingyang, and I combined them with this biography to complete a trilogy on the Three Doctrines.

(The latter novel, a short work by Deng Zhimo, was used by Feng in his *Common Words*.)[14] The prologue is a brief historical survey of Confucian doctrine, beginning with the invention of writing itself. In Feng's view, the Han dynasty provided an ideal combination of scholarship and administration, but the Tang fell from grace by selecting officials on the basis of their poetic skill. His prologue, like his narrative, has a simple didactic tone, and the work is obviously what Feng says it is—an educational text for the young.

Stories

Feng's collections include about forty early and middle period stories, as identified by bibliographical and stylistic evidence. In reprinting them, he corrected and adapted as he thought fit without removing features simply because they seemed archaic. From the dozen stories of which the originals still exist, one can see that he used no simple rule of adaptation.[15] With the exception of one story he cut down to serve as a prologue, there are four that show major changes, all of which were discussed in their original form in Chapter 3.

Two are the interconnected religious stories "Red Lotus Seduces the Priest Yutong" (GJ 29), of which earlier versions appear in the popular miscellanies, and "The Five Abstinences Priest Seduces Red Lotus" (Hong 13, adapted as GJ 30). In the first case, Feng took up the invitation offered by the original and filled out the ending. In the second, he was dissatisfied with the tone on which the story was pitched and with the sketchy way it treated Su Shi's life. He added a prologue, another story of priestly incarnation but on a high moral plane, and inserted into the main story a version of how Foyin became a priest. He also added several pages on the vicissitudes of Su's official career and the firmness of his friendship with Foyin, doing justice to him as public servant, poet, and friend. The adaptation is in the same spirit as his rewriting of the scurrilous story about Liu Yong (Hong 1).

His main change in "The Wrongly Identified Corpse" was the addition of a passage that tells how the erring victim, having killed himself, still manages to claim the life of the blackmailer. Feng was upset by the inequity of the blackmailer's getting away with his crime. After the victim's ghost has possessed the blackmailer and killed him, the narrator continues: "In handing on this story, everybody said that Qiao Jun, though a lecher, had never killed anyone and yet suffered this frightful calamity. From his place in the netherworld how could he ever let Wang Qing get away with his deed? His claiming of Wang's life was a necessity of the Heavenly Principle."[16] Feng's note says that, without this event, the principle of bao would not have been kept. In fact, his notes try to explain the whole action on the basis of bao. Qiao's wife has been guilty of putting the adulterous servant to death. A note reminds us that adultery does not deserve death and that the servant has therefore been unjustly killed.[17] The blackmailing follows as a consequence, and the blackmailer must be paid out in his turn.

The other story, "The Ring" (Hong 20), combines elements of the romance and folly types. Feng disliked the cluster of predictions and warnings and regularly removed one element or the other, but in this story he removed all of them. No doubt he recognized the ambivalence of "The Ring" and chose to recast it, except for an introductory poem, as a romance.

He acknowledges writing one story himself and implies that he rewrote the scurrilous story about Liu Yong, but there is no doubt that he was also responsible for many other stories.[18] The evidence is internal, derived from patterns in the use of sources as well as from characteristic features of style. In *Stories Old and New,* Feng is the probable author of nineteen stories, almost half the collection. In *Common Words,* there are three stories which can be attributed to him, and another thirteen which he may have written. (Even if they are not by Feng, these thirteen must still be the work of a single author.) In *Constant Words,* only one or two stories are attributable to Feng; the majority are by an associate, probably the Langxian who wrote *The Rocks Nod Their Heads.* I shall assume that Feng wrote twenty-two stories (nineteen in *Stories Old and New,* three in *Common Words*) and will consider him the possible author of certain other stories, notably the thirteen in *Common Words.*

He regularly worked from a source or sources, virtually all of which are in Classical Chinese, varying from Classical tales to mere anecdotes. Some stories, for example those with historical subject matter, he selected and pieced together from a chronicle history. In effect, he put the source together himself. At least two of his stories are based on court case fiction. He does not appear to have used plays, and there is no clear evidence that he adapted any chantefables.

"Jiang Xingge Meets the Pearl Shirt a Second Time" (GJ 1), or "The Pearl-Sewn Shirt," the story that Feng placed at the head of his first collection, is based squarely on a Classical tale of a couple of decades earlier, "The Pearl Vest."[19] The briefest abstract of the source would run as follows: A young wife is seduced while her husband is away on business. On discovering the fact, he divorces her but refrains from making her adultery public. She is thus able to marry again, this time as concubine to an official. When her former husband is brought before this official on a murder charge, she threatens suicide unless his life is spared. The official manages to dismiss the charge and allows the pair to remarry.

The principle of bao that lies behind fiction and drama of moral import is here quite plain: the husband's act of grace toward the wife is requited by hers toward him. From a psychological point of view, they have a deep love for each other, which expresses itself in reciprocal action. In an epilogue comment, "The Pearl Vest" adds an optional complexity, introduced by the words "Other people say . . ." The seducer is set upon by thieves and dies brokenhearted. The merchant, who has divorced his own wife, then unwittingly takes the seducer's widow as his second wife, thus achieving a poetic justice. The author comments that if this version is true, "Heaven is too close to us, governing us in all things!"

Feng Menglong, the probable author of the vernacular story, took up the complexity and incorporated it in the main plot. It was inevitable he do so, since the vernacular story abhors loose ends, especially when villains are allowed to go unpunished. But Feng went further, actually placing the theme of heavenly requital at the head of the story. Thus the introduction dwells on the dangers of sex, particularly of adultery: "How would you feel if you had a pretty young wife or a cherished concubine who fell prey to a seducer?" The narrator avows his intention of providing a warning to young men by showing that punishment for adultery cannot be evaded. This is to claim that heavenly bao, the punishment of the seducer, is the story's principal theme. The same claim is made by its title, for Jiang, the merchant, meets up with the pearl shirt again when he marries the seducer's widow, and at that point, the text actually says, "This is the main theme of 'Jiang Xingge's Meeting the Pearl Shirt a Second Time.'"[20] The two wives settle down in marriage to Jiang, but the former widow is now the senior wife, a fact which, the final poem says, is a heavenly punishment for the adulterous woman. The official is rewarded for his magnanimous act with successful descendants, another example of heavenly bao.

Human bao, the reciprocal acts of grace between Jiang and his wife, is still important. When Jiang seals up the cases containing his wife's possessions, the narrator comments: "Because he and his wife had such deep feelings for each other, his heart was cut to the quick, even though they were divorced. The sight of her belongings would only bring her back to his mind, and so he could not bear to open the cases and look at her things." When, in an extraordinary action, he returns the cases to her on the eve of her wedding to the official, "his wife was overcome by remorse. People's reactions varied according to their thinking. Some praised him for his honesty and sincerity, others ridiculed him as a poor fool, while still others condemned him as gutless."[21] Finally, near the end of the story, when the wife has saved Jiang from the charge of murder, the narrator essays an explanation of her motive:

> They had been deeply in love with each other. Although he had had to divorce her because of her wrongdoing, he continued to feel pity for her, and that was why, on the eve of her second marriage, he gave the sixteen cases back to her intact. That one action inevitably made her heart soften toward him. In a high position herself now, and with her husband in dire trouble, how could she fail to come to his rescue? This is what is known as 'being aware of the kindness done to you and repaying it with kindness.'[22]

The reader is likely to find the second bao theme the more compelling. The first is stale, and even its language indicates as much. There is a dual voice or vision in this story, and the reason lies in the twin themes of bao, the one routine, the other refreshing. The first voice can be regarded as part of the tribute paid to the genre and its stock narrator; it is the voice of standard social morality expressing a standard judgment.

The principal changes made in the plot are in the service of the second theme, that of human bao. Their single greatest contribution is to make the reader understand and sympathize with the wife's situation. Feng has set himself the task of shifting the balance of sympathy toward the wife. The reader is told how she originally opposed her husband's going, how he presented her with a fait accompli, how he promised to be back by a certain date but failed, deliberately extending his business journey. Feng pays great attention to the wife's expectations, first raised by the prophecy of a fortuneteller, then dashed. Of course, the diabolical scheme against her honor is found in the source as well, but the episode in which the husband sends her the broken hairpin and silk sash has been added. They were presents from her lover, and her husband broke the hairpin in his rage, but she does not know any of this. She assumes that the broken hairpin must be a matching love token of the sort that parting lovers keep and that the sash is intended as a suggestion of suicide. She concludes that out of love for her (symbolized by the hairpin), her husband wants her to preserve her honor by committing suicide (symbolized by the sash); thus, she tries to hang herself. It is excellent psychological description of a kind rarely found before in the vernacular story. But we should note that the purpose of the psychology is to help us understand and sympathize with the wife's feelings and actions. From the wider view of the workings of bao, it exists to balance the moral equation.

A common feature of the vernacular fiction—its particularistic realism—is conspicuous here, as a comparison between the source and story will show. The tale is spare and direct; virtually every piece of information is necessary to the plot. The story, however, is prodigal with information, most of it only tangentially related to the action. Here is how the attempted suicide ends:

> Saying this, she wept, then placed one stool on top of another, tied the sash to a rafter and proceeded to hang herself. But her allotted span was not yet complete. She had omitted to close the door, and as good luck would have it, Mrs. Wang came in at that moment with the flask of heated wine and saw what her daughter was doing. In her panic she did not stop to put the wine down, just flung herself forward and tried to pull the girl away. But in doing so she kicked over the stools, too, and she and her daughter ended up in a heap on the floor, with the wine all spilled. Mrs. Wang scrambled to her feet and helped her daughter up. "Foolish girl! Here you are in your twenties, a flower still in bloom. How could you think of doing so stupid a thing? Even if your husband does not have a change of heart and actually goes through with the divorce, why, with looks like yours, there will always be someone who will want you. You'll just have to choose a good husband and plan your own happiness in the life you have ahead of you. Now just calm down and take life as it comes—and stop your pining!" (pp. 34a-b)

The narrative method does not differ greatly from that of the early and middle stories, but a number of features are intensified. There is more concern with thought and motive; characters' thoughts are given directly and are commented on. General propositions on a variety of topics are addressed to the reader. Feng does not go so far as Ling Mengchu, but he has freed himself from the earlier story's restraint. His disquisitions on the choice of wives and on the psychology of raised expectations are on a less hackneyed level than the poems, which are the banal stuff of the old Polonius-like narrator. Sometimes, too, the disquisitions lead into a development in the story rather than explaining it ex post facto, a rare feature in the earlier story. Feng also has a more flexible approach to narrative order. The story frequently dips back into the past to explain a point, and sometimes a prediction formula makes a proleptic jump to a new narrative focus. The outstanding case is the wordless meeting between the wife and her seducer, in which the narrator's prophecy first warns us that she will meet a handsome young man and then asks and answers the question "Who was this handsome young man?" As a result, we are able to see the meeting alternately from both sides and appreciate the misunderstanding for what it is.[23]

What strikes the reader is the story's social meaning. A merchant's wife is seduced and falls in love with her seducer, but her love for her husband survives and proves strong enough to bring them back together. No previous story can match this one for its daring. "The Pavilion of Lingering Fragrance" shows a boy and a girl falling in love and forcing their parents to agree to a marriage. A variant with a tragic outcome occurs in "The Ring." But adultery is not involved, and in any case, both stories are on the social level of the romance. Apparently the rules were stricter for the merchant class, in accordance with a different social ethic. In the earlier stories, adulterers are condemned outright and the women portrayed as nymphomaniacs. C. T. Hsia, in an acute observation, has taken this story as an example of the author's siding with the self against society.[24] It is certainly concerned with the difficulty of living up to society's moral code. When a person fails to live up to the code, the author who sides with society condemns him outright, relegating him to some group that must be rejected and from which a warning must be drawn. The author who sides with the self or the individual may or may not attack the particular social law; the essential point is that he shows the person in a sympathetic light as he wrestles with it. Feng's concern with the self in opposition to society is, however, virtually limited to this one matter of sexual love. His concern clearly arises from his attempts to reconcile qing with Confucian morality. Of course, both the wife and the seducer are driven by qing, but only the wife's passive conduct can be regarded as pardonable—at least in the context of Feng's vernacular stories and plays.

"Censor Chen's Ingenious Solution of the Case of the Gold Hairpins and Brooches" (GJ 2) matches its companion. It is a story of heavenly bao in which a man who steals the virginity of his cousin's fiancée ends up losing his own wife to the cousin. The narrator's tone displays a distinct jocularity at various points; he even casts the villain's confession into the form of a popular song. The source of the main story was a lengthy court case story that, with a few exceptions, contains everything vital to the plot.[25] But the source is, for all its ingenuity, a crude piece, an imaginative scenario that had to be developed into a literary work. What Feng did here is what he did later in writing the *New History:* he took the work of a "village schoolmaster" and rewrote it.

The singular feature of both source and story is the wife who goads her unworthy husband into divorcing her and then marries the husband's cousin. The divorced woman is described as chivalrous, the daughter of a gallant father framed by an official. She must have appealed to Feng as an activist example of positive morality. By contrast, the fiancée is an idealized example of traditional virtue. When it dawns upon her that she has given up her virginity to the wrong person and that her real fiancé is the man waiting outside to see her, her mother is quick to suggest that she hush the matter up. The narrative continues:

The girl was silent for a long time. It would be very hard to describe her emotions. Not alarm, no, nor shame, nor anger, nor bitterness—none of those things. She felt an inexpressible pain, as if she were being jabbed with needles. But luckily, she was a woman of great spirit and an idea was already forming in her mind. "Go out and welcome him," she said to her mother. "I know what I shall do." (p. 15b)

Then she hangs herself. It is this kind of scene, with its acute indications of her and her mother's natures, that distinguishes the story from its source.

"Prefect Teng's Ghostly Solution of a Case of Family Property" (GJ 10) was based on a less striking court case story from the same collection. Its main innovation is that a marriage between an old man and a young woman is treated with approval. Together with "Censor Chen's Ingenious Solution," it may be compared with "Prefect Kuang's Solution of the Case of the Dead Baby" (TY 35), a story that may not be Feng's. The latter's source, found in a collection in which Hai Rui, the famous sixteenth-century official, appears as the judge, is much finer, good not merely as rough scenario but also as finished work.[26] The actual process of detection in the source is far simpler than that of the vernacular story, but the taut sequence of temptation, sex, pregnancy, blackmail, murder, and suicide remains much the same. The remarkable feature of both is the sympathetic view taken of a widow's unsuccessful attempt to live up to the social ideal of chastity. This story entirely lacks the jocular tone so often affected by the vernacular narrator.

Feng reprinted three or four stories from the *Pillow* collection and wrote several others in the same vein, reflecting the values of a certain kind of Confucian intellectual. Largely about historical personages, these stories were chosen and developed for their didactic value. They concentrate on two questions that obsessed Feng in his *Sack of Wisdom* and elsewhere: the predicament of the gifted individual who is given no chance to serve his society, and the nature of leadership, especially the leader's relationship to his followers. Most are set in periods of national crisis. As one might expect, their structure is that of bao—human bao and usually heavenly as well. In almost all cases, they have known sources, either Classical tales or informal history.

"Ma Zhou" (GJ 5) (from here on, short titles will be used) is the well-known story of the rise to prominence of Ma Zhou, the Tang writer. Although he lived in a time, Feng tells us, when men of talent were appreciated, he was poor and an orphan, and despite his great knowledge and lofty ambition, he languished in obscurity because he had no one to recommend him. (Although we cannot apply the details to Feng, these stories may be taken as symbolic of his own plight.) The sight of less worthy people succeeding drove him to indulge his formidable capacity for drink. Feng's note on Ma's drinking says, "The discriminating man will pity him for his frustration; the ordinary man will suspect that he lacked character."[27] In a note on the next story, he takes up the point again: "When heroes are in despair, they often devote themselves to wine and sex—take Ma Zhou and Shentu Tai, for example."[28] (Shentu is one of the figures in the companion story.) Ma's extravagant behavior is evidently to be excused as the result of his own sense of frustrated worth.

All such stories involve questions of fate. Ma himself complains of his destiny, and the introductory poem also brings up the question, advising us to wait patiently for the Lord of Heaven to dispose. Although fate is not the instrument of comedy for Feng that it becomes for Ling Meng-chu, such stories of the rise from obscurity of the worthy man have a comic aspect that both source and story exploit. "Ma Zhou" can be regarded as a romance about the success of the eccentric genius whose wild, arrogant behavior is the simple product of his lack of recognition.

"General Ge" (GJ 6) and "Pei Du" (GJ 9) are leadership stories which embody Feng's favorite virtue of magnanimity, but they are also romances. The former tells of the rise of a poor but loyal officer. When, in his superior's presence, he is struck dumb by the beauty of one of the concubines, he expects, when he comes to his senses, to be punished for it. Instead, the incident is overlooked. The officer covers himself with glory in battle, and his superior later marries him to the woman. Finally, as the officer and his wife discuss their good fortune, he realizes that his superior "understood human nature, and valued worth above sex—the conduct of a great man."[29] This brings the narrator to a typical comment on the deterioration of values, especially generosity. He remarks, in the linking passage between the prologue and main story: "People are so pusillanimous they will even hunt out others' faults just to show off their own cleverness."[30] In the second story, both prologue and main story illustrate Pei Du's magnanimity. In his introduction, on the subject of predetermination as shown in physiognomy, Feng argues for a "physiognomy of the heart," asserting that good actions can change one's destiny (and also one's physiognomy). In effect, he is rejecting predetermination and showing his characteristic preference for positive action over passive acceptance.

"Wu Bao'an" (GJ 8) takes up another of Feng's favorite virtues, the compact of friendship, especially between literati. It gives him an opportunity in the prologue to rail against the shallowness of the modern conception of friendship ("a contract of faces") as compared with the friendship of the ancients ("a contract of hearts"). Feng's source is a Tang Classical tale[31] to which he adds a little historical background on Empress Wu, changes the order so as to begin with Guo, the friend, rather than with Wu Bao'an, and inserts the poems of comment ascribed to "a later poet." But his principal change is to trim the letter sent by Guo to

Wu Bao'an. The reason is that the letter in the source asks too much of Wu, thus offending against bao. It is for Wu to volunteer everything but not for Guo to ask everything of him. Guo is described as the complete man, capable in civil as well as military arts, but of the heroic type not "constrained by conventional rules," which explains why he was not recommended for office. Wu appeals directly to Guo, whom he has never met, because he himself lacks formal qualifications (a bugbear of Feng's). The story deals with the bao of friendship and contains values dear to Feng: friendship, leadership, heroism.

Feng included both of the *Pillow* collection's stories of friendship in *Stories Old and New*. It appears from his notes that he appreciated the almost gratuitous gallantry of these exemplary tales and tried to emulate it in his own work. In "Wu Bao'an," Wu asks a favor of a man he knows only by reputation. Guo grants the favor, and then, when he is captured, sends a letter to Wu asking a favor in return. When Wu goes far beyond the request, sacrificing himself and his family to save a friend he has never seen, Feng comments, "Some say that Wu Bao'an abandoned his family for ten years in an effort to ransom a friend he had never even met," and answers the criticism by quoting the saying, "If there is a single person who really appreciates one [zhiji], one will die without regret."[32] Through textual comments and notes in this and other stories, Feng constantly points to the shallowness of latter-day practices as compared with the ancient examples. He says of one of the *Pillow* stories, "It suddenly opens our vulgar eyes," adding, "This is true gallantry—to be prepared to throw away one's own hopes of a career for a friend!"[33] There are numerous echoes of these sentiments in his other work, especially his plays.

In writing "Qian Liu" (GJ 21) and "Mumian An" (GJ 22), Feng turned to a new method of composition. In place of well-formed sources, he now quarried biographical stories from historical works. He turned above all to Tian Rucheng's *Supplement to the Guide to the West Lake*, and from its chronicle history of Hangchow developed these two stories and several prologues, all found in the latter part of *Stories Old and New*.[34]

The former is about the rise of Qian Liu, the King of Wu and Yue in the late Tang and Five Dynasties. It describes itself as a romance of success (*faji biantai*) and was modeled, presumably, on an early story of that same type, "The Meeting of Dragon and Tiger," which Feng reprinted in *Stories Old and New*. The notes insist on heroism and comradeship, although once at least "heroism" is intended ironically. One note consists of a song comparing modern and ancient friendship: "Although vulgar, this song goes right to the heart of society's ills," comments Feng.[35] The latter story is a biography of Jia Sidao, one of the villains of Chinese history, who led the Court into the appeasement policy of accepting the loss of North China. For Feng, the anecdotes about the Emperor disporting himself in Hangchow are not a piece of nostalgic history but an ironic contrast to his duty to retake the North. Jia held power for fifteen years, during which, Feng relates, he successfully hid the true situation from the Emperor. "Later he was stripped of his position and rank and died at the Mumian An, but his death failed to save the country from ruin."[36]

"Sima Mao" (GJ 31) and "Humu Di" (GJ 32), are another pair of parallel stories: both include visits to hell, in which the hero acts the judge's part. Sima Mao is a prodigy whose blunt talk offends the examiners. (The story takes place at a time when offices are sold, but he has neither the money to buy one nor the political pull to be recommended.) He is fifty and a failure when, in his frustration, he gets drunk and writes two poems of complaint about the injustice done to him. He then burns the poems, thus appealing his case to Heaven. His soul is taken to hell, where he is offered a chance to sit as judge for half a day. In the course of his conversation with Yama, the King of Hell, he describes earthly injustices with passion. Feng's note comments, "The injustices in my heart are here all set forth by him."[37] They are predominantly social inequities stemming from wealth and power in the wrong hands.

"Humu Di" begins with the same subject as Feng's play *The Flag of Perfect Loyalty*—the archtraitor Qin Gui and his execution of the patriot Yue Fei. A short passage then brings history down to the Mongol conquest. The narrator dwells on the pleasure seeking of the Emperor's ministers and also mentions Wen Tianxiang's martyrdom at the hands of the Mongols. There is then a complete break, and the narrative reopens with the story of Humu Di, a student frustrated in his noble aspirations for government service. He chances to look at the account of Qin Gui's execution of Yue Fei and seethes with rage. Then he pulls out another book—the posthumous works of Wen Tianxiang. He gets drunk and writes three poems of accusation, declaring what he would do in Yama's position. Like Sima Mao's, his soul is summoned to hell, and he is shown the precise mechanism of cause and effect.

The finest of the historical stories are "Wang Ge" (GJ 39) and "Shen Xiang" (GJ 40). "Wang Ge"'s prologue is based on the *Supplement*, but its main story is drawn from a Classical narrative by Yue Ke, the historian grandson of Yue Fei.[38] It tells of the abortive uprising of Wang Ge, a local magnate. At first sight, Feng's prologue appears to be nostalgic for the Northern Song capital, but it must be read ironically. It begins with anecdotes of the Emperor Gaozong on the West Lake, telling how Gaozong chances to hear a vendor's Kaifeng accent and patronizes her, and how this makes her famous and rich. Another day, he admires a poem on a wine shop screen; the owner of the shop prospers and the poet receives an official post. (The poem is about the joys of idling by the West Lake.) This is the familiar glamorous lore, and it is in that spirit that the *Supplement* reprints it. But the prologue follows it with this passage: "At that time, when the Southern Song was at peace, goodness knows how many people received the Emperor's grace without expecting it. But at the same time there was a man of civil and military abilities famous for his gallantry who never met with the Emperor's favor. He was falsely accused by a knave, and this provoked a ghastly catastrophe which turned into a futile farce. It was all a matter of fate, time, and fortune."[39] The nostalgic episodes are an ironic foil for this man, a genuine patriot, whose career turns into tragedy and farce. Not only is he denied a hearing when falsely accused of seditious intent; he is foolish enough to let himself be goaded into an armed uprising. When he realizes that his defiant gesture will lead nowhere, he contrives to save his family from execution at the cost of his own life. This one success is what the story, formally speaking, focuses on, its full title being "Through His Own Death, Wang Xinzhi Saves His Whole Family."

Wang Ge, the magnate and local power, is the most interesting of Feng's historical characters. He is seen positively but is also condemned for his intemperate folly. He has many of the features Feng admired. He is a self-made man, an entrepreneur who single-handedly develops the iron mines in the district near Anqing to which he moves after a quarrel with his brother. He is a strong and decisive local leader who compels the compliance of local officials and commands the utter loyalty of the people who work for him. He has administrative and military ability, and he is a patriot with a plan to raise troops in an effort to regain the North. It was just such natural leaders that the country needed, in Feng's view, as he points out in the text of this story, in his notes, and in his other works, especially the life of Wang Yangming. Yet when Wang Ge is falsely accused of plotting rebellion and the case is mishandled by cowardly local officials, his pride and anger are too easily provoked. He ignores his daughter-in-law's advice that he give himself up and contest the legal case, and embarks instead on the impulsive course of punishing the local official, establishing his armed power in the area, and then offering his services to the Emperor for an attack on the North. Of course, his actions merely confirm the charge of sedition. His uprising peters out in a series of bathetic acts, such as the burning of a local temple where the offending official has lately stayed.[40] This is what the prologue means, presumably, by "futile farce." (A similar expression is used of abortive rebellions in Feng's introduction to his *Ping yao zhuan*.) He regains a measure of nobility as he coolly plans to save his family and land at the cost of his own life.

The background of his action is also significant. We are told at some length about the disbanding of the local "patriotic force," troops being trained for the retaking of the North. The disbanding, carried out for reasons of political nepotism, spurs Wang Ge to make his proposals to regain the North, proposals that go unheeded, as it would be a "breach of normal practice" to heed a mere commoner. The same phrase recurs in the strictures on government in Feng's other works.

Yue Ke's narrative is a substantial work, but it was not written in the shape of a story, and Feng has treated it freely. He has somewhat improved the character of Wang Ge, who is now more of a hero, less unscrupulous. He does not, for example, seduce the wife of one of his subordinates. Moreover the story is rounded out by the emphasis on his devotion to his family. But the biggest change is Wang's visit to the capital and his proposals for a patriotic war; they are included to make his patriotism and leadership even clearer. Behind Feng's Wang Ge, with his mixture of gallantry and folly and his attribution of failure to destiny, we can see the dim archetype of Xiang Yu, the contender for what became the Han Empire.

"Shen Xiang" is set in the mid-sixteenth century, during the sway of Yan Song and his son Yan Shifan. It begins with a description of the Yans' tyranny, then relates Shen Lian's defiance, his exile, the false accusation of treason brought against him, and his secret murder in jail lest he harangue people on the execution ground. This is historical fiction on the grand scale, like the story of Jia Sidao. The second part of the story is the small-scale, tense account of the pluck and ingenuity shown by his son's concubine in managing, largely by bluff, to save the son from being murdered by his escorts. It is a common type of plot—there are two among Feng's plays—but this is a brilliant specimen. It is hardly necessary to point to the familiar theme of the patriot, a man of civil and military ability, who has the courage to face down the all-powerful Yan Song. Shen Lian knows that his attack on the Yans is a mere gesture, but he makes it nonetheless, hoping it will serve as an example. Even in exile, he is fearless, almost reckless, as he lectures the local residents on loyalty and filial piety and narrates the deeds of the gallant officials of the past:

When he came to a moving subject, sometimes his hair would stand on end, and he would strike the table and roar. At other times, he was all laments and sighing, his tears streaming down. The people of the district, old and young, came and listened enrapt. There were times when he reviled Yan as Yan the Bandit, and the local people would join in in unison, and if any one of them sat silent, the others would round on him and call him disloyal and unrighteous. (p. 8a)

There is also the theme of casual, selfless friendship, as Jia Shi, who knows Shen Lian only by reputation, gives up his modest house to him. And there is the foreign threat, this time from Anda. But it is the last part of the story, the escape and the bluff, that is the most brilliant. It is detailed, protracted, believable—history brought down to the level of mundane reality at which the vernacular fiction excels.

"Su Shi" (TY 3) and "Wang Anshi" (TY 4) are linked by their common subject — the Northern Song statesman and man of letters Wang Anshi. In the former, comic story, he is seen checking Su Shi's intellectual presumption. The latter tells of the nightmarish end of Wang's life, when it is brought eerily home to him, by various human and divine means, just how disastrous his governmental reforms have been to the people. For a long time, the latter was believed to be a Song story expressing the popular feeling against Wang's reforms. But it is actually a genre translation, probably by Feng, of a mid-Ming Classical tale.[41] The tale is itself a work of powerful imagination that welds various anecdotal materials together. Feng's version is quite close to it, if one allows for the freedom of the vernacular author to develop, particularize, and dramatize. Feng has done little, however, to fill in Wang Anshi's past; the story gives only a sketchy account of his rise to power, of his New Laws, and of their effects. Atypically, it has no positive ending, nor does it rest on a structure of bao. Moreover, the reader is interested less in the events themselves than in what they mean to Wang Anshi.

The prologue concerns itself with time and reputation. A man's reputation changes with time, and if he should die while his reputation is at a peak, he will be well remembered. This ushers in the subject of Wang Anshi. If he had died before attaining the highest power, he would have enjoyed a good reputation. But his arbitrary actions while in a position of authority condemn him. It is another story of the decline and fall of a tyrant. But here there is no revenge theme, except for Wang's own slow realization of the contempt in which he is held. The story is built on seven incidents that bring the contempt home to him: some are evidence of human dislike, some are signs of heavenly displeasure, but all affect his mind and drive him eventually to a Buddhist view of life.

Other stories are less concerned with historical issues. "Liu Seven" (GJ 12) is about the Song poet Liu Yong. Feng's preface to *Stories Old and New* condemns the middle period story "Wanjiang Pavilion" as vulgar, as does a note to this story,[42] and one can easily see why. It shows the poet, while a magistrate, arranging to have a singing girl raped by a boatman in order to bend her to his will. Feng turns the incident around to show Liu in a noble light. (A rich man arranges the rape in order to break her tie to her lover; Liu buys her out and marries her to the lover.) Feng certainly used the other text — it is employed piecemeal in several places — but he added a prologue story, as well as accounts of Liu's romance with the singing girl Xie Yuying, his dismissal from office, his carefree life among the singing girls of Kaifeng, his death in penury, and his funeral, paid for by the singing girls.

He insists on a different Liu Yong, a man who is, first of all, a gifted poet: Feng gives a short explanation of the ci lyric and of Liu Yong's innovations in it. He is, secondly, a man of great pride, who cannot endure the life of patronage and who shuns literary friendships. Finally, he is a man of qing: he is true to Xie and she to him. This mixture of talent, pride, and feeling evidently makes him a model for Feng, who defends him from the charge of licentiousness, comparing him in one note to the Soochow eccentric Zhang Xianyi. In another, he says that "Marshal Guo [Ziyi] and Minister Wen [Tianxiang] both devoted themselves to famous courtesans, and yet, when suddenly given power, they sacrificed themselves for their country and forgot their own families. How are pedantic moralists capable of understanding anything like this?"[43]

Liu Yong is also a man whose inability to conform makes him a failure in his career; thus, the story is a condemnation of "respectable" society. His great romance is with a singing girl, and it is the singing girls, not the officials, who appreciate his talent. The editorial notes relish Liu's reaction to his dismissal: "The people in office are all illiterates. How could they allow a genius like me to succeed?"[44] This is another Feng story of the talented man's problem in fulfilling himself in public service.

The most notable of these stories is "The Old Protégé" (TY 18), a story that Feng admits writing.[45] It is about the perennial candidate who, despite his great talents, regularly fails in the examinations. (Its facts are close to Feng's own experience. He had apparently continued to fail in the examinations until, in 1630, he received the status of tribute student, went probably to the National University for a further examination, and finally attained office.) The tribute studentship is an avenue open to the hero of this story from the age of thirty on, but he spurns it, believing he has the talent to succeed in the regular examinations. He does not have the money to go to the National University; besides, only the lesser jobs are open to former tribute students. So he makes a practice of selling his seniority to the man next in line and is fifty-six before he succeeds in the provincial examination. (Feng must have been about fifty when he wrote the story.) If he had wished to take the studentship, he tells people, he could have been a county official:

> The trouble is that this is an examination world. If Confucius had taken the examinations and failed, who would be telling us about his genius? If a village lad, who roughly memorizes a few obsolete eight-legged essays, meets up with a purblind examiner who marks haphazardly, and becomes a jinshi [holder of the highest degree] in his sleep, people will all declare themselves his disciples. (p. 3b)
>
> There are so many injustices that, if one doesn't become a jinshi, one might as well not serve at all. I'd prefer to end my days as an old licentiate and then complain loud and clear to King Yama after my death, hoping to get a chance in the next life, than stoop to take some humble position in which I would have to endure people's spleen and take sedatives the rest of my career! (p. 4)

The story is structured on a bao plot. The hero owes his success to the marking of a single examiner, who happens to be in charge at each of the examinations he passes. The comedy—for it is a comedy—lies in the fact that the examiner does not mean to pass him on any of these occasions;

he is eager to pass younger candidates, on whose allegiance he will depend in his old age. But by a twist of fate, he is thwarted in every move he makes to fail the hero. When he deliberately chooses the crudest paper, feeling it cannot belong to an experienced scholar, his guess is wrong, for the aged hero has been stricken with diarrhea and has had only the briefest time to jot down a few thoughts. What adds to the comedy is the hero's firm conviction that his success is due in each case to the examiner's favor. In fact, he survives the examiner and goes on to educate, and promote the careers of, the examiner's son and grandson.

The prologue takes up the question of the age at which success is achieved, arguing that age itself is not important. Feng launches into a tirade against the fickle moderns who flatter the promising young man but scorn him when, as time goes by, he does not succeed. Age is relative to success: the youthful prodigy may reach his senescence at twelve, while the late developer may be in his youth at seventy. This is comic, but it has its serious side. If the story is relevant to Feng's career, as I assume it to be, he was still able to regard his frustrations with humor.

There are five others in *Stories Old and New* that Feng probably wrote and thirteen in *Common Words* that he may have written. It is no surprise to find stories on Taoism and Buddhism in the work of a man who professed a belief in the Three Doctrines. "Zhang Daoling" (GJ 13) and "Chen Tuan" (GJ 14), both apparently by Feng, are on famous Taoist figures: Zhang was the founder of Taoism as an organized religion and Chen a famous ascetic. Feng's discussion of the three doctrines in "Zhang Daoling" is different from that of his preface to the *Chance Selection*. Here Confucianism is criticized as too ordinary and Buddhism as too austere, while Taoism is valued for its teaching of immortality. Feng's treatment of Chen Tuan is respectful but humorous. After a lively introduction on the nature of sleep, the narrator launches into the story of Chen himself, the leading authority on its enjoyment. He tries hard to make the story plausible, rejecting the popular notion that Chen slept for eight hundred years. In fact, Chen had acquired the technique of hibernation as practiced by animals and could sleep for several months at a time.

"Yang Balao" (GJ 18) is not typical of Feng's work. It is a story of chance and adventure full of piquant coincidences and recognition scenes, all of them taken from the Classical source. What is new is the grim reality of the pirate raids, particularly the plight of the captured women who survive and return home.

"Shan Fulang" (GJ 17) and "Jin Yunu" (GJ 27) are stories of fidelity and betrayal in love, respectively. The problem is one of social caste, for although both men are scholars, one woman is a prostitute and the other the daughter of a beggar. In the first story, the man overcomes the opposition of his family to marriage. (Actually, the couple were engaged as

children, but in the turmoil of the Jurchen invasion, the girl was abducted by mutinous troops and sold to a brothel. There the boy falls in
love with her without realizing who she is.) In the second, an impover-
ished young student marries the daughter of a man who has become rich
by organizing the city's beggars. The student enters the marriage because
he needs money from his father-in-law to further his career, but as he
succeeds, he feels the burden of his wife's shameful origins and tries to
kill her. Eventually, after he has been duly shamed, there is a reconcilia-
tion.

The problem of "Jin Yunu" is in its moral equation: How is the hero to
atone for attempting to murder his wife? He is humiliated before his
peers and beaten by his former wife and her maids, and a note comments: "It would be unsatisfactory if husband and wife were simply to
reunite. With this beating, their reunion gladdens the heart."[46]
Nonetheless, the story, which Feng developed from an anecdote, remains
a problem, in recognition of which it begins in an unusual way: it begins
with the beggars, and only after describing their status, the wealth of the
beggar boss, and his hopes for his daughter, does it raise the question of
her marriage. The disruption of the wedding celebration by the boss's
relatives and friends is intended to explain the bridegroom's reaction. As
much thought has gone into balancing the moral equation here as in "The
Pearl-Sewn Shirt," even if the effort is unsuccessful.

In the thirteen *Common Words* stories that Feng may have written, the
principal theme is that of loyalty or betrayal, especially in love. "Tang
Yin" (TY 26) is about the famous sixteenth-century poet's passion for a
maidservant in a great man's house and about the extraordinary pains he
takes to win her. Like the anecdotes of Feng's anthology *Celestial Air*, it
is an example of qing—the headlong, sentimental passion of the literary
man. In "Fan Xizhou" (TY 12), the positions of hero and heroine are
dramatically reversed in the course of the story. He is the nephew of a
rebel leader and saves her life during the rebellion. They fall in love, but
have to part when the rebellion is crushed. Eventually she is able to induce her father to accept him as a son-in-law. (Meanwhile he has improved his moral position by fighting gallantly under Yue Fei.)

Two other stories tell of love between young scholar and singing girl.
One is the famous "Courtesan's Jewel Box" (TY 32), in which the singing
girl, finding herself betrayed, throws her jewels and then herself into the
river. It is based on a lengthy Classical tale by Song Maocheng, the writer
of the tale that Feng made into "The Pearl-Sewn Shirt." The other,
"Zhao Chun'er" (TY 31), is the story of the singing girl who turns model
wife and gradually reforms her wayward husband—an old theme. A
story which may be grouped with these, although it was not written by
Feng, is the celebrated "Yutang Chun" (TY 24), in which the loyalty of
scholar and singing girl is subjected to countless trials.

"Wang Jiaoluan" (TY 34) is a story of disloyalty in love. The heroine is a poet who expresses the wrong done her in a long plaint, much of which is given. In all of these betrayal stories, the betrayer is a man; there is no equivalent of the disloyal woman of the middle period story.[47]

Only one of the remaining stories can be easily related to Feng's known concerns. "The Luckless Licentiate" (TY 17), the companion piece to "The Old Protégé," is about the relationship of destiny to success. The narrator tells the story so that his audience will "hold their heads high and wait for their day to dawn, without losing heart."[48] It deals with the false friends who attach themselves to a promising young man and then, unlike his fiancée, who proves to be a model of self-sacrificing loyalty, abandon him as he suffers one misfortune after another.

The world of Feng's fiction is larger than that of the early and middle period stories. It is the world of a concerned, educated activist with basically Confucian sympathies, to which is joined a strong romantic streak. This is no longer the cool pragmatist of *Sack of Wisdom* but the impassioned patriot who admires total commitment to an ideal. In issues of private rather than public morality, he is more lenient, except where the principle of loyalty is broken. He is sympathetic to the demands of the instincts, sanctioning them as an outlet for frustrated ambition. There is even a trace of the headlong romanticism of his art songs. Several of his heroes can be seen as symbolizing his personal ideals and frustrations. He is also constantly aware that he is writing for a broad public, and he often provides simple explanations of fact. A couplet in "Fan Xizhou" runs:

A story must cater to the general public if it is to circulate afar.
Speech must deal with moral principle if it is to move men's hearts.[49]

6
Langxian

Constant Words, Feng's third collection of stories, differs radically from the other two, and for an obvious reason. A newcomer has written most of its stories, and it is his writing, and perhaps also his influence on the other selections, that accounts for the difference.[1] Only seven of the forty stories are known to have been in existence before the collection was made,[2] and it is likely that the writer who was responsible for at least twenty-two of the remaining thirty-three was an associate of Feng's, not merely the author of some independent collection that Feng appropriated. In that case, he may be identified as one of the two men whose pseudonyms are attached to *Constant Words*. The annotation is attributed to the Keyi Recluse and the collation to the Master of the Ink-Wild Studio (Molang zhuren). Keyi evidently wrote the preface, dated Nanking, 1627, in which he signs himself the Keyi Recluse of Longxi; there is little doubt that he was Feng Menglong.[3] It is likely, therefore, that it was the Master of the Ink-Wild Studio who wrote the twenty-two stories. The same man also assisted Feng in preparing new editions of the first two collections, probably in 1627.[4]

Study of the unknown author's style suggests that he probably also wrote *The Rocks Nod Their Heads* (*Shi dian tou*), a fourteen-piece collection of stories, with preface and notes by Feng Menglong.[5] This author was thus apparently responsible for some thirty-six stories in the two works.

The author of *The Rocks Nod Their Heads* is identified only by pseudonyms. He is called Langxian, "Free-Spirited Immortal," in Feng's preface, and Tianran Chisou, "Foolish Old Man of Nature," at the head of the text itself. A certain Xi Langxian appears in a volume of art songs edited by Yuan Yuling, for which Feng wrote the preface.[6] He was presumably a friend of Feng's; he is referred to simply as Langxian in the preface. He is the only known Langxian among Feng's acquaintance, but his authorship is still uncertain, and I shall call the man who seems to have written the *Constant Words* and *Rocks* stories simply Langxian.

120

The publisher of the first editions of these two collections brought out one other work of fiction, Feng's *New History of the States*, and Langxian may also have had something to do with its compilation. The two principal commentators on the action — mainly in the form of poems — are the Longxi Recluse (Feng Menglong) and the Bearded Old Man (Ranweng) and the Bearded Immortal (Ranxian), whom I assume to be one and the same person. The latter's opinions are more orthodox than Feng's; at times he seems to conduct a debate with Feng over the moral interpretation of historical events. I think it possible that the Master of the Ink-Wild Studio, alias the Foolish Old Man of Nature, alias the Free-Spirited Immortal, may also have been the Bearded Old Man and the Bearded Immortal. The last named also contributed the final poem to Feng's life of Wang Yangming, which may have been written during Feng's service as assistant county instructor in Dantu in the early 1630s. If these last guesses are correct, Langxian was associated with Feng for several years, beginning about 1627. Everything else about him has to be inferred from his stories.

Theme and Form

Langxian's moral world differs vastly from Feng's. It displays none of Feng's concern for public morality — the morality of patriotism, of competent and magnanimous leadership, of heroic action on the great stage of civil and military affairs. In his stories, success in examinations seems an end in itself, a social and cultural symbol of accomplishment, rather than an opportunity for self-fulfillment. Some of his stories even cast doubt on the validity of career ambitions. Their perspective is far from that of the official. In fact, officials in his stories, even local magistrates, appear as if viewed from another social sphere, as alien, arbitrary, and even menacing figures. Several of his best stories, particularly in *Constant Words*, stress withdrawal from public life, even from social life, into country seclusion, delight in nature, and belief in Taoism. Feng and Langxian, though friends, emerge from their writings as very different people.

No previous stories are as committed to Taoist themes as Langxian's. Four of them are centrally concerned with the attainment of immortality: "The Old Gardener" (HY 29), "Metamorphosis into a Fish" (HY 26), "Du Zichun" (HY 37), and "Yunmen Cave" (HY 38). According to one hint, the hero of "Lu Nan" (HY 29) also becomes an immortal. But Langxian's Taoism was not the rigorous, doctrinal sort. It may be called sentimental, if the term is not taken as disparagement, the Taoism of the artist or poet rather than of the believer or practitioner.

"The Old Gardener" is about a gentle recluse who devotes his life to the care of the flowers in his garden.[7] For him the flowers are sentient beings, and he loves them as if they were children. His burial services for the dead flowers anticipate those of Black Jade in *Story of the Stone*, although their meaning is very different: for Black Jade the dead flowers are symbols of herself, while for the old man the flowers are his friends. Indeed, they are superior to ordinary humanity; he cannot bear to see them sullied by the "foul breath" of vulgar people. Into his paradise there intrudes coarse and violent humanity in the form of the avaricious Zhang with his political connections and his cunning, and the old man is saved from Zhang's machinations only by the help of the flower spirits. The garden and its flowers are freshly and copiously described, in prose passages, set pieces, and poems, a vast change from the perfunctory treatment usually accorded the natural setting in fiction. The garden becomes the center of the story, a microcosm of idyllic innocence rudely violated by the outside world.

The garden in "Lu Nan" is just as central and more elaborate. Not only is it described in loving detail; the story itself is constructed upon the main flowering seasons of the year—plum blossom, peach blossom, tree peony, lotus, cassia, chrysanthemum—as well as the perfect moonlight of the Mid-Autumn Festival. Lu Nan, a historical figure of the sixteenth century, is a different character from the old man; where the latter is humble and saintly, Lu is proud and arrogant in his genius. He is an aesthete and epicurean who has withdrawn from the world in distaste because it will not give him his due, a man to whom the garden brings aesthetic pleasure. Lu's garden, figuratively termed a Taoist paradise, is also invaded, by a cruel and greedy official, a man who is at first merely anxious to cultivate Lu's acquaintance but who eventually becomes so resentful of Lu's contempt that he tries to ruin him. Like the old man, Lu spends time in prison on fabricated charges.

Taoist themes are not so important among the *Rocks* stories, despite the fact that both pseudonyms of the author, "Free-Spirited Immortal" and "Foolish Old Man of Nature," point to Taoism. However, several of the stories show this same interest in flowers. "The Impetuous Student" (*Rocks* 5) gives an account of the jade flowers of Yangzhou; "Mistress Wang" (*Rocks* 10) gives an account of the crabapple; and "Tang Xuanzong" (*Rocks* 13) gives the historical lore of a species of peony.[8]

The theme of reverence for living things, which was found in "The Old Gardener," occurs in other stories in different guises. In "The Foxes' Revenge" (HY 6), a story of foxes that haunt a man who has shot at them and taken away their most treasured possession, a magic text, the blame is laid not on the foxes but squarely on the man himself, for the wanton violence with which he interfered with the sanctity of life. Like the flowers of "The Old Gardener," the foxes can metamorphose themselves at will, and they exact an appropriate revenge. From one (too narrow) point of view, "Metamorphosis into a Fish" can be regarded as an argument against eating fish. While the man turned fish listens in mounting fury and frustration, the men who were his closest colleagues discuss whether to cook and eat him. And when the fish is dead on the kitchen table, and the man's soul has returned to its human body, both he and his stunned friends resolve never to eat fish again. But this last example is a reminder of the place of comedy in Langxian's use of Taoist themes. The prose that links the prologue of "The Old Gardener" to its main story advises the audience to cherish and enjoy flowers: the story "will at least relieve the tedium, even if it doesn't lead you to grasp the Way and become immortals."[9] It suggests the manner in which to view the story—as an inspired Taoist fantasy.

Although Langxian spurned the theme of public morality, he did not reject with it the domestic side of Confucianism. On the contrary. Here he shows himself more orthodox than any writer of the vernacular fiction up to this time, and far more orthodox than Feng Menglong. Despite the insistent moral emphasis in the majority of previous stories, there had, strange to say, been none that was centrally concerned with the key relationship of Confucian morality—filial piety. Apart from one prologue essay in *Stories Old and New*, there is nothing in Feng's first two collections on the subject. Many of Feng's stories, of course, are about the husband-wife relationship, but they concern themselves with its points of strain and emphasize the wife's (or widow's or lover's) interests rather than her self-sacrifice.

Langxian, by contrast, plunges us into the world of the Confucian moral exemplum. One of his stories, "Li Yuying" (HY 27), is based explicitly on an item in the expanded Ming version of the *Lives of Women* (*Lie nü zhuan*), a handbook of suffocating exempla which was approved reading for young women; it is a well-realized story of wicked stepmother and filial children.[10] "Rainbow Cai" (HY 36) is about a daughter who dedicates her life to avenging her parents' murder, even marrying to achieve her end; after she has avenged the murder, she takes her own life. "Wang Benli" (*Rocks* 3) tells of a young son's search for his missing father, a search that succeeds with supernatural help. "The Siege of Yangzhou" (*Rocks* 11) is a gruesome story of a woman who literally sells her flesh to ensure her mother-in-law's survival.

The Confucian obligations are extended even to servants. In "The Old Retainer" (HY 35), the family servant, by diligence and acumen, saves the fortune of the widow he serves, and having done so, steps modestly into the background, not a penny the richer. (This was too much for Li Yu, who wrote a parody to show a worthy retainer succeeding to his late master's property.[11]) The prologue story is about a servant who endures the beatings of a sadistic master because he admires the man's genius. After the servant's death, the master realizes that the servant was the only person who ever truly appreciated him. There are several stories, in both collections, of wives loyal to the death even to foolish husbands. In "The Martyr" (*Rocks* 12), for example, a widow marries her husband's murderer solely to kill him. The same morality is found even in *Constant Words* stories that were not written by Langxian, notably "Chen Duoshou" (HY 9), in which a girl sacrifices herself for a dying fiancé and is rewarded by his miraculous recovery.

This is the familiar heroism of the exemplum, in which the hero or heroine takes an obligation, real or fancied, to supererogatory lengths. It is no different in its workings from Feng's stories on friendship, but it does differ in its nature. Friendship is a relationship between equals, freely entered into, which is often associated with public morality. By contrast, Langxian's is the world of hierarchical relationships within the family in which, naturally, the heroes and heroines are its junior members—its women, children, and servants. Langxian is well aware that his morality conflicts with much current opinion, particularly Feng's: The words of disparagement for Confucian morality—fusty, doctrinaire, old-fashioned—are used frequently in his stories, but ironically, so that their effect on the reader is to praise rather than condemn.[12]

On the crucial question of the moral nature (is it innate or formed by education and other cultural processes?), Langxian takes roughly the same position as Feng; both men saw moral qualities as innate rather than instilled. It might be said that an author who writes of moral heroism, whether in the area of filial piety or of friendship, will tend to take the former position, while an author who, like Ling Mengchu, presents negative examples will seek to blame a lack of character on faulty upbringing. But I find the opposite argument more persuasive; that is, an author with a particular view of human nature will be impelled toward a corresponding kind of fiction, and the springs of human nature as they appear to him will affect the work he does.

Langxian is aware of the importance of a Confucian education, but he sometimes explicitly says that morality is independent of all education. He shows us immoral people who, unlike Ling Mengchu's villains, are immoral by nature, not by some defect in their upbringing. In "Wang Benli," he shows the filial son learning the meaning of filial piety as he pores over his classics, but he also asserts that filial piety is not a matter of class or culture but of the innate character. In "Qu Fengnu" (*Rocks* 4), he shows a girl of the purest moral heroism developing from a corrupt family, and in "Zhang Tingxiu" (HY 20), he describes two daughters, one a model of virtue and the other of vice. In "The Brothel Keeper" (*Rocks* 8), the cruel and greedy Wu, after several shocking acts of extortion and injustice, is deposed from office and becomes the owner of a high-class brothel in Nanking. Langxian never tells us, as Ling certainly would have done, that Wu was, for example, outrageously spoiled by his parents.

His stories often show a clash between elemental good and evil, as in "The Old Gardener," "Lu Nan," and "Li Yuying," in which the noble daughter and the filial son are pitted against a wicked stepmother. His goodness is a natural goodness not necessarily accompanied by shrewdness. Indeed, the good man may be touchingly unworldly, even gullible, provided he is innocent and sincere, while the evil characters are worldly and calculating. The clash sometimes reduces itself to one of innocence versus worldliness. The evil characters manipulate the law. Their motives are greed and cruelty—the reverse of Langxian's favorite virtues. He shows a pervasive cynicism about the world beyond that of his noble and saintly moral heroes.

His moral heroism is similar, in some respects, to his notion of idealistic love. (He has at least five love stories in *Rocks* and one or two in *Constant Words*.) For Langxian, idealistic love means a headlong personal commitment to an ideal, to action that goes beyond prudence, action that is almost selfless. This is not love in the sense of a need that has to be satisfied.[13] The sacred compact, complete with vows of dedication, is its natural expression. It resembles moral heroism in that it shifts action to a higher plane, above that of the ordinary selfish, prudential values. Like moral heroism too, it is admirable in its excess. Most of the love stories have a supernatural sanction, like the stories of moral heroism, and it is sometimes hard to say whether a story of wifely heroism is really a matter of qing or of Confucian duty.

In "Qu Fengnu" (*Rocks* 4), a widow, anxious to keep her hold over her young lover, persuades her credulous and innocent daughter to marry him. It is a cynical arrangement for everyone but the girl, who falls deeply in love with the young rake. She feels spiritually bound by the phony marriage vows she has taken and kills herself when she hears of his death. (The rake, a weak character, has been affected by her devotion and has felt obliged to respond to it.) When they are cremated, there is one part of each which stubbornly refuses to burn away: a tiny figure of him in her breast and of her in his. The blossoming of love in such sordid surroundings suggests the episode near the end of *The Golden Lotus* in which the young prostitute Aijie falls in love with the rake Chen Jingji. (This story's maid, Chunlai, is based lightly on the figure of Chunmei in the novel.)

"The Impetuous Student" (*Rocks* 5) concerns clandestine love and elopement; both lovers are the reincarnation of the participants in an old love story in which the woman was wronged. "Jade Flute" (*Rocks* 9) is based on the well-known tale of the girl who was loved and left and who continued to love until she finally despaired and took her life; she was then reborn as her lover's concubine. "Tang Xuanzong" (*Rocks* 13) is about the neglected palace lady whose prayer to heaven is answered. Finally, the last *Rocks* story, "Pan Wenzi" is an idealistic story of homosexual love, glorified at the end by supernatural means.

Langxian's stories typically favor the inner view. He is the first writer in the vernacular fiction, apart from the author of *The Golden Lotus*, to give it much attention. His heroes sometimes indulge in torrents of emotional thought and his villains in elaborate calculation. Furthermore, he is interested in mental processes beyond cogitation, such as dreams and dreamlike illusion. Dreams are explained as the product of an intensity of thought—that is to say, as the revelation of psychological states.[14] More often than not, they are nightmarish, the result of anxiety. In "The Old Gardener," the old man in jail has a dream in which he is captured in the act of escape. In "Tang Xuanzong," the palace lady dreams of a romance with the Emperor and of the terrible revenge exacted by the jealous Yang Guifei. In "Master Wu" (HY 28), the girl dreams that she is visited secretly by the young man in the boat moored next to hers but that he is discovered by her father and thrown into the river to drown. In "Master Dugu" (HY 25), the wife and her husband, who is traveling home to see her, share a nightmare in which he watches helplessly as she is about to be raped by hoodlums.

Nightmare exists for its own sake, not merely as psychological description; it is one of Langxian's main themes. There is the nightmare illusion of "Metamorphosis into a Fish," which is explained at one point as a dreamlike illusion produced by an excess of thought.[15] The greater part of the story is devoted to the fish-man's sensations, thoughts, and fears, in a brilliant piece of nightmarish comedy. The "Yunmen Cave" presents the eerie experience of a Chinese Rip Van Winkle's return to his native place after the lapse of a lifetime. Langxian may also have been attracted to the Du Zichun story because of its illusory experience. "The Foxes' Revenge" is full of threatening illusions and impersonations. Metamorphosis in Langxian's stories is in the service of illusion, and illusion is in the service of nightmare.

Nightmare does not have to be produced by dream or illusion; it may also spring from events. Its essential quality is surely the helplessness of the subject before some inexplicable threat or the helplessness of an observer before some event he dreads to see. It is a quality found frequently in Langxian's fiction. An innocent hero may be trapped and thrown into jail on a false accusation. This occurs in "The Old Gardener," in which the old man is accused of sorcery and sedition, and also in "Lu Wuhan" (HY 16), in which the villain has been impersonating the hero. In "Zhang Tingxiu," Zhang the cabinet maker is framed by the false accusations of captured robbers who incriminate him as their chief. The same stratagem is used by the victim's false friend in "The Martyr." In "Lu Nan," the vengeful magistrate concocts evidence with which to charge the hero and causes him to languish ten years in jail.

Other traps must surely include "He Daqing" (HY 15), in which the philandering hero wanders into a nunnery from which the nuns never allow him to escape; "Li Yuying," in which, after their father's death, the children are helpless before the malevolence of their stepmother; and "Mistress Wang" (*Rocks* 10), in which a woman is abducted from the center of Hangchow in broad daylight. There are several stories in which the traitor who schemes to bring about the hero's downfall is actually his supposed best friend. "Rainbow Cai" is one long series of traps, broken promises, and escapes. Helplessness before some evil, the sense of being suddenly and inexplicably trapped, marks the best of Langxian's stories, in which entrapment often leads to jail, the symbol of helplessness. It fits one of his main themes—innocence threatened and helpless before the world.

What distinguishes Langxian most from his predecessors is the social locus of his stories, in particular their interest in peasant life. The vernacular story is vastly unrepresentative, with its concentration on cities and towns. (One exception is the inferior middle period story "The Contract.") Earlier fiction has not dealt with the recurrent perils of the farmer's life—floods, droughts, plagues of locusts, bandits, rebels, tax collectors, and corvée enforcers. Even the middle period story, with its interest in the Hangchow silk business, was concerned with marketing rather than with sericulture.

Langxian was interested in the farm not merely as a setting but as a way of making a living. What impresses the reader of "Wang Benli" is less the filial son's search for his father than the reasons for the father's desertion of the family. Langxian's account of the tribulations of the corvée system, particularly in the vicinity of the capital, is extended and graphic, dominating the story. Of course, it also helps to explain why a decent man would desert his wife and infant son, but the story insists on this subject long past the point of necessity and returns to it even when the son is wandering through Shandong in search of his father. The point is made again, in "Zhang Tingxiu," when the Zhang family are driven off the land because of their corvée duties. In "Shi Runze" (HY 18), the activities of the silk farmers, their raising and care of the silkworms, and even their superstitious practices are told with more detail than in any other Chinese fiction before Mao Dun's *Spring Silkworms* (*Chun can*) of 1932. "A Single Copper Cash" (HY 34) takes us to Jingdezhen, the porcelain center, for the first time in Chinese fiction. Its chain of venality and disaster begins with a family working in the industry but evolves into a property dispute between two large and powerful local families. A number of other stories include droughts, floods, and plagues of locusts as part of their causation.

The Langxian story is similar to Feng's in form. The prologue disquisitions are usually longer than Feng's, and some of them make significant points, such as "Li Yuying" with its discussion of the fate of stepchildren in the three social classes. They allude often to exemplary people and even to moral handbooks. (The main stories make frequent allusions to historical personages and also to dramatic characters.) The material of the prologues is not new, except in "Li Yuying" and one or two others, including some ribald stories; they contain the usual reflections on predetermination, success and failure, temptation, and the like, wittily discussed. (Like Feng, Langxian tends to stress the individual's ability to alter his predetermined fate.) The linking passage to the main story generally takes this form: what you have just heard is strange, but by no means so strange as what you are about to hear.

On the configurative level, Langxian's stories are relatively simple. They contain few lines of development and are not subject to the usual process of intensification by coincidence and dovetailing. On the narratorial and focal levels, he indulges in direct address to the reader more than any previous writer. Questions such as "Readers, who do you think he was?" and "Why do you think this happened?" are so frequent as to amount to a form of narrative progression. There are also numerous generalizations, and the narrative moves fluently back and forth between general statement and narrated action. Curiously, there is little moral lecturing, certainly less than in Feng, despite the overt morality of many of the stories. Popular songs are often used to reflect a contemporary opinion, and there are frequent geographical explanations; in "Master Dugu," for example, there is a long, evocative account of the journey upriver to Chengdu that may reflect personal experience. Description is generally in prose, integrated in the narrated action, rather than isolated from it in set pieces. The language of description, as well as of comment, is lively, free, figurative, and often comic. In general, Langxian's language is more expansive than Feng's and his detail more luxuriant.

Sources have been discovered for most of the stories, ranging from Tang Classical tales to a Ming chantefable that Langxian adapted simply by cutting out the verse passages. He favors the Tang period, especially the An Lushan rebellion,[16] on which a good deal of historical background is provided. In several cases, he appears to have combined two or more sources.

Some of his stories seem to be stretched between two emphases: the moral intent as expressed in a conventional plot and some social fact that engaged his interest. "Wang Benli" is a good example. The disastrous effects of the corvée in the North are what concern him, yet the story is on the theme of filial piety. Like other vernacular writers in this period, he is restricted by the accepted notion of what a story is. It is commonly said that a story should be *qi* ("novel"), and the term appears often in prologues and titles, but it is obvious, in addition, that the story has to belong to certain types and to have certain features. Most commonly, particularly in the middle period and after, these types express an underlying moral fable of which the omnipresent structural feature is bao, in its various meanings. Narrators sometimes express an awareness of plot requirements in their dialogue with their readers, as Langxian's does in an extraordinary passage toward the end of "A Single Copper Cash."[17] The writer of the Classical tale had an infinitely greater freedom, as, of course, has the writer of the modern short story. The modern writer could take the corvée of "Wang Benli" and show its effects, with the husband packing up and leaving forever, or devote a story to the marriage of the mat weaver's daughter, or write a largely personal account of the journey upriver to Chengdu. But the option did not exist for Langxian, and the modern reader must get used to his duality of emphases. Story writers after Langxian are divided into those who, like Ling Mengchu and Li Yu, favored the sovereignty of the unitary plot, and those others who overthrew it.

Story Types

Langxian's stories vary somewhat according to the collection in which they appear. The *Rocks* collection has no prologue stories, only prologue disquisitions. And while the Taoistic stories are concentrated in *Constant Words*, the stories of idealistic love predominate in *Rocks*.

The most numerous type in both collections is the story of positive moral example. In *Constant Words,* the three finest are "Li Yuying," "The Old Retainer," and "Rainbow Cai," all of which are magnificently realized despite their simple themes and a tendency to portray villains as prodigies of malevolence. "Zhang Tingxiu" is a long, uneven story of great interest, which may have been based on a Southern drama. The others, "The Brothers Liu" (HY 10), "Zhang Xiaoji" (HY 17), and "Shi Runze," seem a shade too obviously to be the mere actualizations of moral fables; their interest lies mainly in their rural setting. The last of them utilizes a folk tale that was still current in the 1920s, one that was also used by Ling Mengchu.[18] Characteristically, Ling used it to show the immutability of fate, Langxian to show the fruits of virtue.

Of the five stories of Taoism and immortality, the best, in my opinion, are "The Old Gardener," "Metamorphosis into a Fish," and "Lu Nan." The others, "Du Zichun" and "The Yunmen Cave," happen to be those that involved Langxian in the least creative exertion. Both "The Old Gardener" and "Lu Nan" show the clash of his two worlds, the world of natural innocence inside the garden and the world of corrupt reality outside it. As both are well known, I translate here a portion of the third story, "Metamorphosis into a Fish," beginning from the point at which Magistrate Xue's colleagues, assembled to eat a special meal in his memory, first set eyes on the fish that, unknown to them, embodies his soul.

Captain Pei hustled Zhao Gan [the fisherman] out of the door, picked up the fish, and looked at it. It was a golden carp, three feet in length. He gave a sigh of pure contentment. "What a splendid fish! We should send it to the kitchen and have it prepared for dinner." At which Magistrate Xue roared at him: "I'm no fish! I'm your colleague. How can you fail to recognize me? I've had to put up with rudeness from numbers of other people, and I was just looking forward to venting my frustration in front of all of you, but now you take me to be a fish, just like all the others, and want to send me to the kitchen to be cooked! Why, that would be tantamount to murder! Does it mean nothing to you that we've been colleagues all this time? Have you no feeling for me at all?" To which his colleagues paid not the slightest attention.

The magistrate became desperate and felt compelled to continue. "Brother Zou, we graduated together, you and I, in the last year of the Tianbao reign. Back then in the capital, we were the closest of friends, and now we serve together in the same office. We're closer than all the others. How can you sit there and watch me die without uttering a single word?"

At this point, Assistant Magistrate Zou addressed himself to Captain Pei. "In my humble opinion," he said, "we ought not to eat the fish. Near the Lao Zi shrine on Qingcheng Hill there is a large conservation pond. People holding *jiao* services buy fish, turtles, shellfish, and the like and release them in the pond. Since we are dining today on the 'distributed blessings' sent us by the Xue family, we should set the carp free in the conservation pond, as a good karmic deed which would show the deep affection we bore our colleague."

Captain Lei spoke up from beside him. "What an excellent idea, letting the fish go! Karmic theory is something we cannot fail to believe in. Moreover, we have plenty of fine meats for our dinner. We don't need fish."

Hearing this conversation going on above him, the fish heaved a sigh. "You have no sense at all, Brother Zou," he said. "If you want to save me, send me home, not up into the hills where I'm bound to die of thirst. Still, I suppose it's better than dying by the cook's hand. Once I'm in the conservation pond, I'll turn back into my old form, put on my official cap and belt, and take my place in the office. Then I'll watch the reactions of these colleagues of mine, to say nothing of that swine Zhao Gan and the others."

As these thoughts were passing back and forth in his mind, Captain Pei responded:

"Sir, your desire to release the fish accords with heaven and earth's regard for life. It is a suggestion we must pay full attention to. However, the *jiao* service is a Taoist rite, not part of Buddhist doctrine. This is therefore not the occasion for establishing karmic merit. I consider that heaven created the myriad beings especially for mankind's sustenance. If fish, to take just one example, were not consumed by men, the whole world would soon be fish, and the rivers would be blocked to traffic. Human self-perfection takes place entirely within our minds, not our mouths. As the old saying goes, 'Buddha inhabits our minds, while wine and meat visit our stomachs.' And again, 'Abide by Buddhist rules and you'll find yourself unable to take a sip of water.' Do you really believe we would be showing disrespect to our colleague if we ate this fish? Obviously, if we don't cook it, we would be giving up a fine fish quite gratuitously. And how are we to know that, if we don't have it for dinner. it won't be devoured by some otter? It would suffer death, in either case, and I'd rather we were the ones to eat it."

At these words, the magistrate fairly screamed at him: "You see that your two guests want to release me, and yet you, the host, insist on having me for dinner! Obstinate fool! Not only do you show no feeling for a colleague, you have no conception of the way a host should behave!"

Now, as it happens, Captain Lei was an indecisive sort, and seeing that Pei was set on having the carp for dinner, he turned to Zou: "Our respected colleague does not believe in karma, so perhaps it wouldn't be right to release the fish. Moreover, he is our host at today's dinner and wants to serve it to us; as guests we cannot very well refuse. Since we were not the ones who decided to kill the fish, I shall assume that today was the final day of its life span and that there was nothing we could do to save it."

At this the magistrate gave a roar. "Sir, have you no mind of your own! How can you urge both sides on at once? You urged him to release me, and' when he declined, you ought to urge him again, not turn to Brother Zou and persuade him to drop his efforts to save me! I suspect you have pretty thin fare at your place and haven't eaten fish in a long time. Now you're thinking of gorging yourself on a fish dinner, I suppose?"

Then the magistrate felt he had to try Zou as well: "Brother, Brother! You're not just putting up a show of friendship, are you? Giving up after one token effort at persuasion? You've nothing more to say, not even one word? The old saying puts it well: 'When one friend survives the other, you find out what friendship is really worth.' If it weren't that I was dying, I'd never have known that your friendship as a class brother of mine was worth so little! If I ever get away, you just wait till I revert to my old form and come back here! You may be sure I'll follow the example of Captain Zhai and write those lines of his on my office door for you to see! Oh, Brother, Brother! I'm afraid you'll regret this when it's too late to do anything about it." But rant and rave as he might, the host and his guests appeared not to have heard a thing.[19]

The passage conveys the sense of nightmare so prominent in Langxian's stories, this time in a comic context. (Comedy is far more evident among the *Constant Words* stories.) It also shows his close narration and excellent dialogue, to say nothing of his interest in the processes of thought.

Among minor varieties, no fewer than three stories[20] portray the ruthless wickedness of the Buddhist clergy, both monks and nuns. Lest too much be read into this fact, it should be added that Langxian has harsh things to say about the Taoist clergy too, as distinct from Taoist masters and immortals. Two stories, "Prefect Qiao" (HY 8) and "Master Wu," are love stories of erotic intrigue, in which the parents are finally and reluctantly persuaded to allow the lovers (lovers in deed as well as word) to marry. In each case, the girl has vowed her loyalty to her lover and threatens to kill herself unless she is permitted to marry him; to this extent, they are idealistic love stories. Both are comedies and depend on a comic stratagem. In the former, this stratagem consists of the boy's impersonation of his sister as he visits the family into which she is to marry. He is told to share a bedroom with the girl of the household, with predictable results. In the latter, a young man of gargantuan appetite falls in love with an official's daughter on a boat at the next mooring. While the two are in bed asleep in her cabin, the weather changes and her father orders his boat to set sail. By the time the pair wake, the boat is well along the Grand Canal. The girl is forced to hide her lover under her bed and make bizarre excuses to her parents for taking vast quantities of food back to her cabin. Both stories represent a significant change in the tradition of romantic comedy, bringing it down to the level of ordinary reality. Its heroes and heroines are no longer necessarily of special attainments and sensibility, although they are still of the educated class.

Finally, there are two remarkable stories that exemplify Langxian's view of humanity as motivated by greed, lust, and cruelty. This is not his only view of humanity, of course, but in these two stories it dominates: "Lu Wuhan," in which it is counterbalanced by a heroine who kills herself when she realizes the extent of her guilt; and "A Single Copper Cash," in which cynicism is unrelieved. It is a view of humanity as either venal, rapacious, and violent or else timid and temporizing. In its brutal naturalism, "A Single Copper Cash" is reminiscent of Zola.

Its prologue relates the comic adventure of a famous Taoist immortal. Langxian appears to welcome such violent contrasts between prologue and main story, but in this case the contrast has the additional function of juxtaposing his two worlds of selfless innocence and calculating venality. The main story depicts humanity as constrained by base motives which lead to a callous violence. It is the manner in which this vision is embodied in his fiction that distinguishes Langxian at his best, as the following extract shows.

Qiu Yida and his wife, Yang, work in the porcelain center of Jingdezhen, he in moulding forms, she in painting designs. Yang is thirty-six and has had a series of affairs which she has taken care to keep secret from her husband, a harsh and violent man. They have a simple-minded son, Zhang'er, thirteen years of age. The son has quarreled with a boy from the same street over a game of toss penny, and both mothers have been drawn into the fray. Yang's adversary, Sun Daniang, is a notorious street virago who promptly launches into a diatribe against Yang's various infidelities.

Qiu Yida was just returning from the kiln when he heard Sun Daniang's torrent of abuse. He listened, heard everything she was saying, and said to himself: "I wonder whose wife has been misbehaving herself and deceiving her old man, to stir up Old Clapper-Tongue's abuse like this." When he arrived home, he saw his son crying, and on asking the reason, realized it was his family that had incurred the trouble.

Qiu Yida was a hard man, who feared ridicule. Without uttering a word of complaint, he sat down, fuming with anger. In the distance he could still hear the diatribe continuing without pause. It was dusk before it ceased. Qiu Yida drank a few cups of wine, waited till it was dark and the street was quiet, and then called his wife over to interrogate her. "You slut! A fine thing you've been up to, deceiving me! All these men you've been with, what are their names? Come on, out with it! I mean to go and have a word with them."

The woman was afraid of her husband to begin with, and these words struck her ears like a clap of thunder and sent her into a fit of trembling. She did not dare utter a word.

"Filthy slut!" went on Qiu Yida, "You're clever enough when it comes to adultery. Why can't you tell me their names? 'If you don't want people to know something, don't do it.' You managed to deceive your husband, but you couldn't deceive the neighbors. How can I ever hold my head up again? Think now. Out with it! I want the facts."

"It's all lies," she said, "so how can I possibly give you any names?"

"Is it really untrue?"

"Yes."

"If it's not true, why is she accusing you, and why aren't you saying anything to rebut the accusation? You obviously have a guilty conscience and can't answer her. If it's really untrue, if she is really slandering you, the only way you can clear your reputation and restore my good name is to go and hang yourself outside her door tonight. Then I can have it out with her tomorrow."

The woman would not budge from where she was, but with tears streaming down her face, she was driven out of the front door by two or three cuffs from her husband. He threw a rope after her.

"Go on, kill yourself," he shouted, "if you don't, it will prove you are an adulteress." He slammed the door and went inside. Zhang'er wanted to open the door, but his father clouted him over the head, and after crying for a while, the boy went off to bed. Yida was half drunk himself, and he too went to sleep. Yang was left there, a pathetic figure standing alone outside the door. She had no way of escape, either to heaven above or to earth below. All the wrongdoing was hers, and the only solution was to kill herself. She passed the night in grief and rage, and then, afraid that dawn would break first, she hastily picked up the rope and went off to find Liu Sanwang's[21] door.

Now a person about to take her own life is in a state bordering on derangement. The Liu house was actually the third house to the east, but she mistakenly turned in the opposite direction, and after passing five or six houses, came to the seventh, which looked like the Lius'. She hurriedly piled up a few bricks to stand on, attached a rope to the eaves, knotted it around her throat, and hanged herself. What a pity that so capable a woman should have lost her life through a quarrel over a single copper cash! Truly

One more malignant ghost in the world below,
One fewer painter of flowers on earth above.

Now the seventh house belonged to a blacksmith whose nickname was White Iron. Each night, at the fourth watch, he would get up and begin his work. He chanced to be opening his front door to urinate when all of a sudden a cold gust swept over him and set him shivering with fright. He focused his eyes and gave a great start.

More like a damsel in a swing
Than a puppet on a string.

Something was hanging from the eaves, but where did it come from? Terrifying! Still afraid that his eyes might be playing a trick on him, he went back inside, lit a torch, and shone it outside. It was the body of a woman who had just hanged herself. Her breathing had stopped and she was clearly beyond resuscitation. If he were to ignore the body it would be seen at dawn by a constable, and to him that would come as a bolt from the blue, a law case he could never clear himself of! An idea occurred to him. "I'll move it somewhere else, and then it won't have anything to do with me." With his fears weighing heavily upon him, he stepped forward and undid the rope.

White Iron was a man of brute strength, and he lifted the body down easily and carried it on his back out to the main street where, panic stricken, without taking the time to see exactly where he was, he threw it into someone's doorway. Then, without a single backward glance, he went home, still shuddering. He could not face the thought of work that day and went back to bed. And there we leave his story.

Meanwhile Qiu Yida got up before dawn to see what had happened to his wife. At Liu Sanwang's there was no sign of any activity. He went as far as the end of the lane, but there was no trace of her to be found anywhere. He returned home, sat down and pondered. "Don't say the slut has run away!"

Another thought stuck him. "She rarely goes out, and it was pitch dark, so how could she travel?" Another thought: "If she's not dead, the rope must still be there."

He went back to the door. There was no rope on the ground. "She must have hanged herself in the Lius' doorway, and they must have discovered the body and hidden it so that they can deny any knowledge."

Another thought: "Liu Sanwang didn't come home last night. Only Old Clapper-Tongue and the boy were at home, and they would never have the strength to move the body."

Yet another thought: "They would have people to help them, of course, just as insects have legs! I'll wait until they come out and see how they act and what their expressions are. That will tell me the true story."

He waited until the Lius' door opened and Zaiwang emerged and went off to the market to buy cakes and buns, apparently quite unconcerned. Qiu Yida could not make up his mind, and he took another turn up and down the street, but without any success. Returning, he saw Zhang'er still in bed snoring. A fit of anger swept over him, and whipping off the bedclothes, he struck the boy a few blows on the legs which made him leap up out of a sound sleep.

"Your mother has been driven into killing herself by the Lius," he said, "and yet you go on sleeping instead of demanding vengeance!"

By these words Qiu Yida was clearly telling Zhang'er to go and pick a fight with the Lius, so that he could find out what their reaction would be. On hearing that his mother was dead, Zhang'er burst out crying. He hurriedly pulled on his clothes, and, still crying, went straight to Liu Sanwang's doorway and screamed inside:

"Bitch whore, bitch slut! Give me back my mother!"[22]

In this gray realism of drab streets, cramped lives, squalid motives, and casual violence, Langxian is unsurpassed. What strikes the reader is the sense of hopelessness over human bondage, which is what I mean by my reference to Zola. There are signs of influence from *The Golden Lotus* in "Lu Wuhan" and "Qu Fengnu," but this story is indebted for its structure—so many deaths resulting from a trivial quarrel over a copper cash—to the "One Songbird" story of the middle period. A grim view of human limitations was characteristic of the folly story, and Langxian's story belongs to the same type, although the care and detail with which it is told lift it to a different plane. The most remarkable thing about Langxian is that he should have excelled both at Taoistic fantasy and at this kind of naturalism.

Of the moral heroism stories in the *Rocks* collection, "Wang Benli," or to give it its full title, "Wang Benli Goes to the Ends of the Earth in Search of His Father," is the finest. Like many of Langxian's stories, it has its longueurs, for he prefers to give events in full rather than summarize. (In this story, the longueurs are precisely where one would least expect them, in the desperate journeying of the young son.) Its best scenes are the trials of the corvée, which force the father to desert his family. He resolves to flee not only to escape the routine beatings for default but also so that his family, paradoxically, will be better off. He gets ready to travel on some pretext, then tells his wife he will have to move away for the time being. Finally, as he comes to say good-bye and hugs the baby for the last time, he lets out the truth.

> "But that's ridiculous!" she said. "My husband runs away from home, leaving me behind, with a child still not weaned, to maintain the household and meet all our corvée duties!"
>
> "You don't understand how things work," he replied. "Families without a male head are exempt from all duties, even if they have a son, just so long as he is under fifteen. It is also the practice that, when the group leader runs away, the section head has to substitute for him. You don't need to worry about any of that. Just keep the house safe and secure and guard against the danger of fire. You are a thrifty housewife and you'll naturally keep your expenses low. You have your skill as a weaver. But I don't need to tell you any of this. There will be no way to reach me after I have left. They say that all boats meet one day in the eastern sea, but that's just nonsense. From this point on, the love we have had for each other as husband and wife is canceled out, and you must not be concerned about me any more. All I can hope for is that heaven will take pity on us and help my son to grow up, marry, and have children of his own to continue the family sacrifices." And he took the child in his arms and cuddled him.
>
> "My child," he said, "I had hoped to raise you to be a good hard-working son who would support me in my old age. But now I'm leaving you forever while you are still a baby. I will never know what becomes of you, and you will never even know whether I am alive or dead."
>
> At this harrowing moment, his heart broke, and despite himself, two columns of tears spattered down. Hearing his incoherent words, his wife burst out crying and sank to the ground. Afraid that the news of his flight would get out, he quickly put Yuan'er down and, without a glance at his wife, hoisted his belongings onto his back and strode out the door. She scrambled to her feet and rushed after him to try and hold him back. But he broke into a run, dashed out of the gate, and was away. (pp. 63-64)

This is a scene most writers would summarize in a few conventional phrases but which Langxian brings to life by his careful observation. Another example is the scene in which the son finally asks his mother for permission to go in search of his father.

> "That shows a fine filial spirit and a lot of determination," she said. "But does it mean you have to forget your mother now that you know of your father's existence?"
>
> "I owe everything to you," replied Wang Yuan, "The labor of giving me birth, of nursing me as a baby, everything I have from the top of my head to the soles of my feet I owe to you. How could I forget my mother?"
>
> "There you go again!" she said. "It's not just giving you birth and nursing

you that I mean. When your father left home, you were less than a year old, and I had to maintain the household and look after you, my dear, all at the same time. Although we managed to escape the corvée, there was still the worry of using up all our money. And so I slaved away, day and night, without regard for my health. I put up with countless hardships, long days of labor in all kinds of conditions, in heat and cold and in storm, to put together this modest competence and win a measure of respect for your father. Do you think it was easy, bringing you up? You may never have had any of the really serious illnesses, but you've had a whole succession of minor ones. I've constantly had my worry cap on, I can tell you, calling doctors, saying prayers. I don't know how much money I've spent on it, or how much anxiety I've suffered.

"When you were at last old enough to go to school, the school fees were the least of my worries. I was afraid you'd be scared when the teacher scolded you, I was afraid that you'd be bullied by the other children—these fears were constantly weighing on me. Just imagine the worries and hardships I've borne, as a widow all on her own, to bring you up to this stage. Look around you—even with our two shadows, there's still only the four of us. Pathetic, isn't it? But now you want to up and leave me. I'm sorry, it just doesn't seem very reasonable to me. And there's something else I want to add. A father and a mother are the same, yet here I am, someone you've never looked after for a single day in your whole life, and yet you want to go off and search for a father you don't even know. If *this* principle isn't clear to you, what's the use of studying and analyzing filial virtue, I'd like to know? Put aside this idea of looking for your father. My mind is quite made up."

Hearing his mother talk of her many sufferings, Wang Yuan quickly knelt down, his eyes full of tears.

"I have not behaved like a filial son," he said, "and you are prefectly right to reprove me. But one's father and mother correspond to heaven and earth, and to have a mother but no father is to be incomplete. I shall never have peace in my heart while my father is away from home. I beg you to find some way to allow me to go."

"Very well, very well," she replied. "A dragon sires a dragon, a phoenix a phoenix. It is only to be expected that a father without love for his family who begs his way to the other end of the world would sire a son like you who doesn't care about his mother and wants to drift about in the gutter. Get up off your knees. You must at least wait until I have got you married. That will mean the end of my responsibility to you as a mother, and it will also give me the company of a daughter-in-law when you have gone. After your marriage, you can go off any time you wish. I shan't stop you!"

Wang Yuan had no choice but to accept. "I shall do your bidding, Mother," he said. "We'll talk about it again sometime." He got up and went into the study and sat there in utter dejection for quite a long while. (pp. 73-74)

In any discussion of moral heroism, one cannot pass over "The Siege of Yangzhou," the story of a martyrdom so shocking to the modern sensibility that it is omitted in some editions. Yet it is only a degree more gruesome than many other stories of filial sacrifice and martyrdom, which tend to applaud the extreme action, in which the moral will be seen at its strongest. However, one must admit that there are features of this story that live in the imagination as uniquely horrible, and we must suppose that the author chose to develop it—it exists as an anecdote in

Anatomy of Love[23] and before, of course — for that reason. The features are, first, the idea of cannibalism, and second, the matter-of-fact way in which the heroine sets about her self-sacrifice once her mind is made up. Langxian dwells on this in a manner that Feng, in his stories of sacrifice for a friend, does not. Clearly the process of decision, the procedure the heroine goes through, and her husband's humanly craven response are what interest him. It is impossible for the modern reader to accept the premise of the story — that is, the primacy of the heroine's vow to look after her mother-in-law — but one must concede to the author a certain skill in meeting the challenge.

The most notable of the idealistic love stories is "Pan Wenzi," or "Wenzi Makes a Compact over the Mandarin Ducks' Tomb." If only because of its theme, a homosexual love affair, it is new to the vernacular story. There had been idealistic tales of homosexual love in Classical narrative, including one by Feng Menglong based on fact. Before long, in the *Bian er chai*,[24] there would be a whole collection devoted to this theme, which was also taken up with zest by Li Yu in two notable stories.

The introduction is on the unnaturalness and comic absurdity of homosexuality. It is "academicians' love." The various dialectal terms for it are given. This is the kind of thing one might expect of Li Yu, who contrives to join the comic and the romantic. In the passage that introduces the main story, we are told that the incident was at first thought to be romantic and that later it became a joke. But it is also treated with condemnation. When Langxian describes the family background of the two youths, he tells us that Pan's mother was a young concubine whom he resembled, that she spoiled him outrageously, and that he could get his way with his father by throwing a tantrum. The reader prepares for a warning against spoiling his children, but it does not come. When Pan's friend, Wang, is allowed to delay his marriage for the sake of his career, the reader braces for a stricture against letting his children remain unmarried. It does not come, though it is implied. However, when Pan surrenders to the overtures of his friend and they move away to Mount Luofu to live together, the narrator explicitly condemns the two for abandoning their parents and their fiancées. "Are they not the greatest sinners between heaven and earth?" But then his comments suddenly veer away from moral condemnation: "Is this not the strangest thing ever heard amongst men? Is it not the greatest joke of all time?"[25] Thus, although occasional deference is paid to Confucian views of the family, the dominant note is of idealized romance and humor, reinforced by the ribald songs made up by the heroes' schoolfellows.

The heart of the story is, of course, the seduction. How the story writers revel in seduction! Against a background of school and study and debate over the meaning of the Four Books, Wang pursues his scheme to seduce his roommate, Pan. Pan is adamant in his refusal, although he

accepts Wang as his sworn friend. Wang stresses the value of qing, and
even Pan has to agree that qing is something more than what husbands
and wives feel for each other. Finally the seducer conquers, as so often in
later stories of this type, by committing himself irrevocably through a
dire vow to heaven to this one love all his life. This is qing with a
vengeance, and it justifies an appropriate response from Pan.

A few *Constant Words* stories other than the twenty-two I have referred to may also have been written by Langxian. They include "The
Two Magistrates" (HY 1), which resembles "Li Yuying" in some respects,
particularly in the wife's cruelty toward the adopted girl she sees as her
rival; "Licentiate Qian" (HY 7), a romantic comedy matched with
"Prefect Qiao"; and "The Pavilion of Prince Teng" (HY 40), an immortality story, among other things. Feng himself is likely to have written
"The Three Brothers" (HY 2) to match Langxian's "Two Magistrates"; it
contains a passage on the Han system of official recruitment by recom-
mendation of which he heartily approved.[26] "Big Tree Slope" (HY 5) is
given two alternative titles in *Constant Words* and presumably existed independently. An obscene narrative about the goings on in the Jurchen
royal household, "Emperor Hailing" (HY 23), is written in a style quite
distinct from Feng's or Langxian's; it is a clumsy piece of work patched
together out of Classical narrative. The companion piece, "Emperor
Yangdi" (HY 24), is made in the same way from at least four Classical
narratives; it is possible that Langxian constructed it on the model of the
preceding story. Feng's note on "Bai Yuniang" (HY 19), a good story,
compares it favorably with a play on the subject by a "village schoolmaster";[27] it may have been written by Feng or an associate.

There are two other outstanding stories in *Constant Words*—"The Oil
Seller" (HY 3) and "Chen Duoshou" (HY 9). "The Oil Seller" is a novelty
in the romantic comedy because it shows the peerless singing girl falling
in love with a social inferior, the solicitous young oil seller who worships
her. The excellence of the story lies in the convincing way it shows the
girl's mind changing, through persuasion and experience, first into accepting the fact of brothel life and then into concluding that the oil
seller's thoughtful, self-effacing kindness is worth more than the attentions of her other suitors. Appropriately, it is she who proposes marriage.

"Chen Duoshou" is a moral heroism story in which a girl insists on
marrying a fiancé stricken with leprosy. By an odd chance, which can be
taken as a manifestation of heavenly bao, he is cured of the illness, and
they live a happy life together. It is no different from the moral heroism
stories by Langxian, except for the fact that the two are not yet married
and the girl is therefore free to renounce the engagement (though in the
romance it is the betrothal that commits the lovers and is sanctioned by
heaven, not the marriage itself.) The new element in this story is the

gravity of the young man's illness and his consequent despair, which makes the girl's persistence in her moral heroism seem almost willful. From a modern, post-Lawrentian viewpoint, her self-abnegation would be itself immoral. But Lady Chatterley is not imaginable as a heroine in Chinese fiction.

7

Ling
Mengchu

There are strong resemblances between Feng Menglong and Ling Mengchu (1580-1644), the most prolific writer in the genre. Both men came from large cities—Ling from Wuxing (Huzhou) in Zhejiang, across the lake from Feng's Soochow. Both men failed to pass the provincial examinations, and each eventually gained a modest post by means of a tribute studentship, Feng in 1630 at the age of fifty-six, Ling in 1634 at fifty-four. In their respective posts—Ling held a succession of positions in Shanghai and Xuzhou until his death—both proved able administrators. Moreover, each demonstrated his loyalty to the dynasty. In 1643, Ling produced a ten-point plan for eradicating the rebels from his area and died the following year fighting against Li Zicheng's troops.

Like Feng, Ling was active as compiler and editor, although of a more orthodox kind of work. Both men were known as dramatists and critics of the drama, and there are clear parallels between the strong opinions they held on its diction and subject matter. In some cases, the similarities in their work can be attributed to influence. Ling's anthology of dramatic and art song, *Three Kinds of Southern Sound* (*Nanyin sanlai*), clearly influenced Feng's *Celestial Air,* published in 1627; and Ling acknowledges that Feng's story anthologies were the model for his own first collection, published in 1628.

Ling's family was the more distinguished.[1] His father, Ling Dizhi, was a jinshi of 1556 and served as the secretary to a government bureau in Peking until he was demoted in 1564 to the assistant prefectship of Daming in Hebei.[2] He retired soon afterward and spent his time compiling and publishing works of general reference, as well as handbooks on early historical and literary classics. Most of them appeared in the 1570s, some with his younger brother, Zhilong, as collator. Zhilong, having himself failed in the quest for a higher degree, had contentedly returned home to

140

a life of compiling and editing.[3] His dated works, mainly from the 1580s, include editions and versions of the early histories with collected comments. For the most part, the Ling brothers published their works themselves. Editing and publishing must have been a large part of the life in which Ling Mengchu grew up.

He was born in 1580, when his father was fifty-one.[4] He was Dizhi's fourth son, but his two eldest half-brothers, one of them a poet, had died long before, and the third was already an adult. Mengchu and his younger brother must have formed a separate family. In 1597, at seventeen, he won the position of stipendiary, the highest grade of licentiate, but despite at least four attempts, he was unable to pass the higher examination. His frustration is revealed in the reasons he gives for writing his first few vernacular stories: to cheer himself up as he tarried in Nanking after yet another unsuccessful attempt.[5]

In 1600 his father died, and in 1605 his mother, but Ling did not lack for influential friends. Feng Mengzhen (1546-1605, unrelated to Feng Menglong), a celebrated man of letters, who describes Ling Mengchu as a relative by marriage, visited the area in 1602 and the following year took Ling with him on a journey to Soochow.[6] Ling's first known publication was a version of the *History of the Latter Han,* which was published in Nanking in 1606.[7] The preface was written by another famous man of letters, Wang Zhideng (1535-1613). In 1609, Yuan Zhongdao, the youngest of the three Yuan brothers, visited Ling in Nanking. (With his eye for artistic and literary rarities, he noted only the picture by Liu Songnian that Ling had on his wall.)[8] The celebrated Chen Jiru (1558-1639) offered suggestions that Ling adopted in writing one of his plays.[9] Ling also knew Tang Xianzu (1550-1617); a letter of his elicited from Tang a revealing account of his art.[10] In 1623, Ling traveled to Peking in the company of Zhu Guozhen, who had just been appointed minister. Ling's plays and art songs had received recognition by the 1620s, if not earlier. His songs are represented in a 1624 anthology as well as in Feng's *Celestial Air,* and one of his plays was chosen for the *Northern Plays of the Glorious Ming, Second Collection* (*Sheng Ming zaju erji*), which has a preface by Yuan Yuling dated 1629.[11] An editor, Wang Yun, praising Ling highly in a note, says he had searched for years for copies of his plays, and the critic Qi Biaojia also reserved some of his highest ratings for them.[12]

His literary life consisted of a vast amount of compiling, editing, and publishing, as well as of his own creation. In the former activities, he was responsible, in part, for a special kind of fine edition known as a "Min edition," after the family who were the Lings' neighbors in the Shengshe district of Wucheng County. The Lings had intermarried over the generations with the Mins; a member of the Min family collated some of Ling Dizhi's works as early as 1576.[13] It seems to have been Min Qiji, born in the same year as Ling Mengchu, who initiated the fine editions. He had given up the quest for examination success and devoted himself to editing and publishing, something his wealth permitted him to do.[14] But the publishing tradition in the Ling family certainly had an effect on the kind of works published. Dizhi and Zhilong had produced versions of standard historical and literary works for an educated but unspecialized readership, and Zhilong had made a point of assembling critical comments, just as Min Qiji does in his editions.

The obvious feature of the Min editions was their two-color or multicolor printing. From 1616 on, a steady stream of Min editions was issued, published by both Mins and Lings, to which a dozen different editors' names are attached.[15] The most prominent name among the Mins was Min Qiji, and among the Lings, Ling Mengchu.

Min editions bearing Ling Mengchu's name (some have prefaces in his hand) include selections from a number of famous poets. (There are several works by Su Shi.) Ling and his cousin produced separate editions of the *New Account of Tales of the World*. Ling's critical comments are given, alongside those of Li Zhi and others, taken from earlier editions; his own comments resemble the kind of appreciative remarks found in the notes to vernacular fiction.[16] A few of the contemporary commentators may have been his friends and acquaintances. (His references are not always reliable, however.) His name is also on several editions of standard historical and philosophical works, some of them Min editions of works published earlier by his uncle, Zhilong.[17] His editions of *The Western Chamber* (*Xixiang ji*) and *The Lute* (*Pipa ji*), the masterpieces of the Northern and Southern drama, respectively, are in a different category; they are new editions of real scholarly value.[18] His critical anthology, *Three Kinds of Southern Sound,* also appeared in a Min edition.[19]

Ling also published works in black and white, including an edition of the *Poetry Classic*, edited with the help of his eldest son in 1631. It is one of four works he devoted to the *Classic*.[20]

His creative work consisted of Classical poetry and prose, plays both Northern and Southern, Southern art songs, and vernacular stories. None of the Classical poetry and prose is extant. His *City Gate Collection* (*Guomen ji*) and *Second City Gate Collection* (*Guomen yiji*), written during his visits to Peking, apparently contained poems and essays expressing melancholy and ennui.[21] His epitaph, notoriously unreliable, divides his work into serious writing such as the *City Gate* collections and the studies of the *Poetry Classic,* and "leisure-time" writing such as the anthology, the plays, the vernacular stories, and two other titles, one of which may be a volume of art songs.[22] Zhang Xuqu, coeditor of *The Combined Edition of the Songs of Wu* (*Wusao hebian*), recalling his first meeting with Ling in Nanking, says that Ling "considered himself a man

of feeling, and brought out work after work which he had written or
edited, all of which were characterized by their mockery of society and
by their transcendent power."[23]

Ling wrote at least eight Northern plays, of which three survive, and at
least three Southern plays, of which none survive.[24] Three of the Northern plays are based on the same Tang Classical tale, "The Curly-Bearded
Stranger" (*Qiuran ke zhuan*), one centering on Curlybeard, the others on
the girl Red Whisk. One of the Red Whisk plays, *The Impetuous Choice
of a Husband* (*Mang ze pei*), may refer to his own frustrated
ambitions.[25]

Several of his Northern plays seem to treat their heroic subjects in a
partly comic vein. *Song Gongming Throws the New Year Festival Into
Uproar* (*Song Gongming nao yuanxiao*), published as a makeweight in
his second collection of stories, takes as its basis a comic episode in the
Shuihu in which Song Jiang travels to the capital to enlist the aid of the
singing girl Li Shishi, the Emperor's mistress. Ling combines the story
with a related anecdote in which it is the famous lyric poet Zhou
Bangyan, not Song Jiang, who is surprised in Li Shishi's room by an
unexpected visit from the Emperor.[26] Zhou hides under the bed and then
escapes but is unwise enough to include some of the conversation he has
overheard in a new ci lyric. For that offense, he is banished. The play is a
comedy, light and graceful in the scenes between Zhou and the singing
girl, loud and roistering in the other scenes.

Ling also wrote a lost play about Ni Heng, the righteous Confucian
scholar who denounced Cao Cao to his face. Ling's *Ni Zhengping*,
however, according to Qi Biaojia's description, must have been comic or
satirical; it shows a jesting, not a denouncing, Ni Heng.[27] Ling also
wrote a play on Liu Ling, one of the Seven Sages of the Bamboo Grove,
famous for their drinking, and a man for whom, Qi suggests, Ling felt an
affinity. He wrote one somber play on moral heroism and, at Chen Jiru's
suggestion, rewrote a play he had half finished on the Classical tale "Hui
zhen ji" (source of the Western Chamber material) so as to show Yingying returning from the dead to avenge herself on Zhang.[28]

All of his Southern plays appear to have been romances. *The Lapel*
(*Shanjin ji*), from which some song sets are preserved in the *Three Kinds*
anthology, is a thorough reworking of Gao Lian's *Jade Hairpin* (*Yuzan
ji*), a play to which Ling objected on account of its ornate diction.[29] His
songs survive only in the anthologies. The *Celestial Air* describes him as a
"brilliant talent, able to write fine songs at will. Drama and song are but
a fraction of his literary work."[30] Zhang Xuqu's reference to him as a
man of feeling would certainly apply to the songs.

Ling wrote seventy-eight stories in all, forty for his first collection,
thirty-eight for his second. (One story, slightly abridged, was repeated
from the first collection and the *Song Gongming* play added, to bring the

total up to forty.)[31] His "brief introduction" to his second collection, dated 1632, gives the clearest account of how he came to write his stories.

> In the autumn of 1627, after "grazing the skin" and "missing the mark" in my affairs, I was tarrying in Nanking when I idly picked out one or two remarkable situations I had heard of from past and present—items worth recording—and elaborated them into stories as a way of relieving the frustration that oppressed me . . .[32] But whenever my [examination] colleagues visited me, they would ask me for one of my stories to read, and on finishing it, would invariably slap the table and exclaim, "What an amazing thing!" The news was spied out by a book merchant who begged me to let him publish the stories. And so I copied them out, put them together, and obtained forty stories.

Ling apologizes for the commercial success of the stories, in comparison with the work of men who "twist their moustaches, spit blood, dig graves for their old writing brushes, and wear out their ink slabs." Now the bookseller, having had one success, wanted to publish another collection. Ling obliged, in some cases using stories he had got ready before but had not "committed to ink." The reaction of his friends, of course, gave him his title, *Slapping the Table in Amazement* (*Pai an jing qi*).

His preface to the first collection gives a different account.[33] It begins with a justification of the vernacular story. Ling deplores the belief that the only remarkable (or amazing) things are thought to be those outside the range of our eyes and ears—phantasms and the like. The *xiaoshuo* artists of the "Song and Yuan periods" provide him with a wholesome example. "For the most part, they chose recent events from the streets and lanes to offer the palace for its diversion. The language of the stories is generally simple and familiar, and they contain a moral purpose." Although the authors cannot be considered men of "the highest cultivation," theirs is, in general, a minor art that is well worth attention. He distinguishes their work from modern vernacular fiction, the product of a long period of peace and accompanying moral laxity; it is written by "vulgar delinquents just learning how to hold a brush," who are intent on defaming everything and everyone. Their fiction is either absurd or obscene, and Ling recommends it be banned.

The exception to the general condemnation is Feng Menglong, editor of the "Song and Yuan" stories. "Only the *Stories Old and New* and similar works edited by Feng maintain a rather high moral tone and consistently offer moral precepts which demolish the vicious practices of the day." A bookseller, seeing how successful Feng's collections had been, approached Ling in the belief that he too must possess some rare stories worth reprinting. But practically all of the "Song and Yuan" stories had been collected, and Ling decided instead to write his own.

His description of his method of composition tallies with modern scholarship, which has shown that most of his stories, like Feng Menglong's and Langxian's, are elaborations of Classical tales and anecdotes. In general, however, Ling is more beholden to his sources; in one or two cases, he is an adapter rather than a creator. His range of sources is also different. It includes a number of plays and also some long Classical romances from *New Tales Under the Lamplight* (*Jian deng xin hua*). In several stories, he even mentions the source he is using.

He may well have met Feng in Nanking in 1627. Feng's preface to his third collection is dated mid-autumn of that year in Nanking, just at the time Ling tells us he began writing. The examinations gave writers a chance to exchange manuscripts and publishers a chance to strike deals, and Feng may well have been one of the colleagues who slapped the table in amazement over Ling's first stories. The contact between the two men may have extended over a longer period; Ling's first collection was published about a year later, in Soochow.

Dramatic and Fictional Theory

The example for Ling's fiction came to him from Feng, but it came to a man who had already thought long and hard about the values of a vernacular literature. Ling was more than a dramatist and songwriter; he was also a critic with a set of extreme principles in the light of which he reevaluated the whole of Southern drama. His views appear in several places: in his anthology; in an essay on the Southern drama that was published in the anthology but may not have been written for it;[34] in his critical editions of plays; and in the prefaces and introductions he wrote to his vernacular stories. The anthology's "three kinds" are the three sources of sound (heaven, earth, man) as described in the *Zhuang Zi* (*Chuang Tzu*).[35] Adopting them as a scale of values, Ling originally intended to arrange his anthology in three parts but eventually decided merely to label each item as belonging to one of the kinds. His attempts to define his values, and the fact that he applies them to songs and song sets rather than to whole plays, give them more meaning than the simple ratings used by Qi Biaojia and other critics.[36]

Ling's "Notes on the Southern Drama" (*Tan qu za zha*) is, despite its brevity, his main statement of principle. It amounts to a systematic reevaluation of the drama, beginning with a summary historical account and proceeding to reassess the main plays and playwrights. His values are expressed in sweeping historical terms: "When drama originated in the barbarian Yuan, it was professionalism, in general, that was valued, not poetic embellishment. Professionalism in drama was known as its 'authentic nature.'" The early drama was free both of ornateness and erudition. *The Lute* is not one of its canonical models because it was too much affected by the ornate diction of the ci lyric. Ming songwriters down to the sixteenth century were able to preserve the pristine values, but Liang Chenyu, the first exponent of the Kunqu form of the Southern drama, began a trend toward ornateness. Ling attributes Liang's high reputation to the critical vogue of the time; the mid-sixteenth century was the heyday of the so-called Latter Seven Masters of the Archaist school of poetry, and it was one of those Masters, Wang Shizhen, who praised Liang's plays and made them fashionable. Following Liang's lead, the Kunqu playwrights strove to emulate the beautiful lyric (*mi ci*) with its cloying, romantic clichés. At the same time, diction became difficult and allusive, so that songs required endless notes. "Not only is there no trace of the dramatist's authentic language, there is no longer any true expression of human feeling."

The terms translated as "professionalism" (*danghang*) and "authentic nature" (*bense*) had been brought together by Yan Yu in his *Canglang's Remarks on Poetry* (*Canglang shihua*) to refer to a work's or writer's fidelity to the properties of a genre.[37] "Bense," literally "true colors," means for Ling the authentic character of the Southern drama, as illustrated by the earliest plays, with the partial exception of *The Lute*. Liang Chenyu abandoned its authentic character in seeking to import the properties of other genres. In its early history, since drama was performed before uneducated audiences as well as before the Court, it had to be comprehensible at a first hearing and could not afford to be abstruse. How absurd of later dramatists to require an encyclopedic knowledge of their audiences! By the logic of the drama's authentic character, Ling can defend a feature that may appear incongruous. For example, he justifies the opening of scene 15 in *The Lute*, in which a eunuch describes the court in a long passage of parallel prose, by the use of set pieces in vernacular fiction. It belongs to the authentic nature of scenic description, and people who object to it simply do not understand the form. He implies that if the set piece is a property of vernacular fiction, it cannot be considered too mannered for the drama.[38]

"Bense" is usually contrasted with ornateness in language, and hence may come to mean little more than "plain" or "natural," with reference to diction, syntax, and the avoidance of obscurities.[39] As such, it is the main requirement of the ideal vernacular style. But although Ling relished the use of a direct vernacular in both the spoken parts and the songs and sometimes praised diction for its speechlike qualities,[40] he was not under the illusion that raw speech is itself dramatic language. If most of his efforts went into defending dramatic style from the encroachments of lyric diction, he was also intent on defending it against a "harsh and crude" or "low and ridiculous" use of language. This was his main criticism of Shen Jing and his followers, for whom the term "bense" denoted a key principle: Shen "though scrupulous about the rules of prosody, was deficient in talent. He realized it was inappropriate to use allusions and clichés and tried to write a professional, authentic, felicitous diction, but was incapable of it. He merely pulls shallow and vulgar language together . . ."[41] (Tang Xianzu, by contrast, was praised by Ling for his brilliance but criticized for his neglect of the prosodic rules and his use of local dialect.) In his commentaries, Ling praises verbal felicities, startling phrases, conceits, puns, wit, and irony. "Authentic nature" clearly implied a level of taste and art — of literariness.

The value to be accorded bense in its limited meaning of "plainness" was the main nontechnical issue dividing Ming commentators on drama. He Liangjun (1506-1573) put *The Moon Prayer Pavilion* (*Baiyue ting*) above both *The Western Chamber* and *The Lute* because of its greater commitment to plainness and was taken to task by Wang Shizhen for doing so.[42] Wang Jide, modifying his master Shen Jing's position, essentially agreed with Wang Shizhen, on the grounds that plain diction tended to be dreary.[43] Others, such as Xu Fuzuo and Shen Defu, supported He's judgment, but Ling Mengchu was its most thoroughgoing advocate and the only one to use bense as a principle for reevaluating the Southern drama.[44]

Ling's criticism focuses on the work itself, especially its language, and says little about the writer's emotions. He is in accord with Li Zhi, the Yuan brothers, and even Feng Menglong where diction is concerned (it is a condemnation of Wang Shizhen even to recall that he belonged to the Archaist school) but not in terms of the expressive function of literature. It is an approach that fits one's impression of him as an author who stands outside his work as the judge and satirist of his society, detached if not dispassionate. Ling never used his stories, as Feng did, to dramatize his personal aspirations.

Controversies about diction are always about more than diction; they are about the efficacy of language to signify experience and also, generally, about the kinds of experience signified. Ling advocated a plain, direct style for reasons that went beyond its comprehensibility. Indeed, he believed that plain, direct language represents an object truthfully while ornate language obscures or falsifies it.[45] With this belief goes a preference for a certain kind of literary world. Ling found the boudoir world of the exquisite lyric as insubstantial as its language. Similarly, in talking of the structure of the dramatic plot, he showed a distaste for the fantastic event, the supernatural contrivance, accusing modern plays of becoming more and more "remote from human nature and devoid of human reason."

The last point is the burden of his preface to the first collection. "People do not realize," he writes, "that within the range of our eyes and ears, within our daily lives, there are numerous deceptive and illusory things which are not logically predictable." His admiration for the "Song and

Yuan" stories was, apparently, due to their factual nature, their origin in "new events from the streets." His statement claims that the events he narrates are "close to human nature and daily life." If his stories do not quite live up to the claim, and if he later modifies it, that hardly matters. He saw the "authentic nature" of the vernacular story as the here and now of human beings in society, and he wrote accordingly. His stories are mostly about the novel or strange event — the sine qua non of Chinese fiction — occurring within the world of everyday life.

Another admirable feature of the "Song and Yuan" stories was their moral example. Ling declares his moral aim both positively ("The main aim of this work lies in moral exhortation and admonition") and negatively ("This work undertakes not to transgress against the canons of taste"). Its morality distinguishes it from contemporary pornography, just as its setting in everyday life distinguishes it from fantasy. In Ling's view, morality is equally part of the "authentic nature" of the vernacular story. And risqué as some of his stories are, there is no doubt of the commitment of his fiction to a moral view of life.

Fictional Form

Despite its indebtedness to Feng Menglong and his predecessors, the Ling Mengchu story is quite distinct. Ling's heroes are not symbols of himself, as some of Feng's and Langxian's are. His social world also differs from Feng's: merchants play a larger part in it and officials a smaller one. His moral themes refer to common conceptions of reasonable behavior rather than to an absolute code. He is little concerned with moral heroism but appeals instead to the practical morality of good sense and even to an enlightened self-interest. Human character, his stories imply, is decisively shaped by nurture rather than by nature. (In some of these respects, his stories are reminiscent of the Hangchow realistic fiction of the middle period.) He appears to take predetermination more seriously than do his contemporaries, some of whom show moral activism triumphing over a predetermined fate. Finally, his narrator speaks more directly for the implied author than does Feng Menglong's, whose work sometimes displays a dual vision. These tendencies contribute to, and are occasioned by, a different kind of story, one dominated by comedy and satire.

Ling's distinctiveness shows up most clearly on the narratorial and focal levels and in the mode of comment. He gives the narrator a power over the story's interpretation such as he had not had before and grants him a distinct personality. In part, this innovation stems from the kind of story Ling was writing. His are avowedly stories of "moral admonition," which appeal to a clear-cut moral judgment on the part of the reader. In such stories, even the wise saws of the narrator need not be out of place.

In the typical Ling story, the introduction takes up the theme and the prologue story illustrates it. On its own, the main story might be susceptible to several kinds of emphasis, of which the introduction and prologue select one.[46] The introductions are disquisitions, miniature essays, on matters of social concern: ambition, fate, marriage, choosing a son-in-law, female suicide, autopsy, luck in the examinations, the arrogance of the recent graduate, bandits, prostitutes, and assorted follies, vices, and problems. The argument is lively and humorous, using the techniques of the debater rather than of the moral philosopher. Here is part of Ling's introduction to "The Gambler" (II.8) on the psychology of gambling:

> Some people will object to this. They will say, "*I* stop while I'm ahead, and so I never lose." This may sound plausible, but which one of us has the necessary self-control? Some gamblers, with winnings of one thousand, will want ten thousand, and people never stop until they're satisfied. Others are on a winning streak and assume it will go on forever; they are so fired up they won't stop. And still others are afraid they will be derided as cheapskates; they feel they have no choice but to go on gambling. (p. 121)

And in his introduction to "The Hunter" (I. 37), a story that warns against the killing of animals, he says:

> But the argument of greedy people fond of slaughter, like that of pedants and schoolboys, runs as follows: "Heaven created animal life for our sustenance; hence it is no sin to eat meat." Now we don't know if the Lord of Heaven told them this personally, or whether they are simply announcing it on their own authority. But if our ability to eat animals is to be ascribed to Heaven's interest in our welfare, does that mean that, because tigers and leopards are able to eat human beings, Heaven created us for *their* benefit? We get stung by mosquitoes and flies. Does that mean that Heaven created us for *their* consumption? If tigers, leopards, mosquitoes, and flies could speak and write as we can and were to make this case, I wonder if people would let themselves be persuaded by it? Wise and virtuous men have exhorted us throughout the ages not to kill, and their writings are far too voluminous for me to describe. I am just taking this opportunity to slip in these free, lighthearted remarks, to give you a laugh or two and to allow you to decide for yourselves whether I am right or not. (pp. 793-794)

"Against Autopsy" (II. 31) shows Ling's own convictions more clearly than perhaps any other story, although it is still not without an element of comic rhetoric. After describing the law allowing an autopsy in the case of a person who has apparently been beaten to death, Ling mentions the adage "Each new law breeds new corruption," and continues:

> The moment an offical gives permission for an autopsy, the local functionaries who put up the shed need their building money, and the yamen runners, the bearers, and the musicians all need their handouts. The coroners want money for operating, and for washing up afterwards. For the official's desk in the shed, they need money for incense and for ink (both vermilion and black), brushes, ink stones, blankets and cushions, all of which must be provided by the accused. Then there are the unscrupulous aides; you have to provide all kinds of food and drink for them—I can't list it all. And even if your name

emerges from the autopsy as pure as driven snow, you'll still be minus three-quarters of your worldly possessions. What good will it do you even if the plaintiff confesses under examination to bringing a malicious suit? That is why a blackguard with a grudge against someone regards a homicide as a rare piece of good fortune. How simple it is for the official, with a mere stroke of his pen, to give the order "Autopsy!" He thinks it perfectly proper in a case of homicide, but he has no inkling of the harm it can do. (p. 459)

The narrator's wit also appears in his comment on the action. He is fond of puns, humorous similes, and assorted bons mots, so fond, indeed, that he sometimes repeats them. Thus, when the beautiful girl offers herself to her dead sister's fiancé, he is "like a boy lighting a firecracker, excited and petrified all at the same time."[47] Of a promiscuous woman, he remarks, more than once, "She was not someone you would want to erect a chastity arch to." And the hero, approaching his beloved, "melted with desire, like a snowman next to a fire." Typically, the narrator's commentary gently mocks its object, calling attention as much to the speaker's wit as to the action described. It is a step away from the ordinary business of the realistic novelist.

The introductions and comment define an individual narrator, as distinct from the generalized narrator of most previous fiction. In the anti-Zhu Xi story, for example, the narrator reflects in his introduction upon the morality of the stories he has told so far. He is equating himself with the author, in the sort of comment we might expect to find in a preface or in the author's own editorial notes. His references to the source of the story he is telling have a similar significance.[48] In his introduction to one of the cony-catching stories, Ling has his narrator introduce subjects with phrases such as "I remember" and "I have heard," which resemble the formulae of a more personal kind of literature.

Where other authors use digressions as a means of providing general information or of solidifying the social context of the story, Ling's narrator uses them to drive home his own ideas. In "The Sutra Manuscript" (II.1), when a disastrous flood occurs and the cost of necessities soars, the narrator intervenes to attack the usual method of handling such crises, which is to peg food prices.[49] It is an impractical idea based on abstract principles, typically Confucian, he claims. (One of the connotations of "Confucian" for Ling's narrator is "impractical.") It simply drives all goods off the market. His argument is pure classical economics: let demand force prices up until goods are drawn in from other parts of China, bringing prices down again. One cannot say that Ling equates the narrator with the implied author, for the two have different functions, but at least there is no incongruity between them. Like the power and coherence of his comment, this is a feature of Ling's writing that anticipates a major trend in the seventeenth century.

Ling's treatment of time and place also appears to depart from Feng's and Langxian's practice. He is remarkably flexible with time. Several of his stories are built around a single incident related again and again from the differing points of view of each of its participants. In "The New Year's Kidnapping" (II.5), we hear about the kidnapping from three points of view: the servant's, the little boy's, and the kidnapper's.

Ling is unconcerned about visual effect; on some occasions, his stories have less visual quality than the Classical tales that served as their sources. Dialogue is often not placed in a specified setting. He uses set pieces sparingly, and when he does, it is often for an extra significance. In "The Double" (I.2), the merchant is described in all his finery not simply in order to present him to the reader's imagination but for psychological reasons; it is this finery and the luxury it implies that turn the head of the abducted woman. In "The Insoluble Murder" (II.21), there is a single set piece, describing a handsome young monk coming out of a temple. There is no reason whatever to describe him at that point. The reason becomes apparent later, when the monk proves to be the murderer.

On the configurative level, in contrast to the narrator, who has become an individual, the characters have become more generalized. Many of Ling's chief characters are not even fully named, and naming is the basic method of individualizing. The hero of "The Rich Man and the Alchemist" (I.18) is surnamed Pan, but we are never told his personal name. In fact, he is generally referred to not even as Pan but as *fuweng*, "the rich old man"—that is, by the social category to which he belongs. Furthermore, when a character's actions or motives are explained, it is usually with reference to his social type. In "The Jealous Wife" (II.10), for example, we are told that the head of the family, Mo, "has the mentality of a rich man" and hence loves sex, that his wife is the classic jealous woman, and that the noodle seller who is only too happy to marry the pregnant maid has "the mentality of a petty tradesman and seeks a petty gain." Almost every story contains references to the mentality or experience of social types.

Finally, there is the detachment with which Ling's characters are treated. No comparative use can be made of the concept of detachment without some measure of the character's moral standing, that is, his distance from the moral and intellectual norms of the implied author. With this in mind, one can see that Ling's stories run counter to the tendency of the late stories. His technique is to treat his characters with detachment and often with sardonic amusement. The heroes and heroines even of his love stories are presented quizzically, and inside views are restricted to describing a calculation or the immediate motive for an action.

He excels in the unsentimental treatment of character, in the ascription of cynical motives; but the weakness of his method becomes apparent when he attempts to explain a change of heart. The seduction of the abducted wife in "The Double," for example, cannot compare with the seduction in "The Pearl Sewn Shirt" or "The Courtesan and the Oil Seller." In accordance with his use of detachment, Ling scrupulously avoids pathos, either by technical means or simply by avoiding pathetic incident. In "The Lost Daughter" (II.7), we do not hear of the daughter's harrowing experience, or even of the fact that she has been lost, until *after* she has been recovered, and then only briefly, in her own words. Even the victims of his crime stories are guilty of folly and are often just lesser rogues falling foul of a greater rogue. There is no story of Ling's to compare, even remotely, with "Prefect Kuang" (TY 35), which, although a crime story itself, still presents genuine pathos. Ling cannot afford to let pathos subvert his main concerns; hence he diffuses the guilt between criminal and victim.

Comic and Satiric Attitudes

One's initial impression of Ling Mengchu's fiction is of its comic and satiric elements. The features noted above confirm and deepen that impression and demonstrate that comedy and satire broadly determine his technique. Although Ling is thought of as a moralist, not a satirist, one has only to glance at true moralistic fiction to see the extra dimension in his work. His few positive examples represent shrewdness rather than morality, good sense rather than mere goodness. He does not appeal to his reader's sympathies; his whole satiric effort is spent in ridiculing folly and vice. There is an element of comic exaggeration even in his most serious story, "Against Autopsy." If, in its classic definition, satire unites art (or wit or fantasy) with morality,[50] Ling is eminently a satirist. Even some of the objects of his satire have a faintly familiar ring: alchemists, shamans and their dupes, rich men and their "humors," women, especially widows and second wives, even a mild Chinese example of the miles gloriosus ("The Braggart," I.3). In vastly different societies, the satiric temper evidently sought out roughly similar objects for attack.

It is the exemplary nature of his stories, presumably, that has prevented him from being taken as a satirist. Each story is a moral fable that rewards folly and vice with humiliation and punishment. But although punishment is, of course, admonitory, it is also a satirical device. In "The Hunter," for example, the hero is one of those rich young men whom Ling loves to satirize. Having squandered his patrimony, he takes to hunting and rustling in order to make a living. Summoned to hell, he is confronted with the whole population of animals he has killed in a lifetime of blood sports, now grown to menacing size, with pigs and sheep as large as horses and oxen, and horses and oxen as large as rhinoceroses and elephants. He returns home to spend the rest of his life writing out sutras in his own blood. As Ling tells the story, it is impossible to miss the element of comic, even farcical, exaggeration.

His morality is normative, like the morality of most comedy and satire. A number of his stories deal with deviations from the norm, typically obsessions that often resemble the humor, or ruling passion, of European neoclassical comedy. Ling's is a centripetal ethic, seeking the norm (unlike the centrifugal ethic more characteristic of the European novel, which may honor personal aspiration and the transcendence of social norms and conventions). Ling's is also the kind of practical morality that depends on good sense and experience.

Talk of Ling's morality quickly slides off into the area of "good sense and experience," but this is a feature of much comedy and satire. In Ben Jonson's comedy,

> It is not the virtuous man, but the resourceful, clever man who prospers . . .
> This does not mean that the hero of a comedy cannot be virtuous, but only
> that he is a comic hero not because of virtue but because of his good sense.[51]

The weight of praise or criticism, in Ling's stories, is placed more often on practical wisdom or folly than on goodness or wickedness. His wise man knows the ways of the world, and knowing his own limitations also, acts only when he can act effectively. And some of his confidence tricksters are treated leniently, as if in silent tribute to their finesse.

The intellectual position that sustains his fiction is one that is common to certain kinds of satire and comedy, a preference for the pragmatic, for practice over theory. Ling is scornful of Zhu Xi (II.12) because he considers the neo-Confucians impractical theorizers. In the stories attacking alchemical Taoism, he does not go so far as to say that the art itself is absurd — he has too much respect for ancient authority — but that the authentic tradition has been lost and all present-day practitioners are quacks. It no longer has any practical significance.

Ling's morality is linked to his metaphysics but not dominated by it. Despite the stress he places on predestination and the Heavenly Principle, it would be absurd to regard his stories as primarily about metaphysical issues. On the other hand, it would be a mistake to consider the beliefs, trite though they may be, as mere packaging to be discarded after the stories have been unwrapped. They at least provide a philosophical basis for his morality, and in general they do a great deal more: they condition the comic and satiric attitudes of his fiction.

Belief in predestination, expressed often and at length in his introductions, is summed up in a ubiquitous cliché derived ultimately from the *Zhuang Zi*: "One sip, one peck . . ." According to the belief, everything is foreordained, and it is pointless, even positively harmful, to pine or strive. The prologue to Ling's first story, "The Tangerines and the

Tortoiseshell," tells how a thrifty merchant who has scrimped all his life saving money for his sons is finally prevented from giving it to them. The money is not in their destiny, so it simply marches off from under the old man's bed the night before it is to be handed over. It is a familiar folk tale.[52] The main story tells of an indolent but charming young man who is taken along, as a penniless neophyte, on a merchant voyage to the South Seas. But he is destined to become rich, and in a series of fantastically lucky strokes, he makes his fortune on this one trip. The mechanism of predestination is not made clear: It may be karmic, but if so, the causation is not mentioned by the narrator. All one knows is that accurate knowledge of one's fate is available through the physiognomer. Predestination is invoked only about the objects of human desire: riches, marriage, sons, rank. This, in fact, is how the apparent contradiction with the Heavenly Principle is handled; the Principle is active in a separate field, that of crime and punishment, and so no direct clash ever occurs.

Predestination is in part a fictional device, freeing the author from some of the elaborate coincidences and stratagems of the previous story. Its depreciation of the will, and the sense of human limits that it implies, fit Ling's normative, centripetal morality and even his psychology of social types. It also deeply conditions his comedy. Although a doctrine of predestination might have resulted in a grim naturalism, in Ling it is almost always comic. Conversely, the comic story in Ling is generally associated with predestination.

Belief in the Heavenly Principle is summarized in a similar cliché: *Tianli bu rong*, "The Principle of Heaven would not tolerate it." In Ling's stories, the Principle is a popular notion yet still connected with the Principle of the neo-Confucian philosophers. It is a force immanent in nature which, by subtle means, marshalling coincidences, brings injustice to light and punishes crime. (Sometimes it is undetectable, and the slogan means little more than "Crime does not pay.") The Principle is the agent of perfect law, the sublime enforcer of society's moral code. Like predestination, it is a useful fictional device that allows an author to explain his coincidences simply. Most important of all, it provides the clear, simple standards of objective justice that Ling Mengchu the satirist needed. It is generally invoked in Ling's darker satires.

In discussing the artistic structures that result from the comic and the satiric attitudes, it is no longer possible to avoid making distinctions. Unfortunately, the definition of comedy and satire is in a state of comic disarray. Like rival countries claiming the same territory, theorists of comedy and satire have painted the map in their own colors. Oddly, the territory in dispute, the comedy of the social corrective, is regarded as central to both, since it exemplifies the remarks of Aristotle from which all comic and much satiric theory begins. I shall propose instead a simple, practical distinction related to the social effects of a hero's action.

Comedy (or comic structure) deals with a benign stràtagem or some stroke of good fortune that has a socially beneficent effect, frequently that of marriage. Satire of the first stage, lighter satire, deals with a folly, a self-inflicted harm caused by some abnormality or misperception on the part of the hero. In cases where the hero is cheated by rogues, he is actually falling victim to his own avarice or lechery. Satire of the second stage, darker satire, deals with a crime, a grievous harm to society, which must be exposed and punished. In terms of Frye's principle of social inclusion and exclusion,[53] comedy unites society, lighter satire chastises the foolish man and then reclaims him for society, and darker satire excludes the wrongdoer from society. According to this distinction, romantic comedy is true comedy; classical and neoclassical comedy, the comedy of Aristotle's definition as well as the satires of Horace, are lighter satire; and Juvenal is darker satire.

Comedies

About one-third of Ling's stories are either romantic comedies, culminating in marriage, or comedies of luck or reciprocation, in which other objects of social desire are attained. Searching for a phrase to describe them, one settles on "comedies of fortune," implying three senses of the word "fortune": fate, luck, and success.

Most are based on the idea of predestination. No fewer than eight of the romantic comedies have introductions that dwell at length on predestination in marriage (yinyuan). Their protagonists are the passive, unheroic recipients of a good fortune they have done little to earn; they exemplify Ling's advice to accept your fate and not strive unduly to achieve your ambition. They also include most of the exotic and fantastic stories. (I do not say supernatural, for ghosts of the dead, visits to hell, and the workings of the Heavenly Principle belong to the world of Ling's realistic fiction.) Of all Ling's stories, these are the closest to the folk tale. Sometimes their morality is even freed from social norms. In "The Chess Champions" (II.2), for example, the hero's sole concern is to take the girl to bed with him, while she is ready to cheat in order to hold on to her title as chess champion of the Liao. There is a ribald level of comment that would not be used of approved characters in other kinds of story.

Although they possess many of the qualities of the romance, Ling's comedies retain an astringent humor. The best of them, "The Imperial Decree" (I.10), sympathetically describes the problems of a penniless young licentiate in getting a wife. This introduction is followed by a

stroke worthy of Gogol. A decree of the Jiajing Emperor is mistaken in
the provinces as referring to a new draft of single women for the imperial
palace. The rush to escape the draft is on, and the previously un-
touchable licentiate is besieged with offers. There is a wildly comical
passage describing the panic in the village, with seventy-year-old widows
scrambling to get married.

. Ling's romantic comedies, like their European counterparts, are
generally about young love triumphing over parental opposition. The
writer needed a supernatural sanction for an action that must have been
barely conceivable in life. In Feng's collections, the understanding is that
a betrothal is sacrosanct once the parents have given their permission; if
the parents back out, the lovers may call upon the gods for help. This
justifies the children's defiance of their parents, but at the cost of a
restrictive convention. Ling's usual recourse is to his favorite doctrine of
predetermination, but since he gives no explanation, the outcome
generally amounts to sheer luck. Many of his comedies are about fantastic chances, jests and the like, that lead to unexpected but successful
love and marriage. Of course, as a convention, chance also exacts its
price; his characters are the sport of a blind fate.

Ling's other kinds of comedy make more use of the paradox of fate.
His first story, "The Tangerines and the Tortoiseshell," tells of the young
man who, after failing regularly in his own enterprises, makes a vast fortune on a merchant voyage to the South Seas. The story might be thought
a little insipid, were it not for the touches of the exotic: the tangerines,
lovingly described because of their later importance in the story; the
foreign port with its men clamoring for goods; the desert island; the Persian buyer's reception for the returning merchants.

The theme of the story, stressed in the introduction, is Ling's standard
advice that it is useless to try to shape your own fate. (The carpe diem
motif is also mentioned in the introduction, but briefly; it is rare in Ling,
who usually advocates quietism rather than hedonism.) But the central
comic strategy is the paradox of fortune. At each stage, the efforts of the
young man—such as his ingenious but slightly dishonest attempt to
create a vogue for autographed fans in Peking—come to nothing, while
his unpremeditated actions bring him a fortune. The raillery of his companions, serious merchants all, turns to admiration as fortune showers
upon him. It is a luck story, related to a universal folk tale archetype, but
handled with sophistication. And it offers a final paradox that seems to
reflect Ling's satirical view of his society. After making his fortune, the
hero, who is an educated man, does not even consider climbing the ladder of examination success but settles down to the leisurely life of the
master merchant, letting others go out on ocean voyages for him.

. "The Herd Boy" (II.19), which claims to be based on the *Zhuang Zi*, illustrates the *vanitas vanitatum* theme of Taoist thought. It is an account

of the herd boy's days and nights—hard work in the mountains by day, success and glory in the world of his dreams at night. The two lives reflect each other, but inversely, so that success in one life betokens disaster in the other, and the comic strategy consists of the relationship between the two. In his dream life, in his capacity as a statesman, he suggests a compromise plan to get two neighboring countries to withdraw their troops. Ling ridicules him as a Confucian, interested in moral suasion rather than practical things such as defense and counterattack. The two countries are reflected in two dangers, a tiger and a swollen river, which carry off the beasts he is supposed to be watching.

Another example is "The Old Tutor" (II.26), a story of good fortune descending upon a penniless old teacher, rejected, like Lear, by his married daughters. There is a characteristic satirical touch about the way fortune comes. The teacher is discovered by a former pupil, now a censor, and appointed to his staff. After only six months of dispensing favors, he has made enough money to retire. The prologue also shows Ling's satirical approach to social values. A young graduate is appointed to a teaching post in a remote port in Guangdong, where the young men want no instruction, are not interested in the classics, and are already literate enough for the jobs they have, which are, in any case, more remunerative than any they could get with a classical education. However, touched by the teacher's coming, they take up a quick collection and raise enough money to set him up for life.

Satires

Ling's satires, light and dark, match his avowed aims and methods better than do his comedies. His claim that his stories are about strange events grounded in observable reality fits his satires better than his comedies. As for the supernatural elements in his fiction, he asserts that they are at least close to credibility, a statement that seems to refer to the ghosts and the like of his satires rather than to the sheer fantasy of some of his comedies. His purpose as a writer, he declares, putting the matter beyond doubt, is "moral admonition."

Certain social relations are favored over all others by the satirist, especially that of the fool and the knave. The knaves in Ling's fiction are of a wide variety—shamans, alchemists, priests, cony catchers, moneylenders, officials, almost every class and profession in society except the most obvious predators: robbers and bandits. His fools, however, are from a narrow stratum. They are predominantly rich men, usually young, never officials. It is the rich man's avarice and self-deception that make him vulnerable. Satirists have always been fascinated by the rich bourgeois, but the fact that Ling's rich man is young is as important as that he is rich; he fits the Chinese stereotype of the prodigal son. Further-more, Ling's rich man is generally not a nouveau riche, and there is no suggestion that he is condescended to simply because he is not a scholar or official. Ling was fully as critical of scholars and officials as he was of merchants and the landed gentry; they just happen not to be at the center of his fiction.

His satires of folly and crime can be seen as different forms of this knave-fool relationship. The former throw the emphasis on the fool while largely ignoring the knave, apart from tacitly admiring his gall and his skill. The latter put the emphasis on the knave, now seen as a vicious figure. A certain sympathy has to be conceded to the fool, despite the satirist's general detachment. The harm he does is inflicted mainly on himself. He is an absurd figure, prodigal, avaricious, without any sense of fitness or modesty, who is fleeced unmercifully by the knave. The knaves in the folly satires are skilled professionals who seem to be ac-cepted as one of the natural hazards of Chinese life, past which the wise, practical man ought to be able to steer his course. ("This is how we operate," say the confidence men in "The Rich Man and the Alchemist" (I.18) when they are exposed, and then promptly proceed to pull the same trick again, in a more sophisticated form.) But in the crime satires, the knaves are amateurs abusing the power and opportunities that come their way. Whereas the professional knave is acting in an expected social role, the amateur's crime is a dangerous departure from the norm and must be condemned.

About ten stories can be called satires of folly, all of which are built on an obsession that is something like the "humour" of Jonsonian comedy. The rich man of "The Rich Man and the Alchemist" is "a highly educated, articulate, and likable man"[54] who is obsessed with alchemy. In his obsessed state, his intelligence and learning are actually a han-dicap, for alchemy, Ling tells us, is a folly to which the intelligent are particularly susceptible. In moments of discouragement, they can always turn to the ancient authorities to sustain their faith. The obsession, of course, is more than a misperception of reality; it is also prompted by avarice. The rich man of the story is anxious to get the secret of alchemy in order to put it to his own use, and he is quite prepared to seduce the alchemist's concubine into the bargain. Though a mild obsession, it is hardly a generous one, as we see from Ling's prologue:

> But these greedy men of our day, with their throngs of beautiful women, always seeking to extend their property, ruining others to enrich themselves, haggling over every trifle—what can they be like at heart? How preposterous a hope, that by meeting up with a crew of debased Taoists they will be able to practice alchemy, live a life of luxury, and then bequeath their wealth to their children! (p. 364)

The obsession may be gambling; or hunting, together with the sophisticated savagery, as Ling sees it, of gourmet cooking; or prodigality, the posture of the rich young man who is bemused by the heroic ethic and scorns his possessions; or lust; or boasting; or the vanity and emotional bias that warp objective judgment. It is a true obsession, rather than the kind of intellectual hypocrisy we find, alongside genuine obsessions, in Molière and *The Scholars*.

The obsession places the hero at odds with reality and at the knave's mercy. It cannot be appeased; as Ling puts it, satisfying an obsession is "like trying to fill a well by stuffing it with snow."[55] Acts are repeated until a climax is reached which works to purge the obsession. The comic strategy is largely that of character irony, as in all humor fiction and drama, since the reader sees the gap between the hero's perceptions and the reality.

"The Rich Man and the Alchemist," the best of the folly satires, consists of an elaborate confidence trick played on the rich man by a self-styled alchemist and a woman posing as his concubine, a trick that ends with the pair departing not only with the silver used to seed the experiment but also with a large sum that the rich man has paid in reparation for sleeping with the woman. The hero emerges from the incident still believing in the alchemist's powers, blaming himself for the failure of the experiment and congratulating himself on having escaped so lightly. "The Gambler" (II.8) is another rogue and gull story. Gambling, like alchemy, offends against the ideas on predestination that underlie most of Ling's comedies; it amounts to taking an unauthorized part in one's own fate, thus upsetting the prescribed order. "The Braggart" (I.3) is concerned with the self-glorification of the swashbuckler's ethic, which offends against the sense of proper modesty advocated by the satirist. "The Spendthrift" (II.22) is about a prodigal obsessed with the heroic ethic and its contempt for money. Like many foolish heroes, he has a wise and experienced relative. Here is the relative explaining how his father made his money:

"Your late father, the minister, did not build up the family fortune solely from his official earnings; most of it came from sound, thrifty management of his finances. I have seen him myself, working from early in the morning until late at night, his abacus, scales, deeds, and account books always at hand. If anyone was short by so little as a penny, it would show up in his figures, and then his face would darken and he would give the man a frightful tongue-lashing. But if he got even a modest bargain, he would fairly beam with delight." (p. 344)

The spendthrift's friends, knaves all of them, have no trouble rebutting the advice, quoting Li Bai on the heroic ethic.

"The Wife Swapper" (I.32) shows how Ling's delight in ribaldry tends to reshape and distort his satire. "The Cheat" (II.16) is about a rich man who tries to cheat his brothers out of their share in the patrimony, and is then cheated in his turn by his partner in deception. "The Biased Judge" (II.12) relates two stories in which Zhu Xi, in his capacity as an official, is shown up as either incompetent or biased. The prologue shows him using his deductive powers to arrive at the obvious solution to the case. But the rogues have made precisely this calculation and have arranged the evidence accordingly. The main story, developed from an item in the *Yijian zhi*,[56] shows Zhu Xi's objectivity upset by pique and impulsive judgment. Ling was greatly concerned with objective judgment, a characteristic of the satirist; he regularly notes occasions in which the emotions distort objective thinking.

The darker satires, of which there are about twenty, are studies in different shades of crime, vice, and folly. "The Wife Who Eloped" (II.38) tells of a woman whose husband finds out about her adulterous affairs and makes life difficult for her. She decides to run off with one of her lovers but, when drunk, reveals the secret to a cousin. The cousin takes the other man's place, and the woman does not find out until too late. The lover is accused by the husband of abducting her and thrown into jail. The cousin, tiring of her, sells her into prostitution. She is rescued, and the judicial tangle is finally sorted out. Each character is a fool or a rogue or both. Even "The Ginger Merchant" (I.11), the best of Ling's stories of detection, divides guilt between the rogue and his victim to some degree. The victim has a quick temper that causes him trouble on two crucial occasions. Also, he is a student and therefore naïve, in Ling's eyes. "The Filial Son" (I.13) has a more serious tone than most of Ling's stories; it is about the killing of a father, but even here the parents have been guilty of outrageously spoiling their monstrous son.

There is a pervading cynicism about human motives in these satires. "The Theft of the Family Silver" (II.20) warns against trusting even one's relatives. Its rogue is a rich, retired official who cannot resist the temptation to steal the family heirlooms from a naïve young daughter-in-law. Any victims who are not actually to blame prove to be positive figures who find ways of outwitting or getting revenge on the rogues. Pathos, where it is not avoided altogether, is kept at arm's length. As there are few victims who inspire sympathy and admiration, so there are few villains who inspire fear and awe. The basic strategy of Ling's, as of all satire, is that of reduction. He attempts to make folly ridiculous rather than pathetic and evil squalid rather than terrible. From this point of view, the fool's chastisement and the villain's punishment are merely Ling's final satiric touch, his reductive coup de grâce.

Other Writers

Following Feng's and Ling's successes, the story enjoyed a burst of popularity with authors and publishers. Some twenty collections by individual authors, many of them in elaborate editions, survive from the next two decades. For all its popularity, however, the story failed to attract any well-known writers; those whose names can be discovered are all relatively obscure. Their common characteristic, as compared with their predecessors, is a tendency to restrict their thematic range and even to concentrate on a single theme. Theirs are the first specialized collections.

Thematically, they can be divided into two broad categories, according to whether they favor the erotic and romantic on the one hand or the moral and heroic on the other. The former were much influenced by the contemporary emphasis on qing, particularly in Feng's *Anatomy of Love*, and also by the vogue for erotic fiction, such as *The Unofficial History of the Embroidered Couch* (*Xiuta yeshi*) and *The Life of the Foolish Woman* (*Chi pozi zhuan*).[57] The moral-heroic writers combined themes of public morality (as in Feng) with those of private morality (as in Langxian), asserting the interdependence of the two spheres in an orthodox Confucian manner. Their purpose, in the face of imminent national disaster, was to promote a basic moral regeneration throughout society.

The earliest work of the romantic-erotic kind was the *Guzhang juechen*, four ten-chapter stories written in 1629 or 1630, between the publication of Ling's two collections.[58] Its title seems to echo Ling's, and it shares his interest in romantic comedy and social satire. Stories 1 and 3 are long and elaborate romantic comedies which may be seen as precursors of the "brilliant and beautiful" novel of the Qing dynasty, despite their robust sexuality. In plot, they clearly owe much to the complex structure of the Southern drama. Story 4 is a satirical extravaganza that anticipates the novel *Marriage Destinies to Awaken the World* (*Xingshi yinyuan zhuan*) and the story collection *The Cup that Reflects the World* (*Zhao shi bei*).[59] Its satire reaches higher in the social scale than Ling's stories; even the tyrant Wei Zhongxian makes an appearance. It is also unusually free of the constrictions of the bao plot. The "juechen" of the title, meaning ridding oneself of worldly dross, refers to the eremitic ideal declared in the collection's foreword and propounded in this story.

A more typical work is *Antagonists in Love* (*Huanxi yuanjia*), twenty-four stories purporting to illustrate a single theme.[60] The author asserts in his preface that fiction writers have their own field, that of romance, and stakes out for himself a particular area within it: the inevitable progress of the love affair. The affair begins with the first signs of attraction, reaches its climax in sexual love, and then declines; suspicion replaces love and deepens into hatred and violence. Hence love ("huanxi") and hatred ("yuanjia" means "antagonist") are inseparably linked, a notion expounded at one point in the *Anatomy of Love*.[61] But the reader who expects to be led to some broad psychological truth will be disappointed. Apart from the author's erotic intent — he is much concerned with woman's fall from grace—he presents hatred and violence merely as the moral retribution for illicit love. His is a story of moral bao dressed up in a theory of qing, and he handles the calculus of requital with great finesse. I believe that the author was a certain Gao Yiwei of Hangchow, an obscure figure known to us only as the editor and publisher of a handful of plays.[62] For character and incident, he drew freely on his knowledge of vernacular fiction, particularly Feng's stories.[63]

Expanse of Love (*Yipian qing*), a fourteen-piece collection from Hangchow,[64] shares the ostensible moral aims of *Antagonists* but has far more erotic material and is less concerned with retribution. Its real interest is in ribald comedy, based mainly on the notion that men are sexually no match for women. Told in simple language, the stories are distinguished above all by their social locus; many are about uneducated people, some even about peasants. (The author seems to have associated ribaldry with the humble life.) Among more specialized works is *Bian er chai* (Wearing a Cap but Also Hairpins), a Hangchow collection of four five-chapter stories about homosexual love affairs (whence the title) between an older sophisticate and a younger innocent.[65] The older man, at least, is always of the scholar class. The archetype is Langxian's idealistic romance "Pan Wenzi," but whereas Langxian's narrator was tempted to treat the subject with humor, this author is deadly serious. Together his stories make up an argument for the validity of homosexual love.

The major strain of fiction in the 1640s, under the foreign threat, was Confucian moral heroism. Writers rejected the alternative values of reclusive withdrawal and romantic abandon and subordinated the claims of the individual self to social duty. They were cool even toward the utilitarian morality of rewards and punishments (although their heroes are rewarded in the next generation by heavenly bao). Their morality proceeds from conscience, not the social stimuli of shame or vainglory; their heroes persist in principled behavior despite the taunts of their peers. With strong forebodings about the dynasty's fate, these writers show an obsessive interest in its past, especially the strong reigns of the Hongwu and Yongle Emperors, finding cases of moral heroism in the Ming to match or surpass those of ancient times. The social locus of most of their stories is that of the officeholder and the student, and students must surely have been the main public they envisaged.

Collections include *Illusions* (*Huanying*), with a preface apparently of 1643;[66] the *Second Collection of West Lake Stories* (*Xihu erji*),[67] which must have been written before the fall of Peking; *A Pair of Needles* (*Yuanyang zhen*) and *The Brush that Serves as Judgment Goat* (*Bi xiezhi*),[68] by a single author who wrote probably during the short-lived reign of the Prince of Fu in 1644-45; *Alarum Bell on a Still Night* (*Qingye zhong*),[69] published during the equally short-lived reign of the Prince of Tang in 1645-46; and *The Sobering Stone* (*Zuixing shi*),[70] written in the early years of Manchu rule. They present a series of reactions to a catastrophic period of history, from the urgent exhortation of the prewar fiction, through the desperation of some of the wartime stories, to the somber reflections of *The Sobering Stone*.

Little is known of Zhou Ji, author of the *Second Collection of West Lake Stories* (his *First Collection* has been lost), beyond what can be deduced from the work itself. As the title indicates, all of the stories are set, at least in part, in Hangchow, but the author's prime purpose is not to celebrate the city's past. The preface explains that he turned to fiction as a last desperate resort, because his talent was not appreciated. Although the preface was written by a friend, there is every reason to believe that Zhou saw himself in just this light. His prologue to the first story doubles as a prologue to the book and amounts to a personal testament.[71] He implies that fiction is something to which he turns out of necessity but that it is also the means by which he presents his outraged view of society. Throughout the book, his personal frustrations are fused with his contempt for those in authority. His morality is of the absolute, idealistic kind, calling for moral heroism; but at the same time he is a man of letters, presenting his favorite poets to us for our admiration—men with a high degree of amour propre, satirists who do not suffer fools gladly or rogues at all. They are, of course, symbols of himself. It is this subjective element that sets Zhou Ji apart from his peers.

His condescending attitude to fiction impelled him toward a new kind of story. He vastly increased the mode of comment, particularly in his long and convoluted prologues, and he also attempted to assimilate the story to historical narrative. Several of his stories actually go beyond the biographical form to present tracts of Ming political and military history, dense with detail. Whatever one may think of his historical stories—in my opinion, they are not successful—he deserves mention as a master of vigorous, denunciatory vernacular prose.

The Sobering Stone, the last and best work in this strain, comprises fifteen stories by an author who signs himself Master Gukuang (Ancient-Crazy) of Eastern Lu. (Despite the place of origin, he has no perceptible connection with the flourishing Shandong vernacular literature, and most of his stories are set in Jiangsu or Zhejiang.) The title, as the foreword points out, comes from the legendary stone that awakens one from a drunken stupor. The work has a strong moral and patriotic intent, and its narratorial tone is uniformly serious. Gukuang's aim was to celebrate good and condemn evil according to his Confucian lights. He focuses on the lower bureaucracy, up to the level of the county magistrate, and seeks to reinforce an ethic of Confucian duty—that is, the fulfillment of one's social role.

His examples, although set earlier in the Ming dynasty, are clearly a reaction to the dynasty's fall. Stories 1, 2, and 5 show people handling modest responsibility with selfless competence. Story 11, "The Bribe," shows the successful candidate bending beneath the pressures and temptations to which he is subjected. Gukuang is an excellent analyst of motives; he lays before the reader the process by which the immoral decision is made. Even his one venture into fantasy, story 6, "The Metamorphosis of Poet into Tiger," a reworking of a Tang tale,[72] demonstrates his moral concerns. It condemns egocentricity as offending against the ideal of self-fulfillment in one's social role. The poet's psychopathic arrogance is the cause of his ruin.

For all his modesty, the Gukuang hero is a moral activist driven by a sense of duty, an inner-directed man who bears with equanimity the scorn of his colleagues. He has no literary pretensions; they might detract from his effectiveness in his job. Gukuang is not cynical about the legal and adminstrative system, as Ling Mengchu was; he believes it will work if everyone shoulders his responsibilities. The central figure in his moral world is the officeholder, not the merchant; his is an officeholder's morality. Evil is not innate, merely the result of a failure to think through to the principles involved; hence the didactic nature of his book. One cannot help but conclude that Gukuang was a Confucian of the strict school that was the object of so much ridicule in seventeenth-century literature, particularly from Li Yu. Gukuang, for his part, leaves us in no doubt of his contempt for fashionable writers. There were evidently two contrasting types in seventeenth-century life and literature: the puritanical moralist and the bohemian man of letters, each of whom satirized the other unmercifully.

8
Li
Yu

Li Yu (1611-1679/80) is the one author of whom we know as much as we could reasonably hope. He had a wide acquaintance among his fellow men of letters and was well known to the general public. His friend Bao Jun claimed hyperbolically that "there is not a single woman or child in the nation today who has not heard of Liweng of the Lake."[1] His most important writings have survived and are accessible: the collected prose and poetry, including his brilliant book on drama and the art of living, *Casual Expressions of Idle Feeling* (*Xianqing ou ji*); ten plays; two collections of vernacular stories; and the novel *Carnal Prayer Mat* (*Rou putuan*), the solitary classic of Chinese pornography. His works tell of his search for piecemeal patronage on long fund-raising journeys about the country, as he went from one potential donor to the next, with his concubines (a gift from one of them) performing his plays for him. (This last circumstance scandalized some of his contemporaries.) They tell also of his manifold writing, editing, publishing, and bookselling ventures, and of his always precarious finances.

He belonged to the tradition of self-revelation articulated by Yuan Hongdao, and his attitudes, values, and interests are manifested throughout his work. Prominent among them are his aesthetic values. His angle of approach to the arts was that of craft or technique: he was the skilled practitioner explaining his art systematically to the novice. In this vein, he wrote analytical treatises of exceptional clarity on the drama, the domestic arts, and the ci lyric. His criticism is all of a piece; certain broad principles run through it, whether he is explaining how to compose plays or arrange antiques, and in some degree these principles can also be applied to his fiction.

There was something of both the epicurean and the aesthete about him. He was the philosopher and technician of happiness, if happiness is understood as a passive accommodation with reality. His was a philosophy of low expectations, as a means of guarding against disappointment; of not tempting providence; of consoling oneself by thinking of people who are worse off. All of these points are made equally in his stories, his plays, and his essays. His work frequently turns on the notion of a reality principle to which ideals and preconceptions must be made to conform. (Sometimes the process is described as bringing Confucianism up to date by a choice of current, not outmoded, problems within its Five Relations.) Naturally, he believed in a morality fitted to the situation rather than an absolute morality. He tended to go even further, honoring an enlightened self-interest over self-sacrifice to a social ideal. It is no surprise that he was able to accommodate himself to political reality in the shape of the Manchu conquest.[2]

But if stoic and epicurean attitudes offer a way of living one's life without stress and mortification, the chief aim of that life is to achieve sensory pleasure in general and aesthetic pleasure in particular. Writing was itself his keenest delight,[3] and the moments of greatest passion in his writing are those in which he describes the pleasures of the senses. One spring, for example, he had no money with which to buy narcissi, and his family thought that one season's deprivation should not be too much for him to bear.

> "Do you want to take my life away from me?" I replied. "I'd rather lose a year out of my life than miss a narcissus season. Why, it was for the sake of the narcissus that I braved all the snow and traveled back here! If I'm not going to see any, I might just as well have stayed there the whole year and not returned to Nanking at all."
> Unable to restrain me, my family let me pawn some hairpins and earrings and buy narcissi. My passion for the narcissus is no mere quirk. Its color, scent, leaf, and stem set it apart from other flowers. It appeals to me most of all by its winsomeness. You can find girls anywhere with complexions like a peach blossom and waists like a willow frond, girls as sleek as the *mudan* and the *shaoyao*, or as slender as the chrysanthemum and the begonia. But I have never seen a girl to match the calm beauty of the narcissus, or with such quiet, unmoving grace.[4]

For Li Yu there is no hierarchy among sensory pleasures. He is as eloquent on the subject of some favorite taste in food or the ecstasy of a hot bath as he is on the narcissus or on girls caught in a soaking downpour that reveals the lineaments of their beauty. Aesthetic standards are applied to all areas of life and tend to fuse with moral standards. In his drama and fiction, beauty is associated with talent, and beauty and talent together are generally associated with goodness.

The principles behind his aesthetic preferences are stated and restated — design, simplicity, naturalness, refinement, novelty. The important thing in a house "is not splendor but refinement, not exquisite detail and brilliant colors but novelty and elegance." Of these principles, it is novelty, the capacity to surprise, that he insists on most. He inveighs passionately against a writer's imitating others, which he regards as plagiarism, and even against his repeating himself, which he calls self-plagiarism. In his foreword to *Casual Expressions*, he writes: "Of the eight subjects I deal with here, there is not one which is not new. Of the myriad words I have written here, there is not one which is even slightly secondhand." He continues, in a section entitled "A Vow Not to Plagiarize," "In half a lifetime's writing, I have not filched so much as a word of anyone else's work." The principle applies also in fields other than literature. In arranging objets d'art in one's study, the aim should be constant newness; if one fails to rearrange all the time, one's mind will grow stale. "If people wish to enliven their minds, they must first enliven their eyes."[5]

He practiced what he preached. He was continually coming up with new ideas, designs, and inventions, including a heated desk, a new style of letter paper, new designs for windows and partitions, and even a flower stand to fit into his bed. The same happy inventiveness appears in his plays, his stories, and in the *Casual Expressions*, in their organization as well as their subject matter.[6]

He stressed the value of originality in literature more than any other Chinese critic—indeed, probably more than any European critic before the twentieth century. He never appealed to ancient authority. His criteria for a judgment are teleological (for example, the Creator's purpose) or are based on the idea of what is "natural," and he constantly tests his judgment against his own experience.[7] It was the innovative side of Li Yu that most impressed his contemporaries. A typical critique of one of his plays says it "opens up a whole new territory never discovered by previous writers and deserves to be called the ultimate in freshness and novelty."[8]

"Newness is a term of approbation for everything in the world," he wrote, "but far more for literature than anything else." Addressing the novice playwright, he wrote, "If you don't rid your mind of stereotypes, it is hard even to talk about writing plays." The requirement of novelty applies to the matter of a work rather than to its technique. In technical matters, Li Yu urges the novice to follow the precedents, and he is capable of criticizing his contemporaries for rash experimentation with formal features. On the other hand, he says that before beginning a play, the novice should ask himself if the stuff-material has been used before; if it has, it is not worth wasting time on.[9] And in the writing of the ci lyric, where complete originality is impossible all the time, the poet should aim at originality of concept before anything else: "If the concept is extremely novel, it does not matter if the diction is a little old. A bewitching beauty seems all the more beautiful in tattered clothing."[10]

Novelty of subject matter does not, however, extend to the fantastic or the supernatural. Li several times states his allegiance to a Confucian form of philosophical naturalism. Literature should not go outside perceptible human experience, the "range of what we see and hear." With a few exceptions, his plays and stories obey this dictum. Only literature that "speaks of the nature of man and the principles of things" will last.[11] Li Yu disagrees with people who complain that human experience has been exhausted as a subject: the "principles of things" cannot be made new, but the "nature of man" has an infinite subject matter.

His doctrine of newness arises from a conviction that there are no fixed social or literary rules.[12] Social mores, attitudes, institutions are as subject to change as are literary forms, genres, styles. Many of his stories contrast the ideal or conventional view with present reality. In his over-turning of social stereotypes, particularly those of women, Li Yu may, in addition, have intended a liberating effect. Of course, his comic tech-nique consists of overturning a stereotype, and one may therefore be tempted to think that comedy was his sole purpose. But an examination of the sterotypes he chose to overturn, as well as of the facts of his own life, indicates a genuine concern for women.[13]

Social change produces literary change. Why do we need to modernize old plays? he asks, and answers: because attitudes change.[14] The classic Southern play The Lute is already an antique, which the author, were he alive today, would feel compelled to adapt. Old plays are only for specialists; new plays are needed for the entertainment of the modern audience. Writers can be divided into the traditional and the innovative, Li Yu being firmly in the latter category. He prides himself on formal in-novation, for example, on the structure of his drama, on the amount and the quality of its spoken parts, and on the opening device of Carnal Prayer Mat;[15] but when he speaks of historical change in literature, he means change in the social reality with which literature deals.

Dramatic Theory

There is a closer connection between his drama (and dramatic theory) and his fiction than between any other two fields of his work. The aspects of the drama on which he focuses, such as construction, are those most applicable to fiction. And fiction itself is not beneath his notice; he occasionally refers to stories while discussing plays. The copious reflex-ive comment in his fiction also makes use of terms that belong properly to the drama.

Even a superficial reading shows many of the same qualities in his fic-tion as in his plays: the careful design; the suggestion, in the case of the longer stories, of the symphonic structure of the Southern drama; and also the nature and distribution of characters (roles). Many of the plots proved transferable; several *Silent Operas* were made into real operas. To reverse the comparison, Li Yu also emphasized in the drama features that are more prominent in fiction, for example, the spoken parts. It has been suggested that the relative lack of specificity in Li Yu's fiction might be due to his thinking in dramatic terms.[16] But it could also be maintained that his plays are distinguished by their essentially fictional features. Both plays and stories, in fact, are conditioned by his emphasis on concept, which means that characters and background are illustrative rather than representational.

His dramatic theory is distinguished more by its analytical power than by its suggestiveness. By its side, even the best of the traditional dramatic criticism looks like brilliant, scattered notes. But he has purchased a blessed clarity at the price of a certain subtlety. His criticism of his contemporary, the famous critic of the novel and drama, Jin Shengtan, indicates the reason. Li criticizes Jin on the subject of *The Western Chamber* for approaching the play from a reader's point of view: "But his critique of *The Western Chamber* is of the play the literary man delights in, not the play the actors perform." He goes on to assert that Jin would have done better if he had been a dramatist, by which he means not just that Jin is treating a play as a text but that he is ignorant of the processes of composition. Li asserts that "the most remarkable literature in history was created not by men but by ghosts and spirits; the writers were merely the subjects whom the ghosts and spirits possessed."[17]

The argument arises from the different stances of the two critics. Jin was writing as a reader, not a creator. He saw an astonishing subtlety in the works he chose to annotate, and, consistent with his view of the creative genius, he attributed this subtlety to conscious intention. Li was writing as a practitioner, and he knew from his own experience of the part played by the unconscious mind, which he attributed to spiritual agencies. Since it was unconscious, he excluded its work from the criticism he was writing, a reasonable decision for someone composing what is ostensibly a manual for novice playwrights. At the same time, he was no believer in the theory of individual genius, and his attitude toward masterpieces is less than awestruck.

The first requirement of a play, he says, is intelligibility, which is attained by using simple language and a coherent structure. Avoid literary allusions and dialectal expressions: "Good literature in all periods is just speech, after all."[18] He sees the various genres as existing at different levels of diction according to the kind of audience for whom they were, by convention or of necessity, intended.[19] The ci lyric stands between the *shi* poem and the dramatic song, each possessing its proper diction. Dramatic song is based on the vernacular language and is direct in its signification. The ci lyric is not based on the vernacular and pro-

ceeds more by implication than direct statement. Drama is to be distinguished in similar terms from formal prose.

> Prose is written for educated men, hence no one questions its abstruseness.
> Plays are written for both educated and uneducated men, and also for
> uneducated women and children; hence they are valued for their simplicity,
> not their abstruseness. If prose had been instituted for educated and
> uneducated men to read, along with uneducated women and children, the
> sages' classics and commentaries would also have been written solely in simple
> rather than abstruse language, just like present-day fiction.[20]

Simplicity does not mean simple-mindedness or vulgarity, however; a
thought can be profound and yet be expressed simply and directly.
Moreover, the spoken parts of a play should still be attentive to such
refinements as tone pattern. Although there is a set of conventions in the
drama—what would be a natural level of speech for a "painted face"
character would be intolerable for a male lead—vulgarity should be
avoided lest one lose "the style of the literary man" (wenren zhi bi). The
literary man's use of a form that caters to the educated and the
uneducated alike is the heart of the problem. Li Yu approaches it not
with condescension but by treating it as a special challenge; in writing fiction or drama, the author must write intelligibly for the wider public
without discarding the qualities that made him a literary man in the first
place. "If one can display one's talent in simple situations, one is a true
literary master."[21]

Li was not the first critic of the drama to use the concept of structure
(jiegou), but he was the first and only one to give it a prominent place.
"Structure" is not the best English equivalent, for Li is looking at the
drama from the playwright's angle. He means the activity of construction
rather than an immanent form perceived in the completed play. His image of the playwright is that of the maker—the tailor, the builder, the
Creator (zaowu)—who works purposefully from a detailed design. Great
stress is placed on the planning stage: "Only if you keep your hands in
your sleeves at the beginning will you be able to write quickly later on."[22]
The essential requirement of all good construction is a key or controlling
element (zhunao), which is not merely a key person—that would result in
an episodic play—but a key person in a key incident. Li's examples from
The Western Chamber and The Lute show that the key element is the
crux of the plot, the element from which all others derive in terms of
causation. Planning for the play begins with a key element that must
itself, of course, be novel enough to excite interest. Subplots must be
kept to a minimum, lest the play become complicated and the line of
thought divergent; and the stitching must be fine—that is to say, the
play's continuity should appear seamless.

Li Yu discusses construction at different levels, including the verbal,
but it is this emphasis on grand planning and smooth articulation that

distinguishes his criticism and practice in both fiction and drama. The novelty and ingenuity in which he took such pride apply to structure as much as to other features. In talking of coherence, he frequently uses the example of the eight-legged examination essay, anathema to many intellectuals but a respected genre for both Li and Jin Shengtan. The essay required careful planning and tight articulation and thus provided them with an example of complex organization in literature.

The function of the literature Li speaks of is to amuse or to entertain, not to arouse pity or terror or indignation. His view of life impelled him toward comedy; it is hard to imagine a work of his dealing in any ravaging emotion. Pathos is nonexistent; even his serious works do not move the reader. (His poetry occasionally does, though. He wrote some stark and affecting poems on his return home after the sack of his town.)[23] He himself summed up his writing as "matter for amusement," a true description of his drama and fiction. He said that a play should be a pleasant, not a tearful, experience, and his drama and fiction are all comedy, much of it the comedy of sex—romantic comedy, erotic comedy, ribald comedy. He ridiculed all moralizing in literature, by which he meant not only authorial sermons but the subject matter of moral heroism; for in moralizing , all gusto, all piquancy is lost.[24] Didacticism as such he did not exclude from his work; indeed he developed his own brand of philosophical comedy.

Fiction

He wrote three collections of stories, in addition to his one novel, *Carnal Prayer Mat: Silent Operas, First Series; Silent Operas, Second Series;* and *Twelve Structures* (*Shi'er lou*), which has a preface, dated 1658, by Du Jun, a well-known writer. *Silent Operas* (*Wusheng xi*) preceded *Twelve Structures* but cannot be dated precisely. Neither the first series nor the second series has survived as such; their stories exist in a variety of combined editions, the earliest of which was also edited by Du Jun. It consisted of at least eighteen stories, in two sections of twelve and six respectively, which may correspond to the original first and second series. In all, seventeen *Silent Operas* exist, but only twelve are accessible, in what is apparently the latest of the combined editions.[25]

Of his predecessors, Li Yu is closest to Ling Mengchu.[26] Like Ling's, his professed subject is the novel event occurring within human experience; his stories are comedies, with elaborate, witty prologues to control their meaning; and they lack individualizing detail. But his moral values differ from Ling's. He sets out to make values conform to what is natural, sensible, and practicable rather than to affirm a well-established morality. His stories are governed by their basic concept (usually a paradox) and contain a strong element of didacticism. On the level of serial meaning, he makes a far greater use of the comic image. And he was not, like Ling, dependent on written sources.

There is a Li Yu trademark in fiction that is more than just the primacy of the comic idea and the obtrusiveness of the witty comment. Themes and motifs are picked up and reworked in story after story; they unite both of the collections and also the novel. How many polygynous marriages (in which there is no hierarchy of wife and concubine) there are in his stories, and how he dwells on the intricacies of multiple courtship and domestic management! The fact that he had personal experience in plenty is not the point; the comic possibilities of the arrangement intrigued and even obsessed him. There are, too, those gray figures who clearly represent some of Li Yu's personal ideals: wise, self-disciplined stoics and hopelessly generous, artistic innocents. There is the sudden sensuousness of his description of phenomena, reflecting his concern with sensory pleasure, that intrudes on the bright novelty of some comic concept, bringing two modes together. Eroticism, sensuous and evocative, and ribaldry, comic and sometimes grotesque, are regularly intertwined in his writing.

There is ample reason to treat all of his fiction together and ample reason also to go from work to work and show how his fiction changes. I adopt the second method here but will identify the common features as I go.

At the heart of most of Li Yu's stories is a social paradox resulting from the overturning of some cherished myth or stereotype. Bernard Shaw is another example of a writer who used the social paradox (the new soldier, the new woman) in virtually all of his work, and the term "paradoxical farceur," which has been applied to Shaw, would apply equally to Li.[27] The overturning, of course, can be convincing only if it claims to accord with present reality. In *Silent Operas*, the social paradox is more prominent, and the stereotypes are usually those enshrined in literature. Several of its stories are parodies of other vernacular fiction. Story 11 in *Operas* parodies Langxian's "Old Retainer," as it shows the loyal servant inheriting the family property, and *Operas* 7 parodies "The Oil Seller," with the singing girl exploiting and deceiving her naïve admirer.

Other stories upend common themes. *Operas* 1 overturns the theme of the "brilliant and beautiful" couple. Li Yu's story is about a monstrously ugly man with few redeeming qualities who is married to a number of beautiful wives. This, he insists, is the typical reality. *Operas* 10 treats the jealous wife, a fearfully overworked theme in seventeenth-century fiction and drama.[28] Li analyzes jealousy into envy, which may be felt either by men or women, and jealousy proper, which refers to one woman's jealousy of another. Of the latter kind, there is the old jealousy and the new. Drama and fiction, he says, have exhausted jealousy as a subject; but with the aid of this distinction, he is able to find a fresh angle.

Still other stories overturn common beliefs. *Operas* 2 is about a miscarriage of justice that occurs precisely because the magistrate is incorruptible and blinded by his moralism. Li makes much of the paradox that whereas a venal official is likely to be challenged, no one is in a position to challenge the incorruptible one. He is arguing, characteristically, for talent over traditional morality. *Operas* 9 considers the implication of the common belief that devout Buddhist prayer and giving away one's money will produce a son in a hitherto infertile marriage. What if, Li asked himself, a husband were to economize on the alms as soon as his concubine became pregnant? The child is born but as a neuter; then, as the father quickly resumes his prayer and alms giving, it begins to form male genitals. The father's backsliding is crucial to the plot, as the epilogue makes clear. If people feel disposed to emulate the father, says the narrator, in the kind of reflexive comment that occurs throughout Li's stories, they should hope for a writer capable of an interesting dénouement.

Operas 5 is about a mastermind who happens to be both a woman and a peasant. The annotator comments that, in using an illiterate woman as a heroine, Li Yu is "breaking out of the mold."[29] *Operas* 6 is about a homosexual marriage, and that fact is its paradox. It is, the narrator tells us, "a variant form of the Three Obligations and an intercalary point in the Five Relations, a strange event that official history need not record but that unofficial history cannot pass over."[30] *Operas* 3 and 4 are both fate stories in imitation of Ling Mengchu. Story 4, in particular, has elements taken from at least three of Ling's stories, including "The Tangerines and the Tortoiseshell." Naturally, both stories differ vastly from Ling's simple belief in prognostication.

Operas 1, 2, 5, and 6 are the most interesting stories in the collection. In *Operas* 1, Li Yu is not content to state the nature of his parody in the prologue; he works up a fanciful theory that feminine beauty is actually an exquisite karmic punishment for sins in a former life. A beautiful and talented woman will have high hopes for her marriage, but married to a clod, as she will be, she will inflict punishment on herself. Then comes Li's logical conclusion: a girl should consult her mirror at the age of twelve, and if she has serious flaws,

> that is a sign of a superlative fortune; it means she will get an ideal husband. There is no need for her to have her fortune told. If she is not unattractive, it means she can look for a fairly good husband. If she is quite attractive, she will have to be content with a rather poor husband. If by some rare chance she should happen to be really attractive, and clever and talented as well, she must realize that this is the sign of an evil fate in store for her and must prepare herself for marriage to the ugliest and most stupid of husbands . . .[31]

This is, of course, a playful extension of Li Yu's philosophy of low expectations: beauty is a curse because it induces high expectations. Li Yu goes on to describe himself: "The writer of this story is a leading specialist in women's problems." In his epilogue, he returns to the same metaphor:

> I have now finished describing this secret formula of mine for the elixir of life, and I'll pack up my medicine bag and leave. You may heed me or not as you wish — it's no concern of mine. But I do have some words of advice for those stupid and ugly husbands of yours. Your wives are married to you, and they have to put up with it. You are married to them, and you had better count your blessings. You must understand that great beauties do not come within the destiny of a talented man. What sort of man am I, you must ask yourselves, to get such a wife as mine?[32]

The wives suffer from no conventional morality of obligation: like almost all of Li Yu's heroines, they obey an enlightened self-interest. The first wife quickly hits on a method of escaping her foul-smelling husband's attentions; she claims to get religion and sets up a Buddhist sanctuary in the study, where the second wife joins her. The third wife, cruelly tricked into marriage, tries various tactics to escape her fate. At length she prevails upon the other two to share her misfortune and thus lighten it. The women have accepted their fate and used their wits to make the best of it.

But although Li Yu applies the reality principle, he does not do so complacently, as is shown by his treatment of Yuan, the official. While Yuan is in the capital, his jealous wife tricks his two concubines into marriage. One is tricked into marrying the ugly man and promptly kills herself. (The narrator was not sympathetic.) The other is then substituted as his third wife. When Yuan returns home, she pleads with him to take her back, but he coldly chokes her off. "If you had wanted to keep your honor, why didn't you kill yourself?" A little later, the narrator's comment runs, "All her hopes were dashed by Yuan's few words." On which Du Jun's note comments: "It is not that a woman is not as intelligent as a man, just that a commoner is not as powerful as a graduate."[33] Yuan is a forbidding figure, who reads ruthlessly the lesson of social hierarchy.

Li Yu made a Southern drama out of this story entitled *There's Nothing You Can Do About Your Fate* (*Naihe tian*). The play has more comic action than the story and is more symmetrical. (For example, Yuan's wife is ugly, in contrast to the two pretty concubines.) It also has a long military episode in which the hero acquires a good name by donating supplies to the army. But although Li prided himself on breaking dramatic convention by marrying his female lead to the comic villain, he could not forgo the drama's conventional happy ending; the ugly hero is metamorphosed into a handsome husband in the last act.

Operas 2, "A Handsome Lad Arouses Suspicion in Trying to Avoid It," thematically linked to *Operas* 1, is of an ingenuity that defies summary. In some respects, it is a suspenseful detective story, except that no crime is committed. It is also a curious version of a romantic comedy in which the brilliant youth ends up with the beautiful girl, except that she has been married to, and rejected by, a stupid husband. The subject of incest hovers over the story, but only as a suspicion, for no incest ever occurs. The story has spatial symmetry, as in so many of Li Yu's stories, and also a symmetry of events, as suspicions of incest occur in the magistrate's own house and lead to the suicide of his daughter-in-law. Finally, and most characteristically, it has a naturalistic solution for the mystery: the fact that rats steal trinkets for their nests. It is a typical Li Yu concoction, of remarkable wit and craftsmanship, which manages to entertain, to amuse, to shock, and also to make some Shavian points about society.

Geng Erniang, the illiterate peasant of *Operas* 5, is a typical Li Yu heroine. She is clever, deft, practical, fundamentally moral, though her morality accords with an enlightened self-interest. The main story is of her bold and brilliant schemes to escape the marauding rebels with her chastity intact. Her conduct contrasts with that of the other village women, who swear that they will kill themselves before surrendering their honor, and then go happily to bed with their captors the first night. Of course, Erniang has to surrender some lesser intimacies, and the narrator discourses in his introduction on the factors of circumstance and motive in judging behavior (Li Yu is opposed, as ever, to prescriptive moral rules). It is a ribald story, full of details of simulated menstruation, swollen members, diarrhea—the various means by which she succeeds in her attempt to stave off sexual intercourse. Significantly, after getting her captor's booty away from him, she and her husband buy a farm with the money without letting anyone know where it came from.

Operas 6, the story of the homosexual marriage, is, despite its comedy and occasional irony, a sentimental romance. It is a love affair that is comic because it deviates from the norm. There is some contradiction with the prologue and epilogue, which are at pains to assert that only heterosexual love is natural, but it is an intentional contradiction quite common in Li Yu. With great ingenuity, he is able to parody heterosexual courtship, heterosexual marriage, chaste widowhood, and strict motherhood, all in one story. So well does the younger partner bring up his lover's child that he earns the name of a "male Mencius's mother." (The mother of Mencius was the archetype of the woman who devotes her life to her son's moral education.) The story has a quality that might be called comic sensationalism, achieved by pushing a ribald imagination to its limits. (A minor example is *Operas* 9, about the man who prayed for a son.) In this story, the younger partner castrates himself as a gesture of gratitude to his lover, to retain his youthful looks and remove the threat to their relationship of his growing masculinity.

If the title *Silent Operas* indicates that Li Yu thought of his fiction in relation to drama, the title *Twelve Structures* has at first sight a more prosaic justification: a *lou*—a storied building, bower, pavilion, tower, for which the term "structure" is much too general—appears in each story. In fact, the structure, in addition to functioning as an element of the plot, also symbolizes one of the story's meanings. It reflects part of the author's vision, as natural scenery commonly does in European fiction. The choice of a building to express Li's symbolism was natural enough; he was a passionate builder himself and used the builder as a symbol of the literary artist. Furthermore, a building, as a made object, can express the mind and purpose of a character, something that is important in stories propounding a philosophy of life. The buildings have a variety of different uses. In *Structures* 1, with the mirrorlike juxtaposition of its two halves, the pavilion accounts for and symbolizes the love affair that begins there. In *Structures* 3, with its separate tiers for intercourse with human beings, culture, and spirits, respectively, it symbolizes the mind of the wise man who built it. And in *Structures* 12, situated where the town meets the country, it symbolizes the ideal of the reclusive man who wants to influence society without fully joining it.

The *Structures* stories are written in as many as six chapters, permitting a complex plot to be treated coherently. But the main effect is a multiplication of chapter beginnings and endings, which provide even more opportunity for narratorial comment. Most of the prologues in *Structures* are of the same kind as in *Operas*—tightly organized, witty essays that consist of an initial arresting statement, its elaboration into an argument, historical examples and canonical quotations, conclusions, and advice, followed by a link to the main story. But there is also a new kind of prologue in *Structures*, one that proceeds by association and symbolism rather than by logic, the outstanding example of which is *Structures* 4. And in both kinds of prologue, as well as in the epilogue and the chapter endings, there is far more personal reference.

The *Structures* stories are full of references to Li Yu. At least four prologues contain his poems, and some even refer to his own experience. In the prologue to *Structures* 4, he appears as raconteur. "I once made a jesting remark," he says in the linking passage between the prologue and the main story, "which everyone told me was worth preserving and now, dear readers, I would like to ask you your opinion. All frivolous, lewd things have to have something proper about them if they are to last . . ." He is apologizing for the eroticism of the story on the grounds of the procreative function of sex. *Structures* 6 has an oblique, personal prologue of a similar kind. It begins with a poem the author says he wrote twenty

years earlier while buying flowers in the market. The contrast between
the exquisite flowers and their vulgar setting, the marketplace, leads him
circuitously to his subject—antique shops and the good taste they may
represent. *Structures* 12 includes in its prologue not only his poems but
much of his personal experience. *Structures* 2 pleads in its prologue that
parents consult their daughter's interest in arranging a marriage rather
than indulge a whim. "The girl can't arrange her own future and has to
bear all the consequences of her parents' virtuous act. No one else dares
put this argument forward, so you must allow us bolder spirits to do
so."[34]

The information offered by the narrator is not of the old platitudinous
kind. It comes very close to, and sometimes coincides with, what Li
himself writes in his essays. The prologue to *Structures* 10 recommends
abstention from beef and dog meat, which come from the two friends of
man, as a feasible solution for people who cannot abstain from meat
altogether. According to his *Casual Expressions,* this was the practice in
Li's own family.[35] As the narrator has come to resemble a persona of the
author, his opinions have come to resemble Li Yu's, in jest or earnest. To
a great extent, the old narratorial formulae have been changed also, to
suit the new, individual voice.

Structures 1, "The Pavilion of Combined Reflections," exemplifies the
power of the concept in this new kind of Li Yu story. Two men with contrasting attitudes toward life marry into the same family. One is a Confucian moralist of the strict school, a stern father and husband with
puritanical views on morality, while the other is the bohemian, libertine,
and man of talent of seventeenth-century fiction and drama. The puritan
has a daughter, the libertine a son. At length, the two men's differences
lead to a rupture, and they divide the property neatly between themselves. But the children, although deprived of a chance to meet, fall in
love with each other's reflections in the pond that divides the property.
The libertine father comes upon his son's love poems, but although he is
delighted that his son has been having an affair, he is unable to arrange a
marriage between the cousins.

Between these polar types stands a mutual friend who is flexible,
unlike the puritan, and yet no libertine. He is surnamed Lu, meaning
"route" or "way," and his personal name is Ziyou, which phonetically
suggests naturalness and freedom. He it is who works out the ingenious
scheme by which the lovesick boy and girl are married. When the puritanical father finally accepts the fait accompli, the families are reconciled, and the barriers between the properties come down. The concept
dominates the story absolutely, expressing itself in a riot of symbolical
symmetries.

The contrast between puritan and libertine appears several times in Li

Yu's plays, notably in *Be Careful About Your Betrothal* (*Shen luanjiao*).
One soliloquy runs: "As I see it, men of talent and morality belong to two
distinct types: those who uphold libertinism and strenuously oppose
puritanism, and those who do the opposite. In my own opinion, Confucianism is by no means barren of enjoyment; Heaven's design is present
even in our idle feelings. In the last analysis, only by combining libertinism and puritanism can one rank as a scholar or man of letters." In
The She-Phoenixes Seek Their Mates (*Huang qiu feng*), libertinism as the
quest for sexual pleasure is contrasted with frivolity and then accommodated with puritanism. "The word *fengliu* [here meaning "sexual
pleasure," more generally "libertinism"] was given us by Heaven," says
Lü, the hero. "If one is to remain a puritan, one must marry a peerless
beauty in order to satisfy one's desire for sexual pleasure and to exhaust
one's sex drive. Only then can one preserve righteousness all the rest of
one's life and not follow in the paths of wickedness . . ."[36]

Structures 3, "The Tower of the Three Teachers," is an ingenious
mystery story with a natural explanation. The novel idea, which it asserts
as a reality principle, is that it is best not to lay up property for your
children or even to pass it on to them but to sell it before you die. Never
mind if it sells too cheaply—you will get a reputation for magnanimity.
Your children will not be encumbered with the need to maintain it, incur-
ring filial guilt and public ridicule if they fail. The story is as notable for
the clarity and patterning of its ideas as is "The Pavilion of Combined
Reflections." Yu is the wise man who keeps aloof from society in order to
indulge in the traditional artistic and other pursuits of the Chinese intellectual. Tang is the nouveau riche, miserly, avaricious. The two types,
although familiar, have never been so clearly delineated. Yu is "a man of
reclusive temperament with a taste for literature but no desire for
recognition"[37] who has given up any thought of public service and takes
his pleasure in poetry and wine. All his energies are devoted to building
gardens and pavilions. The three things that matter in life, he says, are
the house a man lives in, the bed he sleeps in, and the coffin he is buried
in, but in these objects, one must insist on perfection. Yu's perfectionism
makes him pull buildings down and start again, which gets him into
trouble with his creditors. He represents, of course, the creative artist. In
the one building remaining to him, there are three floors; the first is for
"learning from people," the second for "learning from the past," and the
third, fitted only with an incense burner and a Taoist classic, is for
meditation, for "learning from heaven." Hence the name of both
building and story—"The Three Teachers," a title that indicates the
hierarchy of men's contacts with the universe.

Tang, his neighbor, is the nearest thing to a villain we find in Li Yu's
stories. He extends more and more credit, knowing that Yu's perfectionism will eventually drive him into selling at a bargain. He is inartistic

as well as greedy. Having obtained Yu's main house at a fifth of its real price, he attempts to improve it but succeeds only in ruining the effect. "Just as in a fine landscape one has only to add a plant here or take away a tree there to destroy the artistic conception, this house, because of the changes they made, lost all of the artistry it had possessed. They succeeded only in turning precious metal into base—the very opposite of what they had intended."[38]

Structures 9 is the most patently philosophical of Li Yu's stories. It is concerned with the stoic side of epicurean thinking, the philosophy of low expectations to which Li Yu adhered. If you are blessed with good fortune, regard it as temporary and expect the worst. The reward for this practical philosophy is that you will avoid major disappointment and live to a healthy old age. This is a psychological stance toward life that is to be judged by its effectiveness in giving pleasure and avoiding pain. The protagonist of these views is one Duan, a man in no hurry to take the examinations or get married. "In general, he was of a placid temperament. He was circumspect about his good fortune and constantly kept in mind the thought of a disastrous outcome. Hence he took each day as it came and never entertained any hopes or desires for the future."[39] When he passes the examination, he is afraid that he may have infringed the Creator's taboo, apparently conceiving of every successful man as marked for a fall. His methods of dealing with life are two: modesty or circumspection about good fortune and contentedness with poverty, the latter achieved by reflecting on worse possibilities. Parting, he tells his wife, is worse than death, because parting excites hopes and longings, while death puts them to rest. People longing for each other grow old before their time.

He applies the idea to his wife before setting off on a dangerous mission to the Jurchen, alienating her affections by a display of calculated heartlessness. He applies his own psychological methods to himself during his torture by the Jurchen in order to retain his mental and physical health. He returns home to find a resentful wife, who is, however, both plump and healthy. He manages to explain his ruse to her by demonstrating that a cruel letter he wrote her from captivity was really a palindrome that, if read backward, forms a declaration of love. She takes him back into her affections, and their happiness is complete to the extent that Duan will allow it to be in his philosophy. At least they are free from worry. "The finest erotic device in the entire world," we are told by the narrator, "may be summed up in just one phrase, 'freedom from care.' All the potions peddled on the streets are just quack remedies designed to swindle us."[40]

Opposed to this somber figure is his friend Yu. (Both names reflect their natures.)[41] Yu is a self-styled gallant who cares only for love in marriage.

"We are bound by Confucian principles which inevitably fall short of stirring our emotions and appealing to our interest. That is why the sages who created the world opened up this way for us and placed it among the ethical relations, allowing people to free themselves of prudish restraint. Moreover, if there were no husband-wife relation among the Three Obligations, where would the ruler-subject and father-son relationships come from? How would we practice filial piety, friendship, loyalty, goodness? Clearly, marriage is the most important of the Five Relations and should be entered into as early and as well as possible. Beautiful wives are much harder to find than beautiful concubines, but when one has finally found one, that is the most delightful thing in all of Confucianism."[42]

Yu is a romantic, obsessed with making the perfect marriage and throwing himself headlong into it. The ethic he obeys, for all its gloss of Confucianism, is really that of qing, as Feng and Langxian have used the word. Li Yu is as skeptical about the ethic of qing as he is about self-sacrificial morality; both, in their absoluteness, run counter to his philosophy.

When Yu, who is sent on the same mission as Duan, has to part from his wife, he makes extravagant promises and expresses tender sentiments. As a result, the life of separation tells on him. Love constitutes his life, and he cannot be without it: "Just to think of what they said to each other in bed, of their passion beneath the quilt, made his soul melt and almost expire." Duan tries to explain his method to Yu, as they languish amongst the Jurchen. Yu was not quite convinced. "He may be a very wise man," he said to himself, "but he is simply too callous. If I were in his position, even if I were able to conceive of such a plan, I could never carry it out." Finally, prematurely old at thirty, he returns to find his wife dead. He at last realizes the truth of Duan's theory; Duan's are "the words of a true gallant, not of a puritan."[43]

There is a metaphysical side to the theory as well as a psychological one. The Creator, Li Yu's constant reference, tends to ration happiness and abhors the hubris that springs from good fortune. Yu loses two wives, the narrator tells us, "because his passion for sexual love was too wholehearted, the Creator having a perverse desire to topple all heroes and prevent people from fulfilling their hearts' desires."[44] But Yu succeeds brilliantly in his official career, in which he has never invested any hopes.

The prologue of *Structures* 12 is autobiographical to an exceptional degree. The hero is described as a good writer, a man of placid temperament, unambitious, with the inclination to become a recluse. He is unsuccessful on several occasions in the examinations. At thirty, noticing the first gray hairs, he concludes that it is time for him to withdraw. He burns his writings, keeping only his agricultural books and implements. His paintings and calligraphy he gives to others. When people ask him why he is giving up his writing and art, he replies: "In today's society, true art does not bring one recognition; for that, one must beg help from officials. In calligraphy and painting, one does not need to be really expert to be admired by society . . ."[45] He is a forthright man who loves to point out people's mistakes, and it is for this quality that he is cherished by his cousin Yin.

The rather simple story consists of the recluse's finding the social intercourse of the town onerous and moving into the country, and of his friends' good-natured conspiracy to make country life so unbearable that he will move back. He is badgered and even arrested, but it is all a great hoax, for his friends install him in a house they have built for him just outside town. He is touched by their concern, even if it has taken a strange form, and settles there. Yin builds a chalet next door to gain the benefit of his company and advice. The story ends with the narrator praising Yin rather than the recluse, because the capacity to accept advice is rarer than the capacity to give it. In a graceful final note, Li Yu observes that the usefulness of his books depends on the same receptivity in his readers.

The story anticipates some of the themes of *The Scholars*: the aversion to the ladder of success and the network of social relations, the concern for artistic standards, and the desire for personal cultivation. But in this case, the idea is too weighty for the slight fictional vehicle designed to carry it. A modern scholar remarks that the prologue is a fond reverie by Li of his years in the country and that the main story embodies his hopes for the future.[46] Perhaps the story also reflects his wish for patronage, for the semirecluse is set up by friends who value his advice. It is clear, in any case, that he is a persona of the author's, like the hero of "The Tower of the Three Teachers." The two personae are broadly similar: each is a lofty, deep-thinking person free from wordly ambitions. The grave, reclusive counsellor must be added to Li Yu's various other personae—the inventive genius, the suppliant begging for patronage, the comic master dazzling his audience, the epicurean savoring his sensory delights.

Interesting as his philosophical stories are, the finest, in my opinion, are those in which he gives his peculiar cast to more traditional types. *Structures* 4, "The Summer Pavilion," for example, is basically a romantic comedy in which a handsome young man wins a beautiful bride. In addition to the enterprising young lovers one expects of Li Yu, it has the stern, puritanical father of "The Pavilion of Combined Reflections" and also a novel contrivance that appears to everyone except the hero and the reader to be of supernatural origin.

Its outstanding feature is the tableau of girls picking water lilies. The poem that begins the prologue is on this traditional pastoral theme, and the narrator enumerates the aspects of the water lily that symbolize girls as lovers and wives. The idea and the tableau are picked up again at the beginning of the main story, when the young girls of the household, attending a class taught by the daughter of the house, sneak away to skinny dip in the pond while their mistress slumbers in the pavilion on a summer afternoon. The tableau is lovingly and sensuously described, with an occasional comic touch as the giggling girls examine each other's bodies "like the feudal lords of the seven states comparing each other's treasures."[47]

Unknown to the girls and to the reader, this tableau has been relished by a young gallant in a far-off temple who is equipped with that newfangled invention, the telescope. The tableau, with the girls' subsexual romping in the water and the daughter's punishment of the ringleaders, is described several times in the story, once later in Chapter 1, by the gallant to the matchmaker, and then in Chapter 2, by the matchmaker to the daughter. It is taken up again at the end of the story, when the narrator tells us that the gallant had planned to marry the daughter not merely to secure the "queen of the blossoms" but also to deflower the other blossoms as well, whose secrets he already knows. The tableau is both an integral part of the plot and an image through which Li Yu's delicate eroticism is conveyed.

One can see from this story how he came to elevate dramatic construction so. The first of its three chapters is told from the viewpoint of the daughter's household and ends on a note of mystery: How has the unseen claimant for her hand come to know all about her, even to the skinny-dipping episode and the details of the little girls' bodies? Is he man or ghost? The second chapter essays an answer:

> I assume the gentle reader has not been able to guess how Jiren came to know everything, so let me explain: it was neither man nor ghost that was responsible for these events, and the account was neither completely false nor strictly true; it was all due to a certain object that served him as an eye, by the use of which any flesh-and-blood being can impersonate a disembodied immortal without any fear that people will doubt his word. Although this object did not originate in China, it was something that persons with an interest in exotica would be likely to possess; it was certainly no figment of the imagination.[48]

It was Jiren's achievement to see the possibilities of the telescope, which had hitherto been thought of as a mere curio. With its aid, he surveys the unmarried girls of the district whom he could otherwise never have evaluated.

If Chapter 1 is told from the daughter's side, Chapter 2 is from the gallant's. At its end, in one of Li Yu's reflexive asides, the narrator says he wants to slow down in order to increase the suspense. Although the reader is now in possession of the essential facts, the daughter is not, and the comedy of Chapter 3 arises from her belief that Jiren really is an immortal. She ceases to worry, believing he can accomplish anything. When danger threatens, however, she is quick to fabricate a dream in which her dead mother names Jiren as her husband. After she is married to Jiren, she is at first reluctant to engage in lovemaking, thinking her husband a being of more rarified tastes. The couple acknowledge the telescope's contribution by enshrining it and treating it as a magic oracle, and it never fails to give helpful solutions to their problems. But lest we assume that Li Yu has abandoned his naturalistic stance, he adds: "It is clear that in places where spirit is concentrated, earth and vegetation can produce magical manifestations. It has always been the case that prayer to the gods or prayer to Buddha amounts merely to praying to one's own mind. It does not mean that there really are gods or bodhisattvas."[49]

In justifying his eroticism, the narrator explains something of the sexual psychology of hero and heroine. The hero's passions are aroused by seeing the little girls frolicking in the lily pond and then inflamed by the sight of their wrathful mistress as she appears on the scene. For her part, the heroine is aware of her sexual maturity and careful to banish any provocative thoughts. But after his proposal, her passions can no longer be held in check, and she languishes in illness while despairing of marriage. Sexual love is implicitly recognized as a natural and powerful element of life but not as the spiritual force it comes to be in the ethic of qing.

Structures 7 is about Li Yu's outstanding female character, the maid Nenghong, a resourceful, self-confident young woman whose precursor is the peasant wife of *Operas* 5. Its social paradox lies in the fact that a mere maid dominates the family she serves and actually arranges the marriage of the daughter of the house and of herself to the same man, Pei Seven. Brilliant maids have a long history in Chinese literature, particularly in the soubrette figure of the drama (Nenghong chose her own name in imitation of Hongniang in *The Western Chamber*), but this character is a remarkable development.

Nenghong is at first against Pei's suit of her mistress, but she changes her mind when, in a brilliant stroke, he pays court to her instead. "Go and tell him," she says to the matchmaker,

> "that if he had just been after the mistress, he would not even have been able to marry me, but since he wants to marry me, he need not give up all hope of the mistress. The mistress and I are on an equal footing; there's no question of precedence between us. His family and ours are sworn enemies, and if he had used an outside matchmaker, he'd never have gotten anywhere. Fortunately, the whole family realizes that I have quite a lot of common sense. When the time comes to take some action, they don't ask me formally for my opinion, but they always sound me out, without quite realizing they are doing so. If I say go ahead, they go ahead. If I say better not, they end up unable to do it, even if they had already decided in favor."[50]

Nenghong is the practical schemer who manipulates others for generally good ends, including her own interests. She exploits the family's credulity by bribing a soothsayer to set forth prescriptions for the mistress's bridegroom that she knows only Pei can meet. And after the marriage, she arranges some fake dream interpretations that induce the mistress to propose that Nenghong be raised to the position of wife. In her most notable action, she forces Pei, as a condition of her help, to sign a secret contract to marry her, a contract that spells out her precise conditions. It is one of Li Yu's little surprises that the signing of the contract is the sole purpose of a midnight rendezvous to which she summons Pei and to which he comes expecting to make love. No such thing; she is a practical person, not a romantic. Her freedom from conventional behavior is shown on Pei's and her mistress's wedding night, when the mistress is being shy about going to bed with her husband. Pei grows impatient, and thus it is Nenghong who is the first to celebrate the wedding. The narrator issues a dire warning about the perils of ignoring reality in favor of convention.

As in most of Li Yu's stories, there is much reflexive comment on the progress of the narration. At the end of Chapter 3, the narrator says that telling the story "is just like asking people a riddle. If one were simply to give the answer without making them guess, they would find it exceedingly dull."[51] The same statement is found in *Casual Expressions,*[52] where it refers to the function of suspense in contructing a play.

Structures 5 is also on a well-established theme, that of the thief of genius, the sublime confidence man, of which there are examples in the *Shuihu* and among the early vernacular stories. "Song Four Causes Trouble for Miser Zhang" influenced Ling Mengchu's romanticized "Lazy Dragon" (II.39), and both in turn influenced Li Yu's story. The elements it shares are: a brilliant young thief, who passes the initiation test set by his master; a series of brilliant coups, which include the deception of a stingy or boastful pawnbroker; his good-hearted nature (he is inclined to rob the rich and distribute his gains); his journey to the capital, which he undertakes to prove his mettle; his adept use of disguises and drugs; and his name, which constitutes a clever pun. In all three works, the story is told with suspense, and some of the thief's ploys have to be explained ex post facto.

Li Yu's variation is to present the thief as a sensualist. "All the famous prostitutes and most sophisticated catamites had had affairs with him."[53] Li Yu's thief also reforms of his own volition. Having reached the peak of his profession, he fears that his luck may change and decides to retire. At the same time, he meets a young singing girl whose husband had previously forced her into prostitution. The thief had been her first client. He had given her a sum of money and urged her to give up prostitution, but the husband had kept the money and sold her to a brothel. The thief now offers to buy her out. Her wish is to become a Buddhist nun, and so the thief buys a property that can be divided to make a nunnery. Impressed by her devoutness, he decides to turn the other half into a Taoist temple and study the art of becoming an immortal himself. He pulls a final coup to get the rebuilding completed and sets about his devotions.

Li Yu is not interested in Buddhism or Taoism as religions of abnegation or transcendence but, as in *Carnal Prayer Mat*, as a mythical means of atonement. Most of his uses of religion are comic. Why, for instance, did the thief choose Taoism over Buddhism? "Because the things he had done were like the feats of an immortal, things such as ordinary persons would not even guess at, he concluded that it would be much easier to learn to be an immortal than a bodhisattva." When at last the hero and heroine ascend into the sky, the narrator tells us: "The only things I do not know are in what positions in the East or West Heavens they are installed and what grade of immortal he is and what rank of bodhisattva she is. Around the middle, I would guess."[54]

Of all Li Yu's stories, this has the clearest links to his novel, and I believe the story served as its prototype.[55] There is, first of all, the marvelous thief. In *Carnal Prayer Mat*, he is called Superior to Kunlun, after the Kunlun Slave of the famous Tang tale, and he resembles this thief in his exploits, his amours, and his character. When the hero offers to buy out the singing girl, he actually invokes the name of the Kunlun Slave. There is also the wife forced by her husband to become a prostitute as well as the climactic meeting in the brothel.

Structures 6, "The Hall of Gathered Refinements," is an urbane treatment of a homosexual ménage à trois set against the historical background of Yan Shifan's tyranny. The three men run some high-class boutiques in Peking where they sell books, incense, flowers, and antiques, the four most refined products that can be offered for sale. Yan tries to obtain the youngest partner for himself, but the young man refuses out of loyalty to his "husbands." Yan then has an elderly eunuch who loves flower arrangements, the young man's specialty, drug and castrate him. The young man gains an elaborate revenge by helping to bring charges against Yan to the Emperor and then gloats over Yan at his execution.

The description of the shop and the living arrangements of the three men is light and amusing. A harsh note is struck as Yan's henchman brings pressure to bear on the two older men. Yan has taken a great number of antiques on approval, and his henchman insists to the two senior partners that the young man collect the money personally.

"If you don't have the money collected, it will be taken as a deliberate affront. Is he a customer you can afford to antagonize or insult? If he wanted to sleep with your wives, I could understand your reluctance. Naturally you would risk your lives to stop him. But all we are talking about is a friend of yours, whom you need send along only for Lord Yan's delectation, just like an antique or a painting. Even if it comes back a little the worse for wear, it still won't have lost all its value. Why drop thousands of taels because of a cup of vinegar?

And over and above the money you will have lost, other things will start happening to you; you will never feel quite secure again. I sincerely advise you against a course of action that will bring you nothing but harm."[56]

Li Yu's threatening figures are men in power, as in the portrait of Yuan in *Operas* 1.

In its most shocking episode, the story displays the comic sensationalism that makes some readers turn away from Li Yu in distaste. The castration scene is described as follows:

> The eunuch winked at one of his servants, who substituted some drugged wine and poured it into the young man's cup. Ruxiu drank it and soon began to grow limp. His head lolled forward and he slumped in the easy chair like Chen Tuan in his age-long sleep. Eunuch Sha laughed and called out: "Come on, lads, go to it!" Before the drinking had started, he had hidden the castrators behind the rock garden, and at his summons they now came forward. One tore off the young man's trousers and another bunched up his organs in one hand, and with a light deft cut, sliced them off and threw them on the ground, where they were gulped by the Pekinese dog.[57]

At the end of the chapter, which follows soon after, the narrator asks, "Gentle reader, having read this far, are you able to steel your nerves and feel no anguish at all on behalf of the little shopkeeper?"[58] The reader is more likely to be puzzled by Li Yu's determination to be comic at all costs.

Structures 10 and 11 are concerned, directly or indirectly, with the recent past, the China of rebel slaughter and Manchu invasion. Story 10, the inferior story, deals with the subject directly. Like all writers who accepted Manchu rule, Li Yu employed the horrors of the rebellions as an indirect means of praising the Manchu deliverers. But here he goes further. His hero "thought that in the turmoil of war, he could not hope for a reunion with his wife, and that he would have to wait for an Emperor with a true mandate to emerge and pacify the country first. When the dynasty was established . . ." Starving, he approaches a Manchu camp and is given meat to eat. The story's subject is the noble action of the Manchu general who appreciates the wife's self-sacrificial goodness, dissuades her from suicide, and gives her back to her husband. "This virtuous act," comments the narrator, "is the most memorable thing that has occurred since the dynasty was founded. My only regret is that the general's name could not be ascertained; I did not presume to make one up, and so I have merely referred to him as the General."[59]

The idea behind the story is that moral judgment must take account of circumstance and motive. The heroine has a baby boy, the only one to carry on the family line, and her husband and his family urge upon her the idea that, in this special case, she should sacrifice her chastity to the rebels if necessary, in order to safeguard the baby. She is dissuaded only with the greatest difficulty from her belief that suicide is the only moral course.

The prologue of *Structures* 11 continues the argument with an anecdote about a poem, found in a rebel camp, that falls into the hands of a man of letters. He realizes at once that it must have been written by some high-born woman lamenting her fate; dishonored, she was afraid even to die, because in death she would meet her husband. The little story has an immediacy we rarely find in Li Yu. If a high-born woman could curse the Lord of Heaven for allowing the ruin of country, family, and honor, asks the narrator, how must the inarticulate commoner have felt?

Despite its account of rebel atrocities at the end of the Song, the main story is an extravaganza of everything Li Yu has to offer: comic ideas and imagery, intricate construction, surprises, shocks. It clearly parodies the structure of contemporary drama. Unlike other Li Yu stories, which rely largely on human ingenuity, it is a welter of coincidence. The narrator refers to the subject twice. Before the main story, he praises "the Creator's cleverness in arranging people's destinies,"[60] and in a passage near the beginning of Chapter 4, he remarks:

> As it turns out, the Creator's cleverness is a hundred times that of man. It is just as if he were deliberately arranging events so that someone can turn them into a play or a story. He has separated the two couples and then reunited them. He has reunited them and then separated them. What mental energy it must have taken! These events can be termed novel and ingenious to the ultimate degree![51]

Here are some of the coincidences: A young man, abducted from his family as a child, adopts a father who turns out to be his real father. He then adopts as his mother a woman who turns out to be his real mother. Finally, he buys from the rebels a girl who turns out to be his lost fiancée. The story is full of shocking novelties combined with a little ribaldry. A rich old man whose son has been abducted as a child decides to adopt an heir, and in order to find one who is not after his money, he dresses in rags and goes about the country offering himself for adoption as a father. There is also a human market, in which the rebels sell off, in sacks, all the women they have captured. And finally, there is the identification of the lost son, whose only distinctive feature is that he was born with a single testicle, a ribald variation on the birthmarks by which identities are conventionally established in the dramatic romance.[62] If ever a story deserved the standard praise accorded to Li Yu's work, it is this.

Zhuoyuan's *Cup That Reflects the World*

The exuberance of Li Yu's comic imagination was more than matched by the author of *The Cup That Reflects the World* (*Zhao shi bei*),[63] written a few years later. But although both men specialized in social comedy, their work differs in almost every other respect. Li Yu's is the comedy of concept, in which the paradoxical idea governs the story absolutely, so that its plot is neatly illustrative and its characters are embodied attitudes. The *Cup* author's comedy is perceptual, arising from his observation of society. His imagination focuses on the comic scene, not the comic plot, and his stories appear loosely structured beside those of his predecessors. His fiction also lacks the element of personal reference found in Li Yu's, and although it takes a satirical view of its society, it gives no hint of the political conditions of its time.

The title refers to the magic cup in which King Jamshyd of Persia could see the whole world revealed.[64] The author is known only by a pseudonym as the Master of the Zhuoyuan Pavilion. The preface refers to a visit to Hangchow "this winter" by Ding Yaokang, author of *Sequel to the Jin Ping Mei* (*Xu Jin Ping Mei*), a fact that seems to date the work to 1661.[65] Its four long stories are each of a single chapter, though they list several paired headings beneath the title; this appears to be a way of indicating the richness of the story's content without the encumbrance of chapter divisions. The stories are written in a lively, colloquial style which exploits classical allusions for their comic value and makes free use of rhetorical devices. The prologues are brief expositions that suggest the worldly, earthbound wit of Ling Mengchu rather than Li Yu's farcical play of ideas. Apart from the prologues, the author's use of the mode of comment is sparing; for occasional stretches, he works in the vein of character irony,[66] the dominant technique of *The Scholars*, to which this collection bears a slight resemblance.

"True Love in the Garden of the Seven Pines," the first story, is a satirical version of the "brilliant and beautiful" romance. The naïve hero consciously seeks a grand amour under the influence of romantic literature. The story's distinction lies in its social satire, particularly of the young man, who is an aesthetic snob as well as a moral prig. Although, in his naïveté and romantic passion, he is subject to one comic mishap after another, his intellectual ability is never questioned. He is the brilliant young man seen quizzically, like the hero of Ling Mengchu's "Chess Champions."

"Deception in the Baihe Quarter," the second story, is a savage satire of the pseudointellectual who makes a living as a guest (*youke*), visiting people in high positions around the country, impressing them with his talents and receiving patronage, an activity in which Li Yu had some experience. The prologue is on the distinction between the authentic and the inauthentic in life and literature: a man "ought to mold his character from his very bones, to bring forth his writing from his heart, and to wring his wealth from the calluses on his hands. If his character is not molded from his bones, it will be base; if his writing is not brought forth from the heart, it will be meretricious; and if his wealth is not wrung from his calluses, it will be worthless."[67] The pseudointellectual is bent on wringing money from anywhere but his calluses. This is the weakest of the four stories; the author's distaste for the charlatan is so strong as to turn the work into a tirade.

The other two stories show a progressively wilder imagination. One is full of exotic lore, and the other is a scatological fantasy. Story 3, "On a Journey to Vietnam a Jade Horse Miniature is Exchanged for Crimson Velvet," is intent on comparing the customs of the Vietnamese favorably with those of the Chinese. Its exotic feature is the manner in which the crimson dye is obtained from that fabulous animal, the ape-like *xingxing*, a process of which there are many fanciful descriptions in anecdotal literature.[68]

The hero of the final story, "The Miser Makes a Fortune from New Pits," is the head of a family that becomes known as the New Pits Mus. They live in a remote valley, to which night soil, the main source of fertilizer, cannot be imported. Hence such night soil as the village itself produces becomes all the more precious.

> Patriarch Mu came up with an idea. "On my trips to town," he said to himself, "I see cesspits all along the road, although we have none in our village. We are obviously wasting this precious resource. What I have in mind will prove a more lucrative business than any other I know of." He summoned tile workers and had three cesspits dug below the large room at the front of his house. He divided the room into cubicles and had the walls whitewashed. Then he bustled off to town to ask a relative of his for a quantity of paintings and calligraphy to stick on the walls.
>
> "Everything is ready to go. All I need is the name tablet," he said, surveying his handiwork. So he invited the local elementary school teacher to think up a name. The teacher thought for a while. "I test my pupils all the time," he said, "but the lines all come from classical poets. Now you are asking me to come up with something entirely of my own. That's murderously difficult!" The patriarch then brought out wine and tidbits as if making a formal request for a literary composition. The teacher could scarcely refuse. And so, with his wine cup in his hand, he ran through his mind the names of all the halls in and around town but could not come up with a single title. Then a thought struck him. "Hold off with the wine for a moment," he announced with great satisfaction. "I want to compose the title before indulging myself." Mu promptly set to work grinding up the pungent ink. The teacher nibbled the end of his brush, dipped it in the ink until it was fully loaded, and then, with immense care and concentration, wrote three characters.
>
> "Read it to me, won't you?" said Mu, "so that I can memorize it."
>
> "Here is your title—Nobilitas Hall," declared the teacher. Mu asked him to explain what it meant. The teacher had merely copied it from the memorial arch in front of Board Chairman Xu's house in town and had no idea what it meant, and so had to improvise. "It is a very apt title," he said, "highly auspicious for business success. There is a classical allusion behind it which I will explain another time." He departed without even drinking his wine.
>
> Old Mu was thoroughly embarrassed. He prepared two boxes of gifts and went to the school to thank him. "This is much too considerate of you," said the teacher. "Why go to all this expense a second time on my account?"
>
> "There is another matter on which I would like to enlist your help," said Mu, drawing a hundred or more sheets of red paper from his sleeve.

"You want me to write a couplet for your gate?"

"No," said Mu. "I have recently set up these three lavatories and I am afraid people may not know about them. I want to post these notices to attract custom. I'd like you to write the following: 'The sweetly scented New Pits of the Mu family respectfully solicit the patronage of gentlemen from near and far. Toilet paper provided by the establishment.'"

The teacher realized that the text was already prepared, that he had merely to copy it out, and that there was no problem. In a few hours he had finished the task. (pp. 70-71)

The New Pits prosper, just as Mu had hoped. (Money and excrement are implicitly associated.) To his chagrin, however, his son enrolls in the Academy of Gambling, in which the text, taught in the manner of the Confucian classics, is none other than the *Classic of Cards* (*Pai jing*) by Feng Menglong. To Mu's son it comes as a revelation: "He had always thought of *madiao* as a game, but having heard the professor's exposition, he realized it was based on the grandest principles and was far more profound than mere literary composition."[69] But all of this has little to do with the story's announced theme (the danger of acting from anger) or with its outcome. Zhuoyuan, for his own satirical purposes, has begun the dismantling of the formal and moral framework of the traditional story.

9
Aina

It is appropriate to end this history with Aina's *Idle Talk under the Bean Arbor* (*Doupeng xianhua*)[1]—appropriate, but also misleading. As the last of the principal collections, his book marks a decisive break not merely with the compromise form that Feng and his contemporaries had adopted, and Li Yu and the *Cup* author had modified, but also with the basic model and method of vernacular fiction itself. However, the vernacular story did not come to a stop with Aina. Oblivious to his changes, it continued to be written throughout the eighteenth and nineteenth centuries, sometimes well, most often indifferently. The most notable examples are described in an appendix that will give some perspective on the genre's later history.

The author of *Idle Talk under the Bean Arbor* is given as "Aina jushi," which may mean either "the recluse Aina" or "the Buddhist layman Aina." "Aina" means a Buddhist cassock woven with artemisia and hence favors the interpretation "layman." But although the commentator refers to the author as "Man of the Way Aina," he also compares him to Han Yu as a scourge of Buddhism. Thus, it is best to take "jushi" in a neutral meaning. The commentator provides a little other information: Aina had traveled widely and written numerous poems about scenic places, and his poetry and plays were well known to the public.[2] A highly allusive preface refers to the author's brilliance, his frustration in his studies, and his wide reading. Despite the claim that Aina was a celebrated author, he is probably to be identified as one Wang Mengji, an obscure Hangchow writer known to us only as the reviser of a novel about Ji Dian (Ji the Crazy), the eccentric Buddhist saint.[3] Even if he was not Wang himself, Aina must certainly have been one of Wang's friends.

Wang Mengji's revision of the Ji Dian novel was published in 1668, and it is likely that *Idle Talk* appeared soon afterward. Its elaborate first edition seems to be a product of the seventeenth century.[4] A play, *Idle Dramas under the Bean Arbor* (*Doupeng xianxi*), which dramatizes three of the stories told in *Idle Talk*, survives in a Kangxi (1662-1722) edition.[5]

Moreover, the frame story of *Idle Talk* is set not in the first decades of the Qing dynasty, but after a considerable period, with the result that only the older people present can remember the rebellions of the 1630s and 1640s.[6]

Framework

Aina introduces his book as a continuation in narrative form of a volume entitled *Bean Arbor Verses* (*Doupeng yin*) by a fellow townsman of an earlier generation: "But I didn't care to write poetry, and so I sought out some amusing stories instead, which I casually arranged into a number of chapters, with the aim of extending the meaning implicit in the *Bean Arbor*."[7]

A bean arbor is the setting in which all of the book's stories are told. It is a simple frame of bamboo poles, with strings for runner beans to climb along, which serves as a refuge from the heat for people of little or no means. As the weather turns hot and the beans provide some shade, the locals, including the owner of the bean arbor, a schoolmaster or two, and a number of youths, men, and women (though no stories are told by women, and their presence seems to be forgotten) gather to talk and tell stories. The book purports to record twelve such meetings at various times between the spring and autumn of one year. At every meeting but the twelfth, one or two stories are told as part of the discussion; at the twelfth, a teacher from the public school in the county town comes to the bean arbor under the impression that a philosopher Dou—he mistakes the word for "bean" for a man's surname—is holding forth there. A slightly absurd figure, he is only too happy to stay and deliver a rigid, neo-Confucian discourse. His visit worries the group; with attention now focused on them, they are concerned that their meetings will come to the ear of authorities cracking down on heresies and seditious activity. It is autumn, anyway, and they resolve to hold no more meetings. Symbolically, the bean arbor collapses at that very moment, as someone leans too heavily against one of its uprights.

The twelve meetings under the bean arbor constitute a frame story, the first in the history of Chinese fiction. It is fruitless to speculate as to why the frame story had not appeared earlier, but it is worth noting that its use in this book did not lead to any imitations.

The narratorial situation is more or less specific, unlike the generalized situation of most vernacular fiction. In the account of each meeting, there is a background narrator and one or more foreground narrators; in all, at least nine different narrators are employed. The most important of the foreground narrators is the old tutor who is responsible for one of the two stories of Chapter 1, the one story of Chapter 2, and for the reminiscences in Chapter 11. Two other people tell two stories apiece, in Chapters 3 and 4, and 6 and 7, respectively. We are not told who tells the stories of Chapters 5 and 9 and must assume he is to be equated with the background narrator and perhaps with the host of the bean arbor as well. Although the narrators are not named or closely described, they define themselves well enough to give point to their stories. There is a generation gap between the cynical and worldly-wise narrators of Chapters 1 and 2 and the romantic young men in their audience, who are tired of hearing stories about women as witches and femmes fatales. And the old tutor is asked by his host in the eleventh meeting to tell of a catastrophic period of history, the late Ming, which the audience are too young to have known themselves.

There are other disputes that have nothing to do with a difference in age. There are arguments over Buddhism; the young man who tells the savagely anti-Buddhist stories of Chapter 6 is himself attacked for being too harsh. The philosopher who blunders into the last meeting is criticized for his theory of a pitiless cosmos. The background narrator never attempts to adjudicate; it is left to the reader to evaluate the often conflicting stories. In addition to the disputes, there is much detail to solidify the setting of the frame story. There is joking and byplay among the audience. Some speakers are too bashful to speak and have to be urged and reassured. And some canny rustics absent themselves on one occasion for fear they will be expected to stand treat.

The setting is used to indicate the amount of time a story takes to tell and, much more importantly, the time that elapses between meetings. The twelve meetings span the life of the bean, from planting to withering, and time is fixed for us by reference to the growth of the plants and the development of flowers and pods. Much ingenuity is expended in deriving the topic of each chapter — associatively, symbolically, allusively — from the subject of beans. Chapter 11, for example, deals first with autumn, as the background narrator tells us why the season is crucial for the farmer. The sign of a good autumn is the growth of the white bean. Hence the luxuriant bean arbor means a good harvest. This is the time in which the peasants enjoy a brief spell before the bumper crops have to be brought in. How fortunate that the country is at peace! In time of war, all of this prosperity would be jeopardized. Beans thus symbolize a good harvest, and a good harvest is dependent on peace, and the subject of war and peace leads the narrator to ask the old tutor to set before the younger members of the audience the full horror of the late-Ming rebellions.

Not only does the *Bean Arbor* replace the stock narratorial situation and dispense with narratorial judgment; it also relaxes the requirements of plot so that even the lecture and discussion of Chapter 12 can qualify. The chapter ends in a new and arresting way. After the philosopher has departed and the bean arbor has collapsed, a member of the audience complains of the effect his Confucian pedantry will have on the moral stories by which he and his friends encourage Buddhist prayer. The old tutor, who has regaled his listeners with the horrors of civil war in the preceding session, replies in the last, remarkable sentence of the book, "This sort of bigotry has led to the destruction of many more things in the world than just this bean arbor!"[8] The ambiguities of this statement would not have been tolerated by earlier writers. Even if they could have entertained the thought, their fiction, ending on such a note, would have seemed to them incomplete.

Similarly, stories begin in an original fashion. Here is the beginning of the first of the two main stories of Chapter 10:

> Now let me turn to my main theme. It was just after the Dragon Boat Festival in the fifth month. The gentry had just attended the dragon boat races, and now there was little going on. Some of the idlers found life so quiet they were thoroughly bored. They gathered at spots along the Shantang river or at teahouses and antique stalls near the inner gate of Tiger Hill Temple, standing on one foot like egrets on the sand, waiting anxiously for someone they knew to happen by. Suddenly a small group of people approached from the outer gate. Leading the party was a gentleman who [a head-to-toe description of the group follows]. He came swaggering up the hill, but the idlers judged him to be from the Northwest and so paid him little attention. They watched as he went up to Thousand Man Rock, looked about him, and then climbed to the King of Heaven Temple and bowed four times before the image of Maitreya. A few junior monks with subscription books tucked under their arms came up and engaged him in talk, seeking a donation. (pp. 126-127)

On the focal level, this is completely new. If there are models for Aina's narrative, they would appear to be Classical prose and casual oral fiction (as distinct from the professional variety). His stories are indebted for their terseness and vivid diction to Classical ideals, but they also simulate the voice of the raconteur.

Some of the most memorable passages in his book are first-person accounts, often reported at second or third hand. Chapter 9 is notable for a prologue in which the background narrator (perhaps representing Aina) relates that he once spent several years in the capital and became well acquainted with its police force. (The institutions he mentions are those of the Ming.) He gives a direct account of the disclosures made to him by a police agent. The agent is speaking:

> "The robbers we arrest are often not the real culprits. Those we have arrested recently were all cultivated by us in advance and held in readiness, so that when the higher-ups put pressure on us, we were able to deliver."
> I was astonished. "Surely you can't cultivate robbers like so many melons or cabbages?" I asked. (p. 109)

After a detailed account of how the agents deliberately corrupt naïve young men, the agent continues:

"Then a few veteran thieves are brought in to tempt the youth with stories of
how easy it is to get money. Hardly aware of what is happening, he is inveigled
into some quiet place and pulls off a couple of jobs. With easy money to hand,
he relaxes, eats well, fills out — like a regular haohan. Then if something goes
wrong in Peking and there is a bit of an emergency, they quietly arrest him to
take the rap. The stolen goods don't check out, and the youth is being framed,
of course, but these young fellows are ready to throw their lives away and feel
no resentment at all. Trussed up on the execution ground, they still insist on
singing their last songs, while the real professional thieves who pull off the
robberies are safe and sound in their homes. At the end of each month, and
then again at the end of the quarter, a little money is collected and donated to
them. After all, if the real thieves were arrested, what would the agents and
chiefs do?" (pp. 109-110)

Meaning

Aina's fiction is not to be judged by the usual standards. He is more concerned with the striking descriptive fact than with the presentation of action and character, with the story's interpretation rather than with
dramatizing it for the reader. Brilliant vignettes, vivid details lodge in the
mind — the classic virtues of anecdote. His object is the fiction of ideas,
although in a different sense from Li Yu's philosophical stories. (The
commentator traces fiction back to the *Zhuang Zi* in order to put Aina's
stories in their proper context.)[9] The absence of comment, and hence of
authoritative judgment, in his fiction means that all the various sides of a
problem can be presented. He revels in the luxury of ambiguity.

Aina wrote no stories of the standard Confucian virtues, except
loyalty, about which he is skeptical. When he is concerned with morality
at all, it is the morality of quixotic altruism, like that of the knight-
errant. Nor does he favor the ideals of romantic love or otherworldly
withdrawal. His gaze is fixed on the larger, philosophical issues of the
nature of historical causation. Is the universe beneficent or maleficent or
both (that is, a dualism)? Is it merely uncaring? In his bleakest moments,
he imagines a kind of Malthusian universe that acts mechanically to curb
overpopulation with new wars. The reason for his anguished concern — it
appears indirectly from his fiction — was the Manchu invasion and oc-
cupation of China. Under the shock of this inexplicable event, his fiction
questions the very basis of belief in a morally determined universe. His
concern is with the way men should conduct themselves in the new situation — not merely whether they should accept or oppose, join or stand
aloof, but how they can adjust their minds to a new perception of cosmic
order. (One of the stories recommends, symbolically, the Lethe of
drunken stupor.) In the light of his questioning, he is moved to attack
some old virtues by debunking the legends in which they are enshrined.
These concerns are not expressed in every chapter — there is other, more
orthodox subject matter — but they dominate the book.

It does Aina less than justice to present these ideas as if they were part of a treatise. They are true fictional ideas that need to be appreciated in their own medium. His presentation is one of extraordinary obliqueness, as both the preface writer and the commentator, in his final critique, take care to point out. The preface says that Aina feels the emotions of the poet Su Shi but employs the method of Dongfang Shuo—that is to say, the wit and indirection of satire. The final critique, after praising the eloquence of the philosopher's denunciation of Buddhism, then urges the importance of a "good reading" and states that Aina's fiction delivers its warning ironically and subtly ("between the lines").[10] To interpret it straightforwardly would be like reading the *Shuihu* as standing for sedition or *The Golden Lotus* for obscenity.

Much of his material is myth in the sense of sanctified legend. In the course of questioning the moral nature of the universe, he subjects myth to satirical treatment, in the manner of Lu Xun in his *Old Stories Retold* (*Gushi xinbian*). Among contemporary works, his satirical use of myth may be likened to that of Dong Yue's *Supplement to the Western Journey* (*Xiyou bu*), in which the time machine of Monkey's dreaming imagination carries him to fabled personalities in other ages. But a truer comparison is with seventeenth-century drama, which often satirizes historical and legendary figures; at least one of his myths, that of the beautiful Xishi, had been subjected to satirical treatment in the drama before the time of Aina's book, and three of his stories were soon to be adapted.

The best approach to his meaning is through the twelfth and final chapter, "Proctor Chen's Discourse on Heaven and Earth," which is more than a convenient, if enigmatic, way of ending the book. There is no preparation for it, although the eleventh chapter, about the horrors of the civil strife that preceded the Manchu conquest, introduces the subject of recent history and strikes a terrible note. Chen Gang, the proctor of the official Confucian school, is a pompous, even absurd, figure. One villager nudges another and tells us who he is. His personal name is Gang ("hard" or "rigid"), and his other names are Wuyu ("Sans Desire") and Wugui ("Sans Ghosts"). He is stubborn, rigid, biased, and dogmatic, but he has read every book in existence and can discourse with fluency on the principles of heaven and earth. Chen's lecture reveals his self-regard, his sense of being driven ("having no alternative"),[11] which is greater than that of Mencius, in "following the sage kings and Confucius in the attempt to eliminate three thousand years of error."

At the request of the audience, who wish to know about "the time before heaven and earth existed," he launches into a lecture (complete with diagram) on the origins of the world and then into an attack on Buddhism, Taoism, and the popular religion, destroying favorite metaphysical assumptions with ease.[12] But as the villagers press him harder with their questions, he is placed more and more on the defensive. He is asked about the existence of Yama, the King of Hell, and the city god, to whom one appeals for intercession with Hell. He disposes of these figures by finding anachronisms and inconsistencies in the legends surrounding them. He sidesteps the next question, about miracles performed with the aid of the city god, by acknowledging that such miracles occur but only in very restricted circumstances, as performed by the spiritual essence of martyrs and the like—a respectable notion for a neo-Confucian. The questioners ask about witchcraft, demons, and unnatural happenings. Chen explains them all as portents of disaster. The sages seldom spoke of them because they wanted to treat the normal rather than the abnormal, whereas the Buddhists and Taoists seize on such things to scare people. When the world is about to undergo a great upheaval, the elements themselves become demonic, and only the highest qualities of character and moral cultivation can avert disaster.

The audience persists. If such things are not divine in origin, how can they succeed? They cite a popular rebellion that occurred during the Ming dynasty, complete with the standard mythology and apparatus, including a wizard's book.[13] Chen acknowledges that demons and witches belong to the category of spirits and immortals; they have stolen the natural secrets of heaven and earth. When a historical cycle is about to end, demons and witches may help to bring it about. They are the proximate causes in a predestined revolution, but they are still just agents, and they suffer the consequences of their own impiety. Belief in supernatural beings is of no use to humanity and may well be harmful.

The audience now asks why, when the ruler of the Jurchen was crossing the Yangzi, the waters did not even come up to his horse's belly, and why, when the Mongol Crown Prince was fleeing north and came to a river, he was presented with a golden bridge in the sky over which to make his escape. Are these not unnatural happenings? Both are sensitive historical examples. The Jurchen and the Mongols were responsible for the two invasions of China that, before the Manchu invasion, had most deeply seared the memory. Each stands easily as a symbol for the Manchus, the Jurchen particularly, since the Manchus traced their descent from them. Thus, with these two examples, the audience is really asking for a metaphysical explanation of the Manchu seizure of China. Chen's answer is along the same lines as before, with one gruesome addition, the notion of the universal ether (qi, "material force") as an automatic regulator of population size.

"The creative force of heaven and earth tends to supplement a state of insufficiency and reduce a state of excess. Before the Xia and the Shang, there was only a tiny population, and so Heavenly Destiny produced many sages to increase and nurture the people. After eight hundred years of peace under the Zhou house, there was a huge population, and the wicked and violent people far outnumbered the good. The Way of Heaven abhors a plethora of people, and so it produced men with a passion for slaughter to fight each other. For example, it produced Bai Qi, who buried alive the four hundred thousand men of the Zhao army, and it allowed Robber Zhi to rampage throughout the country and then die in his own home at a ripe old age. It helped the Jin [Jurchen] ruler get back over the river so that he could ravage the Central Plains, and it gave the Crown Prince of the Yuan a golden bridge so that he could preserve his line. It is not that the Way of Heaven acted in ignorance; it acted in order to reduce a surplus. For example, when the Will of Heaven desired the restoration of the Han, the river miraculously froze solid so that Guangwu could cross."[14]

The extraordinary thing about Chen's answer is his equation of the Jurchen and the Mongols (and through them, the Manchus) with the most notorious butcher in Chinese military history, Bai Qi, and the most celebrated case of an evil man succeeding in life, that of the robber Zhi. (Zhi posed the classic problem for anyone trying to explain the moral working of the world.) Moreover, his reference to the Han restoration could easily apply to the present.

No doubt the questioners were troubled about the reasons for the conquest of China. But Chen's answer makes the identification with the Manchus even stronger; they are the temporary instruments of a universe that can, as circumstances require, either create or destroy. No wonder the audience rather abruptly thanks him for his instruction, offers him an obscure warning about Taoists and Buddhists, subjects he has not mentioned in some time, and decides to hold no more meetings.

Thus this last, remarkable section of the book deals with the metaphysical causes of China's situation. It is not the only concern of this chapter; part of the function of Chen's discourse is to counterbalance the mythical material of other chapters. But it is the main concern, as the remark that closes the book indicates: "This sort of bigotry has led to the destruction of many more things in the world than just this bean arbor!" The old man who makes the remark is blaming Confucian dogma for the fall of the Ming, just as Chen has blamed it on fate. But Chen, as we have seen, is a satirized figure, and the book ends with a condemnation of him and all he stands for. Surely his opinions are not to be accepted at face value? In this case, as in others, Aina is presenting a problem from several sides. There is apparently no clear and simple cause for a complex historical problem, and it would be a mistake to suppose that Chen Gang can be ignored. His ideas of historical cycles, of impersonal forces in control of things, of creation and destruction as two sides of a single principle, are all notions with which Aina toys in other chapters.

Chapter 11, "In Death, Captain Dang Beheads His Enemy," had already broached the question of responsibility for the collapse of the Ming, as well as the metaphysical justification for suffering. (There may have been a general influence from the eleventh story of Li Yu's *Struc-*

tures.) The chapter contains two anecdotal stories, both told by the old tutor, who has recently returned to the village on a visit. The Ming collapse is traced to the first great Manchu victory in Liaodong in 1619 and is described through the Chongzhen reign (1628-1644). Government incompetence led to the rise of the roving bandits, the rebels of the late Ming. Yuan Chonghuan's murder of Mao Wenlong left Mao's troops to form the nucleus of the first of the rebel bands. Another cause was the cutback in the imperial postal system, for the unemployed couriers and assistants swelled the ranks of the rebels. The discussion is thus modest and responsible. There is no imputation of moral degeneracy, as in *The Sobering Stone*, nor nostalgia for the vanished dynasty. All the emotion in the narrative is reserved for the rebels' sadism and the horrors of war.

The first of the chapter's two stories appears to be based on an item in Feng Menglong's *Survey*,[15] and in Aina's hands it retains its anecdotal character.

A traveler was riding through the thinly populated countryside of Luoyang County in Henan when a sudden storm occurred. There was no place to shelter from it, and he was forced to find temporary refuge under the eaves of a cottage. But the rain kept pouring down and by nightfall had shown no sign of stopping, and he had no choice but to ask for a place to sleep. An old man came out of the cottage.

"My house is very small," he said, "and I'm afraid I can't put you up. You'll have to go on to the next village, about twenty or thirty *li* from here, where you'll find an inn."

It was getting dark, and the traveler had no stomach for a forced march at that hour of the night. He noticed that the cottage also had a side room of good size that was not in use, and he pleaded again and again with the old man.

"The room is not fully occupied," said the man, "and I have no objection to your staying the night, but my brother is using it, and it wouldn't be suitable for you to share it with him."

"Since he is on his own, why shouldn't it be suitable?"

"Well, if one encounters a man in desperate straits, it must be because of a karmic bond," said the old man. "But don't be shocked when you meet him."

"I have been traveling all over the country for a dozen years now, and I have met every kind of man from the highest and noblest to the basest and most vicious. Why should I be shocked on coming here?"

As he spoke, they walked over to the room. The old man rapped lightly on the door and, hearing a noise inside, slipped the bolt and pushed it open. The traveler followed him in and, on suddenly looking up, was confronted with the sight of a headless man standing to the left of the door.

"Help! A ghost! A ghost!" he wailed as, mouth still agape, he crumpled to the floor. The old man quickly helped him to his feet.

"I warned you not to be shocked, and you insisted you would be all right. Why are you in such a state?"

The traveler was struck dumb for a long while, then asked, "How did it happen?"

"Sit down," said the old man, "and I will tell you all in good time." He pointed at the headless man and continued:

"My brother was out in Tongguan the year before last selling textiles when he was forced to flee home to escape a band of roving brigands. Then, when he was only thirty li from here, he was caught by local bandits and beheaded. In the night wolves came and began to eat the corpses. When they got to my brother's body, his soul heard a great voice shouting: 'Off with you, vermin! The officers who assess valor in battle have not been to do their accounting yet. You have no right to start eating.' Soon there arrived a group of men on horseback who checked off the names of all those lying there dead. But they could not find my brother's name in their register. They consulted another register and found that he should merely have been wounded, not killed; he still had another four years of his allotted span.

"Next day, my brother's mind suddenly cleared, but when he put his hand to his head, he felt only the protruding stump of his neck bone. That night I was still in my hideout in the village when I heard someone knocking on the door. It was my brother's voice! There was not a lamp left in the whole village, and so I had to help him in in the dark. He told me in great detail of the disaster that had befallen him in the neighboring village. Only as dawn slowly broke did I see that he had no head and that I had been up half the night talking to a headless man. That is when the shock hit me. His body was still warm, and his limbs had not become stiff. He made a gurgling noise in his throat, so I took some flour paste and rice gruel and fed it in with a teaspoon. When he had had enough, the gurgling stopped. This has been going on for over a year now. Recently he has learned a technique of mat weaving and spends every day at it. It brings in a little money, and that is what we live on." (pp. 144-145)

The seventh chapter, "On Mount Shouyang, Shu Qi Switches Loyalties," is the outstanding example of the satirical reworking of myth or sanctified early legend. Bo Yi and Shu Qi are the famous brothers who, as the Zhou dynasty overthrew the Shang, refused to eat the grain of the new dynasty and retreated to the fastness of Mount Shouyang, there to gather food in the wilds until their death. Aina makes a radical change in the story by having Shu Qi, after arriving on the mountain, rethink his decision and leave his brother in order to seek service with the Zhou. In a dream, a heavenly messenger confirms him in his action by explaining that there is a historical cycle regulating affairs, and that the time for the Shang has run out. There is, as will appear, a good deal of similarity between this notion of a historical cycle and that of Proctor Chen. And the effect of the notion in this instance is the same as that of the old tutor's discussion in Chapter 11: both lead to a reluctant acceptance of the new dynasty. The critique makes it clear that the story is also intended as satire of some forms of Ming loyalism, particularly that of the men who retreated into eremitism, the "phony high-minded."

Aina anticipates Lu Xun's story "Gathering Ferns" (*Cai wei*).[16] (Wei, or ferns, are the wild vegetation the brothers live on.) It is easy to see why the story attracted them both. As it is told in *Records of the Historian*,[17] Bo Yi and Shu Qi were the sons of a hereditary ruler under the Shang. When their father died, neither would take the throne; the father had designated Shu Qi his heir, but Shu Qi, being the younger, could not accept, while Bo Yi could not flout his father's wishes. When the revolution against the Shang broke out, the brothers threw themselves into the path of the Zhou columns and were spared only by Jiang Ziya's intercession. They then retired to Mount Shouyang. Their case has presented a perennial problem to Confucian thinkers.[18] On the one hand, the brothers remained admirably loyal to the old dynasty; on the other, that dynasty had lost its moral authority.

A given writer's attitude to the story depends on his own historical situation and the intellectual stance he takes toward it. It is no accident that the brothers are treated with reverence in the works of the loyalists of lost causes, as in the poetry of Wen Tianxiang, martyred under the Yuan. Bo Yi and Shu Qi are common allusions in Yuan poetry and again in the early decades of the Qing: a noted Ming loyalist, Zhang Huangyan (1620-1664), even named his poetry *Gathering Ferns.*[19] Writers such as Aina and Lu Xun, however, who oppose the tendency to romanticize the past, adapt the legend to make the brothers look foolish. Lu Xun makes Bo Yi senile and the actions of the brothers absurd and even contemptible. Aina treats Bo Yi as a loner out of touch with reality and makes Shu Qi think better of his loyalism.

Here is Shu Qi's soliloquy as, half starved, and with the mountain now swarming with malcontents and dissidents, he rethinks his decision:

"What a mistake it was to come up here! My elder brother, Bo Yi, ought to have succeeded my father as ruler of the feudatory state. It was his duty, both by age-old ethical principle and also by the ancestral precepts of the Shang. Wei Zi fled, Bi Gan died for his admonitions, Ji Zi feigned madness, and their noble deeds have all been duly written up. We were enfieffed, in a bond of loyalty, over many generations, and could not simply follow the herd in ignorance. But I am only the second son of the Lord of Guzhu, after all, and in a very different position from my brother. I could have taken a great deal less upon myself. Running up against the Zhou army, without thinking what I was doing, I joined my brother in hurling wild accusations at them, an act that almost cost us our lives. If it hadn't been for Jiang Ziya's presence—he and my brother were old friends, as patriarchs of Donghai and Beihai—and for his declaring us men of honor and helping us up and leaving us by the side of the road, we would never have been spared. My life would have been cast away on a desperate throw of the dice. But the army passed on, and it is now quite obvious that the Shang house cannot eke out an existence.

"I was in a confused and volatile state of mind when I came up here. I assumed there would be just the two of us on the mountain and that our actions would put us in the top rank for all time. But recently we have been joined by many who are merely looking for an excuse to indulge their pride, as well as by a good number who are pretending to be recluses in the hope that they will one day be summoned to court. As for the supply of ferns on the mountain—they need no cultivation and are free of taxes—these people rise early in the morning to get the first choice and pick the shoots clean. Our faces are as shriveled as dried cabbage leaves, and our ribs are as bent as the window frames of a ruined house. Not long ago, we used to throw out our chests, square our shoulders, and confront anyone, no matter who, but now our bellies are slack and empty and we simply cannot go on.

"It suddenly occurs to me that there are really only two things men seek in this world — fame and money.[20] Some people consider my brother sagelike, virtuous, pure, benevolent, and austere, thus giving him his due as a great man. But if anyone were to couple my name with his, it would be only as a casual compliment. If I were to continue under his auspices, even if I made a name for myself, I would still be just a hungry ghost injecting himself into someone else's affairs. Suppose we declared a righteous rebellion; if, by some chance, we were to falter, I would inevitably be branded the instigator. By this reasoning, I am like the man who picks up a sugar cane end: the more he chews on it, the less enjoyment he gets. Now as I look back, my one consolation is that it is still not too late to act. As the ancients said, 'Better a glass of warm wine while you're alive than empty fame after you're dead.' At present my brother's resolve is as hard as iron, unshakable. If I were to explain to him my desire to leave, he would never accept it. Better by far to seize this opportunity, now that he is over at the back of the mountain picking ferns, to take my stick and my rude basket and slowly make my way to the front of the mountain to look around. If there is any chance, I shall leave."[21]

The arguments are palpably self-serving, and Shu Qi is condemned out of his own mouth. But before concluding that Aina is therefore propounding loyalty to the Ming, one should read further.

As Shu Qi leaves the mountain, he is stopped and interrogated by its animal denizens. Before the brothers arrived on the mountain, the animals had not even heard of the change of dynasty, but they were so impressed by the brothers' example that they became strong loyalists and even dropped their predatory ways. Shu Qi now persuades them that they were wrong to ape the high-minded recluse and even to alter their predatory natures, an action that merely suspends the operation of karma. Congratulating himself on his glibness, he decides in short order to serve the Zhou.

But he has to pass through one more confrontation on his way to the capital to seek preferment. Sheltering from a black cloud, he takes refuge in a forest, where he is menaced by a squadron of soldiers, all in black armor and carrying black flags. They are horribly mutilated, and it dawns on Shu Qi that they are the legions of the dead, Shang soldiers whose loyalty and sense of injustice have enabled them to endure as ghosts. They are determined to make an example of Shu Qi the traitor. Help arrives, in the form of the immortal in charge of the fortunes of nations. He explains that the rise and fall of dynasties is a natural process, a function of time, like birth and death, or like the seasons, and that to oppose the process is to flout the Law of Heaven. Rebellion will not help the Shang; it will merely cost lives. The soldiers still object to Shu Qi's lack of loyalty and filial piety. "What official of a new dynasty is not the child of the preceding dynasty?" demands the immortal in response. Even animals should follow their natures, to create and destroy. The dissidents ask: "Surely the Highest Heaven is not in favor of destruction?" The immortal replies: "Creation and destruction belong in truth to a single principle."[22] The immortal's doctrine resembles Proctor Chen's idea that the cosmic forces may create or destroy merely to balance the population. Common to both is a controlling force, engaged in procreation and destruction, that is not primarily concerned with morality.

This is how the story ends:

> Suddenly the tigers and leopards fled away. From the die-hards' ranks there issued a roar as if the heavens were trembling and the earth cracking. The black clouds and fog turned into a golden mist which faded away into the distance. The earth was covered with thousands upon thousands of blue lilies which seemed to burst into sight in midair. Shu Qi stood up. It had all been just a prophetic dream, and now he understood the immortal's meaning. He was confident that his decision to serve the Zhou was the right one. He would first acquit himself well in his service and win fame. There would be time enough afterward to go back to the Western Mountains and look for his brother's bones.[23]

Opportunist though Shu Qi is, he has clearly chosen the reasonable path. Aina's writing forces the reader to see Shu Qi, the opportunist and realist, as well as his loyalist opponents as objects of satire. This view is similar to the balance of judgment called for in Chapter 12. In Shu Qi's case, Aina is just following out the logic of his idea. If the cosmos does not work in a moral way, it would be misleading to show Shu Qi, as a moral man, accommodating himself to historical necessity. Far better to show a shrewd man unbound by moral principle who acts according to the dictates of a calculated self-interest. Only then can the irrelevance of morality to cosmic causation be brought home to the reader.

Chapter 8, the companion story, "With the Transparent Stone Master Wei Cures the Blind," is an attempt to restate the philosophical problem of Chapters 7 and 12 in terms of Taoist and Buddhist fantasy. The story combines many myths: the belief that each emperor is the embodiment of an arhat sent down from heaven; the myth of the goddess Nüwa, who repaired heaven and had a stone left over (the most famous use of which is in the *Story of the Stone*);[24] and the legends of Chen Tuan, of Maitreya, the Buddha of the future, and several others. The story's answer to the question that obsessed Aina is that historical change is the product of a dualism, one element of which is destructive and the other creative. Disillusionment is expressed in Aina's finest image: two blind men, their sight restored, cannot bear to look at the reality of the world—except through a glorious drunken haze. (Drunkenness, the critique informs us, was Aina's own recourse from his private sense of desperation.)

Two arhats in heaven compete for permission to descend first to earth at a time of dynastic change. There is no pretense that this occurs at any other time than the transition from Ming to Qing, for a piece of drama played in the course of the story is about Li Zicheng's capture of Peking.[25] The competition is won by Lightning, and he descends first, followed by Free-and-Easy. Lightning destroys his part of the world, and when the people complain, Heaven is enraged, but *with the people*, and sends down its hosts to atomize them. Free-and-Easy tries to help, but is warned by a heavenly emissary that he is interfering with karma— "karma" here must mean something like the natural processes of the world—and that he must stop. He goes to Mount Hua, where Chen Tuan has awoken after a thousand-year sleep and is foretelling the future.

Two blind men, Late But First and Cleverer Than Confucius, also set out for Mount Hua in search of a magical cure for blindness and suffer various knockabout adventures on the way.[26] Arriving at the mountain, they are purged of their "filthy blood and flesh" and no longer feel hunger. But Chen cannot help them; their karmic crime—this is "karma" in its usual meaning—is too grave. Despairing, the two men go to Free-and-Easy, who cures them with the magic stone he has found. However, once cured, they are forced to leave the mountain, for only immortals can live there. With their newfound sight, they gaze out over the red dust of the world and begin to weep, seeing only "mirage and illusion." It would have been better to remain blind. Again they appeal to Free-and-Easy for help.

He considers. He cannot put them in a sack he has borrowed from Maitreya because, although it can hold three thousand worlds, it is reserved for paragons of virtue. Instead, he borrows a large jar from Du Kang and tells the two to crawl inside. The jar's mouth is narrow, but inside it is vast,

> all gentle slopes and open country, with no sign of city walls or buildings. Enjoying the pleasant breeze and the warm sunshine, they strolled to a marketplace. The inhabitants seemed friendly and proved gracious and hospitable. They were quite without passion, either of joy or anger, open and easygoing, wearing nothing on their heads. Some sang songs and chanted poetry, others played games of chance or took part in contests of strength, shouting freely at each other but without prejudice or rancor. They needed no cloth for their clothing, nor grain for their food. They were naïve and innocent, aware neither of the height of heaven nor the depth of earth. They knew neither summer's heat nor winter's cold, neither night nor day. They traveled whenever they wanted, without need of ships, vehicles, donkeys, or horses. They slept whenever they wanted, without need of bed or bedclothes. They mingled innocently with the birds, beasts, and fish. They were never afflicted with pains, itches, or illnesses. They tilled the land just as they wished. They were never pressed to pay taxes or rents. Truly, 'Inside the pot, time stands still. It is a paradise, not the world of men.' Then the two men were made to sit on top of the Kunlun Mountains, where they opened their eyes wide and saw the Lightning Arhat strike with his thunder, wind, hail, and rain and scour away the fires of karmic retribution and the ashes of destruction. And afterward they accompanied the Free-and-Easy Arhat as he came out and wandered free of the world, calmly enjoying the blessings of peace.[27]

That is how the chapter ends. Du Kang is the inventor of wine, and the paradise into which the two men have crawled is the beatific world of alcoholic illusion. The only equanimity for those able to see the reality around them is to be obtained in the refuge of drunkenness, from which height of abstraction, symbolized by the Kunlun Mountains, one can bear to watch the dualism that controls human affairs going about its business.

There are two other stories that, like the story of Bo Yi and Shu Qi, debunk old legends. Chapter 1, "Jie Zhitui Traps His Jealous Wife in Fire," is on the hackneyed subject of female jealousy.[28] In the *Bean Arbor*, the subject arises in the course of a dispute between the older and younger men. The latter are romantics who want love stories of the "brilliant and beautiful" type, while the older men present themselves as realists in insisting that talent, beauty, morality, and a good destiny are not to be found in any one woman. One of the older men takes up the story of the hero Jie Zhitui, a model of self-sacrificing loyalty, who shares his prince's exile but is overlooked when the prince gains power. As narrated in *Records of the Historian*, Jie retreats to a hermit's life on Mount Mian with his mother and refuses to emerge.[29] The prince, now the king, belatedly recalls his obligation and sends emissaries who, unable to find him, resort to smoking him out. Jie chooses to perish in the flames.

Aina has altered the story drastically. A wife named Shi You replaces Jie's mother. The epitome of jealousy, she really belongs in a separate legend altogether.[30] During the nineteen years of Jie's absence from the country, her jealousy has festered. Returning, he heads straight back to join her, without waiting for any reward, and she virtually imprisons him on the mountain with her. When the emissaries try to smoke him out, Jie, unable to face his friends, sets a fire of his own and forces Shi to die with him in its flames. The story is a sardonic comment on women and marriage but devoid of the moralizing that usually accompanies that theme. What Aina has done is to strip away all the legend's moral authority.

Its companion story, "Fan Li Gives Xishi a Watery Burial," is another antiromantic story that springs from the same kind of dispute as in Chapter 1. The elderly narrator, again insisting that there are no women with the qualifications needed for the "brilliant and beautiful" romance, runs through an astonishing list of famous women to show how they fall short in one respect or another. The young listeners counter with the example of Xishi, heroine of the play *Washing the Silk* (*Wan sha ji*),[31] which has just been performed in a neighboring village. Was the resurgence of the kingdom of Yue not due to her patriotic self-sacrifice? The narrator staunchly denies the truth of the legend, declaring that the unofficial histories he has read tell quite a different tale.[32]

According to the legend, Xishi was a beautiful peasant girl who, at the urging of Fan Li, a supporter of the defeated King of Yue, agreed to be offered to the King of Wu. She succeeded in her mission of so beguiling and corrupting the king that he fell prey to his enemy. In most forms of the legend, Fan Li, fearing that the King of Yue will eventually turn against him, takes Xishi and sets off with her over the lake. In some versions, they even become immortals. The sardonic narrator will have none of this. According to him, Xishi was not even beautiful; she merely appealed to the jaded tastes of the time with her fresh and unadorned looks. When Fan Li put his monstrous proposition to her, she "dumbly followed him," having, as the narrator tells us, no one to tell her what was proper. It took a hefty bribe to one of his ministers even to get her installed in the palace of the simple-minded King of Wu. At this point, the narrator attacks her virtue and her wisdom:

> Now when the King of Wu treated you so generously, you should have used your influence to help the King of Yue get back to his own country and enabled Wu and Yue to live in peace with one another, while at the same time helping the King of Wu to build up his power. By thus betraying neither Wu nor Yue, you would have gone down in history as one of the most remarkable of heroines. (p. 21)

After the success of his scheme, Fan Li is suspect in both countries—he was born in Wu—and is deeply suspicious of Xishi, who knows where he has hidden a cache of money. He drowns her and flees. The young listeners protest at this distortion of history. What proof does the narrator have? He cites a number of nonexistent works, and a lively debate begins. It is possible to see in this story something more than the mere pleasure of debunking a hoary legend. It is Xishi's extreme patriotism, one might say her nationalism, that the narrator attacks. As the King of Wu's concubine, she should have preferred the sensible, realistic goal of making peace between the two countries.

One or two other chapters may relate to these themes. Chapter 6 contains a story that denounces some of the most powerful members of the Buddhist priesthood for faking the evidence of their spirituality. It is preceded by a diatribe against the clergy and their supporters—dismissed officials, high-minded recluses, and the like. The close connection between the Ming loyalists and Buddhism may be the cause of the diatribe. Chapter 3 shows the hero aiding in the foundation of a new dynasty, the Tang; it may exemplify Aina's view of historical necessity. The remaining stories are less remarkable. Chapters 4 and 5, like Chapter 3, honor the knight errant's reckless altruism, while Chapter 10 is a ribald satire of the confidence men of the tourist area of Soochow. (Part of it has been translated above.)

Chapter 5 refers to the word "xian" ("idle"), which forms part of the book's title: "Only in times of idleness does the conscience emerge."[33]

The background narrator then declaims against the man who succeeds in the examinations but promptly misuses what he has learned. Gaining office, he jettisons his childlike heart. By contrast, these uneducated rustics "have their feet planted on firm ground and their hearts in accord with heaven." Quixotic altruism and the leisure that offers us the chance to contemplate the world and ourselves—these are almost the only values to come unscathed through Aina's gauntlet of ironies.

Appendix:
Later
Collections

Charming Stories of the West Lake (*Xihu jiahua*) is a collection of sixteen stories with a 1673 preface.[1] Although the author was aware of Zhou Ji's West Lake fiction,[2] he shared neither his political passions nor his personal rancor; he genuinely celebrates the romantic lore of Hangchow's cultural history. The West Lake was a literary and spiritual retreat, and many of the stories are about famous poets and religious figures. The introduction to Chapter 10 even attempts to equate the religious with the poetic genius. For an understanding of the author's views, the key stories are the first and the last, about Ge Hong and Shen Zhuhong, respectively. Ge was the Taoist philosopher who gave up a brilliant career for a life of contemplation in the hills above the West Lake. Shen was a late Ming scholar who renounced his ambitions "when fame was his for the taking" in order to enter the Buddhist priesthood, even though his doing so left his family without an heir. A long debate ensues between Shen and a neighbor—Shen's arguments are in the form of ci lyrics—on the relative merits of Confucian service and religious withdrawal. In other stories, all of which are based on well-known material, the tragic and heroic themes are noticeably downplayed in comparison with the romantic and idyllic.[3] There is a consequent loosening of the problem-and-solution plot structure, and although the stories are gracefully written, they are undeniably a little bland.

Portraits of Society (*Renzhong hua*),[4] comprising five stories, and *Multicolored Stones* (*Wuse shi*) and *Eight Fairylands* (*Ba dongtian*),[5] comprising eight stories each, are alike in combining the moral fable with the romantic comedy, sometimes in the same work, as in the "brilliant and beautiful" novel. (They also, perhaps reflecting their times, show public service as either onerous or dangerous.) The latter two were written by the anonymous author of a "brilliant and beautiful" novel. Both collections are notable for prefaces that set out candidly the principles behind their fiction. The stones of *Multicolored Stones* resemble those -

with which the goddess Nüwa repaired the vault of heaven, but whereas
she used real stones to repair a real vault, the author uses literature to
repair the moral Way of Heaven. The *Eight Fairylands* preface contains
a neo-Confucian defence of the ideal (*li*) as an intrinsic part of the world
of reality. Both prefaces, in fact, are a defense of fiction as moral fable.
It is refreshing to find the moral fable defended for its own sake, even if
the stories it leads to are no different from other fiction.

Refined Words to Awaken One from Dreams (*Xing meng pianyan*)[6]
consists of twelve stories based on Classical tales in Pu Songling's
(1640-1715) *Liaozhai's Record of Strange Events* (*Liaozhai zhiyi*). The
author has chosen as sources those that were closest to the world of the
vernacular story — well-rounded tales concerned with human relations
from a moral viewpoint. Although he disguises only thinly his indebtedness to Pu Songling, his stories exploit the vernacular genre for all
its worth, adding detail and even historical background. Four are
romances, the rest problem stories of domestic life. His moral world is
similar to that of Ling Mengchu, except that he places a greater emphasis
on romance; one story, number 9, even shows a clash between the differing values of prudential morality and qing.

Shi Chengjin, born in Yangzhou in 1659, was the first writer in the
history of the vernacular story to sign his work with his own name, a fact
that says much about the nature of his fiction. He was a tireless
pedagogue, a man of simple aesthetic pleasures and deep moral and
religious convictions, who published numerous didactic works of his own
composition. The omnibus collection of his writings, *Family Treasure*
(*Chuanjia bao*), contains one hundred and twenty works of all forms and
sizes, published between 1692 and 1739.[7] Its foreword lists many others
as yet unpublished. His work is addressed to a wide range of readers,
from those requiring the simplest practical advice to those drawn to
transcendental Buddhism. The singular feature of *Family Treasure* is
that it is all in the vernacular. In his 1739 preface, Shi gives the reason:

> Illiterate and semiliterate ordinary folk make up the vast majority of people,
> and it would be incongruous to try to address them in an abstruse Classical.
> They would not understand, and it would amount to saying nothing at all . . .
> Highly lettered scholars will naturally despise this book for its simplicity and
> vulgarity, but it will bring no small benefit to the illiterate and semiliterate of
> the world.

The vernacular permitted the less literate to read his works and the illiterate to understand them when read aloud.

His stories were published in 1726 in a volume entitled *Scent of
Flowers From Heaven (Yu hua xiang)*,[8] an allusion to the preaching of
the Buddhist master Yunguang in Nanking. It contains forty pieces in-
terspersed with short essays, followed by a supplement entitled
Understanding Heavenly Pleasures (Tong tianle). The volume is subtitled
Recent Events in Yangzhou, Newly Published (Xinke Yangzhou jinshi).
Shi's declared purpose was to record in colloquial language such recent
events in Yangzhou as demonstrated the working of moral bao.

Although he was aware of some previous vernacular fiction, including *Twelve Structures*,[9] he dispenses with its narrative method entirely. He is the narrator, and he presents his stories to us as true; some of them he can vouch for himself; others were his friends' experience; still others were casual oral fiction.

The interest of his stories lies mainly in their matter, for example, the Manchu siege of Yangzhou, and also in their presentation of Shi's ideals. The first story, "The Studio of Present Enlightenment" (*Jinjue lou*), is of key importance in the latter respect. It is the picture of a genuinely happy man, high-minded, unbound by convention, contented with the humble life, given to meditation, and taking his pleasure in the arts, especially painting. He builds himself a studio outside town—he resembles certain of Langxian's and Li Yu's heroes—and does a little painting for a living. He has only two close friends, a gardener and a priest named Indolence. When he is invited to go to the capital as an artist, Indolence dissuades him, and he simply hides until the great man's emissary gives up and goes away. There is a distinct similarity between this picture and that of Wang Mian in the prologue chapter of *The Scholars*, written a decade or two later.

Du Gang's *Stories to Delight the Eye and Awaken the Heart* (*Yumu xingxin bian*),[10] published in 1792, was the last important collection. With its echoes of Feng Menglong, Ling Mengchu, Li Yu, Aina, and others, it sums up many of the themes and emphases of the genre.

Du, who came from Kunshan in Soochow prefecture, also wrote a long fictionalized history, which appeared in 1793.[11] According to the publisher's preface in *Stories to Delight*, he was a learned man, disappointed in his ambitions, who wrote for his own amusement. His stories are fact, and therefore superior to mere fiction. Since the narrator speaks directly for the author, information can be gleaned from the stories themselves. Story 15 reproduces as its prologue a long Classical narrative from the posthumous manuscript of Du's teacher. Several stories are set in very recent times and may be drawn from his own observation. In story 6, he refuses to give the names of the characters because "the principals in the case are still alive." He also shows a wide range of reading, from Mencius to Fang Bao (1668-1749). More significantly, story 5, although set in the Jiajing reign of the Ming, seems to refer to the political conditions of his own time. The story is about the Li Fuda case of 1527, and it follows the historical sources closely.[12] Guo Xun, Marquis of Wuding, a confidant of the Emperor, had interceded in Li Fuda's behalf. Under criticism from his officials, after it was revealed that Li was actually the leader of a seditious sect, the Emperor condemned Li to death. He could not, however, bring himself to punish Guo. When the censors renewed their criticism, he flew into a rage, overturned the case, freed Li Fuda, and clapped the censors in jail. It was a "disaster for officialdom."[13] Du's story faults the censors for their relentless criticism, and his epilogue tries to reconcile this new note of prudence with his usual moral activism:

People who put forward this view are not trying to turn us into sycophants or temporizers . . . To sum up, one ought to be forgiving in criticizing others for their misdeeds. Leaving them room for maneuver means leaving yourself room for retreat. There is no need to let yourself be swayed by the emotions of the instant into driving them to utter extinction. Such is the wisdom of personal survival—something to which the scholar-gentry should pay close attention. (pp. 112-113)

I believe he is referring to the situation at the court of the Qianlong Emperor at the time of writing. For ten years, the high officials had been contending with the Emperor's corrupt and feared favorite, Heshen (1750-1799), and Du's warnings convey his misgivings about pressing the campaign too far.

Du was profoundly influenced by his reading in the vernacular story. He turned stories by Feng, Ling, and Li Yu into prologue stories.[14] His last story resembles the final chapter of *The Bean Arbor*, "Proctor Chen's Discourse on Heaven and Earth." Du Gang's prologue is pure disquisition, a set of answers to questions on the existence of hell and its connection with Buddhist belief. It is, as the narrator explains, a reprint of the "Discourses on Hell" (*Diyu lun*) of the Ming loyalist Wei Xi (1624-1681).[15] Wei, as a Confucian, is here arguing with a great deal of sophistry for the existence of a hell prior to Buddhism. (Hell and Buddhism were two of the subjects dealt with by Proctor Chen.) Du's main story has a narrative basis, but it, too, is composed largely of a master's answers to his disciples.

Other stories have a more general connection with earlier fiction. The outstanding case is story 15, about a surgeon who kidnaps people in order to amputate the organs he needs for his transplant operations. It is distantly related to the demon story of the early period, sharing the mysterious meeting; the incarceration in a remote place; the sympathetic young informants, here the doctor's sons; the sight of other victims killed or dismembered; the suspenseful escape; and even some of the characteristic language.[16] It amounts to a transformation of the old demon story.

The Du Gang story is told in two or three carefully structured chapters, like Li Yu's, except that the chapter endings are not used for banter. He begins with a poem referring specifically to the story and follows it with a compact essay on the relevant moral point. There is then a prologue story, which may occupy the rest of the first chapter. Typically, another short essay introduces the main story. There is a good deal of comment, both moral and explanatory, in the course of the story. The narrator's tone is serious, even indignant, sometimes ironic, never ribald except for scatological humor. He gives little description and includes no set pieces as such. His is an economical style, without linguistic exuberance or striking imagery.

In general, his stories come within the preferred sphere of Ling Mengchu and Li Yu; they select the novel or piquant event from within tangible reality. There is a good deal of satire, some of it denunciatory.

The court case type is combined in story 6 with romantic comedy and in story 8 with moral heroism. Story 15 is the transformation of a demon story, and story 5 is the political story already mentioned. The rest are on well-established moral themes: filial piety, including the ultimate case of the virtuous daughter-in-law; brotherhood; friendship, including one story of the ideal patron; and the knight errant's universalistic ethic. The collection has a greater moral weight than any other except *The Sobering Stone*.

Du's stories are preoccupied with the relation of the moral act to predestination; fully half of them discuss the question. Story 1 remarks:

> People are always saying that separation in life or by death is determined in advance by Fate and that nothing they do can alter it. They do not realize that, although it is determined in advance, the power to change it rests entirely with them. (pp. 1-2)

Story 2 describes the passive virtues as appropriate only for ordinary women and goes on to tell of a heroine who, by cleverness and wit, found a solution to her family's problems. The epilogue sums up, "Readers of this book should reflect that if people will do good deeds, there is no heavenly intent that cannot be reversed."[17]

Story 10 subordinates geomancy, another determinant, to the virtuous will: "Readers, which do you think is the more important factor in the well-being of your descendants, the Principle of Heaven or the Principle of Earth?"[18] Du's belief in moral activism shows up throughout his book. There are several stories of moral heroism of the kind seen in Feng Menglong, Langxian, and Gukuang. Like the last author, whom he most closely resembles, Du is suspicious of the mere writer. The teacher in his final story tells his disciples to "put practical action before literature."[19] The puritan has the last word.

Notes

1. LANGUAGE AND NARRATIVE MODEL

1. Yuan Jiahua et al., *Hanyu fangyan gaiyao* (Peking, 1960), p. 24, divides the present-day Northern dialects into four main regional types. This is the type formerly known as Lower Yangzi Mandarin.

2. It was originally a Prague School notion. Erich Auerbach applied it to medieval Latin; see Auerbach, *The Literary Language and Its Public in Late Latin Antiquity and in the Middle Ages,* tr. Ralph Manheim (London: Routledge and Kegan Paul, 1965), pp. 249-252. See also Wang Li et al., *Wenxue yuyan wenti taolunji* (Peking, 1957). Although Classical was no longer an ordinary spoken medium, it retained an oral dimension for literary and pedagogical purposes.

3. Auerbach, *Literary Language,* pp. 249-252.

4. Wang Li, *Hanyu shigao* (Peking, 1958), II, 211.

5. See B. Havránek, "The Functional Differentiation of the Standard Language," in Paul L. Garvin, ed., *A Prague School Reader on Esthetics, Literary Structure, and Style* (Washington: Georgetown University Press, 1964), pp. 1-18.

6. See Auerbach, *Literary Language,* pp. 197, 255, 262.

7. *Xianqing ou ji, Li Yu quanji* (Taibei, 1970), V, 1928-1930.

8. Zhou Zumo, "Cong wenxue yuyan de gainian lun Hanyu de yayan, wenyan, guwen deng wenti," *Wenxue yuyan wenti taolunji,* pp. 28-42, claims that Han Yu's prose style was in some respects close to the Tang spoken language.

9. See Bernhard Karlgren, "Excursions in Chinese Grammar," *Bulletin of the Museum of Far Eastern Antiquities* 23(1951): 107-133.

10. See Charles A. Ferguson, "Diglossia," *Word* 15 (1959): 336; Fred W. Householder, "Greek Diglossia," *Word* 15 (1959): 100-129; D. S. Mirsky, *A History of Russian Literature* (New York: Knopf, 1949), pp. 3-4.

11. Barbara Ruch proposes the word "vocal" for oral Japanese literature that has ties to the written language, reserving "oral" for literature in which the producer of a story or the audience or both are illiterate; see "Medieval Jongleurs and the Making of a National Literature," in John W. Hall and Toyoda Takeshi, eds., *Japan in the Muromachi Age* (Berkeley: University of California Press, 1977), pp. 286-287.

12. See Gao Mingkai, "Tangdai Chanjia yulu suo jian de yufa chengfen," *Yanjing xuebao* 34(1948):49-84.

13. See the Seoul, 1965, fac. ed. of a 1245 edition. It was composed in 952 or a little after. See Arthur Waley, "A Sung Colloquial Story from the *Tsu-t'ang chi,*" *Asia Major* n.s. 14.2(1969):243.

14. On the sujiang, see Wang Zhongmin et al., *Dunhuang bianwenji* (Peking, 1957), I, 3-4.

213

15. See the *Dunhuang bianwenji*, I, 389. The *Sou shen ji* manuscript, which was clearly intended for reading, makes use of some of the bianwen's characteristic expressions for the passage of time (e.g., *bu jing xunri*, "before long").

16. One indication is that the vernacular versions of Classical tales contained in the *Sou shen ji* manuscript are not "genre translations." Ju Daoxing's direct rendition of Classical narrative into the vernacular, without any use of an oral model, is only rarely paralleled in later literature.

17. See Li-li Chen, "Some Background Information on the Development of *Chu-kung-tiao*," *Harvard Journal of Asiatic Studies* 33(1973):224-237.

18. See the Taibei, 1962, reprint of the 1878 edition. The work was compiled by Xu Mengxin.

19. See Glen Dudbridge, *The Hsi-yu Chi; A Study of Antecedents to the Sixteenth-Century Chinese Novel* (Cambridge: Cambridge University Press, 1970), pp. 25-45.

20. See the *Zhongguo gudian xiqu lunju jicheng* (Peking, 1959) edition.

21. To the five illustrated pinghua should be added the *Wudai shi pinghua*, the *Xuanhe yishi* (one edition of which has the word "pinghua" attached to its title at one point), and the *Xue Rengui zheng Liao shilüe*, which has certain formal similarities to the pinghua.

22. See B. L. Riftin, *Istoricheskaia epopeia i fol'klornaia traditsiia v Kitae; ustnye i knizhnye versii "Troetsartviia,"* (Moscow, 1970).

23. See the Peking, 1954, edition, pp. 36-44. It is translated in Richard G. Irwin, *The Evolution of a Chinese Novel: Shui-hu-chuan* (Cambridge, Mass.: Harvard University Press, 1953).

24. Juan 17636-17661. On the relationship of the *San fen shilüe* and the *Sanguo zhi pinghua*, see Nagasawa Kikuya, *Shoshigaku ronkō* (Tokyo, 1937), pp. 190-191.

25. The word "huaben" was adopted as the regular term for the genre only in this century. On its early usage, see Charles J. Wivell, "The Term 'Hua-pen,'" in David C. Buxbaum and F. W. Mote, eds., *Transition and Permanence: Chinese History and Culture* (Hong Kong: Cathay, 1972), pp. 295-306.

26. Translated in Dudbridge, *The Hsi-yu Chi*, pp. 25-29.

27. Lü Shuxiang, *Hanyu yufa lunwenji* (Peking, 1955), pp. 6-11, 148ff.

28. *Xianqing ou ji*, pp. 2288, 2294.

29. The authority on this subject is Zhang Zhigong; see his *Chuantong yuyan wenfa jiaoyu chutan* (Shanghai, 1962), pp. 25ff.

30. Reprinted in *Zhongguo jindai wenlun xuan* (2 vols., Peking 1959 and 1962; photographic ed., Nagoya, n.d.), II, 511.

31. Wang Li, *Hanyu shigao*, I, 3, and II, 211.

32. E.g., Fu Sinian, "Wen yan heyi caoyi," *Xin qingnian* 4.2 (February 1918).

33. Guo Shaoyu, "Zhongguo yuci zhi tanxing zuoyong," in his *Yuwen tonglun* (Shanghai, 1941).

34. Kōsaka Jun'ichi, *Chūgoku no hachi daishōsetsu* (Tokyo, 1965), pp. 97ff.

35. See the Peking, 1975, facsimile edition. The preface contrasts the language of the pinghua with that of this novel. Xu Nianci, writing in the early years of this century, explained the popularity of Lin Shu's translations from European fiction into Classical Chinese by saying that the majority of readers were of the lettered class and found Lin's impeccable Classical more palatable than a vernacular style; see *Zhongguo jindai wenlun xuan*, II, 508.

36. P. 231.

37. For the sociolinguistic argument, see J. B. Pride, *The Social Meaning of Language* (Oxford: Oxford University Press, 1971), p. 18: the high variety in a state of diglossia must "lack power of a certain sort."

38. *Culture, Language, and Personality: Selected Essays* (Berkeley: University of California Press, 1960), p. 81.

39. See Yan Fu, "Guowen baoguan fuyin shuobu yuanqi," *Zhongguo jindai wenlun xuan*, p. 198; Qiu Tingliang, "Lun baihua wei weixin zhi ben," ibid., p. 178; Chu Qing, "Lun wenxueshang xiaoshuo zhi weizhi," in A Ying, ed., *Wan Qing wenxue congchao* (*Xiaoshuo xiqu yanjiu juan*) (Peking, 1960), pp. 28ff.

40. See the articles listed in n. 39. The point is made again in Guo Moruo's "Aihu xinxian de shengming," *Renmin ribao* (May 31, 1952).

41. Percy Lubbock, *The Craft of Fiction* (London: J. Cape, 1921); Roman Ingarden, *The Cognition of the Literary Work of Art* (Evanston: Northwestern University Press, 1973); Northrop Frye, *Anatomy of Criticism* (Princeton: Princeton University Press, 1957); Wayne C. Booth, *The Rhetoric of Fiction* (Chicago: Chicago University Press, 1961); Roland Barthes, *S/Z*, tr. Richard Miller (New York: Hill and Wang, 1974); Gérard Genette, "Discours du Récit," *Figures III* (Paris: Editions du Seuil, 1972), pp. 65-282.

42. E.g., R. H. Robins, *General Linguistics: An Introductory Survey* (London: Longmans, 1964), p. 12.

43. See Roman Jakobson and M. Halle, *Fundamentals of Language* (The Hague: Mouton, 1956).

44. For example, Genette's "Discours du Récit."

45. Genette, *Figures III*, pp. 203-211.

46. In general, see Nils Erik Enkvist, "On Defining Style," in Enkvist, John Spencer, and Michael J. Gregory, *Linguistics and Style* (Oxford: Oxford University Press, 1964). The two main kinds of definition of style are "choice" and "deviation from a norm," which clearly stem from an emphasis on either the speaker's or the listener's experience, respectively. Since the critic approaches the work initially in the capacity of a listener or reader, the latter kind of definition is the correct one.

47. See Paul Hernadi, *Beyond Genre: New Directions in Literary Classification* (Ithaca: Cornell University Press, 1972), Ch. 5.

48. By "description" is meant not only the outer scene as rendered in words (*jing* in Chinese critical theory) but also the inner scene of the observer's thoughts and feelings (*qing*), as well as the interactions of one with the other.

49. The narratorial situation in a work of fiction may be referred to as its "simulated context." Note that Lin Shu's translations of Dickens were done in Classical without the oral model, while Lu Xun's translations of Jules Verne were done in the vernacular with full use of it. For a general typology of Chinese narrative without reference to language or model, see Andrew H. Plaks, "Towards a Critical Theory of Chinese Narrative," in Plaks, ed., *Chinese Narrative: Critical and Theoretical Essays* (Princeton: Princeton University Press, 1977).

50. See Chapter 9.

51. See, e.g., Pamela Gradon, *Form and Style in Early English Literature* (London, Methuen, 1971).

52. *Wu Song* (Nanking, 1959).

53. Coordinate comment, except for numerous questions addressed by the narrator to himself and to the audience, is slight among the bianwen. Parallel prose decription, though common, is not set off by markers.

54. See the Shanghai, 1957, reprint of what is probably a Yuan dynasty edition. Note that Luo Ye appears to distinguish the mode of comment (*jianglun*) in oral narrative from the mimesis of action (see p. 5). His distinction between dull and exciting passages is not that between scene and summary but approximates it in effect.

55. "Sur la théorie de la prose," in Tsvetan Todorov, ed. and tr., *Théorie de la littérature* (Paris: Editions du Seuil, 1966), p. 202.

56. See the facsimile edition (Taibei, 1960) of the first (Tianxu zhai) edition, T. Y. Li, ed.

57. Although signed with a pseudonym, the preface has generally been credited by scholars to Feng.

58. In the *Sanchao beimeng huibian*, 149: 11a-b. The passage is discussed in n. 6 of Chapter 2.

59. For an attempt at two such comparisons, see my article "The Making of *The Pearl-Sewn Shirt* and *The Courtesan's Jewel Box*," *Harvard Journal of Asiatic Studies* 33(1973): 124-153.

60. *The Rise of the Novel* (Berkeley: University of California Press, 1957), pp. 80-81.

61. See the Appendix.

62. On bao in Chinese society, see the seminal article by Lien-sheng Yang, "The Concept of 'Pao' as a Basis for Social Relations in China," in John K. Fairbank, ed., *Chinese Thought and Institutions* (Chicago: University of Chicago Press, 1957), pp. 291-309.

63. See James J. Y. Liu, *The Chinese Knight-Errant* (Chicago: University of Chicago Press, 1967), pp. 1-12. Note that many of the works that are the subject of this study are also treated, in a different scholarly approach, by André Lévy in his *Le Conte en langue vulgaire du XVIIe siècle* (Lille: Université de Lille, Service de reproduction des thèses, 1974).

2. THE EARLY PERIOD

1. The *Sixty Stories* edition, published by Hong Pian about 1550, is described in Chapter 3. References are to Tan Zhengbi's modern edition, published under the title *Qingping shantang huaben* (Shanghai, 1957). Stories are referred to as Hong (for Hong Pian), with their position in the Tan Zhengbi edition. Feng's three collections are *Stories Old and New* (*Gujin xiaoshuo*), *Common Words to Warn the World* (*Jing shi tongyan*), and *Constant Words to Awaken the World* (*Xing shi hengyan*). Stories are referred to as GJ (for gujin), TY (for tongyan), or HY (for hengyan), with their position in the collection. (In previous writings, the *Gujin xiaoshuo* has been abbreviated as KC.) Page references are to the facsimile editions by T. Y. Li published in Taibei in 1958-59. The composition of the three collections is described in Chapter 5.

2. See my book *The Chinese Short Story: Studies in Dating, Authorship, and Composition* (Cambridge, Mass.: Harvard University Press, 1973), especially Chapter 7, (hereafter cited as CSS). Some support is given the rough dating by the fifteenth-century chantefables, which were not accessible at the time CSS was written. All the editions appear to be by the same publisher, and some are dated in the 1470s. Although they belong to a different genre, they share many of the features of the huaben. Despite one serious anomaly—two late criteria appear in one of them—they fit the dating pattern of the huaben, combining early and middle criteria but showing none of the features of the earliest stories. See the facsimile edition, *Ming Chenghua shuochang cihua congkan* (Shanghai, 1973).

3. "Encounter in Yanshan" (GJ 24) is in Group A; "The Pavilion of Lingering Fragrance" (TY 29), "Lin Ji's Good Deed" (Hong 11), and "The Meeting at Jinming Pond" (TY 30) are in Group B. The prologue of the last story is also based on a tale. For their relationship to their sources, see CSS, pp. 174-182.

4. CSS, pp. 183-185. They include "Zhou Shengxian" (HY 14), "The Jade Guanyin" (TY 8), "A Den of Ghosts" (TY 14), and "The Monk with the Love Letter" (Hong 2).

5. See Masuda Wataru, "'Wahon' to iu koto ni tsuite," *Jimbun kenkyū* 16.5 (1965): 22-33.

6. See 149: 11a-b. The informant was an aide to Shao Qing, rebel and pirate, who was pardoned and given a high post by Shaozong. See Ye Yuhua, "*Shuihu xie Song Jiang da Fang La fei chu xugou*," *Zhonghua wenshi luncong* 8 (October 1978): 76. It seems likely that the Shao Qing legend was one of the elements in the eventual Shuihu complex.

7. See CSS, pp. 161-163.

8. "Madam White" (TY 28), p. 2.

9. The *Bao Daizhi chu shen zhuan*. See the *Ming Chenghua shuochang cihua congkan*.

10. See CSS, pp. 208-209.

11. See the final poem, p. 18.

12. Pp. 1b-2, 3, 7b.

13. For example, "Song Four Causes Trouble for Miser Zhang."

14. P. 11b. For the meaning of the last phrase, cf. "Encounter in Yanshan" (GJ 24), p. 20.

15. Pp. 3a-b, 1b.

16. "The Meeting of Dragon and Tiger" (GJ 15), "The Fairy's Rescue" (GJ 33), "A Den of Ghosts" (TY 14), "The Three Monsters of Luoyang" (Hong 8), "The Three Pagodas of the West Lake" (Hong 3), and "The Dream of Qiantang" (see CSS, pp. 10, 234). The first four are Group A stories. Something resembling a poem chain is found in Chapter 110 of the *Shuihu quanzhuan;* it is a series of poems on the West Lake, similar to those of "The Three Pagodas" and "The Dream."

17. See his note on p. 2, and also a note to "The Fairy's Rescue" (GJ 33), p. 1b.

18. Cf. "The Honest Clerk" (TY 16), a Group B story of a shop manager who virtuously but circumspectly repulses the advances of his employer's wife. The story ends: "Fortunately, he was a man of complete integrity. He was never besmirched by her and hence was never involved in the disaster that befell her. But many indeed are the people who are misled by money and sex! Hardly one man in ten thousand is the equal of Zhang Sheng."

19. Pp. 12, 15, 16, 20b.

20. On the composition of this story, see CSS, pp. 175-177. A Classical item that contains two extra songs is found in Tian Yiheng's *Shi nü shi*, of which the preface is dated 1557.

21. P. 15.

22. Cf. Jaroslav Průšek, "The Creative Methods of the Chinese Medieval Story-tellers," in *Chinese History and Literature: Collections of Studies* (Dordrecht: Reidel, 1970).

23. The gist of the prologue, together with some of the poems, is found in two different Yuan works; see CSS, p. 164. It belongs to a common type of Song and Yuan Classical tale that features poems written and exchanged.

24. The meaning of the word *luosuo* as applied to the rings is unclear.

25. Pp. 16, 29b.

26. Quoted from CSS, p. 188. The type is related to the lamia theme in international folklore. See especially Nai-tung Ting, "The Holy Man and the Snake-Woman," *Fabula* 8.3(1967): 145-191.

27. P. 15. The words *heng bo* ("cross waves") of the next-to-last line apparently refer to sidelong glances flashed from beautiful eyes.

28. Pp. 8b, 10b.

29. Note that "Zhou Shengxian," p. 1b, has a set piece on sex that is related to this. It is really a pagoda poem, with couplets expanding from one to seven syllables but with irregular rhymes.

30. P. 4a-b.
31. CSS, p. 197.
32. CSS, pp. 179-180, 189.
33. Pp. 38b, 16b, 25, 39.
34. It was also a category in oral fiction named *chuanqi*; see Luo Ye's *Zuiweng tanlu*, pp. 3-4.
35. Note the bracketing of one hero in "The Toy Pavilion" (TY 37).
36. See Luo Ye, pp. 3-4.
37. P. 4.
38. P. 4b.
39. Notably "The Golden Eel" (TY 20, Group A), "Fifteen Strings of Cash" (HY 33, Group C), and "The Five Abstinences Priest Seduces Red Lotus" (Hong 13, Group C).

3. THE MIDDLE PERIOD

1. See CSS, Chapter 5.
2. See CSS, p. 131.
3. See Tian Rucheng, *Xihu youlan zhiyu* (Peking, 1958), 20: 368, and CSS, p. 140.
4. See CSS, pp. 141-142.
5. As noted by André Lévy in his *Etudes sur le conte et le roman chinois* (Paris: Ecole Française d'Extrême-Orient, 1970), p. 168.
6. The Liu Yong story (Hong 1) has been generally supposed to have come from a Yuan play on the strength of a song it contains. But the song is represented as sung by the boatman, not the hero, and hence it could not have come from a Northern play. Tan Zhengbi, p. 5, n. 1, Fu Xihua, *Yuandai zaju quanmu* (Peking, 1957), p. 200, and CSS, p. 138, n. 14, are all in error. For the set to which the song belongs, see *Shengshi xinsheng* (Peking, 1955), pp. 470-472, and other anthologies.
7. The only first-rate story among them, "The Apotheosis of Ren the Filial Son" (GJ 38), may well not have been based on a play. Fu Xihua lists two or three related plays, none of which seems to have used precisely this stuff-material; see pp. 346-347.
8. See the 1718 *Qiantang xianzhi* 19:12b.
9. Ibid. 10:35.
10. See the preface by Kong Tianyin to Hong Pian's edition of *Tang shi ji shi*.
11. His edition of *Liuchen zhu Wen xuan*. Two of the works published by Hong Pian appeared in other editions at about the same time. There is a *Tang shi ji shi* edited by Zhang Zili, whose preface is dated the first month of 1545; it must have appeared just before Hong's and may explain why Kong Tianyin is so specific in telling us about the circumstances of Hong's discovery of the text. There was also a Soochow edition of *Liuchen zhu Wen xuan* by Yuan Jiong in 1549 entitled *Liujia Wen xuan*; see *Zengding Siku jianming mulu biaozhu* (Peking, 1959), p. 877.
12. As a contemporary example, note the four stories published by the Jianyang publisher Xiong Longfeng, probably in the 1590s, which apparently had no collective title. (They are now known as *Xiong Longfeng sizhong xiaoshuo*; see the Shanghai, 1958, edition.)
13. See the edition in the Naikaku Bunko. There is also a Shanghai, 1915, edition. On Gu's sequels, see *Zhongguo congshu zonglu* (Shanghai, 1959), I, 758. Several titles are also attributed to Gu's Soochow contemporary Yuan Jiong; see the *Zengding Siku jianming mulu biaozhu*, p. 550.

14. Precisely this point is made by Hong Pian's Hangchow contemporary Lang Ying (b. 1487) in his *Qixiu leigao* (Peking, 1959), p. 330, in a note on the word "xiaoshuo." Lang sharply distinguishes the use of the word in Gu's titles from its application to the cihua chantefables. W. L. Idema's belief that Lang was contrasting Hong Pian's *Sixty Stories* with the chantefables springs from a misjudgment of the *Sixty Stories*; see his *Chinese Vernacular Fiction: the Formative Period* (Leiden: Brill, 1974), pp. 28-29. Hong's imitation of Gu's title was no doubt a commercial device, but it may also have been an assertion of the right meaning of the word "xiaoshuo" in the spirit of Lang Ying's note. Lang circulated his notes before publishing them (at some time after 1552).

15. See CSS, pp. 122-123.

16. In the *Zuiweng tanlu*, pp. 88-90.

17. Liezhuan 49.

18. *Han shu*, 50.

19. See the *Qingsuo gaoyi* (Shanghai, 1958), *houji*, pp. 172-174. The source has been reordered and treated freely; the local shrines have been added. "The Red Snake" is itself related to the Tang tale "Liu Yi," as the vernacular story implies, in its *Gujin xiaoshuo* form at least; see p. 11.

20. See Fu Xihua's *Yuandai zaju quanmu*, pp. 216-217, for the editions of the play. The original source was the *Hou Han shu*, liezhuan 71.

21. See CSS, pp. 150-151.

22. P. 224.

23. See my article "Sources of the *Chin P'ing Mei*," *Asia Major* n.s. 10. 1 (1963): 33-35.

24. TY 20, p. 1b.

25. HY 33, p. 16.

26. See Lang Ying, *Qixiu leigao*, pp. 653-654.

27. See CSS, pp. 133-134.

28. P. 3.

29. GJ 38, p. 10.

30. P. 15.

31. There were at least four plays on the subject; see CSS, p. 137, n. 1. Cuckoldry of a naïve hero was a common subject in both the Northern drama and the *Shuihu*.

32. Pp. 156-157.

33. See CSS, pp. 10, 148, and also C. T. Hsia, "Time and the Human Condition in the Plays of T'ang Hsien-tsu," in W. T. de Bary, ed., *Self and Society in Ming Thought* (New York: Columbia University Press, 1970), pp. 273-274. There are two versions of the story, one of which is closer to a Classical tale. The romances the heroine pores over are well-known early-Ming Classical tales of the "brilliant and beautiful" kind. Another story, "The Decorated Lantern" (in *Xiong Longfeng sizhong xiaoshuo*) is a romantic comedy about an elopement to which both sets of parents are eventually reconciled.

34. For example, "Zhao Bosheng" (GJ 11) is a romance of success in which a young poet meets the Emperor in a teashop (the latter is in disguise) and impresses him with his talent and his character.

35. The comment is probably Feng's; he makes the same point elsewhere in his writings. Note that Feng's *Qing shi leilüe* (see Chapter 4) contains a Classical tale on the same stuff-material; it is a good deal closer to the idealistic romance, even adding poems by the heroine (see CSS, p. 92).

36. For the editions and their locations, see CSS, p. 10.

37. A connection could be made with the saints' lives which formed a flourishing vernacular (and Classical) genre in the Ming and after, and even

with the Miaoshan legend itself, for which see Glen Dudbridge, *The Legend of Miao-shan* (London: Ithaca Press, 1978).

38. "Foyin" (HY.12).

39. See CSS, pp. 142-147.

40. See my article "The Authorship of Some *Ku-chin hsiao-shuo* Stories," *Harvard Journal of Asiatic Studies* 29(1969): 195-197. Note that the second entry in Fu Xihua's *Yuandai zaju quanmu*, p. 336, appears to be a mistake; it may well refer to the mid-sixteenth-century play by Xu Wei. The Xu Wei play *could* have been the object of the miscellany's reference, which is not to say that it had anything to do with the story's development.

41. The texts have been republished in facsimile under the collective title *Ming Chenghua shuochang cihua congkan*.

42. The full title appears in several forms. Before the table of contents, it is *One Hundred Court Cases Decided by Academician Bao: A Newly Published Simple Language Version in a Capital Edition, with Illustrations Added (Xinkan jingben tongsu yanyi zengxiang Bao Longtu baijia gong'an)*. The editor is given as one An Yushi. The sole surviving copy is preserved in the Hōsa Bunko, Nagoya. A fragmentary 1597 edition, textually very close to this, is preserved in the National University, Seoul.

43. For an account of the relevant works and their relationship, see Y. W. Ma, "The Textual Tradition of Ming *Kung-an* Fiction: A Study of the *Lung-t'u kung-an*," *Harvard Journal of Asiatic Studies* 35(1975): 190-220.

44. See my "*Judge Bao's Hundred Cases* Reconstructed," due to appear in the *Harvard Journal of Asiatic Studies* 40. 2 (1980).

45. The *Bao Daizhi chu shen zhuan*.

4. FENG'S LIFE AND IDEAS

1. Wing-tsit Chan, tr., *Instructions for Practical Living and Other Neo-Confucian Writings by Wang Yang-ming* (New York: Columbia University Press, 1963), p. 18.

2. Ibid., p. 22.

3. See the Peking, 1962, edition.

4. For the preface by Guqu Sanren, see the original edition in the Peking University Library. (The modern facsimile edition does not carry the preface.) "Taixia" is explained in the preface as the title of a tune associated with the Taoist immortal Taiji Zhenren. There is reason to suppose that the preface writer was Feng; see n. 73 below.

5. The *Bu xue chusheng*, now in the Palace Museum, Taibei. It is reprinted in Lu Qian's *Yinhongyi suo ke qu* (Taibei, 1961). Yuan Hongdao held a similar negative view of the effect of the examinations on poetry; see Guo Shaoyu, *Zhongguo wenxue pipingshi* (Shanghai, 1948), p. 274.

6. See his preface to Wang Jide's *Qu lü (Zhongguo gudian xiqu lunzhu jicheng)*, IV, 47-48.

7. References to Feng's plays are to the modern facsimile edition, *Mohan zhai dingben chuanqi* (Peking, 1960), 3 vols.

8. There is a copy of an early-Qing edition in the Harvard-Yenching Library. For a general account of Feng's attitude to vernacular fiction, see Ono Shihei, *Tampen hakuwa shōsetsu no kenkyū* (Tokyo, 1978), pp. 23-43.

9. It was published in 1620 under the title of *Bei Song San Sui ping yao zhuan*, then republished after the blocks had been destroyed in a fire with the added title

of *New Ping yao zhuan* (*Xin Ping yao zhuan*). Copies of both editions are preserved in the Naikaku Bunko.

10. The Wang Yangming biography is contained in a trilogy compiled by Feng entitled *Sanjiao ounian* (see Chapter 5).

11. See his "Tongxin shuo," contained in the *Fen shu* (Peking, 1961), pp. 97-99. The essay was written in the form of a preface to the *Western Chamber* play (*Xixiang ji*). The "child's heart" as a criterion of authenticity was stressed by Luo Rufang (1515-1588); Luo's views on the matter were brought together with Li Zhi's by Yuan Zongdao in his *Baisu zhai leiji* (Shanghai, 1935), p. 283. On the critical attitude implied by Li's theory, see James J. Y. Liu, *Chinese Theories of Literature* (Chicago: Chicago University Press, 1975), pp. 78-81.

12. See particularly Wong Siu-kit, "Ch'ing in Chinese Literary Criticism" (Ph. D. diss., Oxford University, 1969), pp. 150-161, on Li Mengyang and Yang Shen.

13. References to the *Qing shi leilüe* are to the Jiezi Yuan edition, which appears identical to the late-Ming edition in the Shanghai Library. The literature on qing and morality in the late Ming is too large and varied to describe here. See, e.g., Wei Yong's "Yue rong bian" in his *Zhenzhong mi* (preserved in the Peking University Library) and in numerous anthologies. It asserts that all great men are also men of great qing; when their ambitions to serve the state are thwarted, they turn to qing—that is, to sexual love. (This is an idea expressed in the notes to Feng's stories; see Chapter 5.) Note also Zhou Quan's "Yingxiong qi duan shuo" contained in the late-Ming prose anthology *Bing xue xi* (Shanghai, 1935), II, 144-145; the whole piece is translated by Lin Yutang as "On Heroes and Women" in his *Importance of Understanding* (Cleveland: World Publishing Co., 1960), pp. 117-118. Zhou explicitly condemns the notion of the femme fatale: "It is often said that 'the great heroes of history met their match in woman.' By this people mean that the love of a woman is a dangerous thing . . . I beg to differ. I think that what makes heroes heroes is that they love in greater measure than others and are capable of greater devotion to something, with their heart and soul in it."

14. See Feng's preface to the *Xilou meng,* a revision of Yuan Yuling's *Xilou ji,* but not the drastic revision he published under the title of *Chujiang qing.* The edition is preserved in the Naikaku Bunko.

15. The ethics of F. H. Bradley are probably the closest in the European tradition to the kind of Confucian ethics Feng adhered to. See his *Ethical Studies,* rev. ed. (Oxford: Clarendon, 1927), especially "Duty for Duty's Sake" and "My Station and Its Duties." The self is realized in moral action by fulfilling one's duties in one's various stations in life, as son, as friend, as public servant. Feng was distinctly more orthodox than most of the men who influenced him, and it is the relationship of the standard notion of moral duty to qing that is the point of strain (and hence the point of interest) in his ethics.

16. In the local history he wrote, the *Shouning daizhi* (preserved in the Ueno Library), Feng describes himself as a "Changzhou man of Wuxian registration" (*Xia,* p. 36). Ye Ru's "Guanyu Feng Menglong de shenshi" and "Guanyu *San yan* de zuanjizhe," both published in *Ming Qing xiaoshuo yanjiu lunwenji* (Peking, 1959), are also an indispensable source of information on Feng. As Ye Ru shows, one cannot be quite sure that Feng survived into 1646.

17. See the colophon by Feng Duling, or Feng Mengxiong, Menglong's younger brother, which is included in the 1924 edition of Wang Jingchen's *Sihou bian.*

18. See Ye Ru's "Guanyu Feng Menglong de shenshi," p. 35; he does not say which source uses this term.

19. He is said to have written the best poem at the spiritualist séance described in *Taixia xinzou,* 1:21b; on his appetite and position, see *Gujin tangai,* 9:7.

20. He was a close friend of the Donglin partisan Yao Ximeng (1579-1636) and of the Fu She members Hou Tongzeng (1591-1645) and Hou Qizeng; see Yao's *Xiang yu ji,* 10:34b-37b and the *Hou Zhongjie gong quanji,* 10:12b. The inaccessible anthology *Wujun wenbian* by Gu Yuan contains seventeen prose pieces, mostly of a routine nature, which Fan Yanqiao attributes to Feng Menglong. ("Feng Menglong de *Chunqiu hengku* ji qi yiwen yishi," *Jianghai xuekan* [September 1962]: 38.) But one of them, the colophon to Wang Jingchen's *Sihou bian,* is attributed to Feng Mengxiong in the 1924 edition, which obtained it from the *Wujun wenbian.* Even in the 1924 edition, there is some ambiguity; Menglong's style, Youlong, is attached to the piece. From Fan Yanqiao's account of the author's evident close friendship with Yao and the Hou brothers, it seems most likely that all of the pieces were really by Mengxiong, not by Menglong.

21. The anecdotes about Feng's wit and drinking are collected in Rong Zhaozu's "Ming Feng Menglong de shengping ji qi zhushu xukao," *Lingnan xuebao* 2.3(1931): 103-104.

22. Ibid.

23. For Yuan's play *Ruiyu ji,* see Jiao Xun's *Ju shuo* (*Zhongguo gudian xiqu lunzhu jicheng*), VIII, 131. Li Yu's (Li Xuanyu) is the famous *Qingzhong pu;* see the *Guben xiqu congkan,* first series (Shanghai, 1954). (Li's style is given here to differentiate him from the Li Yu of Chapter 8.) There is a slight but inconclusive similarity between the pseudonym Feng used in the *Zhi nang* in 1626 and a pseudonym attached to a contemporary account of the Soochow riots, the *Kaidu chuanxin.* (See the *Song tian lubi,* 32:1-14b.) The former was Dongwu zhi jiren, "The Singular Man of Eastern Wu," and the latter Wushimen jiren, "The Singular Man of Wu Market Gate."

24. On Mei Zhiyun, see the 1882 *Macheng xianzhi,* 32:25b and 18:58, where he is described as belonging to the Fu She of the "Three Wu" area.

25. See his *Ying zhi ji* (preserved in the Naikaku Bunko), 6:15b. Feng Mengxiong's friendship with Yao Ximeng and the Hou brothers could also be mentioned.

26. I assume he is the "Mei of Chu Huang" who is listed as a founding member; see Zhu Tan, "Mingji Nan Ying she kao," *Guoxue jikan* 2.3 (September 1930): 541-588. Mei was also a close friend of Wu Yingji (1594-1645), a powerful member of the Donglin; see *Macheng xianzhi,* 32:13.

27. See Li Changgeng's preface to the *Chunqiu hengku.*

28. A copy is preserved in the Academia Sinica, Taiwan; it has a preface by Li Shuyuan, who says that he has not met Feng. Li was known as the compiler of a model handbook of examination essays; see Zheng Zhenduo, *Jiezhong de shu ji* (Shanghai, 1956), p.93. The preface makes it clear that Feng's work was intended as an introductory guide, to take the place of the established *Chunqiu kuangjie.*

29. It is entitled *Chunqiu ding zhi can xin.* There is a copy in the Naikaku Bunko.

30. According to Mei Zhiyun's preface to his own handbook, the *Chunqiu yin shi* (preserved in the Naikaku Bunko), Zhang was the leader of the study group. Mei criticizes Feng's handbooks for being too comprehensive, for including material of little relevance.

31. There is a copy in the Harvard-Yenching Library.

32. An edition is preserved in the Peking Library. (It contains only the *Mencius* and part of the *Analects.*) For the preface by Chen Renxi (1579-1634), see his posthumous works, *Wumeng yuan yiji* (preserved in the National Central Library), 2:3-4.

33. Feng describes his composition of the work in his preface to the expan-

sion (*Zhinang bu*). The title was a nickname applied to a number of learned men in ancient times, notably Chao Cuo.

34. Copies of the edition are preserved in the Naikaku Bunko, the Library of Congress, and the Gest Collection at Princeton. The first preface is dated 1605, the second 1614. Feng is in debt to it for the basic idea of a classified anthology on wisdom, and also for a couple of categories, many items, and some comments.

35. Feng says in his preface to the *Supplemented Sack of Wisdom* that the first version had twenty-seven juan, which is incorrect; it had twenty-eight. The *Supplemented Sack* adds items and makes changes in the order.

36. From his preface. The image of the well is taken from Li Zhi, speaking of the Way. See the *Cang shu* (Peking, 1959), II, 517.

37. 1:11. The first version began with an item from the *Huainan Zi* about Confucius' groom, on which Feng's comment is: "People communicate with each other according to their kind. Our pedantic Confucians are betraying the country by trying to expound the classics to peasants." It reflects Feng's interest in audience and medium. He goes on to extract from the story a further moral on the absurdity of literary and other qualifications in life. (Zi Gong possessed them and failed; the groom lacked them and succeeded.) The item came through the *Zhi pin* (2:25) from the *Huainan Zi* (18) and the *Lü shi chunqiu* (2) versions; the comment is Feng's. In the *Supplemented Sack*, items like this are replaced at the beginning by anecdotes about harsh but salutary measures, the first of which is a drastic action carried out by Confucius himself as an administrator.

38. A copy of an edition entitled *Gujin xiao* is preserved in the Peking Library. (It was formerly in Zheng Zhenduo's possession.) It contains a preface by "Member No. 5 of the rhyming society" as well as a 1620 preface by Feng (under the pseudonym Long Ziyou), written in the Mohan zhai. The annotation is attributed to Yuan Yuling. The publisher of the edition is given as the Mohan zhai, presumably Feng himself. Its text appears to be identical to that of the *Gujin tangai*, of which a facsimile edition is available (Peking, 1955). Soon after the publication of the *Gujin xiao*, Feng must have decided to reserve the word "xiao" for jokes rather than anecdotes. Li Changgeng's preface to Feng's *Taiping guangji chao* (preserved in the National Central Library and in the Gest Collection at Princeton), which is dated the ninth month of 1626, mentions two previous works by Feng—Guide to the Annals and the "Tanyu"—by which I assume he means the *Gujin tangai*. In a general sense, the *Gujin tangai* belongs to the tradition begun by the *New Account of Tales of the World*. On the latter, see the translation by Richard Mather (Minneapolis: University of Minnesota Press, 1976).

39. Especially the *Chutan ji* (Peking, 1974), of which a number of items are repeated in the *Survey*. There is a much closer connection with Xu Zichang's *Peng fu bian* (preserved in the Library of Congress), which has a 1619 preface. It covers much the same ground as Feng's work, but its contents are not classified.

40. Cf. the *Pi dian xiaoshi* (A Short History of Idiosyncrasy and Craziness) by Hua Shu, whom Feng describes in the *Survey* as a friend. It has a preface by Yuan Hongdao, which may not be authentic. It is part of Hua's anthology *Qingshuige Kuai shu shizhong* (preserved in the Library of Congress), which has a 1618 preface.

41. 2:16.

42. There are blocks of seemingly uniform, recent Soochow items, e.g., at the end of juan 5.

43. 1:19-20; 2:14-15; 25:5b.

44. Its effects are evident in other seventeenth-century satire. Cf. the "Headless Men" items in 20:20-21 with the story told in the eleventh section of the *Bean Arbor*.

45. The *Taiping guangji chao*.

46. A copy is preserved in the Ueno Library in Tokyo.

47. 1:47a-b, on schools; 1:50a-b; 1:53a-b; 2:64a-b; 1:12.

48. 1:17. Feng is described in the 1683 *Dantu xianzhi*, 21:24b, as serving as assistant instructor (*xundao*) during the Tianqi reign period (1621-1627), but the dating must be wrong. It can be inferred from the *Dantu xianzhi* that the magistrate Feng refers to here, Shi Que, was in office from about 1631 to 1634.

49. 2:5, in a note; 2:61; 2:48b.

50. There appears to have been a third work by Feng of a similar kind, the *Zhongxing congxin lu*, arranged according to four moral categories, which was published in the Prince of Fu's time. See Yao Jinyuan, *Qingdai jinhui shumu* (Shanghai, 1957), p. 200. The haste with which these works of Feng's were prepared is obvious. Parts were sent out to the printer, he tells us, as soon as they were ready.

51. See the copy described in the *Xuxiu Siku quanshu tiyao* (Taibei, 1971), history section, p. 338; it equals juan 7-12 of the *Jiashen jishi*, which is described below.

52. References are to the *Xuanlan tang congshu* edition. It is in thirteen juan, with an extra juan appended. Elsewhere the work exists in fourteen juan; see the *Xuxiu Siku quanshu tiyao*, history section, p. 338. The work includes dates down to the middle of the eighth month, but it must have been written in 1644, because of Feng's age. The hero of one of the accounts of revolt against the Ming troops is Feng's friend Qi Biaojia. (*Jingkou bianlüe*). The juan of commemorative poetry and prose seems to show that Feng was in touch with such younger writers as You Tong (1618-1704) and Lu Shiyi (1611-1672). Lu also contributes "Fourteen Proposals for the National Resurgence."

53. It is entitled *Zhongxing weilüe*. There is a Ming edition in the Naikaku Bunko and also a 1646 Japanese edition, which Nagasawa Kikuya has reproduced in his *Min Shin shiryōshū* (Tokyo, 1974), I, 183-208. According to Ye Ru's "Guanyu Feng Menglong de shenshi," the *Weilüe* was published in the ninth month of 1645. It was published by the Prince of Tang and begins with his edicts. Note that the *Peking Diary* (*Yandu riji*), which is often attributed to Feng, is described by him as an anonymous manuscript that he merely edited.

54. *Ming shi zong*, 71:23. Feng uses the pseudonym Master of the Seven Delights in his preface to the *Chance Selection on the Three Doctrines* (*Sanjiao ounian*), which he probably wrote in the 1630s; see Chapter 5.

55. See the *Siku quanshu zongmu tiyao* (Taibei, 1971), 25:79.

56. His preface to *Sack of Wisdom* was selected by Wei Yong of Soochow for his *Bing xue xi*, of which the preface is dated 1643; see the Shanghai, 1935, edition, pp. 71-73. (This is the same collection that reprints Dong Sizhang's preface to Feng's lost anthology of art song, the *Wanzhuan ge*.) Feng was a friend of Wei's and wrote a colophon for his *Zhenzhong mi* (preserved in the Peking University Library). On the alleged pieces by Feng in the *Wujun wenbian*, see above, n. 20. Note that the *Qingyuan wenxian*, which the *Dictionary of Ming Biography* (p. 507) describes as collated by Feng, was actually collated by a different Feng Menglong. An annotated edition of the *Songs of Chu* which is preserved in the Naikaku Bunko was mistakenly attributed to Feng by Dong Kang; see his *Shubo yongtan* (1930; rpt., Taibei, 1967), p. 64.

57. See the edition by Guan Dedong (Peking, 1962), which is based mainly on the Ming MS copy in the Shanghai Library. (It preserves only eight of the original ten juan.) Wang Jide described the edition on the day he received it; see

his *Qu lü* (*Zhongguo gudian xiqu lunzhu jicheng*), IV, 181. Wang's preface is dated 1610, but he evidently kept adding items to a final section well after that date. If any reliance can be placed on the order in which the item appears, he must have seen the edition after 1616. (On p. 170, he refers to the two parts of Zang Mouxun's *Anthology of Yuan Drama*, the second part of which appeared only in 1616.) If the anecdote connecting Feng with Xiong Tingbi is true, the edition must have appeared before 1619, for in that year Xiong was reappointed to an army command; see Tan Qian, *Guo jue* (Peking, 1958), V, 5135, 5138. (The anecdote tells how Feng was accused of promoting immorality by bringing out this song book and one of the gaming handbooks.)

58. 1:7b. For Dong Sizhang's "The Sneeze," see 3:24.

59. Pp. 6b-7. See also the introduction, p. 10. Note that the *Shange* has a tenth juan of Tongcheng (Anhui) popular songs. All of the *Shange* songs are translated by Cornelia Töpelmann in *Shan-ko von Feng Meng-lung* (Wiesbaden: F. Steiner, 1973).

60. According to Guan Dedong, it was still current in the Qing; see introduction, p. 10.

61. P. 1.

62. P. 36.

63. The edition is preserved in the Naikaku Bunko. Feng is sometimes credited with the authorship of the numerous works of the pseudonymous Fubo Zhuren ("fubo" refers to drinking games), which consist of jokes, songs, and riddles. Ten of Fubo's works are collected in a *Shi qing shizhong* (preserved in the Peking Library), which also goes by the title of *Po chou yixi hua shizhong*. Seven of his works also exist in a *Fubo shanren qizhong*. Because some of these works are actually selections from Feng's song anthologies, the other works, such as the *Huangshan mi* (riddles) and the *Jia zhu tao* (songs), have also been attributed to Feng, with little foundation. The overlapping between the riddles in juan 8 of the *Guazher* and those of the *Huangshan mi* is not substantial.

64. The *Xianxian pian*, preserved in the Naikaku Bunko.

65. Preserved in the Hōsa Bunko, Nagoya. Its preface has the cyclical characters for 1617. The compiler, who appears under the pseudonym of Wanyu Zi, is included in the *Caibi qingci* of 1624 as the author of several dramatic songs. (The *Caibi qingci* is now in the Palace Museum in Taiwan.)

66. 1:51.

67. The *Xiao fu* exists in what could be a late-Ming edition (preserved in the Naikaku Bunko). The work is best known in a version entitled the *Expanded Treasury of Jokes* (*Guang Xiao fu*), which rearranges its contents into simpler categories, omits the prefatory essays that stood before each section as well as much of the comment, and actually, despite the title, contains less than half the jokes of the original. It expands Feng's preface by inserting a vernacular passage in the middle of it. Feng was given to republishing his work, but it is hard to see why he would reorganize this book so drastically and yet make do with a crudely altered preface. I doubt that it is his work. (For the *Guang Xiao fu*, see the Shanghai, 1936, edition.) The *Treasury* draws heavily on the joke section in Deng Zhimo's *Xianxian pian* (juan 5, entitled "Hongtang"). But, although it mentions a *Xiaolin ping* twice, the jokes do not appear in Yang Maoqian's 1611 joke book of that name (preserved in the Naikaku Bunko). Like the *Treasury*, Feng's expositions of the card game known as *madiao* or *yezi*, *The Classic of Cards in Thirteen Sections* (*Pai jing shisan pian*) and the *Rules of Madiao* (*Madiao jiaoli*), contain much local reference. (See the Ming edition of the *Shuo fu*, continuation, juan 39).

68. *The Act of Creation* (London: Macmillan, 1969), pp. 35-97.

69. See the preface to his *Romantic Dream* (*Fengliu meng*). Although Feng's

manual, the *Mohanzhai xinpu,* does not survive, many passages from it were copied into Shen Zijin's *Nan jiugong shisan diao cipu* (abbreviated title *Nanci xinpu*) of the early Qing.

70. See his preface to Wang Jide's *Qu lü.* The critique of this play is preserved in the *Quhai zongmu tiyao* (Peking, 1959), 9:410; it claims the subject was an event of 1600-1601 in Soochow, to which the play was written in angry reaction.

71. See, e.g., Shen Defu, *Wanli yehuo bian* (Peking, 1959), 25:643, where the low quality is blamed on "actors with a little writing ability" and "the semieducated with a modicum of musical knowledge." According to his preface, Zang Mouxun compiled his *Anthology of Yuan Drama* partly in reaction against the lack of contemporary standards. Feng, in the preface to his revised *Pair of Heroes,* lays the blame on "village schoolmasters," i.e., the semieducated, and old actors who wrote plays as vehicles for themselves.

72. It is first mentioned in the *Taixia xinzou* of 1627.

73. In Shen Ziyou's "Jutong sheng xiaozhuan" in the *Nanci xinpu,* Feng is described as "selecting" the *Taixia xinzou;* presumably the compiler, Guqu sanren, was Feng. In 1644, Feng visited Shen Zijin and urged him to revise his uncle Shen Jing's manual, and in the spring of the following year, he repeated the advice to Zijin and his brother Ziji. (See Shen Zinan's preface and Zijin's "Supplementary Account.") In 1647, Zijin received the manuscript of Feng's manual from his son and made grateful use of it in the *Nanci xinpu.* Qian Nanyang, in his "Feng Menglong *Mohanzhai cipu jiyi,*" *Zhonghua wen shi luncong* 2: 281-310 (Peking, 1962), assembles the passages of Feng's manual from the *Nanci xinpu* and offers a critique of Feng's, Zijin's, and other contemporary manuals.

74. 10:27.

75. The *Romantic Dream,* preface.

76. His concern with technical questions was apparent even in his early, lost collection of dramatic songs, the *Wanzhuan ge;* some of its contents with their original notes have been reprinted in the *Taixia xinzou.*

77. See the introduction to the *Mohanzhai dingben chuanqi,* which is based on the *Xinqu shi'erzhong* anthology and some editions of single plays.

78. 12:18b-22. Lü Tiancheng's *Qu pin,* of which the preface is dated 1610, repeats the notion that the play deals with a real event. (*Zhongguo gudian xiqu lunzhu jicheng,* VI, 237.)

79. 1:15.

80. See the *Quhai zongmu tiyao,* p. 399.

81. See the critique, as well as the notes to 1:7b (scene 5) and 2:9b (scene 23). *The New Gardener* is mentioned in Feng's *Sack of Wisdom* and hence was revised before 1626.

82. 1:11b (scene 6).

83. In editing *Snow-Sprinkled Hall* (*Saxue tang*) by the unidentified Hubei writer Mei Xiaosi, Feng's tone is respectful, and I believe the author must have been his friend Mei Zhiyun or some relative from Macheng. In adapting the plays of Yuan Yuling and Li Yu (Xuanyu), Feng's tone is one of straightforward criticism; Yuan and Li are his juniors and protégés. Yuan was a commentator in the *Survey* and in the *Taixia xinzou.* He also edited the *Happiness Complete* (*Wanshi zu*), which Feng had adapted from an old play; see the critique preserved in the *Quhai zongmu tiyao,* p. 423. The play's final poem talks of composing "new songs" in the peace of a government office of a town in the hills, which may mean that the edition was prepared while Feng was magistrate of Shouning. During the 1630s, Yuan's work seems to follow Feng's. Feng intended to write—or more likely adapt—a fictionalized history of the Han; one

appeared, carrying Yuan's studio name, Jianxiao ge. Yuan also wrote the *Sui shi yiwen* in the same genre. Some of the plays he edited resemble Feng's in their format and editorial attitude. On Yuan Yuling, see Robert E. Hegel, "*Sui T'ang yen-i* and the Aesthetics of the Seventeenth-Century Suzhou Elite," in Andrew H. Plaks, ed., *Chinese Narrative: Critical and Theoretical Essays* (Princeton: Princeton University Press, 1977). Note that Feng also edited some plays apart from those in the *Mohanzhai dingben chuanqi*: the *Sha gou ji* and the *San bao en*, both in the *Guben xiqu congkan*. For the latter, by his protégé Bi Wei, he wrote a preface dated 1643. One or two other plays are attributed to Feng, less reliably.

84. 10:23-24; 7:12-13b; 1:18b-21b. The Three Eternal Things are moral power, worthy acts, and meritorious words. Feng also edited some earlier collections of art song.

85. The *Shike pian*, an anthology compiled by Ma Jiasong with a preface of 1630, includes items from a *Qing shi* that do not appear in the *Qing shi leilüe*. Ma quotes on numerous occasions from *Sack of Wisdom*, with due attribution to Feng. The *Shike pian* is preserved in the Palace Museum, Taibei. There is also a *Qing zhong* in eight juan compiled by Song Cunbiao, whose preface is dated 1626. Preserved in Peking Library, it contains dozens of Classical tales, including the tales by Song Maocheng that had served as sources of "The Pearl-Sewn Shirt" and "The Courtesan's Jewel Box."

86. The "Life of Zhang Run" appears in *Guazher*, 5:41b-43, and in *Anatomy*, 4:6-7b. For the "Life of Wansheng," see *Anatomy*, 22:5-6. Wan was from Hubei, and Feng may have encountered him during his time in Macheng. For the "Life of Ai-sheng," see *Anatomy*, 13:34b-35b; Feng knew her as a singing-girl in Soochow. Feng is explicitly credited with each of these, but he must also have written others, including the romantic story involving his friend Qiu Tan of Macheng; see *Anatomy*, 6, "Qiu Changru." Qiu was a minor poet who was a close friend of both Li Zhi and Yuan Hongdao; he sent Feng songs for his *Guazher* (see juan 4).

87. See CSS, p. 89.

88. In "Changsha yiji," 6:10b, Feng argues with the editor's comment. In "Rongyan Zheng-sheng," 16:6b-7, his is the third and last comment.

89. 5:28a-b. Feng has a strong statement on this very subject in *Guazher*, 1:4b.

90. See 17:20 and 16:6b-7, respectively.

5. FENG'S VERNACULAR FICTION

1. See the *Wanli yehuo bian*, 25:652. (The earliest edition of the *Wanli yehuo bian* is a 1660 movable-type edition which was used in the *Zhongguo gudian xiqu lunzhu jicheng*, vol. 4; this passage is virtually identical in it.) The item is important evidence for the date of the first edition of *The Golden Lotus*. Shen says he discussed the offer with Ma Zhijun, who was then in charge of the Soochow customs office. Ma's posthumous works, the *Miaoyuan tang quanji* (preserved in the National Central Library), make it clear that he took up his Soochow post in 1613 and that by 1616 he was back in Peking. André Lévy's suggestion that Ma took up his post in 1616 is inadmissible ("About the Date of the First Printed Edition of the *Chin P'ing Mei* — Notes Toward A Clarification," *Chinese Literature: Essays, Articles, and Reviews I*[January 1979]: 46). There is other evidence in the *Wanli yehuo bian* that Ma's service in Soochow took place before that time and that in 1617, he was actually demoted in the sexennial review in Peking (see 24:618-619 and 28:723-724). Feng is sometimes credited with the Nongzhu Ke preface, dated Winter 1617, which is attached to the earliest extant edition of the novel, but no evidence has been offered.

2. See Xu's *Shuzhai manlu* (preserved in Peking Library), 6:8a-b. Xu's preface is dated the winter of 1612. In a diary entry for 1614, Yuan Zhongdao mentions receiving a copy of the *Shuihu* edition from the hand of Yuan Wuya (Shudu). On the edition, see Wang Liqi, "*Shuihu quanzhuan* Tian Wang erzhuan shi shui suo jia?" in *Wenxue yichan zengkan*, I, 182-183. Li Yu, in the preface to his edition of the *Sanguo* (preserved in the Bibliothèque Nationale), reports hearing that Feng Menglong had labeled the *Sanguo, Shuihu, Xiyou,* and *Jin Ping Mei* the "four greatest and most remarkable books in the world."

3. The writer of the preface says he intended to make his own selection of one hundred stories but was forestalled. The preface reflects the ideas of Feng's *Stories Old and New* preface and may have been written by Feng, despite the lavish praise it heaps upon him.

4. Feng is credited with at least three letter-writing handbooks, but there is no reason to believe he had anything to do with them. One is the *Rumian tan*, supposedly compiled by the famous writer Zhong Xing and checked by Feng, of which the Naikaku Bunko has a late-Ming edition. Another is the *Zhe mei jian* (in the Naikaku and the Harvard-Yenching), purportedly compiled by Feng and annotated by a member of the Yu publishing family (the Yus seem to have made the most capital out of Feng's name). A third, the *Shu shu huotao*, with a 1645 preface attributed to Feng, reached Japan; see the *Hakusai shomoku* (Kansai University, 1972), II, 25, 30. Several fictionalized histories of the mythical period are attributed to Feng and Zhong Xing; see Sun Kaidi, *Zhongguo tongsu xiaoshuo shumu,* rev. ed. (Peking, 1957), pp. 23-24. One of them, the *You Xia hezhuan* (in the Peking Library), has a preface dated 1635. One or two Qing novels are also attributed falsely to Feng; e.g. the *Xing ming hua* (in the Harvard-Yenching) and also a Qing collection of stories, *Twelve Jokes (Shi'er xiao),* preserved in Peking University Library. A version of the *Tanju biji* miscellany that is published by the Yu family also carries a preface by Feng; see Sun Kaidi, *Riben Dongjing suo jian Zhongguo xiaoshuo shumu,* rev. ed. (Peking, 1958), pp. 135-140. It reprints a few vernacular stories, including one or two of Feng's, but it also contains stories Feng is known to have despised. There is a distinct similarity in the way Feng's name appears in several of these works. There is no possibility that Feng wrote the vernacular version of the *Lienü zhuan,* the *Gujin lienü zhuan tongsu yanyi.* Liu Ts'un-yan has shown that the version must have appeared after 1667; see his *Chinese Popular Fiction in Two London Libraries* (Hong Kong, 1967), pp. 101-102, 301-302. Feng's name is on the title page of some editions of the *Wuchao xiaoshuo,* a vast collection of xiaoshuo completed in 1632-33, probably added by a publisher; see CSS, p. 86, n. 61. R. H. van Gulik suggests that Feng was involved in the publication of Lü Tiancheng's erotic novel *The Unofficial History of the Embroidered Couch (Xiuta yeshi),* but the pseudonym used is not Feng's and there is no other evidence to associate Feng with it; see *Erotic Colour Prints of the Ming Period* (Tokyo, privately printed, 1951), p. 128. The novel is respectfully referred to in Feng's *Celestial Air,* however.

5. See the writer's "The Composition of the *P'ing yao chuan,*" *Harvard Journal of Asiatic Studies* 31(1971): 201-219.

6 *Bei Song san Sui ping yao zhuan* (in the Naikaku Bunko), 1620 ed., Ch. 14, pp. 7-9.

7. See the *Lieguo zhizhuan* (preserved in the Naikaku Bunko), 9 ("Wu Wang Xi Zi bajing").

8. The Naikaku edition was not the first in twelve juan. Juan 4 carries the rubric "checked by Zhu Huang of Soochow," and there are other editions that bear Zhu's preface. An eight-juan edition is preserved in the Hosa Bunko, Nagoya.

9. See juan 3, under "Qi Xiang Gong xi mei xian Peng Wang."

10. See Chs. 78, 82.

11. Particularly Guan Zhong, in Ch. 15 and after. By contrast, Jie Zhitui (Ch. 37) and Qu Yuan (Ch. 93) are little stressed.

12. There are some tense and macabre passages reminiscent of Suetonius, e.g. Ch. 32 on the senility and death of Duke Huan of Qi, Ch. 50 on the coup d'état in Qin, and Ch. 58 on the madness of the Duke of Qin.

13. The only surviving copy is preserved in the Sōkōdō Collection of the Tōyō Bunka Kenkyūjo of Tokyo University. A Manchu translation exists under the (Chinese) title of *Sanjiao tongli xiaoshuo*; see Sun Kaidi, *Zhongguo tongsu xiaoshuo shumu*, p. 222. The Wang Yangming life was published as a separate item in Japan.

14. TY 40. Previously it had existed as a fifteen-chapter novel. In the trilogy it has the same format as in the TY edition.

15. I.e. GJ 4, 7, 16, 20, 29, 30, 35; TY 6 (prologue only), 33, 38, 40. Earlier vernacular versions of TY 1 and HY 11 exist in the fragmentary copy of a nameless popular miscellany in the possession of Lu Gong, the two surviving parts of which are entitled *Xiaoshuo chuanqi*. See his *Ming Qing pinghua xiaoshuo xuan* (Shanghai, 1958), introduction, p. 4.

16. TY 33:20b.

17. TY 33:13b.

18. See CSS, pp. 76-86.

19. See "The Making of *The Pearl-Sewn Shirt* and *The Courtesan's Jewel Box*," pp. 128-139.

20. P. 41b.

21. P. 35a-b.

22. P. 44b.

23. P. 8b.

24. *The Classic Chinese Novel* (New York: Columbia University Press, 1968), pp. 316-321.

25. See CSS, p. 237.

26. The *Hai Gangfeng Xiansheng juguan gong'an zhuan,* published in 1606. The first edition is preserved in the Peking Library. This is the last item, no. 71. The author of the story makes the servant boy more naïve than in his source and has the widow, when faced with blackmail, kill the boy as well as herself.

27. P. 1b.

28. P. 4.

29. P. 11b.

30. P. 2.

31. See CSS, p. 77.

32. P. 8.

33. GJ 16:1b, 2, respectively.

34. See my article "The Authorship of Some *Ku-chin hsiao-shuo* stories," *Harvard Journal of Asiatic Studies* 29(1969): 191-197.

35. P. 12b.

36. P. 2.

37. P. 5b.

38. See Yue Ke's *Ting shi* (*Congshu jicheng* edition, juan 6), "Wang Ge yaochen." André Lévy has argued against my attribution of this story to Feng Menglong, largely on the grounds that it contains anachronisms that a learned man like Feng would not commit; see "A propos des deux versions relatives au récit de la rebellion de l'entrepreneur Wang Ge à la fin du XIIᵉ siècle," *Etudes d'histoire et de littérature chinoises offertes au Professeur Jaroslav Průšek* (Paris: Bibliothèque de l'Institut des Hautes Etudes Chinoises, 1976), pp. 181-187. But

Lévy has neglected to check Feng's known works, in which a surprising number of the anachronisms (and other features he cites) occur.
39. P. 3.
40. See Feng's note on p. 20b: "What did it have to do with the temple god?"
41. See Hanan, "The Authorship of Some *Ku-chin hsiao-shuo* Stories," p. 199.
42. P. 6b.
43. P. 12b.
44. P. 13.
45. In his preface (1642) to Bi Wei's play *San bao en*, which is based on this story.
46. P. 13.
47. Perhaps TY 2, about Zhuang Zi and his wife, a Chinese equivalent of the Widow of Thebes story in Petronius, could be considered an exception. (The introduction is on one of Feng's favorite themes, but there is no other indication that he might have written it.) Note that "Gui yuanwai" (TY 25) deals with disloyalty of another kind and shows the karmic punishment of a family of ingrates.
48. Pp. 2b-3a.
49. P. 5b.

6. LANGXIAN

1. See CSS, pp. 66-70, in which the newcomer is designated "X."
2. The seven stories that certainly predated the collection are 11-14, 21, 31, and 33. Story 5, which is given alternative titles in the text, presumably predated it.
3. The preface by Wu'ai jushi to *Common Words* says that Longxi jun showed him several juan that he had recently printed (sic) and asked him to suggest a title. The preface is dated the twelfth month of 1624. The preface to *Constant Words*, dated mid-autumn of 1627 and written in the same studio in Nanking (Qixia shanfang) in which Wu'ai had met Longxi jun, is signed Keyi jushi of Longxi. (The preface repeats some of the ideas of the *Stories Old and New* preface.) Feng may have been in Nanking at three-year intervals for the provincial examinations; presumably he stayed on Mount Qixia. The notes to *Common Words* are by Keyi zhuren, who is no doubt the Keyi jushi of *Constant Words*.
4. A reprint of *Stories Old and New* entitled *Clear Words to Instruct the World* (*Yu shi mingyan*) must have appeared by 1627; it is referred to in *Constant Words* and in Ling Mengchu's first collection. There are editions of both *Common Words* and *Clear Words* that give the commentator as Keyi jushi and the collator as Molang zhuren, just as in *Constant Words*. The edition of *Common Words* may be the actual edition Feng and his associate produced. (See Sun Kaidi, *Zhongguo tongsu xiaoshuo shumu*, pp. 92-93, for a description.) Two editions of *Clear Words* survive, but one is a later compilation that includes some *Constant Words* stories, and the other is a mere fragment; see Sun Kaidi, pp. 91-92. The likelihood is that Feng and his associate reissued the two works in 1626-1627.
5. See CSS, pp. 70-74, in which Molang's stories in *Constant Words* and Langxian's in *Rocks* are compared. Closer investigation of language and themes does nothing to diminish the case for common authorship, but it cannot be regarded as proven. Note that the first story in *Rocks* cannot be ascribed to Langxian on stylistic grounds, although it fits well thematically. (See CSS, p. 72.) For the editions of *Rocks*, see Sun Kaidi, *Zhongguo tongsu xiaoshuo shumu*, pp. 97-98. I have consulted the Ming edition in the Tōyō Bunka Kenkyūjo for Feng's notes, but references in my text are to the Shanghai, 1935, edition. The book's title refers to the legend of a priest's sermon (given on Tiger Hill in Soochow) that

moved even the nearby rocks and made them nod their heads—another image of moral didacticism.

6. The *Bu xue chusheng*. The point was noted by Ye Dejun in his "*Shi dian tou de zuozhe he laiyuan*," *Tiandi* 6(March 1944). The *Bu xue chusheng* contains many art songs by a certain Zhang Shoulang of Hubei interspersed with a few by Xi Langxian.

7. A principal source of the main story is to be found in the *Wanxuan qingtan* (preserved in the Library of Congress), 4:17b-19, "Wanzhong qibian."

8. Cf. *The Old Gardener*, p. 13b, which has similar lore.

9. P. 6.

10. The source is Mao Kun's (1512-1601) *Gujin lienü zhuan*, juan 8, "Li-shi Yuying." The Harvard-Yenching Library has the 1591 edition.

11. See Chapter 8.

12. E.g., in HY 22:5, the hero is ironically condemned in this fashion.

13. See the discussion of "perfect qing" in the prologue of *Rocks* 9.

14. See, e.g., HY 25:29b, HY 39:4, *Rocks* 13, p. 348.

15. P. 6b.

16. HY 6, 25, 26, 30, 35 (prologue), 38, and *Rocks* 9, 11, and 13 are all set in the Tang. HY 25 and *Rocks* 9 are largely about Wei Gao, while HY 30 and *Rocks* 11 have the An Lushan rebellion as background. HY sources are dealt with in CSS; see "Index to the Extant Stories," pp. 242-245. The main stories of *Rocks* 2, 5, 6, 9, 10, 11, 12, 13, and 14 are related in some fashion to narratives in the *Anatomy of Love*; see "Li Miaohui" (1:5b-7), "Mo juren" (3:14b-15b), "Zhou Liu nü" (2:2b-3), "Wei Gao" (10:23-24b), "Wang Congshi qi" (2:22a-b), "Zhou Di qi" (14:72), "Shen-tu shi" (1:8b-9b), "Tang Xuanzong" (4:18b), and "Pan Zhang" (22:10b), respectively. See Harada Suekiyo, "*Jōshi* ni tsuite," *Taidai bungaku* 2.1(1937): 53-60, and Hua-yuan Li Mowry, "*Ch'ing-shih* and Feng Meng-lung," (Ph.D. diss., Berkeley, 1976), pp. 503-519. Few, however, are actually based on those versions; *Rocks* 9, for example, shares material with other versions, including plays. *Rocks* 3 is apparently based on a tale in Jiao Hong's *Guochao xianzheng lu*, 112:39; see Tu Lien-che, "Mingren xiaoshuo ji qi dangdai qiwen benshi juli," *Tsing-hua Journal of Chinese Studies* 7.2 (1969): 156-175.

17. HY 34:36b.

18. Cf. the prologue of Ling's "Tangerines and the Tortoiseshell" with an incident in the main story of HY 18.

19. HY 26:18-19b. Pp. 18a-b were missing in the Naikaku copy; the facsimile edition has supplemented the text from another edition. The "distributed blessings" are the meats remaining from a sacrifice.

20. HY 15, 22, 39.

21. I.e., the husband of Sun Daniang.

22. Pp. 11-14.

23. *Anatomy of Love*, 14:72, copied from *Taiping guangji* (270).

24. See p. 162.

25. P. 376.

26. HY 2:4b. Cf. the notes on 4b and 5 with Feng's comments in his *Sack of Wisdom*, 3:2b, 11:8, and 14:5.

27. P. 10b, upper-margin note.

7. LING MENGCHU

1. The main sources for Ling's life are the clan genealogy *Ling shi tongpu* of 1805 and the county and prefectural histories, the *Wucheng xianzhi* of 1746 (see 6:28b) and 1881 (see 10:18b, 16:8, and 31:17), and the 1874 *Huzhou fuzhi* (see

59:27-29b). An epitaph by Zheng Longcai is included in the genealogy and (in part) in the *Huzhou fuzhi*. The genealogy has not been accessible, and I am depending for knowledge of it on a chronological account of Ling's life by Ye Dejun entitled "Ling Mengchu shiji xinian," which appeared in four installments in the *Huabei ribao* in 1947, and has been reprinted in Zhao Jingshen, ed., *Xiqu xiaoshuo congkao* (Peking, 1979), II, 577-590. Ye also wrote an article in the Shanghai *Dagong bao* of January 8, 1947, showing that much of what Zheng says of Ling in his epitaph is false ("Shu Zheng Longcai zhuan Ling Mengchu muzhiming hou"). An article by Li Houji in the *Guangming ribao* of May 4, 1958, is based uncritically on the epitaph.

2. The genealogy, which gives a string of higher positions, is not borne out by the local histories; see the 1854 *Daming fuzhi*, 10:33.

3. See Wang Shizhen's preface to Zhilong's *Han shu pinglin*, of which the foreword is dated 1581. It includes comments by his father, Ling Yueyan, as well as by He Liangjun, Wang Shizhen, and others. At least a dozen works compiled by Zhilong exist, dated from 1576 to 1589. Zhilong had changed his name from Yuzhi.

4. See Ye Dejun's article for these and the following details.

5. See Ling's "brief introduction" to his second collection, *Erke Pai an jing qi* (Taibei, 1960). The original is in the Naikaku Bunko.

6. See Feng Mengzhen's diary, contained in his *Kuaixuetang ji*, 60:3b. (The work is preserved in the Naikaku Bunko.) For poems written by Feng on this occasion, see juan 63-64. Ling brought along two Buddhist works, one of them a collection of Su Shi's and Huang Tingjian's Chan meditations, and the two men annotated it together. Much later, in 1621, after Feng's death, Ling published it, attaching a colophon Feng had written in the other work. (See the *Dongpo Chanxi ji*, preserved in the Naikaku Bunko.) It was not the only Buddhist work he annotated. The Library of Congress contains an edition of the *Vimalakīrti sutra* with a copious commentary by Ling, who describes himself as a "disciple of Buddha."

7. See the original edition in the Naikaku Bunko. Ling was obviously imitating his uncle Zhilong, who had published a *Shi ji zuan* in 1579 and a *Han shu zuan* in 1583; both are preserved in the National Central Library. Wang Zhideng, the writer of the preface, was a relative of Ling's closest friend, Wu Zaibo, a writer of art songs; see the *Heng qu zhu tan* (*Zhongguo gudian xiqu lunzhu jicheng*, vol. 4), p. 270.

8. See his *Youju shi lu* (*Yuan Xiaoxiu riji* edition, Shanghai, 1935), p. 50.

9. See Qi Biaojia, *Yuanshantang jupin* (*Zhongguo gudian xiqu lunzhu jicheng*, vol. 4), p. 145.

10. *Tang Xianzu ji* (Peking, 1962), II, 1345. Tang's words as quoted in Ling's *Notes on the Southern Drama* (*Tan qu za zha*) are drawn from this undated letter.

11. See the facsimile edition (Shanghai, 1963).

12. See his *Yuanshantang jupin* and *qupin*.

13. See the *Zuo Guo yuci*, part of the *Wenlin qixiu* collection of Dizhi's (preserved in the Harvard-Yenching Library).

14. See K. T. Wu, "Colour Printing in the Ming Dynasty," *T'ien Hsia Monthly* (August-September 1940): 37-39.

15. In the Min editions, the text is in black and the notes and punctuation in red. Third, fourth, and fifth colors may be used to differentiate the various critics' comments. A modern collector had 136 different Min editions, of which fourteen had Ling Mengchu's name on them; see Tao Xiang, "Ming Wuxing Minban shumu," *Qinghe* 5.13(May 1937): 1-10. It is by no means the complete number of extant editions.

16. The Harvard-Yenching has both editions. Yingchu's colophon explains their relationship.

17. The *Lü shi chunqiu* in the Harvard-Yenching has a preface by Zhilong "written in the hand of his nephew Ling Mengchu," but it is actually a Min edition of 1620. Ling Mengchu's biographies in the local histories also attribute to him editions of historical works that really belonged to his uncle, for example an edition of Ni Si's *Shi Han yitong buping*, of which there is a copy in the National Central Library.

18. The *Huike chuanju* (1919) contains the whole of Ling's *Western Chamber* but rearranges it. For his *Lute*, there is a modern facsimile edition, n.d.

19. See Li Yu's (style Xuanyu) preface to the 1668 edition, which is attached to the modern facsimile edition of the *Three Kinds*. Note that Ling's original edition was collated by Yuan Yuling.

20. I.e., the *Shengmen chuan Shi dizhong*, of which the edition in the National Central Library is dated 1631. For his other, lost works on the *Classic,* see the *Siku quanshu zongmu tiyao* and the *Huzhou fuzhi*, 58.

21. See the *Siku quanshu zongmu tiyao.*

22. Quoted in Li Houji's article in the *Guangming ribao* of May 4, 1958. The work is the *Yan zhu ou.*

23. *Wu sao hebian* (Shanghai, 1934), 4:76.

24. See the *Mingdai zaju quanmu*, pp. 178-182, and the *Mingdai chuanqi quanmu*, pp. 343-344. Nine Northern plays are listed, of which three are extant. One of the nine was the first draft of the *Diandao yinyuan*, and was probably never published. Fu Xihua reports hearing of an extant Min edition of the *Diandao yinyuan;* see p. 180.

25. Zhao Jingshen, "*Qiuran ke zhuan* yu *Bei Hongfu,*" *Yinzi ji* (Shanghai, 1946), pp. 46-47, describes Sun Zijing's preface as implying that Ling's most appreciative friend, on the analogy of the play, is a woman. The preface is not reprinted together with the only accessible text, Zhou Yibai, ed., *Mingren zaju xuan* (Peking, 1958). Ling's own introduction dwells on the lack of recognition of outstanding men, a point that is echoed in Red Whisk's last song in the play.

26. Of the two works Ling lists as sources, the *Gui er ji* of Zhang Duanyi is accessible; see the Peking, 1958, edition, 2:55-56.

27. *Yuanshantang jupin*, p. 155.

28. Ibid., p. 145.

29. See the *Celestial Air*, 6:7b. Zhao Jingshen, "Ling Mengchu de *Shanjin ji,*" *Ming Qing qutan* (Shanghai, 1957), p. 115, reports hearing of an extant edition. The *Three Kinds* note on this play says the *Yuzan* had lost all "authentic feeling."

30. For the apparent plot of Ling's play *Xuehe ji*, see Bei Ying, comp., *Quhai zongmu tiyao bubian* (Peking, 1959), pp. 140-142.

31. For the principal changes made in the story, see Wang Gulu's edition of the *Chuke Pai an jing qi* (Shanghai, 1957), p. 444, n. 8, and p. 445, n. 15. No attempt to disguise the repetition has been made; the story keeps its title and even its place in the collection (23). The fact that it was a Ling play that was added would seem to rule out any merely arbitrary action by a publisher. The story must have been retained to round out the number.

32. Reproduced at the end of T. Y. Li's edition of the *Erke Pai an jing qi* (Taibei, 1960). For the first of the two allusions, see the *Taiping yulan* (Peking, 1960), 744:3305. Jia Jian was a famous archer whom the king ordered to shoot at an ox. His first arrow grazed the beast's back, shaving its hair; the second did the same for its belly. The second allusion is to a sentence from the *Doctrine of the Mean* (*Zhongyong*), 14.3 ("misses the center of the target"). It speaks of the superior man's conduct in an analogous situation. Presumably both allusions refer to Ling's examination experiences.

33. See the edition edited by T. Y. Li (Hong Kong, 1966). It was based on the original edition preserved in the Jigendō at Nikko.

34. It makes no mention of the "three kinds," and therefore seems to be earlier. Fu Xihua, *Mingdai zaju quanmu*, p. 178, lists a *Rules of Drama* (*Qu lü*) by Ling, I do not know on what evidence.

35. Book 2 (*Qi wu lun*).

36. Li Yu's (style Xuanyu) preface describes it as the best work of its kind. Ling's nephew Yanxi's colophon to the *Lute* says Ling had already published *The Lapel* and his edition of *Western Chamber*, but does not mention the *Three Kinds*. One may suppose that the former works came out about 1620 and the *Three Kinds* a little later but well before 1627. (It is mentioned in the *Celestial Air*).

37. Guo Shaoyu, *Canglang shihua jiaoshi* (Peking, 1961), p. 103, comments on the meaning of these terms in this context. Bense in the sense of the authentic nature of a person (e.g., a hero) is rarer in Ling's dramatic criticism, although common in the notes to his stories. Sometimes he uses the term *qujia bense* ("dramatists' bense") to distinguish it from other kinds.

38. He also defends moralistic discussion — even the quoting of the Confucian classics — on the grounds that it had belonged to the Yuan drama.

39. It is used in different ways by sixteenth-century critics such as Tang Shunzhi and Li Zhi. Note that the *Celestial Air* editors try to separate the two terms, using "danghang" to distinguish the diction of drama from that of poetry and "bense" to distinguish it from that of lower forms. In the latter case, it means "ordinary speech that does not cross over into coarseness or vulgarity"; see 12:18.

40. He traces the descent of drama from the old *yuefu*, whose diction was formed from "dialect and ordinary language."

41. The *Celestial Air*, compiled by followers of Shen Jing, contains numerous subtle ripostes to Ling's ridicule of their master. The editors delight in pointing out that, on at least one occasion, Ling placed a Shen Jing song set in his highest or heavenly class (characterized by "simplicity, naturalness, professionalism, and authenticity") without realizing its authorship.

42. See He Liangjun's *Qu lun* and Wang Shizhen's *Qu zao* (*Zhongguo gudian xiqu lunzhu jicheng*, vol. 4), p. 6 and pp. 33-34, respectively.

43. See his *Qu lü* (edition cited above), pp. 121, 149.

44. See Shen's *Gu qu zayan* and Xu's *Qu lun* (editions cited above), p. 210 and pp. 235-236, respectively.

45. In the *Three Kinds, sanqu*, 2:5a-b, Ling notes that popular songs such as the *Guazher* render human feelings better than the contemporary drama. On p. 6b, he uses the image of cutting through the skin and flesh to get to the bone of meaning.

46. All references are to the editions prepared by T. Y. Li. The stories are referred to by the collection in which they appear and by their order within it; thus I.1 means the first story in the first collection. The short titles are for mnemonic purposes; they do not necessarily reflect any part of the actual titles.

47. I. 23, 485.

48. E.g., in I.19, 20, 25, 28; II.12, 17, 37, etc. In his editions, Wang Gulu lists numerous sources.

49. The same point is made in *Sack of Wisdom*, 8:9.

50. Expressed most notably by Dryden in his "A Discourse Concerning the Original and Progress of Satire," 1693.

51. L. J. Potts, *Comedy* (London: Hutchinson, 1948), p. 124.

52. Wolfram Eberhard, *Typen Chinesischer Volksmärchen* (*FF Communications* no. 120, Helsinki, 1937) and *Volksmärchen aus Süd-ost-China, Sammlung Ts'o Sung-yeh* (*FF Communications* no. 128, Helsinki, 1941). The folk tale is no. 177 in the first work, no. 114 in the second.

53. Northrop Frye, *Anatomy of Criticism*, pp. 163-165.

54. P. 365.

55. II. 8, 122.

56. See the Shanghai, 1927, edition, *zhi geng*, 10:4b-5.

57. See the block print editions in the Academia Sinica and the Harvard-Yenching Library, respectively. According to Wang Jide's *Qu lü*, the former was written by his friend Lü Tiancheng in his youth, i.e., about 1600.

58. The original edition, of which the "appreciation" (*tici*) is dated the beginning of 1631, is preserved in the Naikaku Bunko. Chs. 1-14 were reprinted in Dairen in 1916 and Chs. 31-40 by Lu Gong in his *Ming Qing pinghua xiaoshuo xuan*. Only the author's surname, Wu, and his pseudonym, the Carefree Man of the Metal and the Wood (Jinmu sanren), are known. The writer of the preface is from Soochow, but most of the commentators are from Hangchow. One of the commentators uses the pseudonym of Deng Zhimo.

59. Wang Shouyi describes what he believes to be a Shunzhi (1644-1661) edition of the former; see the *Guangming ribao*, May 28, 1961 (*Wenxue yichan* no. 365). For the latter, see Chapter 8.

60. The earliest extant edition is that by the Shangxin ting.

61. See juan 14, "Enmity from Love" (*qingchou*). The compiler's comment begins by explaining the term "huanxi yuanjia," stressing the causative connection of love with hatred. The intensities of love and hatred are related to each other: "If one doesn't love, one doesn't hate, and if one doesn't hate, one doesn't love." At the end of his final story, which ends in a happy reunion, the author comments that it runs counter to all the others; he evidently conceived of the collection as a whole.

62. The preface, purporting to be by the author, is signed by the Fisherman Recluse of the West Lake (Xihu yuyin) at the Shanshui Lin, the name of a studio. The Shanshui Lin published two volumes of plays in the late Ming, one of which was the *Four Great Follies* (*Si da chi*), a tetralogy on the traditional vices of Lust, Drink, Avarice, and Wrath. (A copy is preserved in the Harvard-Yenching Library.) One of the plays, that on avarice, is actually described in story 12 of *Antagonists in Love*. The Shanshui Lin edition of the tetralogy has no compiler's or editor's name, but the other extant Shanshui Lin edition, that of Fan Wenruo's *Huayan zhuan*, carries the line "Corrected by Yiwei of the West Lake." (See Fu Xihua, *Mingdai zaju quanmu*, pp. 344-345.) Yiwei can almost certainly be identified with Gao Yiwei of Hangchow and the West Lake, the late-Ming adapter and editor of two Southern plays, one of which survives, carrying a similar attribution: "Corrected (*dingzheng* is used in each case) by Gao Yiwei of Qiantang," i.e., Hangchow. (See Fu Xihua, *Mingdai chuanqi quanmu*, pp. 228-229, for both plays; the Japanese import record of the lost play carries a similar line.)

63. E.g., story 3 was influenced by "The Pearl-Sewn Shirt" and "Prefect Kuang"; story 4 was also influenced by the "Pearl-Sewn Shirt;" and story 5 uses some of the setting of "The Old Gardener."

64. See the copy in the Tōyō Bunka Kenkyūjo (Sōkōdō). Note that the *Baduan jin* preserved in the Peking University Library reprints at least five stories from *Expanse of Passion*.

65. The sole extant edition is now in the Palace Museum, Taibei. The title refers to its theme of homosexuality: "Wearing a cap (like a man) but hairpins (like a woman)." The same author wrote another collection of four erotic stories, the *Yi chun xiang zhi* (see Sun Kaidi, *Zhongguo tongsu xiaoshuo shumu*, p. 110) and was also involved with *The Jealous Wife* (*Cu hulu*), a novel on a henpecked husband theme that is preserved in the Naikaku Bunko. A number of other anonymous erotic or romantic collections exist from the late Ming, most of them not easily accessible. They include *Tan xin wu* and *Tian cou qiao* by the same author (see Sun Kaidi, pp. 107 and 98, respectively); *Wugeng feng* (Sun Kaidi,

p. 99); and *Baiyuan zhuan* (Sun Kaidi, p. 155). Lu Gong notes a fragmentary *Bi hua nao* and Tien-yi Li a *Jin fen xi*, which may be closer to the erotic-romantic strain than to the moral-heroic. (See *Ming Qing pinghua xiaoshuo xuan*, introduction, p. 5, and "Riben suo jian Zhongguo duanpian xiaoshuo lüeji," *Tsinghua Journal of Chinese Studies,* n.s. 1.2 (April 1957): 71-73.) The *Twelve Jokes* (*Shi'er xiao*), of which only four survive in the Peking University copy, makes a spurious attempt to suggest Feng Menglong's authorship; it consists of expanded sex jokes on a lower level than those of *Expanse of Passion.* Several other works, such as the *Baduan jin,* are secondary anthologies.

66. On the editions, see Sun Kaidi, p. 97, and Liu Xiuye, *Gudian xiaoshuo xiqu congkao* (Peking, 1958), pp. 48-57. Twenty-four stories from *Illusions,* and ten from Ling Mengchu's second collection, are included in the "variant edition" of the *Erke Pai an jing qi* preserved in the Bibliothèque Nationale; they carry comments by Lu Yunlong, the late-Ming publisher, and his friends. A work which could well be included with these is *Qishi'er chao renwu yanyi* (preserved in the Naikaku Bunko), a collection of pious stories about figures from the Confucian Four Books, which has a 1640 preface.

67. See the Shanghai, 1936, edition. A Ming edition is preserved in the Naikaku Bunko.

68. See Sun Kaidi, *Riben Dongjing suo jian Zhongguo xiaoshuo shumu,* pp. 192-194. A mimeographed copy of *Needles* was issued by Dongbei People's University in 1957.

69. Three stories are reprinted in Lu Gong, *Ming Qing pinghua xiaoshuo xuan,* pp. 85-122. Lu Gong attributes the authorship to a certain Yu Lin, who also, apparently, wrote a novel about Yang Guifei at the court of Tang Xuanzong; see p. 84.

70. The original edition is preserved in the Peking Library. There is also a Shanghai, 1956, edition.

71. The prologue's introduction is about Qu You, author of *New Tales Under the Lamplight,* and about Xu Wei, author of a play about Ni Heng, the righteous Confucian scholar, denouncing the tyrant Cao Cao. Zhou clearly sees himself in two roles: as a gifted writer forced to lower himself, like Qu You, to write fiction in order to make a living, and as one who, like Xu Wei, excoriated his contemporaries by historical example.

72. Originally from the *Xuan shi zhi,* it appears under the title of "Li Zheng" in the *Taiping guangji* (427) and as "Ren hu zhuan" in the *Gujin shuohai.*

8. LI YU

1. See his preface to Li's collected works, *Yijia yan,* in the *Li Yu quanji,* I, 9. Although the print of the *Li Yu quanji* is sometimes barely legible, it is the most convenient edition for reference. It does not include the *Rou putuan,* however; references here are to the Meiji period Japanese edition. Liweng was Li Yu's style. On his life, see Sun Kaidi's "Li Liweng yu *Shi'er lou,*" published as an introduction to the Yadong edition (Shanghai, 1949) of the *Shi'er lou* stories and reprinted in the *Li Yu quanji,* vol. 15. Helmut Martin, *Li Li-weng über das Theater* (Taibei, 1958), provides some biographical information and a comprehensive bibliography. Nathan Mao and Liu Ts'un-yan include a brief biography in their *Li Yu* (Boston: Twayne, 1977).

2. See *Shi'er lou* (*Twelve Structures*) 10 and 11, as discussed below. The Naikaku Bunko contains a *Sketch of Ancient and Modern History* (*Gujin shilüe*) by Hushang Liweng (Liweng of the Lake), which displays the same attitudes. (On a list of banned books under the Qing, it is a work that Li Yu scholars have

assumed to be lost.) It is an outline of history in twelve juan, from Pangu's creation of the world up to 1644, which vastly increases its coverage as it approaches
the terminal date; juan 12 is on the first few months of 1644. It accords great
respect to the Manchus, and its stress in the last couple of juan is on the atrocities
committed by the late-Ming rebels. (Some of the details appear to have been used
by Aina in writing the eleventh section of his *Idle Talk under the Bean Arbor.*

3. See the *Xianqing ou ji* (*Li Yu quanji*, vol. 6), VI, 2800.

4. V, 2648-2649.

5. V, 2339; 1911; 1915. IV, 2517.

6. Dong Yue, author of the highly innovative novel *Xiyou bu* (*Supplement to
the Western Journey*), of which the preface is dated 1641, was also an amateur inventor. See Liu Fu, "*Xiyou bu* zuozhe Dong Ruoyu zhuan," *Bannong zawen erji*
(Shanghai, 1935), pp. 95-96.

7. VI, 2739-2740 (on walking), 2766-2771 (on sex), 2731-2732 (on sleep), and
2790 (on medicine).

8. See the general critique to the *Mistake with the Kite* (*Fengzheng wu*), *Li Yu
quanji*, VII, 3221.

9. *Xianqing ou ji,* I, 1949; 1952; 2009; 1950.

10. The *Kui ci guanjian,* item 6; see *Li Yu quanji*, III, 1293.

11. See the section "Avoid the Fantastic" in the *Xianqing ou ji,* I, 1959-1962. It
appears to show Ling Mengchu's influence.

12. II, 2056.

13. His play *Ideal Marriage Destinies* (*Yizhong yuan*) has preface and notes by
a woman poet and artist, Huang Jie. In one of her notes, she complains bitterly of
her treatment by the public. See also p. 2248, in which Li Yu claims he can be
called the *zhiji* (appreciative friend) of woman.

14. See the *Xianqing ou ji,* II, 2106-2116, "Turning the Old into the New."

15. See the critique at the end of Chapter 2 of *Carnal Prayer Mat* on the novel's
unorthodox opening.

16. See Sun Kaidi's "Li Liweng yu *Shi'er lou*," pp. 6658-6659.

17. *Xianqing ou ji,* II, 2091; 2092. On Jin Shentan's criticism, see John Ching-
yu Wang, *Chin Sheng-t'an* (New York: Twayne, 1972).

18. See the *Kui ci guanjian*, item 12 (p. 1293).

19. See the *Kui ci guanjian* and several sections of juan 1 of the *Xianqing ou ji*,
especially "Value Clarity and Simplicity" (pp. 1969-1974) and "Avoid the Superficial" (pp. 1978-1979). Li Yu charts a middle course through the Scylla and
Charybdis of diction, as Ling Mengchu does, advocating the compromise
achieved by the Yuan playwrights. Another section, pp. 1983-1985, advises
against pedantic and allusive diction.

20. *Xianqing ou ji,* I, 1984.

21. P. 1798; p. 1984.

22. P. 1938.

23. See his letter to Han Ziqu, *Li Yu quanji*, I, 514: "In general, my poetry,
prose, and miscellaneous writings are all material for laughter."

24. *Xianqing ou ji,* I, 1976.

25. See Sun Kaidi, *Riben Dongjing suo jian Zhongguo xiaoshuo shumu*,
pp. 152-172, for an account of the extant early editions. There are three: (1) the
Wu sheng xi heji, a fragment, now in the Peking University Library; (2) the *Liancheng bi quanji*, a manuscript copied from an edition after it was imported into
Japan, which is now in the Lüda Municipal Library; (3) an edition entitled
Wusheng xi of twelve stories, the sole copy of which is in the Sonkeikaku Bunko
in Japan. (This last edition has been republished in facsimile both in the *Li Yu
quanji* and separately.) Both (1) and (2) contain a preface by Du Jun, in which he
says that Li showed him the first and second collections of the *Wusheng xi.* (The

word "second" is missing in [2] and the whole double page is lacking in [1]). Du says he combined and republished them, making reductions to cut costs for the purchaser. It seems, therefore, that there were six different editions, assuming all were actually printed and published: (a) and (b), the two collections Li Yu gave to Du Jun; (c), the combined edition he edited; (d), the *Wusheng xi heji*, edition (1) above, which is a later edition of the one by Du Jun; (e), the *Liancheng bi quanji*, edition (2) above, a still later edition; (f), the *Wusheng xi*, a selection from one of the combined editions (c, d, e).

The *Liancheng bi quanji* was divided into a main section and a *waibian* of twelve and six stories, respectively (see the *Hakusai shomoku,* nos. 4-5, p. 4). The manuscript contains only four of the six waibian stories. It is possible that the twelve represent the old first collection, and the six the old second collection. (Whether Du Jun actually cut any stories out one cannot say.) The *Wusheng xi* contains seven stories from the main section and four from the waibian. Its seventh story is not in the *Liancheng bi* manuscript, although scholars of Li Yu's fiction, following Sun Kaidi, have assumed it to be there, equating it wrongly with no. 3 in the manuscript. The *Wusheng xi* stories correspond, in order, to the following *Liancheng bi* stories: 5, 4, 2, 6, waibian 1, waibian 3, nothing, waibian 4, waibian 2, 10, 11, 8. It appears that the anthologist began by selecting from the initial stories of the main section, went on to the waibian, and then came back to the later stories of the main section. The whole work was probably in three fascicules, which he took in the order 1, 3, 2. I suggest that story 7 of the *Wusheng xi* corresponds to one of the two missing waibian stories. We thus have seventeen extant stories from the combined edition, not sixteen. Sun Kaidi gives synopses of the five inacessible *Liancheng bi* stories (pp. 159-169).

26. Li Yu's only Classical tale, the "Qinhuai jian'er zhuan," uses the same stuff-material but probably not the same source as Ling Mengchu's I.3, the miles gloriosus story. (See *Li Yu quanji,* I, 242-250.)

27. John Simon, *New York Times Book Review* (February 29, 1976).

28. Li Yu also wrote a more orthodox story on female jealousy, no. 7 in the *Liancheng bi*. See Sun Kaidi's synopsis, pp. 164-165.

29. Pp. 5345-5346, upper-margin note.

30. See *Li Yu quanji,* XIII, 5387.

31. XII, 5080-5081.

32. Pp. 5082; 5160-5161.

33. Pp. 5142-5143; 5148.

34. XIV, 5992; 5888.

35. *Xianqing ou ji,* V, 2571.

36. XI, 4812 (act 2); VIII, 3698 (act 2).

37. XIV, 5936. The meaning "three teachers" is implied by the actual title.

38. P. 5947.

39. XV, 6354.

40. Pp. 6433-6434.

41. See Sun Kaidi, "Li Liweng yu *Shi'er lou*," XV, 6670.

42. Pp. 6355-6356.

43. Pp. 6407; 6420; 6426.

44. P. 6434.

45. P. 6548. "True art" is miswritten. The translation follows the Yadong, 1949, edition.

46. See Sun Kaidi, "Li Liweng yu *Shi'er lou,*" pp. 6673-6677.

47. XIV, 5998.

48. P. 6011.

49. P. 6047.

50. XV, 6246.

51. P. 6255.

52. *Xianqing ou ji*, II, 2086.

53. XIV, 6077.

54. Pp. 6106; 6128.

55. Nathan Mao and Liu Ts'un-yan, pp. 92-95, note numerous connections between Li's stories and his novel, but not these. They give credence to a highly questionable cyclical date attached to one edition of the novel and set its composition in Li Yu's youth. (R. H. van Gulik challenges the value of this edition; see his *Erotic Colour Prints of the Ming Period*, p. 94.) The evidence is in the other direction, as Helmut Martin has concluded; see his *Li Li-weng über das Theater*, pp. 299-301.

56. XIV, 6159-6160.

57. Pp. 6173-6174.

58. P. 6175.

59. XV, 6456; 6476.

60. P. 6480.

61. P. 6528.

62. Li Yu actually turned it into a play called *The Ingenious Finale* (*Qiao tuanyuan*), with the aid of some material from *Operas* 5. In the more decorous world of the drama, the means of identification has been changed to a sixth toe on the left foot.

63. For the preface, see the *Guyi xiaoshuo congkan* (Shanghai, 1928), which is based on the Japanese edition of the 1764-1771 period. (The Chinese work entered Japan in 1693.) References to the text of the stories are to the Shanghai, 1957, edition.

64. The glass or cup of the title is mentioned in several well-known Ming works, notably Shen Defu's *Wanli yehuo bian* (supplement, juan 4, p. 936). It came to the notice of the Chinese as an image used in a flowery letter to the Hongwu emperor from Timur of Samarkand. (For the text of the letter, see the *Ming History*, 332, under "Samarkand.") The letter compares the Emperor's mind to a "world-reflecting cup" (*zhao shi zhi bei*). According to E. Bretschneider, *Medieval Researches from Eastern Asiatic Sources* (London, 1910), II, 260, n.1065, the allusion is to Jamshyd's Cup, a common image in Persian poetry. (Cf. Fitzgerald's *Rubaiyat*.) Note that the author of the *Cup* stories appears to refer to himself in the poem that introduces the last story.

65. See Ding's *Jianggan cao*, his collected poems for the years 1660-1661. (The *Jianggan cao* forms part of the *Ding Yehao xiansheng yigao*, preserved in Peking Library.) He was sent in 1659 to a post in Fujian, and passed through Hangchow on his way there, as well as on the way back. (He fell ill shortly after his arrival in the post.) Mention of "this winter" could therefore be either the end of 1659 or the end of 1660. I assume the latter, since he evidently left during the winter. Ding's novel was apparently published during his visit; the preface is by someone from the West Lake, and the edition appeared in 1660.

66. Character irony refers to the gap between a character's pretensions and beliefs and the reality.

67. P. 25.

68. See Robert H. van Gulik, *The Gibbon in China, An Essay in Chinese Animal Lore* (Leiden: E. J. Brill, 1967), pp. 26-29. To the essentials of the legend, which goes back to the *Shan hai jing*, the author has added other anecdotal material (perhaps from the *Survey of Talk*, 35), as well as some comic touches of his own.

69. P. 81.

9. AINA

1. References are to the Shanghai reprint of the Hanhai lou edition, which appeared probably in the middle of the eighteenth century. It is in the Peking Library, as is the earliest extant edition, which was apparently published in the early Qing. The latter is a large-format edition, with illustrations, but fragmentary; only the first seven sections survive. In addition to the Hanhai lou, there are editions from 1781, 1795, 1798, and 1805. (In editions after the first, the "na" of "Aina" is written differently.) In 1795, a *Little Bean Arbor* (*Xiao Doupeng*) appeared, by Zeng Yandong, a *juren* graduate of 1792; see the Shanghai, 1935, reprint of the 1890 edition. Although inspired by the *Bean Arbor*, it is a collection of Classical tales, with no frame story. The *Bean Arbor* itself has received little attention from scholars. It was described briefly by Zheng Zhenduo in his 1931 article "Ming Qing erdai de pinghua ji," *Zhongguo wenxue yanjiu* (Peking, 1959), pp. 447-449; Sun Kaidi listed the editions in his *Zhongguo tongsu xiaoshuo shumu*, p. 104; Zhao Jingshen devoted a short article to it, in his *Xiaoshuo luncong* (Shanghai, 1947), pp. 94-97; and André Lévy, in the most substantial study so far, introduced the collection and summarized the stories' contents in his "Etudes sur trois recueils anciens de contes chinois," *T'oung Pao* 52.1-3 (1965): 110-137.

2. See the critique at the end of Chapter 12. "Chuanqi" is assumed to mean plays, not Classical tales.

3. A fragmentary copy of the revised novel, the *Ji Dian quanzhuan*, is preserved in the Peking Library; it was formerly in Zheng Zhenduo's possession. (There is also a complete edition in the Lüda Municipal Library, an edition I have not seen.) The author's name is given in the edition as Xiangying jushi, but he is identifiable from his seal as Wang Mengji. Xiangying is described as from the West Lake. The illustrations are matched with signed poems. Some are clearly by Wang himself, but one is by "Aina jushi." (Oddly, his seal, which accompanies the name, writes "na" differently, with the silk radical.) The commentator on the *Ji Dian quanzhuan* is named Purple-Bearded Man of the Way, from Jiaxing; the commentator on *Idle Talk under the Bean Arbor* is named Purple-Bearded Crazy Stranger, also from Jiaxing. In his preface, Wang refers to the West Lake as Holy Lake (*Sheng hu*); the *Idle Talk* gives Aina's native place as Holy Water (*Sheng shui*). *Idle Talk* uses the term *ze* for its sections, as does the *Ji Dian quanzhuan*.

4. Preserved in Peking Library.

5. On the edition, see Wu Xiaoling, "Qingdai juqu tiyao bazhong," *Wenxue nianbao* 5 (1939): 45-46. The *Doupeng xianxi* forms part of a collection of three Northern plays entitled *Three Illusions* (*Sanhuan ji*) which was appended to a collection of eight Southern plays republished in a Nanking edition of the Kangxi period. (The title of the Nanking edition was *Xiuke chuanqi shizhong*, in blatant disregard of the nature and quantity of its contents.) Li Yu's name was on both the eight-play collection as editor, and also on this, no doubt spuriously in the latter case, at least. A manuscript of *Three Illusions* is preserved in Peking University Library. *Idle Dramas,* which calls for the erection of a bean arbor on stage, is adapted from the debunking stories of Jie Zhitui (Chapter 1), Xishi (Chapter 2), and Bo Yi and Shu Qi (Chapter 7). Its plays, in very colloquial language, are more overtly didactic than the stories, and in a different way; they include much conventional bao morality.

6. The background narrator of Chapter 9 describes his own experience in the capital under the Ming. If we equate his experience with the author's, Aina must have visited Peking in 1640 at the latest.

7. P. 1.

8. P. 169.

9. See the end of Chapter 2.

10. See p. 170.

11. P. 164. The same phrase (*bu de yi*) was used by the Confucian zealot Yang Guangxian, famed for his tirades against the Jesuits, in the title of a tract published in 1665. See the Taibei, 1969, reprint of the 1928 edition.

12. Much of his neo-Confucianism is actually derived from Zhu Xi's works. His attacks on Buddhism are a simplified version of those made by a long line of Confucian philosophers from Zhu Xi himself to Aina's contemporary Yan Yuan.

13. P. 168. Although it appears to be fictional, the rebellion has a general resemblance to that led by Tang Sai'er in 1420.

14. Pp. 168-169. That heaven should act to preserve a balance is a familiar idea in the *Classic of Changes*. The particular application appears to be Chen's alone, however.

15. See 20:20; Aina has evidently combined two items.

16. "Cai wei," translated by Yang Hsien-yi and Gladys Yang as "Gathering Vetch" in *Old Tales Retold* (Peking, 1961), pp. 54-80. Lu Xun completed his story about the time the modern edition of the *Bean Arbor* appeared. There is no mention of it in his collected works.

17. *Shi ji*, 63. Sima Qian also had doubts about a beneficent providence.

18. Wang Anshi proposed a neat, historian's answer, suggesting that the *Records of the Historian* includes accretions that distort the thinking of Confucius and Mencius, who had merely praised the brothers for rejecting King Zhou. Thus, the brothers' attempt to block the insurgent army and their retreat to the mountain are just accretions. Wang's and others' solutions to the conundrum of the brothers are collected by Liang Yusheng in his *Shi ji zhi yi* (*Congshu jicheng* edition), XXVII, 1113-1115. Aina's appears to be the first thorough debunking of the brothers.

19. *Cai wei yin*; see *Eminent Chinese of the Ch'ing Period*, p. 42.

20. A distortion of the *Analects*, 4.5.

21. Pp. 84-85. Zhao Jingshen takes this as a satirical portrait of a traitor. True, but we are also meant to conclude that Shu Qi is doing the smart, practical thing.

22. Pp. 91; 92.

23. P. 92. The blue lily is the blue lotus, a common image for the eyes of the Buddha.

24. The magical stone of the title is described in Chinese materia medica, and the more fanciful accounts of it claim that it is capable of curing blindness. The play *Kongqing shi* by Aina's contemporary Wan Shu deals with this stone. The name of the arhat Zizai, translated as Free-and-Easy, represents the Buddhist concept of *Īśvara*: "free from resistance," "free from delusion."

25. The play is called *Li Chuang fan shenjing*.

26. For the origin of the comedy, see a joke in Zhao Nanxing's *Xiao zan*, contained in Wang Liqi, *Lidai xiaohua ji* (Shanghai, 1957), p. 288.

27. P. 104. The "world inside the pot" refers to a Taoistic legend that exists in several different forms. Here, of course, it is the world of the wine pot. Note that the depredations of Lightning refer to the three calamities of Buddhist thought — fire, water, and wind — the means by which the world is destroyed.

28. Female jealousy obsesses the comic writers of the seventeenth century. The novel *Marriage Destinies to Awaken the World* (*Xingshi yinyuan zhuan*) is largely concerned with it, as is *The Jealous Wife* (*Cu hulu*). Several of Pu Songling's tales and also a play are devoted to it. Li Yu, of course, endeavored to find a fresh approach.

29. *Shi ji* 39. See also the *Zuo zhuan*, Duke Xi, 24.

30. It exists in various forms, in most of which Shi You is the name of a wind.

31. By Liang Chenyu (b. 1510). Wang Daokun's *Wuhu you* provides a similar romantic ending. (See the *Guben Xiqu congkan*, first series, and the *Sheng Ming zaju erji*, respectively.)

32. Note the debunking play *Fu Xishi* by the seventeenth-century Xu Shiqi. On Xu and his play, see Zeng Yongyi, "Qingdai zaju gailun," *Zhongguo gudian xiju lunji* (Taibei, 1975), pp. 130-133. Another, anonymous debunking play, *Dao Wansha*, is reprinted in the *Guben xiqu congkan*, third series.

33. P. 56.

APPENDIX: LATER COLLECTIONS

1. The original fine edition is preserved in the Peking University Library. Reference here is to the Shanghai, 1956, edition. The compiler is given as Molang Zi of Soochow, a name that appears on several other works of fiction, and which has presumably been taken from that of Feng's associate in *Constant Words*. A Molang Zi from the West Lake was involved in a seventeenth-century novel about Ji Dian; see Sun Kaidi, *Zhongguo tongsu xiaoshuo shumu*, p. 174. A Molangxian zhuren of the Three Wu wrote the novel on the female martyr, *Hai liefu bailian zhen zhuan*, which is preserved in the Bibliothèque Nationale. (The martyrdom is said to have occurred in 1667.) The novel's preface is by Wolu zhuren, who uses the name "Ink-Crazy" on his seal, a name that Feng Menglong commonly employed. (There is a pattern here; the *Twelve Jokes* was attributed to the Master of the Ink-Crazy Studio, and its preface was by Yiwolu sheng.) Except possibly for the novel about Ji Dian, the other works seem remote from the *Charming Stories*.

2. He adapts its first story to form his twelfth.

3. E.g., the story of Little Green (Xiaoqing), as found in the *Anatomy of Love* 14, about a concubine oppressed by a jealous wife, a story made more poignant by the poems she leaves describing her plight. (There is evidence, some of it conflicting, that Little Green was a fictional creation; see Yagisawa Hajime, "*Shōseiden* no shiryō," *Shūkan Tōyōgaku* 6 (1961): 64-78, and two earlier articles in the *Kangakkai zasshi*, 4.3 and 5.2, in 1936 and 1937, respectively. Note that the characters for "little" and "green" make up the character for "qing.") The author of the *Charming Stories* feels compelled to explain why he has introduced a note of tragedy into the blissful world of the West Lake, and in his epilogue he considers the question of whether we should feel sorry for Little Green. Some people, he says, meaning the author of the Classical tale, are impressed by her talent and feel sad over her death. He thinks differently. If she had not been cruelly treated, her life would have been transitory. Her tragedy has immortalized her. Note that Molang Zi includes a vernacular story or two among his Classical sources, most notably "Madam White"; it is smoothed out and simplified to make story 15.

4. Lu Gong reprints four of the five stories of the Xiaohua xuan edition in his *Ming Qing pinghua xiaoshuo xuan*. (On the edition, which he describes as "about 1650," see p. 122; his reasons for placing the work's composition in the Ming, however, are invalid.) Several other collections from the latter half of the seventeenth century, most of them of the same general type, may be listed here. The *Flower-Laden Ship* (*Zai hua chuan*), published in Hangchow in 1659, contains four four-chapter erotic stories of inferior quality. It is preserved in Peking University Library. The *Awakening Bell* (*Jingwu zhong*) also contains four four-chapter stories. It is by an author who also wrote a short "brilliant and beautiful" novel and a short erotic novel. (See Sun Kaidi, *Zhongguo*, pp. 141, 158.) The Caoxian tang edition of the collection is preserved in the Mukyukai, Machida, Japan. Its fourth story is about the female martyrdom of 1667 (see n.1 above).

Brocaded and Embroidered Garments (*Jinxiuyi*) consists of two stories of six chapters each, which were imported into Japan in 1695. Their titles are "Exchanging the Wedding Dress" ("Huan jiayi") and "Changing the Embroidery Design" ("Yi xiupu"). See Kudō Takamura, "Oda Kakusai Shi kyūzō Shina shōsetsu no nisan," *Kangakkai zasshi* 6.2 (July 1938): 119. The collection is also preserved in the Mukyūkai. The same author was also responsible for two other six-chapter stories that go by the general title of *All is Illusion* (*Dou shi huan*) and that exist in an early-Qing edition; see Sun Kaidi, *Zhongguo*, p. 102. *Snippets of Raw Silk* (*Shengxiao jian*), preserved in the Peking Library, contains eighteen stories (Sun, p. 106, gives the figure incorrectly as nineteen), ascribed to different authors, although they are clearly the work of one. They are not particularly erotic, as Sun's classification would indicate, but are concerned with moral problems, some of a mildly erotic nature. They contain numerous popular songs. The title has the words "Shengtan waishu" attached to it, claiming a connection, probably spurious, with the famous critic Jin Shengtan. The *Fei ying sheng*, originally of eight stories, survives in a ten-work collection entitled *Xiaoshuo shizhong*, mostly "brilliant and beautiful" novels, which was in the possession of the late Kuraishi Takejirō of Tokyo (story 4 is missing). All of the extant seven are set in the Ming, but from a Qing perspective. The *Fengliu wu*, preserved in the Peking Metropolitan Library, contains eight stories written in the Qing. For this work, see André Lévy, *Le Conte en langue vulgaire du XVIIe siècle* (Lille: Université de Lille, Service de reproduction des thèses, 1974), esp. pp. 146, 160, 186.

5. The original edition of the *Wuse shi* is in the Lüda Municipal Library. There is also an 1885 Japanese edition. The original edition of the *Ba dongtian* is in the Naikaku Bunko. The novel, the *Kuai shi zhuan*, has been inaccessible; see Sun Kaidi, p. 141. The novel was imported into Japan in 1728. A manuscript copied from the *Wuse shi* was circulating in Japan in 1731, and one copied from the *Ba dongtian* in 1739; see Kudo Takamura, "Oda Kakusai Shi kyūzō Shina shōsetsu no nisan," p. 121. Sun Kaidi (p. 103) suggested that the author was Xu Shukui, who is famous as the writer whose poem so enraged the Qianlong Emperor that he had Xu's corpse dug up and mangled. All for a double entendre! Nor did the brutalities stop with Xu's corpse. But the suggestion as to his authorship cannot be accepted with any confidence. It is based on the title, *Wuse shi*, of a work in the list of Xu's proscribed writings, but the work is labeled a play, not fiction. The *Zhanggu congbian* (Taibei, 1964), pp. 226-262, contains the sheaf of documents relating to the case. The *Wuse shi* is listed in two documents of 1778 (pp. 227, 231). There is some irony in the suggestion of authorship, even if it does not carry conviction; *Fairylands* 7 tells of a man accused of writing a subversive poem under the Jurchen, a poem that praised the Southern Song and attacked Qin Gui.

6. The Harvard-Yenching Library has a copy of the Jiashi xuan edition. The sources of stories 9 through 12 are consecutive stories in the *Records,* juan 3. Three of the tales used, the sources of 2, 7, and 10, were developed by Pu himself into ballads or plays. Note that the author makes some changes of terminology; the reader is addressed as *kanshu de*, and the narrator refers to himself as *wo zuoshu de*, ("I, the writer").

Two inaccessible works also date from the first half of the eighteenth century: the *Zhenzhu bo*, by Xu Zhen, a prolific novelist who wrote romantic and erotic novels as well as a fictionalized history; the *Erke Xingshi hengyan*, in forty chapters, of which the original edition exists, from the Yongzheng (1723-1735) period. For these works, see Sun Kaidi, *Zhongguo tongsu xiaoshuo shumu*, pp. 101, 102.

7. The Harvard-Yenching has a copy of the 1739 edition.

8. *Scent* contained forty stories and *Understanding* twelve. They survive only in reduced form in the *Family Treasure,* thirty-four and ten stories, respectively.

9. See the *Zhenfu pu xuji*, 28b, in which is discussed the idea behind "The Three Teachers."

10. There is a Shanghai, 1957, edition of the original 1792 edition.

11. I.e., the *Nan Bei shi yanyi*, of which the original edition is preserved in the Harvard-Yenching Library. Du's collected works, the *Jin shi ji*, are noted in the 1880 *Kun Xin liangxian hezhi*, 38:28.

12. See the *Ming History* 206, in the biography of Ma Lu.

13. P. 94.

14. E.g., the prologue of story 10 has been adapted from Ling's II.12, the story about Zhu Xi; the emphasis has been changed, and Zhu is no longer a conceited figure. The prologue to story 13 has been taken from HY 2, and that to story 14 from Feng's "Wu Bao'an" (GJ 8). The prologue of story 4 is parallel to *Operas* 5, and the main story of 4 appears to echo *Sobering Stone* 4. There are several other similarities.

15. It is contained in the *Wei Shuzi wenji*, which is part of the *San Wei quanji*, the combined collections of the three Wei brothers. The prose works of the Wei brothers were proscribed in the Qianlong period because of their attitude toward the Manchu conquest. Note that the main story of story 16 is about the seventeenth-century moralist Zhu Yongchun.

16. It contains the image "his legs were like a beaten cock in a cockfight," which is found in the "Den of Ghosts" (TY 14), and also the formula "If he had not looked, all would have been well, but . . .," which is common in the demon and folly stories.

17. P. 45.

18. P. 252.

19. Pp. 366. *Stories to Delight* was not the last collection. *Ghosts and Spirits* (*Guishen zhuan*), also entitled *Requital is Inevitable* (*Zhong xu bao*), of eighteen chapters, exists in an 1859 Canton edition preserved in the British Library. It was obviously written in Canton; most of the stories are set there, some in precise locations. The structure is often loose, and it is possible that some of the stories may have originated in the drama. There is much interaction of men and spirits, as advertised. The social locus is generally below that of the educated class. In the latter half of the collection, most of the stories appear to be reworkings of earlier fiction, including at least one from *Longtu's Court Cases* and one by Feng Menglong, "Prefect Teng" (GJ 10). The *Suhua qingtan* comprises two collections of stories by Shao Binru which were published in Canton in 1870. (See Sun Kaidi, pp. 104-105; the Harvard-Yenching Library has an 1896 edition.) They are stories of moral bao in a mixture of Classical, Mandarin, and Cantonese, which use both Classical and vernacular narrative methods, dispense with all prologues, and concentrate comment in a distinctly marked epilogue. Shao was also responsible for a collection of Classical moral tales, the *Jixiang hua* (preserved in the Harvard-Yenching), the preface of which refers to yet another collection of vernacular stories. Shao's preface to the *Suhua qingtan* mentions the need to speak in simple language so that women and children may understand. He has selected his stories from ancient sources in the time left over from his studies. He has told them orally (Shao was something of a preacher) and found that they absorbed his listeners, and now he is committing them to print. The *Yu ping mei* has been inaccessible. It exists in an 1896 edition; see Sun Kaidi, p. 105. It includes simplified versions of some stories from Ling's first collection. Hu Shiying notes a 40-piece collection entitled *Ji chun tai* with an 1899 preface (*Huaben xiaoshuo gailun*, Peking, 1980, p. 656). He also notes three earlier collections not previously described: *Huzhong tian* of the late Ming and *Yun xian xiao* and *Bie you xiang* of the early Qing (pp. 510, 639, 645).

Bibliography

COLLECTIONS OF STORIES IN ENGLISH

(For a listing of translations in other languages, together with plot synopses, see André Lévy, *Inventaire analytique et critique du conte chinois en langue vulgaire* [Paris, Institut des Hautes Etudes Chinoises, 1978–].)

Acton, Harold and Lee Yi-hsieh. *Four Cautionary Tales*. New York, A. A. Wyn, 1947. A reprint of *Glue and Lacquer*. London, Golden Cockerel Press, 1941.

Birch, Cyril. *Stories from a Ming Collection: Translations of Chinese Short Stories Published in the Seventeenth Century*. Bloomington, Indiana University Press, 1958. Paperback ed. by Grove Press.

Bishop, John Lyman. *The Colloquial Short Story in China: A Study of the San-Yen Collections*. Harvard Yenching Institute Series 14. Cambridge, Mass., Harvard University Press, 1956.

Chang, H. C. *Chinese Literature: Popular Fiction and Drama*. Edinburgh, Edinburgh University Press, 1973.

Dolby, William. *The Perfect Lady by Mistake and Other Stories by Feng Menglong (1574–1646)*. London, Elek, 1976.

Ma, Y. W. and Joseph S. M. Lau, eds. *Traditional Chinese Stories: Themes and Variations*. New York, Columbia University Press, 1978.

Scott, John. *The Lecherous Academician and Other Tales by Master Ling Mengchu*. London, Rapp and Whiting, 1973.

Wang Chi-chen. *Traditional Chinese Tales*. New York, Columbia University Press, 1944. Reprinted by Greenwood Press, New York, 1968.

Yang Hsien-yi and Gladys Yang. *The Courtesan's Jewel Box: Chinese Stories of the Xth–XVIIth Centuries*. Peking, Foreign Languages Press, 1957.

Yang, Richard F. S. *Eight Colloquial Tales of the Sung*. Taibei, The China Post, 1972.

INDIVIDUAL STORIES IN ENGLISH

"Big Tree Slope" (HY 5). "On Big Tree Slope a Faithful Tiger Acts Best Man," in *The Perfect Lady by Mistake and Other Stories*.

"The Braggart" (I.3). "The Story of a Braggart," in *The Courtesan's Jewel Box*.

"The Bribe" (*Sobering Stone* 11). "The Henpecked Judge Who Loses a Governorship," in *Traditional Chinese Stories*.

"The Brothers Liu" (HY 10). "Brother or Bride?" in *Four Cautionary Tales*. "The Two Brothers," in *The Courtesan's Jewel Box*.

"The Case of the Leather Boot" (HY 13). "The Boot that Reveals the Culprit," in *Traditional Chinese Stories*.

"Censor Chen's Ingenious Solution of the Case of the Gold Hairpins and Brooches" (GJ 2). E. C. Chu, tr. "The Clever Judgement of Censor Chen Lien," in *China Journal* 10: 59–66 (1929).

"Chen Duoshou" (HY 9). "The Everlasting Couple," in *Four Cautionary Tales*. "The Couple Bound in Life and Death," in *Traditional Chinese Stories*.

"Chen Kechang" (TY 7). "P'u-sa Man," in *Eight Colloquial Tales of the Sung*.

"The Courtesan's Jewel Box" (TY 32). "The Courtesan's Jewel Box," in the collection of that name. "Tu Shih-niang Sinks the Jewel Box in Anger," in *Traditional Chinese Stories*.

"A Den of Ghosts" (TY 14). "Ghosts in the Western Hills," in *Eight Colloquial Tales of the Sung*. "A Mangy Taoist Exorcises Ghosts," in *Traditional Chinese Stories*.

"Encounter in Yanshan" (GJ 24). Yang Hsien-yi and Gladys Yang, trs. "Strange Encounter in the Northern Capital," in *Chinese Literature* (December, 1961): 46–68.

"The Fairy's Rescue" (KC 33). "The Fairy's Rescue," in *Stories from a Ming Collection*.

"Fan Xizhou" (TY 12). "The Re-union of Feng Yü-mei," in *Eight Colloquial Tales of the Sung*. "The Twin Mirrors," in *Chinese Literature: Popular Fiction and Drama*. "Loach Fan's Double Mirror," in *Traditional Chinese Stories*.

"Fifteen Strings of Cash" (HY 33). "The Judicial Murder of Ts'ui Ning," in *Traditional Chinese Tales*. "Fifteen Strings of Cash," in *The Courtesan's Jewel Box*. "The Mistaken Execution of Ts'ui Ning," in *Eight Colloquial Tales of the Sung*. "A Joke over Fifteen Strings of Cash Brings Uncanny Disaster," in *The Perfect Lady by Mistake and Other Stories*. "The Jest that Leads to Disaster," in *Traditional Chinese Stories*.

"The Foxes' Revenge" (HY 6). "The Foxes' Revenge," in *The Courtesan's Jewel Box*.

"Friends in Life and Death" (Hong 22). "Fan Chü-ch'ing's Eternal Friendship," in *The Colloquial Short Story in China* (translates the GJ 16 version).

"The Ghost Appears Three Times" (TY 13). "The Clerk's Lady," in *Chinese Literature: Popular Fiction and Drama*.

"Han Five Sells Love at Newbridge" (GJ 3). "Chin-nu Sells Love at Newbridge," in *The Colloquial Short Story in China*. "Han Wu-niang Sells Her Charms at the New Bridge Market," in *Traditional Chinese Stories*.

"He Daqing" (HY 15). "The Mandarin-Duck Girdle," in *Four Cautionary Tales*.

"The Honest Clerk" (TY 16). "The Honest Clerk," in *The Courtesan's Jewel Box*. "Chang, the Honest Steward," in *Eight Colloquial Stories of the Sung*.

"The Jade Guanyin" (TY 8). "The Jade Kuanyin," in *Traditional Chinese Tales*.

"The Jade Worker," in *The Courtesan's Jewel Box*. "Carving the Jade Goddess Kuan-yin," in *Eight Colloquial Tales of the Sung*. "Artisan Ts'ui and His Ghost Wife," in *Traditional Chinese Stories*.

"Jiang Xingge Meets the Pearl Shirt a Second Time" (GJ 1). See "The Pearl-Sewn Shirt."

"Jin Yunu" (GJ 27). "The Beggar Chief's Daughter," in *The Courtesan's Jewel Box*. "The Lady Who was a Beggar," in *Stories from a Ming Collection*.

"Lazy Dragon" (II.39). "The Merry Adventures of Lazy Dragon," in *The Courtesan's Jewel Box*.

"Li Cuilian the Quick-Tongued" (Hong 7). "The Shrew," in *Chinese Literature: Popular Fiction and Drama*.

"Licentiate Qian" (HY 7). "Marriage by Proxy," in *The Courtesan's Jewel Box*. "The Perfect Lady by Mistake," in *The Perfect Lady by Mistake and Other Stories*.

"Lu Nan" (HY 29). "The Proud Scholar," in *The Courtesan's Jewel Box*.

"Ma Zhou" (GJ 5). "Wine and Dumplings," in *Stories from a Ming Collection*.

"Madam White" (TY 28). Yang Hsien-yi and Gladys Yang, trs. "The White Snake," in *Chinese Literature* (July 1959): 103–139. "Madame White," in *Chinese Literature: Popular Fiction and Drama*. "Eternal Prisoner under the Thunder Peak Pagoda," in *Traditional Chinese Stories*.

"Master Wu" (HY 28). "Love in a Junk," in *Four Cautionary Tales*.

"The Monk with the Love-Letter" (Hong 2). "The Monk's Billet-doux," in *The Courtesan's Jewel Box* (translates the GJ 35 version).

"The Oilseller" (HY 3). "The Oil Peddler and the Queen of Flowers," in *Traditional Chinese Tales*. "The Oil Vendor and the Courtesan," in *The Courtesan's Jewel Box*. "The Oil Peddler Courts the Courtesan," in *Traditional Chinese Stories*.

"The Old Gardener" (HY 4). "The Flower Lover and the Fairies," in *Traditional Chinese Tales*. "The Old Gardener," in *The Courtesan's Jewel Box*.

"The Old Retainer" (HY 35). "Old Servant Hsü," in *Traditional Chinese Stories*.

"One Songbird Causes Seven Deaths" (GJ 26). "Master Shen's Bird Destroys Seven Lives," in *The Colloquial Short Story in China*. "The Canary Murders," in *Stories from a Ming Collection*.

"The Pearl-Sewn Shirt" (GJ 1). "The Pearl-Sewn Shirt," in *Stories from a Ming Collection*. "The Pearl Shirt Reencountered," in *Traditional Chinese Stories*.

"Prefect Kuang's Solution of the Case of the Dead Baby" (TY 35). "The Case of the Dead Infant," in *Traditional Chinese Stories*.

"Prefect Teng's Ghostly Solution of a Case of Family Property" (GJ 10). "The Hidden Will," in *The Courtesan's Jewel Box*. "Magistrate T'eng and the Case of Inheritance," in *Traditional Chinese Stories*.

"The Rich Man and the Alchemist" (I.18). "The Alchemist and His Concubine," in *The Courtesan's Jewel Box*. "The Swindler Alchemists," in *Traditional Chinese Stories*.

"Shen Xiang" (GJ 40). "A Just Man Avenged," in *The Courtesan's Jewel Box*.

"Song Four Causes Trouble for Miser Zhang" (GJ 36). "Sung the Fourth Raises Hell with Tightwad Chang," in *Traditional Chinese Stories*.

"Su Shi" (TY 3). "Wang An-shih Thrice Corners Su Tung-p'o," in *The Colloquial*

Short Story in China.

"The Tangerines and the Tortoiseshell" (I.1). "The Tangerines and the Tortoise Shell," in *The Courtesan's Jewel Box.*

"The Three Brothers" (HY 2). "The Three Brothers," in *Traditional Chinese Tales.*

"The Two Magistrates" (HY 1). "Two Magistrates Vie to Marry an Orphaned Girl," in *The Perfect Lady by Mistake and Other Stories.*

"Wang Anshi" (TY 4). "The Stubborn Chancellor," in *Eight Colloquial Tales of the Sung.*

"The White Falcon" (TY 19). "The White Hawk of Ts'ui, the Magistrate's Son, Led to Demons," in *Eight Colloquial Tales of the Sung.*

"Wu Bao'an" (GJ 8). "The Journey of the Corpse," in *Stories from a Ming Collection.* "Wu Pao-an Ransoms His Friend," in *Traditional Chinese Stories.*

"Yang Wen" (Hong 15). "Yang Wen, the Road-Blocking Tiger," in *Traditional Chinese Stories.*

REFERENCE WORKS

Auerbach, Erich. *The Literary Language and Its Public in Late Latin Antiquity and in the Middle Ages,* tr. Ralph Manheim. London, Routledge and Kegan Paul, 1965.

Ba dongtian 八洞天 (Eight Fairylands). Qing ed. (Naikaku Bunko.)

Baduan jin 八段錦 (Eight Pieces of Brocade). Qing ed. (Peking University Library.)

Baiiia gong'an. See *Bao Longtu gong'an.*

Bao Daizhi chu shen zhuan 包待制出身傳. In *Ming Chenghua shuochang cihua congkan.*

Bao Longtu baijia gong'an 包龍圖百家公案. 1594 ed. (Hōsa Bunko, Nagoya.)

Barthes, Roland. *S/Z,* tr. Richard Miller. New York, Hill and Wang, 1974.

Bei Ying 北嬰. *Quhai zongmu tiyao bubian* 曲海總目提要補編. Peking, 1959.

P: Wei 畢魏. *San bao en* 三報恩. In *Guben xiqu congkan,* Second Series.

Bian er chai 弁而釵 (Wearing a Cap but Also Hairpins). Late-Ming ed. (Palace Museum, Taibei.)

Booth, Wayne C. *The Rhetoric of Fiction.* Chicago, Chicago University Press, 1961.

Bradley, F. H. *Ethical Studies.* Rev. ed. Oxford, Clarendon, 1927.

Bretschneider, E. *Medieval Researches from Eastern Asiatic Sources.* London, Kegan Paul, Trench, Trübner and Co., 1910.

Bu xue chusheng 步雪初聲. Late-Ming ed. (Palace Museum, Taibei), reprinted in Lu Qian 盧前, ed., *Yinhongyi suo ke qu* 飲虹簃所刻曲. Taibei, 1961.

Caibi qingci 彩筆情辭. Comp. Zhang Yu 張栩. 1624 ed. (Palace Museum, Taibei.)

Chan, Wing-tsit, ed. and tr. *Instructions for Practical Living and Other Neo-Confucian Writings by Wang Yang-ming.* New York, Columbia University Press, 1963.

Chen, Li-li. "Some Background Information on the Development of the *Chu-kung-tiao,*" *Harvard Journal of Asiatic Studies* 33: 224–237 (1973).

Chen Renxi 陳仁錫. *Wumengyuan yiji* 無夢園遺集. 1635 ed. (National Central Library.)

Chi pozi zhuan 癡婆子傳 (Life of the Foolish Woman). Meiji period ed. Kyoto. (Harvard-Yenching Library.)

Chu Qing 楚卿. "Lun wenxueshang xiaoshuo zhi weizhi" 論文學上小說之位置. In A Ying 阿英, ed., *Wan Qing wenxue congchao* 晚清文學叢鈔 (*Xiaoshuo xiqu yanjiu juan*). Peking, 1960.

Cu hulu 醋葫蘆 (The Jealous Wife). Late-Ming ed. (Naikaku Bunko.)

Da Tang Sanzang Fashi qu jing ji 大唐三藏法師取經記 (Record of How the Priest Tripitaka of the Great Tang Fetched the Sutras). Fac. ed. of S. Song (?) ed., published together with, and under the title of, the *Da Tang Sanzang qu jing shihua*. Peking, 1955.

Daming fuzhi 大名府志. Comp. Guo Chengxian 郭程先. 1854 ed.

Dantu xianzhi 丹徒縣志. Comp. Bao Tianzhong 鮑天鍾. 1683 ed.

Dao Wansha 倒浣紗. Qing ed. In *Guben xiqu congkan*, Third Series.

Deng Zhimo 鄧志謨. *Xianxian pian* 洒洒篇. Late-Ming ed. (Naikaku Bunko.)

Ding Yaokang 丁耀亢. *Jianggan cao* 江干草. In *Ding Yehao Xiansheng shi ci gao* 丁野鶴先生詩詞稿. Qing ed. (Peking Library.)

———— *Xu Jin Ping Mei* 續金瓶梅 (Sequel to the *Jin Ping Mei*). Block print ed. (Berkeley.)

Dong Kang 董康. *Shubo yongtan* 書舶庸譚. Taibei, 1967.

Dong Yue 董說. *Xiyou bu* 西遊補 (Supplement to the *Western Journey*). Fac. ed. of 1641 ed. Peking, 1955.

Doupeng xianhua 豆棚閒話 (Idle Talk under the Bean Arbor). Early-Qing ed., incomplete. (Peking Library.) Also Shanghai, 1935 ed., based on the eighteenth-century Hanhailou ed.

Doupeng xianxi 豆棚閒戲 (Idle Dramas under the Bean Arbor). In *Sanhuan ji* 三幻集 manuscript. (Peking University Library.)

Du Gang 杜綱. *Yumu xingxin bian* 娛目醒心編 (Stories to Delight the Eye and Awaken the Heart). Shanghai, 1957 ed., based on the first (1792) ed.

———— *Nan Bei shi yanyi* 南北史演義. First (1793) ed. (Harvard-Yenching Library.)

Dudbridge, Glen. *The Hsi-yu chi: A Study of Antecedents to the Sixteenth-Century Novel*. Cambridge, Cambridge University Press, 1970.

———— *The Legend of Miao-shan*. London, Ithaca Press, 1978.

Eberhard, Wolfram. *Typen Chinesischer Volksmärchen*. FF Communications, no. 120. Helsinki, 1937.

———— *Volksmärchen aus Süd-ost-China, Sammlung Ts'ao Sung-yeh*. FF Communications, no. 128. Helsinki, 1941.

Eikhenbaum, Boris. "Sur la théorie de la prose," in Tsvetan Todorov, ed. and tr., *Théorie de la littérature*. Paris, Editions du Seuil, 1966.

Eminent Chinese of the Ch'ing Period, ed. Arthur W. Hummel. Washington, United States Government Printing Office, 1943–1944.

Enkvist, Nils Erik, John Spencer, and Michael J. Gregory. *Linguistics and Style*. Oxford, Oxford University Press, 1964.

Erke Pai an jing qi 二刻拍案驚奇. (Variant edition, containing stories from *Erke Pai an jing qi* and *Huanying*.) Qing ed. (Bibliothèque Nationale.)

Fan Yanqiao 范烟橋. "Feng Menglong de *Chunqiu hengku* ji qi yiwen yishi"

馮夢龍的春秋衡庫及其遺文佚詩, *Jianghai xuekan* (September 1962), p. 38.

Fan Yuchong 樊玉衡. *Zhi pin* 智品 (Classification of Wisdom). Ming ed. (Naikaku Bunko.)

Fei ying sheng 飛英聲. In *Xiaoshuo shizhong* 小説十種. (Formerly in Kuraishi Takejirō's possession.)

Feng Menglong 馮夢龍. *Bei Song San Sui ping yao zhuan* 北宋三遂平妖傳. 1620 ed. (Naikaku Bunko.) Also the second edition, subtitled *Xin Ping yao zhuan* (New *Ping yao zhuan*). (Naikaku Bunko.)

——— *Chujiang qing* 楚江情 (Adaptation of Yuan Yuling's *Xilou ji*). In *Mohan zhai dingben chuanqi*.

——— *Chunqiu hengku* 春秋衡庫. Late-Ming ed.

——— *Chunqiu ding zhi can xin* 春秋定旨參新. Late-Ming ed. (Naikaku Bunko.)

——— *Fengliu meng* 風流夢 (Romantic Dream, an adaptation of Tang Xianzu's *Peony Pavilion*). In *Mohan zhai dingben chuanqi*.

——— *Guang Xiao fu* 廣笑府. Shanghai, 1936.

——— *Guazher* 掛枝兒. MS copy, incomplete. (Shanghai Library.) Also a Peking, 1962 ed., ed. Guan Dedong 關德棟.

——— *Gujin tangai* 古今譚概 (Survey of Talk). Fac. ed. of Ming ed. 2 vols. Peking, 1955.

——— *Gujin xiao* 古今笑. 1620 ed., republished as *Gujin tangai*. (Peking Library.)

——— *Gujin xiaoshuo* 古今小説 (Stories Old and New). Fac. ed. of first (Tianxu zhai) ed. 2 vols. Taibei, 1958.

——— *Handan meng* 邯鄲夢 (Adaptation of Tang Xianzu's *Handan ji*). In *Mohan zhai dingben chuanqi*.

——— *Huang Ming da ru Wang Yangming Xiansheng chu shen jing luan lu* 皇明大儒王陽明先生出身靖亂錄. In *Sanjiao ounian*. Also a Meiji period Japanese edition.

——— *Jiashen jishi* 甲申紀事. In *Xuanlantang congshu*.

——— *Jing shi tongyan* 警世通言 (Common Words to Warn the World). Fac. ed. of first (1624) ed. 2 vols. Taibei, 1958.

——— *Jingzhong qi* 精忠旗 (Flag of Perfect Loyalty). In *Mohan zhai dingben chuanqi*.

——— *Jiujia yong* 酒家傭 (Servant in the Wine Shop). In *Mohan zhai dingben chuanqi*.

——— *Liang jiang ji* 量江記 (Measuring the River). In *Mohan zhai dingben chuanqi*.

——— *Lin jing zhi yue* 麟經指月 (Guide to the *Annals*). 1620 ed. (Academia Sinica.)

——— *Madiao jiaoli* 馬吊脚例 (Rules of Madiao). In *Shuo fu* (continuation, juan 39). (Ming ed., Naikaku Bunko.)

——— *Meng lei ji* 夢磊記 (Dream of Rocks). In *Mohan zhai dingben chuanqi*.

——— *Mohan zhai dingben chuanqi* 墨憨齋定本傳奇. 3 vols. Peking, 1960.

——— *Nü zhangfu* 女丈夫 (The Heroine). In *Mohan zhai dingben chuanqi*.

——— *Pai jing shisan pian* 牌經十三篇 (Classic of Cards in Thirteen Sections). In *Shuo fu* (continuation, juan 39). (Ming ed., Naikaku Bunko.)

——— *Qing shi leilue* 情史類略 (Anatomy of Love). Late-Ming ed. (Shanghai Library). Also Qing ed. by the Jiezi yuan.

———— *Sanjiao ounian* 三教偶拈 (Chance Selection on the Three Doctrines). Late-Ming ed. (Tōyō Bunka Kenkyūjo.)

———— *Shange* 山歌, ed. Guan Dedong. Peking, 1962.

———— *Shouning daizhi* 壽寧待志 (Provisional History of Shouning). Late-Ming ed. (Ueno Library.)

———— *Shuangxiong ji* 雙雄記 (A Pair of Heroes). In *Mohan zhai dingben chuanqi*.

———— *Sishu zhi yue* 四書指月 (Guide to the Four Books). 1630 ed., incomplete. (Peking Library.)

———— *Taiping guangji chao* 太平廣記鈔. 1626 ed. (National Central Library.)

———— *Taixia xin zou* 太霞新奏 (Celestial Air Played Anew). 1627 ed. (Peking University Library.) Also modern fac. ed. without preface, n.d.

———— *Wanshi zu* 萬事足 (Happiness Complete). In *Mohan zhai dingben chuanqi*.

———— *Xiao fu* 笑府 (Treasury of Jokes). Qing ed. (Naikaku Bunko.)

———— *Xin Guan yuan* 新灌園 (Adaptation of Zhang Fengyi's *Guan yuan ji*). In *Mohan zhai dingben chuanqi*.

———— *Xin Lieguo zhi* 新列國志 (New History of the States). Late-Ming ed. (Harvard-Yenching Library.)

———— *Xing shi hengyan* 醒世恒言 (Constant Words to Awaken the World). Fac. ed. of first (1627) ed. 3 vols. Taibei, 1959.

———— *Zhi nang* 智囊 (Sack of Wisdom). Edo period Japanese ed.

———— *Zhi nang bu* 智囊補 (Supplemented *Sack of Wisdom*). Early-Qing ed. (Harvard-Yenching Library.)

———— *Zhongxing shilu* 中興實錄 (Veritable Records of the National Resurgence). Included in the *Jiashen jishi*.

———— *Zhongxing weilue* 中興偉略. 1645 ed. (Naikaku Bunko.) Also a 1646 Japanese ed., reproduced in Nagasawa Kikuya, ed., *Min Shin shiryōshū* 明清資料集. Tokyo, 1974.

Feng Mengzhen 馮夢禎. *Kuaixuetang ji* 快雪堂集. 1616 ed. (Naikaku Bunko.)

Ferguson, Charles A. "Diglossia," *Word* 15: 325–340 (1959).

Frye, Northrop. *Anatomy of Criticism, Four Essays*. Princeton, Princeton University Press, 1957.

Fu Sinian 傅斯年. "Wen yan heyi caoyi" 文言合一草議, *Xin qingnian* 4.2 (February 1918): 185–189.

Fu Xihua 傅惜華. *Mingdai chuanqi quanmu* 明代傳奇全目. Peking, 1959.

———— *Mingdai zaju quanmu* 明代雜劇全目. Peking, 1958.

———— *Yuandai zaju quanmu* 元代雜劇全目. Peking, 1957.

Gao Lian 高濂. *Yuzan ji* 玉簪記. In *Guben xiqu congkan*, First Series.

Gao Mingkai 高名凱. "Tangdai Chanjia yulu suo jian de yufa chengfen" 唐代禪家語錄所見的語法成分, *Yanjing xuebao* 34: 49–84 (1948).

Genette, Gérard. "Discours du récit," *Figures III*. Paris, Editions du Seuil, 1972.

Gradon, Pamela. *Form and Style in Early English Literature*. London, Methuen, 1971.

Gu Yuanqing 顧元慶. *Gu shi sishijia xiaoshuo* 顧氏四十家小說. Ming ed. (Naikaku Bunko.) Also a Shanghai, 1915 ed.

Guben xiqu congkan 古本戲曲叢刊. Shanghai and Peking. First Series 1954, Second Series 1955, Third Series 1957.

Gui Dong 鬼董. In *Zhibuzu zhai congshu*.

Guishen zhuan 鬼神傳. Canton, 1859 ed. (British Library.)

Gujin Lienü zhuan tongsu yanyi 古今列女傳通俗演義. Qing ed. (National Central Library.)

Guo Moruo 郭沫若. "Aihu xinxian de shengming" 愛護新鮮的生命, *Renmin ribao*, May 31, 1952.

Guo Shaoyu 郭紹虞. *Canglang shihua jiaoshi* 滄浪詩話校釋. Peking. 1962.

―――― *Zhongguo wenxue pipingshi* 中國文學批評史. Shanghai, 1948.

―――― "Zhongguo yuci zhi tanxing zuoyong" 中國語詞之彈性作用. In his *Yuwen tonglun* 語文通論. Shanghai, 1941.

Guzhang juechen 鼓掌絕塵. Late-Ming ed. (Naikaku Bunko.) Chapters 31–40 are reprinted in Lu Gong, ed., *Mnig Qing pinghua xiaoshuo xuan*.

Hai Gangfeng Xiansheng juguan gong'an zhuan 海剛峯先生居官公案傳. Comp. Li Chunfang 李春芳. First (1606) ed. (Peking Library.)

Hai liefu bailian zhen zhuan 海烈婦百鍊眞傳. Qing ed. (Bibliothèque Nationale.)

Hakusai shomoku 舶載書目. Comp. Ōba Osamu 大庭脩. 2 vols. Kansai University, 1972.

Hanan, Patrick. "The Authorship of Some *Ku-chin hsiao-shuo* Stories," *Harvard Journal of Asiatic Studies* 29: 190–200 (1969).

―――― *The Chinese Short Story: Studies in Dating, Authorship, and Composition.* Cambridge, Mass., Harvard University Press, 1973.

―――― "The Composition of the *P'ing-yao chuan*," *Harvard Journal of Asiatic Studies* 31: 201–219 (1971).

―――― "The Making of *The Pearl-sewn Shirt* and *The Courtesan's Jewel Box*," *Harvard Journal of Asiatic Studies* 33: 124–153 (1973).

―――― "Sources of the *Chin P'ing Mei*," *Asia Major* n.s. 10.1: 23–67 (1963).

Harada Suekiyo 原田季清. "Jōshi ni tsuite" 情史に就て, *Taidai bungaku* 2.1: 53–60 (1937).

Havránek, B. "The Functional Differentiation of the Standard Language," in Paul L. Garvin, ed. and tr., *A Prague School Reader on Esthetics, Literary Structure, and Style*. Washington, Georgetown University Press, 1964.

He Liangjun 何良俊. *Qu lun* 曲論. In *Zhongguo gudian xiqu lunzhu jicheng* vol. IV.

Hegel, Robert G. "*Sui T'ang yen-i* and the Aesthetics of the Seventeenth-Century Suchou Elite," in Andrew H. Plaks, ed., *Chinese Narrative: Critical and Theoretical Essays*. Princeton, Princeton University Press, 1977.

Hernadi, Paul. *Beyond Genre: New Directions in Literary Classification*. Ithaca, Cornell University Press, 1972.

Hong Mai 洪邁. *Yijian zhi* 夷堅志. Shanghai, 1927.

Hong Pian 洪楩. *Liushijia xiaoshuo* 六十家小說 (Sixty Stories). Ed. Tan Zhengbi 譚正璧 under the title *Qingpingshan tang huaben* 清平山堂話本. Shanghai, 1957.

Hou Tongzeng 侯峒曾. *Hou Zhongjie gong quanji* 侯忠節公全集. Late-Ming ed.

Householder, Fred W. "Greek Diglossia," *Word* 15: 100–129 (1959).

Hsia, C. T. *The Classic Chinese Novel: A Critical Introduction*. New York, Columbia University Press, 1968.

―――― "Time and the Human Condition in the Plays of T'ang Hsien-tsu," in W. T. de Bary, ed., *Self and Society in Ming Thought*. New York, Columbia University Press, 1970.

Hua Shu 華淑. *Pi dian xiaoshi* 癖顚小史. In his *Qingshuige Kuai shu shizhong* 清睡閣快書十種. 1618 ed. (Library of Congress.)

Huangshan mi 黃山謎. Shanghai, 1935.

Huzhou fuzhi 湖州府志. Comp. Zhou Xuejun 周學濬. 1874 ed.

Idema, W. L. *Chinese Vernacular Fiction: The Formative Period.* Leiden, Brill, 1974.

Ingarden, Roman. *The Cognition of the Literary Work of Art*, tr. Ruth Ann Crowley and Kenneth R. Olson. Evanston, Northwestern University Press, 1973.

Irwin, Richard G. *The Evolution of a Chinsee Novel: Shui-hu-chuan.* Cambridge, Mass., Harvard University Press, 1953.

Jakobson, Roman and M. Halle. *Fundamentals of Language.* The Hague, Mouton, 1956.

Jia zhu tao 夾竹桃. Comp. Fupo zhuren 浮白主人. Peking, 1959.

Jiao Hong 焦竑. *Guochao xianzheng lu* 國朝獻徵錄. Fac. ed. of 1616 ed. 8 vols. Taibei, 1965.

Jiao Xun 焦循. *Ju shuo* 劇說. In *Zhongguo gudian xiqu lunzhu jicheng* vol. VIII.

Jin Ping Mei cihua 金瓶梅詞話. Fac. ed. of late-Ming ed. 5 vols. Tokyo, Daian, 1963.

Jingu qiguan 今古奇觀 (Remarkable Stories New and Old). 4 vols. Shanghai, 1933.

Jingwu zhong 警悟鐘 (The Awakening Bell). Qing ed. (Mukyūkai, Machida, Japan.)

Jinxiu yi 錦繡衣 (Brocaded and Embroidered Garments). Qing ed. (Mukyūkai, Machida, Japan.)

Huanxi yuanjia 歡喜冤家 (Antagonists in Love). Shangxin ting 賞心亭 ed.

Huanying 幻影 (Illusions). Late-Ming ed., incomplete. (Peking Library.) Another late-Ming ed. under the title of *Sanke Pai an jing qi.* (Peking University Library.) 24 stories in *Erke Pai an jing qi* (variant ed.), q.v.

Ju Daoxing 句道興. *Sou shen ji* 搜神記. In *Dunhuang bianwenji.*

Kaidu chuanxin 開讀傳信. In *Song tian lubi* 頌天臚筆. Comp. Jin Risheng 金日升. 1629 ed.

Karlgren, Bernhard. "Excursions in Chinese Grammar," *Bulletin of the Museum of Far Eastern Antiquities* 23: 107–133 (1951).

Koestler, Arthur. *The Act of Creation.* London, Macmillan, 1969.

Kōsaka Jun'ichi 香坂順一. "*Sangoku engi* no gengo" 三國演義の言語. In *Chūgoku no hachi daishōsetsu* 中國の八大小說. Tokyo, 1965.

Kudō Takamura 工藤篁. "Oda Kakusai shi kyūzō Shina shōsetsu no nisan" 織田確齋氏舊藏支那小說の二三. *Kangakkai zasshi* 6.2: 118–124 (July 1938).

Kun Xin liangxian hezhi 崑新兩縣合志. Comp. Wang Kun 汪堃. 1880 ed.

Lang Ying 郞瑛. *Qixiu leigao* 七修類稿. 2 vols. Peking, 1959.

Lévy, André. "About the Date of the First Printed Edition of the *Chin P'ing Mei*—Notes Toward a Clarification," *Chinese Literature: Essays, Articles, and Reviews* 1: 43–48 (January 1979).

——— "A propos des deux versions relatives au récit de la rebellion de l'entrepreneur Wang Ge à la fin du XIIe siècle," in *Etudes d'histoire et de littérature chinoises offertes au Professeur Jaroslav Prušek.* Paris, Bibliothèque de l'Institut des Hautes Etudes Chinoises, 1976.

——— *Le Conte en langue vulgaire du XVIIe siècle: vogue et déclin d'un genre narratif de la littérature chinoise.* Lille, Université de Lille, Service de reproduction des thèses, 1974.

—— *Etudes sur le conte et le roman chinois.* Paris, Ecole Française d'Extrême-Orient, 1971.

—— "Etudes sur trois recueils anciens de contes chinois," *T'oung Pao* 52.1–3: 97–148 (1965).

—— *Inventaire analytique et critique du conte chinois en langue vulgaire.* Vol. 1, 1978; vol. 2, 1979 (in progress). Paris, Institut des Hautes Etudes Chinoises.

Li Houji 李厚基. "Guanyu 'Er Pai' de zuozhe Ling Mengchu" 關於「二拍」的作者凌濛初. *Guangming ribao*, May 4, 1958.

Li Tien-yi 李田意. "Riben suo jian Zhongguo duanpian xiaoshuo lueji" 日本所見中國短篇小說略記, *Tsing Hua Journal of Chinese Studies* n.s. 1.2: (April 1957): 63–83.

Li Yu 李漁. *Fengzheng wu* 風箏誤 (The Mistake with the Kite). In *Li Yu quanji*.

Li Yu (attribution). *Gujin shilue* 古今史略 (Sketch of Ancient and Modern History). Qing ed. (Naikaku Bunko.)

Li Yu. *Huang qiu feng* 凰求鳳 (The She-Phoenixes Seek Their Mates). In *Li Yu quanji*.

—— *Kui ci guanjian* 窺詞管見. In *Li Yu quanji*.

—— *Li Yu quanji* 李漁全集, ed. Helmut Martin. 15 vols. Taibei, 1970.

—— *Naihe tian* 奈何天 (There's Nothing You Can Do About Your Fate). In *Li Yu quanji*.

—— *Qiao tuanyuan* 巧團圓 (The Ingenious Finale). In *Li Yu quanji*.

—— *Rou putuan* 肉蒲團 (Carnal Prayer Mat). Meiji period Japanese ed.

—— *Shen luanjiao* 慎鸞交 (Be Careful About Your Betrothal). In *Li Yu quanji*.

—— *Shi'er lou* 十二樓 (Twelve Structures). In *Li Yu quanji*. Also Shanghai, 1949 edition. 2 vols.

—— *Wusheng xi* 無聲戲 (Silent Operas). In *Li Yu quanji*.

—— *Wusheng xi heji* 無聲戲合集. Qing ed., incomplete. (Peking University Library.)

—— *Xianqing ou ji* 閒情偶寄 (Casual Expressions of Idle Feeling). In *Li Yu quanji*.

—— *Yijia yan* 一家言. In *Li Yu quanji*.

—— *Yizhong yuan* 意中緣 (Ideal Marriage Destinies). In *Li Yu quanji*.

Li Yu 李玉 (style Xuanyu 玄玉). *Qingzhong pu* 清忠譜. In *Guben xiqu congkan*, Third Series.

Li Yunxiang 李雲翔. *Jinling baimei* 金陵百媚 (Hundred Beauties of Nanking). 1618 pref. (Naikaku Bunko.)

Li Zhi 李贄. *Cangshu* 藏書. 2 vols. Peking, 1959.

—— *Chutan ji* 初潭集. 2 vols. Peking, 1974.

—— "Tongxin shuo" 童心說. In *Fen shu* 焚書. Peking, 1961.

Liang Chenyu 梁辰魚. *Wansha ji* 浣紗記. In *Guben xiqu congkan*, First Series.

Liang Yusheng 梁玉繩. *Shi ji zhi yi* 史記志疑. *Congshu jicheng* ed.

Lin Yutang. *The Importance of Understanding.* Cleveland, World Publishing Co., 1960.

Ling Dizhi 凌迪知. *Zuo Guo yuci* 左國腴詞. In his *Wenlin qixiu* 文琳綺繡. Ming ed. (Harvard-Yenching Library.)

Ling Mengchu 凌濛初. *Chuke Pai an jing qi* 初刻拍案驚奇. Ed. Wang Gulu 王古魯. 2 vols. Shanghai, 1957.

—— *Dongpo Chanxi ji* 東坡禪喜集. Ming ed. (Naikaku Bunko.)

—— *Erke Pai an jing qi* 二刻拍案驚奇. Ed. Wang Gulu. 2 vols. Shanghai, 1957. Also Taibei, 1960 ed., ed. Tʻen-yi Li, based on the original ed. in the Naikaku Bunko.

—— *Hou Han shu zuan* 後漢書纂. 1606 ed. (Naikaku Bunko.)

—— *Mang ze pei* 莽擇配 (Impetuous Choice of a Husband). In Zhou Yibai 周貽白, ed., *Mingren zaju xuan* 明人雜劇選. Peking, 1958.

—— *Nanyin sanlai* 南音三籟 (Three Kinds of Southern Sound). Fac. ed. of late-Ming editions. Shanghai, 1963.

—— *Pai an jing qi* 拍案驚奇, ed. Tien-yi Li. 2 vols. Hong Kong, 1966.

—— *Pipa ji* 琵琶記 (The Lute). Ed. Ling Mengchu. Modern fac. ed. of original ed. Shanghai, n.d.

—— *Song Gongming nao yuanxiao* 宋公明鬧元宵 (Song Gongming Throws the New Year Festival into Uproar). In *Erke Pai an jing qi*.

—— *Tan qu za zha* 譚曲雜劄 (Notes on the Southern Drama). In *Nanyin sanlai*.

—— *Xixiang ji* 西廂記 (Western Chamber). Ed. Ling Mengchu. In Liu Shiheng 劉世珩 ed., *Huike chuanju* 彙刻傳劇. 1919.

Ling Zhilong 凌稚隆. *Han shu pinglin* 漢書評林 Ming ed.

—— *Han shu zuan* 漢書纂. Ming ed.

—— *Shi ji zuan* 史記纂. Ming ed.

Liu Fu 劉復. "*Xiyou bu* zuozhe Dong Ruoyu zhuan" 「西遊補」作者董若雨傳. In *Bannong zawen erji* 半農雜文二集. Shanghai, 1935.

Liu, James J. Y. *The Chinese Knight-Errant*. London, Routledge and Kegan Paul, 1967.

—— *Chinese Theories of Literature*. Chicago, University of Chicago Press, 1975.

Liu Tsʻun-yan. *Chinese Popular Fiction in Two London Libraries*. Hong Kong, 1967.

Liu Xiuye 劉修業. *Gudian xiaoshuo xiqu congkao* 古典小說戲曲叢考. Peking, 1958.

Longtu gongʼan 龍圖公案. Guiwen tang ed., 1821.

Lu Gong 路工. *Ming Qing pinghua xiaoshuo xuan* 明清平話小說選, First Series. Shanghai, 1958.

Lu Xun 魯迅. "Cai wei" 采薇 (Cathering Ferns). In *Gushi xinbian* 故事新編. *Lu Xun quanji* ed. 1948. Translated as "Gathering Vetch," in Yang Hsien-yi and Gladys Yang, *Old Stories Retold*. Peking, 1951.

Lubbock, Percy. *The Craft of Fiction*. London, J. Cape, 1921.

Luo Ye 羅燁. [*Xinbian*] *Zuiweng tanlu* 新編醉翁談錄 (Notes of the Drunken Old Man). Shanghai, 1957.

Lü shi chunqiu. 1620 ed. by Ling Mengchu. (Harvard-Yenching Library.)

Lü Shuxiang 呂叔湘. *Hanyu yufa lunwenji* 漢語語法論文集. Peking, 1955.

Lü Tiancheng 呂天成. *Qu pin* 曲品. In *Zhongguo gudian xiqu lunzhu jicheng* vol. VI.

Lü Tiancheng (attribution). *Xiuta yeshi* 繡榻野史 (Unofficial History of the Embroidered Couch). Ming ed. (Academia Sinica.)

Ma Jiasong 馬嘉松. *Shike pian* 十可篇. Late-Ming ed. (Palace Museum, Taibei.)

Ma, Y. W. "The Textual Tradition of Ming *Kung-an* Fiction: A Study of the *Lung-t'u kung-an*," *Harvard Journal of Asiatic Studies* 35: 190–200 (1975).

Ma Zhijun 馬之駿. *Miaoyuan tang quanji* 妙遠堂全集. 1627 ed. (National Central Library.)

Macheng xianzhi 麻城縣志. Comp. Pan Yifu 潘頤福. 1882 ed.

Mao Kun 茅坤. *Gujin Lienü zhuan* 古今列女傳. 1591 ed. (Harvard-Yenching Library.)

Mao, Nathan and Liu Ts'un-yan. *Li Yu*. Boston, Twayne, 1977.

Martin, Helmut. *Li Li-weng über das Theater*. Taibei, 1968.

Masuda Wataru 增田涉. "'Wahon' to iu koto ni tsuite" 「話本」ということについて, *Jimbun kenkyū* 16.5 (1965): 22–33.

Mather, Richard, tr. *A New Account of Tales of the World*. Minneapolis, University of Minnesota Press, 1976.

Mei Xiaosi 梅孝巳. *Sa xue tang* 灑雪堂. In *Mohan zhai dingben chuanqi*.

Mei Zhiyun 梅之熉. *Chunqiu yin shi* 春秋因是 .Qing ed. (Naikaku Bunko.)

Ming Biographical Dictionary, ed. L. Carrington Goodrich and Chaoying Fang. 2 vols. New York, Columbia University Press, 1976.

Ming Chenghua shuochang cihua congkan 明成化說唱詞話叢刊. Fac. ed. Shanghai, 1973.

Mirsky, D. S. *A History of Russian Literature*. New York, Knopf, 1949.

Mowry, Hua-yuan Li. "*Ching-shih* and Feng Meng-lung." Ph.D. diss., Berkeley, 1976.

Nagasawa Kikuya 長澤規矩也. *Shoshigaku ronkō* 書誌學論考. Tokyo, 1937.

Ono Shihei 小野四平. *Tampen hakuwa shōsetsu no kenkyū* 短篇白話小說の研究. Tokyo, 1978.

Ping yao zhuan 平妖傳. 20 chapters. Ming ed. (Tenri University Library.)

Plaks, Andrew H. "Towards a Critical Theory of Chinese Narrative," in Plaks, ed., *Chinese Narrative: Critical and Theoretical Essays*. Princeton, Princeton University Press, 1977.

Potts, L. J. *Comedy*. London, Hutchinson, 1948.

Pride, J. B. *The Social Meaning of Language*. Oxford, Oxford University Press, 1971.

Průšek, Jaroslav. "The Creative Methods of the Chinese Medieval Story-tellers," in Průšek, *Chinese History and Literature: Collections of Studies*. Dordrecht, Reidel, 1970.

Pu Songling 蒲松齡. *Liaozhai zhiyi* 聊齋志異. 3 vols. Peking, 1962 ed.

Qi Biaojia 祁彪佳. *Yuanshantang jupin* 遠山堂劇品. In *Zhongguo gudian xiqu lunzhu jicheng* vol. VI.

———*Yuanshantang qupin* 遠山堂曲品. In *Zhongguo gudian xiqu lunzhu jicheng* vol. VI.

Qian Nanyang 錢南揚. "Feng Menglong *Mohanzhai cipu jiyi*" 馮夢龍墨憨齋詞譜輯佚. In *Zhonghua wen shi luncong* II. Peking, 1962.

Qiantang xianzhi 錢塘縣志. Comp. Wei Yuan 魏嶀. 1718 ed.

Qingsuo gaoyi 青瑣高議 (attributed to Liu Fu 劉斧). Shanghai, 1958.

Qingye zhong 清夜鐘 (Alarum Bell on a Still Night). Selections in Lu Gong, *Ming Qing pinghua xiaoshuo xuan*.

Qingyuan wenxian 清源文獻. Comp. He Qiong 何炯. Ming ed. (Naikaku Bunko.)

Qishi'er chao renwu yanyi 七十二朝人物演義. 1640 ed. (Naikaku Bunko.)

Qiu Tingliang 裘廷梁. "Lun baihua wei weixin zhi ben" 論白話爲維新之本. In *Zhongguo jindai wenlun xuan.*

Qizhen ji 欹枕集 (Leaning on the Pillow). In *Liushijia xiaoshuo.* Comp. Hong Pian.

Qu You 瞿祐. *Jian deng xinhua* 剪燈新話 (New Tales under the Lamplight). In *Jian deng xinhua, wai erzhong.* Shanghai, 1957.

Quhai zongmu tiyao 曲海總目提要. 3 vols. Peking, 1959.

Renzhong hua 人中畫 (Portraits of Society). In Lu Gong, *Ming Qing pinghua xiaoshuo xuan.*

Renzong ren mu 仁宗認母. In *Ming Chenghua shuochang cihua congkan.*

Riftin, Boris. *Istoricheskaia epopeia i fol'klornaia traditsiia v Kitae: ustnye i knizhnye versii "Troetsartviia."* Moscow, 1970.

Robins, R. H. *General Linguistics: An Introductory Survey.* London, Longmans, 1964.

Rong Zhaozu 容肇祖. "Ming Feng Menglong de shengping ji qi zhushu xukao" 明馮夢龍的生平及其著述續考, *Lingnan xuebao* 2.3 (1931): 95–124.

Ruch, Barbara. "Medieval Jongleurs and the Making of a National Literature," in John W. Hall and Toyoda Takeshi, eds., *Japan in the Muromachi Age.* Berkeley, University of California Press, 1977.

Rumian tan 如面談. Late-Ming ed. (Naikaku Bunko.)

Sanguo zhi pinghua 三國志平話. Fac. ed. of Yuan ed. Shanghai, 1929.

Sanguo zhi tongsu yanyi 三國志通俗演義. Fac. ed. of 1522 ed. 8 vols. Peking, 1975. Also a Qing ed., ed. Li Yu. (Bibliothèque Nationale.)

Sapir, Edward. *Culture, Language, and Personality: Selected Essays.* Berkeley, University of California Press, 1960.

Sha gou ji 殺狗記. Ed. Feng Menglong. In *Guben xiqu congkan,* First Series.

Shao Binru 邵彬儒. *Jixiang hua* 吉祥花. 1870 ed.

——— *Suhua qingtan* 俗話傾談. Canton, 1896 ed.

Shen Defu 沈德符. *Gu qu zayan* 顧曲雜言. In *Zhongguo gudian xiqu lunzhu jicheng* vol. IV.

——— *Wanli yehuo bian* 萬曆野獲編. 3 vols. Peking, 1959.

Shen Zijin 沈自晉. *Nan jiugong shisan diao cipu* 南九宮十三調詞譜. Modern fac. ed. of early-Qing ed., n.d.

Shen Ziyou 沈自友. "Jutong sheng xiaozhuan" 鞠通生小傳. In *Nan jiugong shisan diao cipu.*

Sheng Ming zaju erji 盛明雜劇二集. Comp. Shen Tai 沈泰. Fac. ed. of 1629 ed. in *Sheng Ming zaju.* Shanghai, 1963.

Shengshi xinsheng 盛世新聲. Fac. ed. of Ming ed. Peking, 1955.

Shengxiao-jian 生綃剪 (Snippets of Raw Silk). Qing ed. (Peking Library.)

Shi Chengjin 石成金. *Chuanjia bao* 傳家寶 (Family Treasure). 1739 ed. (Harvard-Yenching Library.)

——— *Tong tianle* 通天樂 (Understanding Heavenly Pleasures). In *Chuanjia bao.*

——— *Yu hua xiang* 雨花香 (Scent of Flowers from Heaven). In *Chuanjia bao.*

——— *Zhenfu pu xuji* 眞福譜續集. In *Chuanjia bao.*

Shi dian tou 石點頭 (The Rocks Nod Their Heads). Ming ed. (Tōyō Bunka Kenkyūjo.) Also the Shanghai, 1935 ed.

Shi shuo xin yu 世說新語 (New Account of Tales of the World). Multicolor editions by Ling Mengchu and Ling Yingchu 凌瀛初, respectively. (Harvard-Yenching Library.)

Shi'er xiao 十二笑 (Twelve Jokes). Qing ed. (Peking University Library.)

Shiqing shizhong 適情十種. Late-Ming ed. (Peking Library.)

Shuihu quanzhuan 水滸全傳. Variorum ed. of the "full" editions of the novel. 3 vols. Peking, 1954.

Si da chi 四大癡 (Four Great Follies). Late-Ming ed. (Harvard-Yenching Library.)

Siku quanshu zongmu tiyao 四庫全書總目提要. In *Heyin Siku quanshu zongmu tiyao ji Siku weishou shumu jinhui shumu*. Taibei, 1971.

Song Cunbiao 宋存標. *Qing zhong* 情種. 1626 ed. (Peking Library.)

Sun Kaidi 孫楷第. "Li Liweng yu *Shi'er lou*" 李笠翁與十二樓. In *Shi'er lou* (Shanghai, 1949). Reprinted in *Li Yu quanji* vol. XV.

—— *Riben Dongjing suo jian Zhongguo xiaoshuo shumu* 日本東京所見中國小說書目. Rev. ed. Peking, 1958.

—— *Zhongguo tongsu xiaoshuo shumu* 中國通俗小說書目. Rev. ed. Peking, 1957.

Taiping guangji 太平廣記. 5 vols. Peking, 1959.

Taiping yulan 太平御覽. 4 vols. Peking, 1960.

Tan Qian 談遷. *Guo jue* 國榷. 6 vols. Peking, 1958.

Tang shi ji shi 唐詩紀事. Ed. Hong Pian. Ming ed. (Naikaku Bunko.) Also 1545 ed. by Zhang Zili 張子立 (Harvard-Yenching Library.)

Tang Xianzu 湯顯祖. *Mudan ting* 牡丹亭 (Peony Pavilion). In *Guben xiqu congkan*, First Series.

—— *Tang Xianzu ji* 湯顯祖集. 4 vols. Peking, 1962.

Tao Xiang 陶湘. "Ming Wuxing Minban shumu" 明吳興閔板書目, *Qinghe* 5.13 (May 1937): 1–10.

Ting, Nai-tung. "The Holy Man and the Snake-Woman," *Fabula* 8.3: 145–191 (1967).

Tian Rucheng 田汝成. *Xihu youlanzhi* 西湖遊覽志 (Guide to the West Lake). Peking, 1958.

—— *Xihu youlan zhiyu* (Supplement to the Guide to the West Lake). Peking, 1958.

Tian Yiheng 田藝蘅. *Shi nü shi* 詩女史. 1557 ed. (Palace Museum, Taibei.)

Töpelmann, Cornelia. *Shan-ko von Feng Meng-lung*. Wiesbaden, F. Steiner, 1973.

Tu Lien-che 杜聯喆. "Mingren xiaoshuo ji dangdai benshi juli" 明人小說記當代奇聞本事舉例, *Tsing Hua Journal of Chinese Studies* 7.2 (1969): 156–175.

Van Gulik, Robert H. *Erotic Colour Prints of the Ming Period*. Tokyo, privately printed, 1951.

—— *The Gibbon in China: An Essay in Chinese Animal Lore*. Leiden, E. J. Brill, 1969.

Waley, Arthur. "A Sung Colloquial Story from the *Tsu-t'ang chi*," Asia Major n.s. 14.2: 242–246 (1969).

Wan Shu 萬樹. *Kongqing shi* 空青石. In *Yungshuangyan sanzhong* 擁雙艷三種. 1686 ed.

Wang Daokun 汪道昆. *Wuhu you* 五湖遊. In *Sheng Ming zaju*.

Wang Jide 王驥德. *Qu lü* 曲律. In *Zhongguo gudian xiqu lunzhu jicheng* vol. IV.

Wang Jingchen 王敬臣. *Sihou bian* 俟後編. 1699 ed. (Naikaku Bunko.)

Wang, John Ching-yu. *Chin Sheng-t'an*. New York, Twayne, 1972.

Wang Li 王力. *Hanyu shigao* 漢語史稿. 3 vols. Peking, 1958.

Wang Li et al. *Wenxue yuyan wenti taolunji* 文學語言問題討論集. Peking, 1957.

Wang Liqi 王利器. *Lidai xiaohua ji*. 歷代笑話集. Shanghai, 1957.

—— "*Shuihu quanzhuan* Tian Wang erzhuan shi shui suo jia?" 水滸全傳田王
二傳是誰所加. In *Wenxue yichan zengkan* I. Peking, 1957.

Wang Mengji 王夢吉. *Ji Dian quanzhuan* 濟顛全傳. 1668 ed., incomplete. (Peking
Library.)

Wang Shizhen 王世貞. *Qu zao* 曲藻. In *Zhongguo gudian xiqu lunzhu jicheng*
vol. IV.

Wang Shouyi 王守義: "*Xing shi yinyuan* de cheng shu niandai" 「醒世姻緣」的
成書年代. *Guangming ribao*, May 28, 1961.

Wang Zhongmin 王重民 et al. *Dunhuang bianwenji* 敦煌變文集. 2 vols. Peking,
1957.

Wanxuan qingtan 萬選清談. Ming ed. (Library of Congress.)

Watt, Ian. *The Rise of the Novel*. Berkeley, University of California Press, 1957.

Wei Xi 魏禧. *Wei Shuzi wenji* 魏叔子文集. In *Ningdu San Wei quanji* 寧都三魏全
集. 1845 ed.

Wei Yong 衛泳. *Bing xue xi* 冰雪攜. Shanghai, 1935.

—— "Yue rong bian" 悅容編. In his *Zhenzhong mi* 枕中秘. Late-Ming ed.
(Peking University Library.)

Wivell, Charles. "The Term 'Hua-pen,' " in David C. Buxbaum and F. W. Mote,
eds., *Transition and Permanence: Chinese History and Culture*. Hong
Kong, Cathay, 1972.

Wong Siu-kit. "Ch'ing in Chinese Literary Criticism." Ph.D. diss., Oxford
University, 1969.

Wu, K. T. "Colour Printing in the Ming Dynasty," *T'ien Hsia Monthly* 11:30–44
(1940).

Wu Song 武松. 2 vols. Nanking, 1959.

Wu Xiaoling 吳曉鈴. "Qingdai juqu tiyao bazhong" 清代劇曲提要八種 *Wenxue
nianbao* 5 (1939): 45–52.

Wucheng xianzhi 烏城縣志. Comp. Hang Shijun 杭世駿. 1746 ed.

Wucheng xianzhi. Comp. Zhou Xuejun 周學濬. 1881 ed.

[*Xinbian*] *Wudai shi pinghua* 新編五代史平話. Shanghai, 1954.

Wuji baimei 吳姬百媚. Comp. Wanyu Zi 宛瑜子. 1617 ed. (Hōsa Bunko, Nagoya.)

Wuse shi 五色石 (Multicolored Stones). Japanese ed., 1885.

Xihu jiahua 西湖佳話 (Charming Stories of the West Lake). Shanghai, 1956.

Xing meng pianyan 醒夢駢言. Qing ed. by the Jiashi xuan 稼史軒. (Harvard-
Yenching Library.)

Xing ming hua 醒名花. Qing ed. (Harvard-Yenching Library.)

Xiong Longfeng sizhong xiaoshuo 熊龍峯四種小說. Shanghai, 1958.

Xiyou ji 西遊記. 2 vols. Peking, 1954.

Xu Fuzuo 徐復祚. *Qu lun* 曲論. In *Zhongguo gudian xiqu lunzhu jicheng* vol. IV.

Xu Mengxin 徐夢莘. *Sanchao beimeng huibian* 三朝北盟會編. 4 vols. Taibei,
1962 reprint of 1878 ed.

Xu Nianci 徐念慈. "Yu zhi xiaoshuo guan" 余之小說觀. Originally published in

Xiaoshuo lin. Reprinted in *Zhongguo jindai wenlun xuan*, II, 504–512.

Xu Zichang 許自昌. *Peng fu bian* 捧腹編. 1619 ed. (Library of Congress.)

—— *Shuzhai manlu* 梣齋漫錄. Late-Ming ed. (Peking Library.)

Xuanhe yishi 宣和遺事. Peking, 1954 ed.

Xue Rengui zheng Liao shilue 薛仁貴征遼事略. Ed. Zhao Wanli 趙萬里. Shanghai, 1957.

Xuxiu Siku quanshu tiyao 續修四庫全書提要. 13 vols. Taibei, 1972.

Yagisawa Hajime 八木澤元. "Shōseiden no shiryō" 小青傳の資料, *Shūkan Tōyōgaku* 6 (1961): 64–78.

Yan Fu 嚴復. "Guowen baoguan fuyin shuobu yuanqi" 國聞報館附印說部緣起. In *Zhongguo jindai wenlun xuan*.

Yang Guangxian 楊光先. *Bu de yi* 不得已. Taibei, 1969 reprint of 1928 ed.

Yang Lien-sheng. "The Concept of 'Pao' as a Basis for Social Relations in China," in John K. Fairbank, ed., *Chinese Thought and Institutions*. Chicago, University of Chicago Press, 1957.

Yang Maoqian 楊茂謙. *Xiaolin ping* 笑林評. 1611 ed. (Naikaku Bunko.)

Yao Jinyuan 姚覲元. *Qingdai jinhui shumu* 清代禁燬書目. Shanghai, 1957.

Yao Ximeng 姚希孟. *Xiang yu ji* 響玉集. 1640 ed.

Ye Dejun 葉德均. "Ling Mengchu shiji xinian" 凌濛初事跡繫年. In *Xiqu xiaoshuo congkao*.

—— "Shi dian tou de zuozhe he laiyuan" 石點頭的作者和來源, *Tiandi* 6 (March 1944).

—— "Shu Zheng Longcai zhuan Ling Mengchu muzhiming hou" 書鄭龍采撰凌濛初墓誌銘後. (Shanghai) *Dagong bao*, January 8, 1947.

—— *Xiqu xiaoshuo congkao* 戲曲小說叢考. Ed. Zhao Jingshen. 2 vols. Peking, 1979.

Ye Ru 野孺. "Guanyu Feng Menglong de shenshi" 關於馮夢龍的身世. In *Ming Qing xiaoshuo yanjiu lunwenji*. Peking, 1959.

—— "Guanyu San yan de zuanjizhe" 關於三言的纂輯者. In *Ming Qing xiaoshuo yanjiu lunwenji*. Peking, 1959.

Ye Yuhua 葉玉華. "Shuihu xie Song Jiang da Fang La fei chu xugou" 「水滸」寫宋江打方臘非出虛構, *Zhonghua wen shi luncong* 8 (October 1978): 71–86.

Yipian qing 一片情 (Expanse of Passion). Late-Ming ed. (Tōyō Bunka Kenkyūjo.)

Yongle dadian 永樂大典. Shanghai, 1955–1960.

You Xia hezhuan 有夏合傳. Late-Ming ed. (Peking Library.)

Yu, Anthony C., tr. *The Journey to the West*. Vol. 1, 1977; vol. 2, 1978. Chicago, Chicago University Press.

Yu Shaoyu 余邵魚. *Chunqiu lieguo zhizhuan* 春秋列國志傳. 12 juan. (Naikaku Bunko.)

Yuan Jiahua 袁家驊 et al. *Hanyu fangyan gaiyao* 漢語方言概要. Peking, 1960.

Yuan Yuling 袁于令. *Sui shi yiwen* 隋史遺文. Taibei, 1975.

—— *Xilou meng* 西樓夢. Feng Menglong, ed. Qing ed. (Naikaku Bunko.)

Yuan Zhongdao 袁中道. *Youju shilu* 遊居柿錄. *Yuan Xiaoxiu riji* ed. Shanghai, 1935.

Yuan Zongdao 袁宗道. *Baisu zhai leiji* 白蘇齋類集. Shanghai, 1935.

Yuanyang zhen 鴛鴦針 (A Pair of Needles). Mimeographed ed. of 1957 by

Dongbei People's University. (Based on the Qing ed. now in Lüda Municipal Library.)

Yue Ke 岳珂. *Ting shi* 桯史. *Congshu jicheng* ed.

Yueming Heshang du Liu Cui 月明和尚度柳翠. In *Yuanqu xuan*.

Zaihua chuan 載花船 (Flower-Laden Ship). 1659 ed. (Peking University Library.)

Zang Maoxun 臧懋循. *Yuanqu xuan* 元曲選. 4 vols. Peking, 1961.

Zeng Yandong 曾衍東. *Xiao Doupeng* 小豆棚 (Little *Bean Arbor*). Shanghai, 1935 reprint of 1890 ed.

Zeng Yongyi 曾永義. "Qingdai zaju gailun" 清代雜劇概論. In his *Zhongguo gudian xiju lunji* 中國古典戲劇論集. Taibei, 1975.

Zengding Siku jianming mulu biaozhu 增訂四庫簡明目錄標注. Peking, 1959.

Zhang Duanyi 張端義. *Gui er ji* 貴耳集. Shanghai, 1958.

Zhang Fengyi 張鳳翼. *Guan yuan ji* 灌園記. In *Guben xiqu congkan*, First Series.

Zhang Mingbi 張明弼. *Ying zhi ji* 螢芝集. Late-Ming ed. (Naikaku Bunko.)

Zhang Qi 張琦. *Heng qu zhu tan* 衡曲塵譚. In *Zhongguo gudian xiqu lunzhu jicheng* vol. IV.

Zhang Xuchu 張旭初. *Wu sao hebian* 吳騷合編 (Combined Edition of the *Songs of Wu*). Shanghai, 1934.

Zhang Zhigong 張志公. *Chuantong yu wen jiaoyu chutan* 傳統語文教育初探. Shanghai, 1962.

Zhanggu congbian 掌故叢編. Taibei, 1964.

Zhao Jingshen 趙景深 "Ling Mengchu de *Shanjin ji*" 凌濛初的衫襟記. In his *Ming Qing qutan* 明清曲談. Shanghai, 1957.

——— "*Qiuran ke zhuan* yu *Bei Hongfu*" 虯髯客傳與北紅拂. In his *Yinzi ji* 銀字集. Shanghai, 1946.

——— *Xiaoshuo luncong* 小說論叢. Shanghai, 1947.

Zhao Nanxing 趙南星. *Xiao zan* 笑贊. In Wang Liqi, *Lidai xiaohua ji*.

Zhao shi bei 照世杯 (The Cup that Reflects the World). *Guyi xiaoshuo congkan* ed., Shanghai, 1928. Also Shanghai, 1957 ed.

Zhe mei jian 折梅箋. Late-Ming ed. (Naikaku Bunko.)

Zheng Zhenduo 鄭振鐸. *Jiezhong de shu ji* 劫中得書記. Shanghai, 1956.

——— "Ming Qing erdai de pinghua ji" 明清二代的平話集. In his *Zhongguo wenxue yanjiu*. Peking, 1959.

Zhongguo congshu conglu 中國叢書綜錄. 3 vols. Shanghai, 1959.

Zhongguo gudian xiqu lunzhu jicheng 中國古典戲曲論著集成. 10 vols. Peking, 1959.

Zhongguo jindai wenlun xuan 中國近代文論選. 2 vols. Fac. ed. of Peking, 1959–1962 ed. Nagoya, n.d.

Zhongyuan yinyun 中原音韻 (Sounds and Rhymes of the Central Plain). In *Zhongguo gudian xiqu lunzhu jicheng* vol. I.

Zhou Ji 周楫. *Xihu erji* 西湖二集 (Second Collection of West Lake Stories). Shanghai, 1936 ed.

Zhou Quan 周銓. "Yingxiong qi duan shuo" 英雄氣短說. In Wei Yong, *Bing xue xi*.

Zhou Zumo 周祖謨. "Cong wenxue yuyan de gainian lun Hanyu de yayan, wenyan, guwen deng wenti" 從文學語言的概念論漢語的雅言, 文言, 古文等問題. In Wang Li et al., *Wenxue yuyan wenti taolunji*.

Zhu Tan 朱倓. "Mingji Nan Ying She kao" 明季南應社考, *Guoxue jikan* 2.3

(September 1930): 541–588.

Zhu Yizun 朱彝尊. *Ming shi zong* 明詩綜. 1705 ed.

Zui xing shi 醉醒石 (The Sobering Stone). Early-Qing ed. (Peking Library.) Also Shanghai, 1956 ed.

Zutang ji 祖堂集. Fac. ed. of 1245 ed., Seòul, 1965.

Glossary

Aina jushi 艾衲居士
Bai yue ting 拜月亭
Baiyuan zhuan 百緣傳
bao 報
Bao Jun 包濬
baojuan 寶卷
bense 本色
Bi hua nao 筆花鬧
Bi xiezhi 筆獬豸
bianwen 變文
biji 筆記
bu jing xunri 不經旬日
cairen 才人
caizi jiaren 才子佳人
Chen Jiru 陳繼儒
chuanqi 傳奇
ci 詞
cihua 詞話
cun xuejiu 村學究
danghang 當行
daoqing 道情
dingzheng 訂證
Dong Sizhang 董斯張
Dongwu zhi jiren 東吳之畸人
Dou shi huan 都是幻
Doupeng yin 豆棚吟
duoqing 多情
Du Jun 杜濬
faji biantai 發跡變泰
Fan Wenruo 范文若
Feng Duling (i.e. Feng Mengxiong) 馮杜陵
Feng Menggui 馮夢桂
Feng Menglong 馮夢龍

Feng Mengxiong 馮夢熊
fengliu 風流
Fengliu wu 風流悟
Gao Yiwei 高一葦
gong'an 公案
guanhua 官話
Guazher 掛枝兒
Guo men ji 國門集
Guo men yi ji 國門乙集
Gukuang 古狂
Guqu sanren 顧曲散人
Han Ziqu 韓子蘧
haohan 好漢
heng bo 橫波
Heshen 和珅
Hong Pian 洪楩
Hong Zhong 洪鍾
Hongtang 哄堂
huaben 話本
Huang Jie 黃介
Huanyuan qiyu xiaoshuo 幻緣奇遇小說
Ji Dian 濟顛
jiang shi 講史
jianglun 講論
Jianxiao ge 劍嘯閣
jiao 醮
jiegou 結構
Jin fen xi 金粉惜
Jin Shengtan 金聖歎
Jin shi ji 近是集
jing 景
"Jinjyue lou" 今覺樓
Keyi jushi 可一居士

263

Kong Tianyin 孔天胤
Langxian 浪仙
Li Changgeng 李長庚
Li Chuang fan shenjing 李闖犯神京
Li Fuda 李福達
Li Shuyuan 李叔元
Li Yu 李漁
Li Yu (Xuanyu) 李玉 (玄玉)
Li Zhi 李贄
Li Zicheng 李自成
Liancheng bi quanji 連城璧全集
Ling Mengchu 凌濛初
Ling shi tongpu 凌氏通譜
Ling Yanxi 凌延喜
Ling Yueyan 凌約言
Longxi jun 隴西君
lou 樓
Lu Shiyi 陸世儀
Lu Xianzhi 陸顯之
Lu Yunlong 陸雲龍
Luo Rufang 羅汝芳
luosuo 落索
madiao 馬吊
Mao Wenlong 毛文龍
Mei Zhihuan 梅之煥
mi ci 麛詞
Min Qiji 閔齊伋
Mohanzhai xinpu 墨憨齋新譜
Molang zhuren 墨浪主人
mudan 牡丹
Ni Zhengping 禰正平
Nongzhu Ke 弄珠客
pinghna 平話
qi 奇
qi 氣
Qi Biaojia 祁彪佳
Qile zhai gao 七樂齋稿
qing 情
Qiu Tan 丘坦
Qiushan 秋山
Qixia shanfang 棲霞山房
Ranweng 髯翁
Ranxian 髯仙
ruhua 入話
Ruiyu ji 瑞玉記
San fen shilue 三分事略
sanqu 散曲
shange 山歌

Shanjin ji 衫襟記
Shanshui Lin 山水鄰
Shao Qing 邵青
shaoyao 芍藥
Shen Defu 沈德符
Shen Jing 沈璟
Shen Lian 沈鍊
Shengshui 聖水
Shi Que 石碏
shuhui 書會
Song Maocheng 宋楙澄
Sou shen ji 搜神記
su 俗
su jiang 俗講
Sun Zijing 孫子京
Taiji zhenren 太極眞人
Tan xin wu 貪欣悮
tanci 彈詞
Tang Sai'er 唐賽兒
Tang Shunzhi 唐順之
Tang Xianzu 湯顯祖
taozhen 陶眞
Tian Rucheng 田汝成
Tianli bu rong 天理不容
Tianran Chisou 天然癡叟
Tianran qiao 天然巧
Tong chi 童癡
waibian 外編
Wang Jingchen 王敬臣
Wang Mengji 王夢吉
Wang Shaotang 王少堂
Wang Shizhen 王世貞
Wang Zhideng 王穉登
Wanzhuan ge 宛轉歌
wazi 瓦子
Wei Zhongxian 魏忠賢
Weilin Zi 爲霖子
wenren 文人
wenren zhi bi 文人之筆
wenyan 文言
Wolu zhuren 卧廬主人
Wu Yingji 吳應箕
Wu Zaibo 吳載伯
Wu'ai jushi 無礙居士
Wugeng feng 五更風
Wujun wenbian 吳郡文編
Wushimen jiren 吳市門畸人
Xi Langxian 席浪仙

xia 俠
xian 閒
Xiangying jushi 香嬰居士
xiaoshuo 小說
Xiaoqing 小青
Xihu yuyin 西湖漁隱
xingxing 猩猩
Xiong Tingbi 熊廷弼
Xu Shiqi 徐石麒
Xu Shukui 徐述夔
Xu Wei 徐渭
Xu Zhen 徐震
xuan 玄
ya 雅
Yan Jun 顏鈞
Yan zhu ou 燕筑謳
Yanju biji 燕居筆記
yezi 子葉
Yi chun xiang zhi 宜春香質
yinyuan 姻緣
Yiwolu sheng 亦臥廬生
youke 遊客
You Tong 尤侗
Yu Lin 于鱗
Yu ping mei 玉瓶梅
Yu shi mingyan 喻世明言
Yuan Chonghuan 袁崇煥

Yuan Hongdao 袁宏道
Yuan Jiong 袁褧
Yuan Shudu (Wuya) 袁叔度 (無涯)
Yuan Yuling 袁于令
Yuan Zhongdao 袁中道
Yuchuangji 雨窗集
yulu 語錄
Yutao ji 鬱陶集
zaju 雜劇
zaowu 造物
Zhang Huangyan 張煌言
Zhang Xianyi 張獻翼
Zhang Wocheng 張我城
Zhang Yu 張譽
Zhanzhan waishi 詹詹外史
Zheng Longcai 鄭龍采
Zhenzhu bo 珍珠舶
zhiji 知己
Zhong Xing 鍾惺
Zhongxing congxin lu 中興從信錄
Zhu Guozhen 朱國楨
Zhu Huang 朱篁
zhugongdiao 諸宮調
zhunao 主腦
Zhuoyuan ting zhuren 酌元亭主人
Zizai 自在

Index